"... a must have introductory hospitality marketing textbook f(
hospitality marketing. Book clearly explains various hospitality n.
and strategies with clear examples, marketing insights and cases. It is full of important and
relevant information for those who are new to hospitality marketing."
– **Professor Fevzi Okumus**, *CFHLA Preeminent Chair Professor,*
*Rosen College of Hospitality Management,*
*University of Central Florida*

"...a well-structured and easy to understand hospitality marketing textbook full of important
information for those of us who are new to the topic. The fourth edition of this introductory
textbook explains you how to successfully apply the principles of marketing to a real-life
work situation within the hospitality industry with examples and case studies"
– **Professor Dimitrios Buhalis**,
*Bournemouth University Business School*

"This book with the addition of social media marketing, user-generated content and the
role of technology makes it a must-have for hospitality students and a valuable reference for
academics in the relevant field."
– **Catherine Prentice**, *Professor of Marketing, University of*
*Southern Queensland, Australia*

"Dogan Gursoy, Francis Buttle and David Bowie have delivered a hospitality marketing book
that satisfies my 3Cs: it is complete, current, and comprehensive. The book has everything
you need to know about the subject, has lots of current examples and data, and covers each
topic very thoroughly. The book is well organized, contains several great case studies, and
offers its readers many thoughtful and useful insights."
– **Dr. Chekitan S. Dev**, *Singapore Tourism Distinguished Professor*
*at Cornell University's Nolan School of Hotel Administration*
*and author of 'Hospitality Branding'*

"The fourth edition is current and easy to read, a great resource for hospitality students.
The theory is applicable globally, and the case studies illustrate well the points made. Each
chapter is laid out clearly and lends itself to guide a weekly learning programme. Formatting
the book following the customer lifecycle gives the book a clear progressive flow."
– **Xavier Font**, *Professor of Sustainability Marketing,*
*University of Surrey, UK*

"A well-established as 'essential reading' hospitality marketing book with completely
refreshed and updated content, stronger emphasis on social media and online marketing
and much wider geographic reach of destination case studies. The logical pre-encounter,
encounter and post-encounter marketing structure it offers as well as the exploration of
new roles of technology, artificial intelligence, service robots and the metaverse in marketing
should appeal to academics, students and hospitality practitioners alike."
– **Alexandros Paraskevas**, *Chair in Hospitality Management,*
*London Geller College of Hospitality and Tourism,*
*University of West London*

"This is an outstanding marketing book dedicated to the hospitality sector – full of thought-
provoking insights and practical examples. The logical and accessible way it covers the whole
planning, implementation and evaluation process makes this an essential text for students,
instructors and practitioners seeking a comprehensive overview of hospitality marketing."
– **Peter Lugosi**, *Professor of Culture and Organisation,*
*Oxford Brookes University*

# Hospitality Marketing

*Hospitality Marketing* is an introductory textbook which shows readers how to apply the principles of marketing within the hospitality industry.

The fourth edition contains examples and case studies exemplifying how ideas and concepts discussed within its chapters can be successfully applied to a real-life work situation, with an emphasis throughout on topical issues such as sustainable marketing, corporate social responsibility and relationship marketing. It also describes the impact that the Internet has had on both marketing and hospitality, using a variety of tools including a wide range of Internet learning activities. This fourth edition has been updated to include:

- New content on social media marketing, user-generated content, group-buying behaviour, franchising, internationalization, non-predictable factors affecting sales and marketing such as COVID-19, the role of marketing in creating a competitive advantage and the role of events and experiences in marketing.
- New extensive exploration of the role of technology in marketing including the use of artificial intelligence, service robots and the metaverse to develop and deliver service and/ or to measure customer experience.
- Updated online resources including a PowerPoint deck, a test bank of questions and added links to YouTube and Instagram content.
- New/updated international case studies including many more from Asian and African destinations.

This book is written specifically for students taking marketing modules within hospitality courses and is a valuable resource to promote learning.

**Dogan Gursoy** is the Taco Bell Distinguished Professor in Hospitality Business Management at Washington State University in the School of Hospitality Business Management and the editor of *Journal of Hospitality Marketing & Management*. He is also the recipient of the 2021 ICHRIE Lifetime Research Achievement Award and the 2019 University of Delaware's Michael D. Olsen Research Achievement Award. Dr. Gursoy is recognized as one of the leading researchers in the hospitality and tourism area. He is consistently ranked as one of the top 10 hospitality and tourism researchers in the world based on the publications in top hospitality and tourism journals. Dr. Gursoy's research has high impact and is widely cited. Dr. Gursoy also receives frequent invitations to give keynote speeches at international hospitality and tourism conferences. He is also an active member of several industry and academia associations.

**Francis Buttle** taught marketing to hospitality management students at the University of Massachusetts, Amherst and the University of Surrey. He became a full professor of marketing, relationship marketing and customer relationship management in graduate schools of management in the UK and Australia. He has published 14 books and over 150 peer-reviewed articles. He continues to mentor academic colleagues, consult for businesses and not-for-profits and serve as an expert witness in legal cases.

**David Bowie**, MBA, worked in the hospitality and tourism industry for over 30 years as a manager, a director and then as a marketing consultant. He taught undergraduate and postgraduate marketing at the School of Hospitality Management, Oxford Brookes University for 21 years. His research interests include hotel branding and destination marketing.

# Hospitality Marketing

## Principles and Practices

### Fourth Edition

Dogan Gursoy, Francis Buttle
and David Bowie

Routledge
Taylor & Francis Group

LONDON AND NEW YORK

Cover image: Getty Images

Fourth edition published 2023
by Routledge
4 Park Square, Milton Park, Abingdon, Oxon, OX14 4RN

and by Routledge
605 Third Avenue, New York, NY 10158

*Routledge is an imprint of the Taylor & Francis Group, an informa business*

First edition published by Routledge 2004
Third edition published by Routledge 2016

*British Library Cataloguing-in-Publication Data*
A catalogue record for this book is available from the British Library

*Library of Congress Cataloging-in-Publication Data*
A catalog record for this book has been requested

ISBN: 978-1-032-03036-4 (hbk)
ISBN: 978-1-032-03026-5 (pbk)
ISBN: 978-1-003-18634-2 (ebk)

DOI: 10.4324/9781003186342

Access the companion website: www.routledge.com/cw/gursoy

# Contents

# Figures

# Tables

# Case studies

# Marketing insights

# Preface

Most readers of this textbook will be university undergraduate or college students studying hospitality and/or tourism marketing for the first time. Our main objective in writing the book has been to provide you with an easy-to-read text, which presents a review of modern marketing theory in the context of the hospitality industry. The many examples we have included will give you a better understanding of hospitality marketing practice.

The book has the following special features:

- The book's unique structure examines marketing activities before, during and after the customers' experience of the hospitality encounter. This helps you understand what has to be done to attract customers, provide them with an experience that meets their expectations and motivate them to return.
- There are 15 chapters, one for each of the key marketing topics you need to understand.
- Many helpful learning activities such as searches of relevant company websites and visits to hospitality units as a customer to collect information are embedded in each chapter. You will then need to analyze and evaluate your findings.
- A companion website www.routledge.com/cw/gursoy which contains a student section with further information, case studies and hospitality contact details. For instructors, there is a separate section, which provides additional teaching resources.

# Structure

The structure of the book is divided into the following sections:

- *Part A: Introduction*. A single chapter, which introduces the key concepts of marketing in the hospitality industry, including market demand, the marketing concept, the special characteristics of service industries, the PESTE environment and the hospitality marketing mix.
- *Part B: Pre-encounter marketing*. This section consists of eight chapters and discusses all the marketing activities that companies have to carry out to attract customers. Chapters include marketing research; understanding and segmenting customers; competitive strategies; developing, locating, pricing and revenue management, distributing and communicating the offer.
- *Part C: Encounter marketing*. This section comprises three chapters, which are concerned with managing the customer experience while consuming the hospitality offer. They include managing the physical environment, managing the service process and managing customer-contact employees.
- *Part D: Post-encounter marketing*. These two chapters discuss post-encounter marketing and explain the importance of customer satisfaction and developing mutually beneficial longer-term relationships with customers.
- *Part E: The marketing plan*. The final chapter builds on the previous chapters, and explains how to write a marketing plan for a hospitality business.

# Learning features

Each chapter contains the following features to aid understanding:

- *Chapter objectives*: Each chapter begins with bullet points highlighting the main features and learning to be covered in the chapter.
- *Activities*: Short practical activities are located at appropriate 'break' points throughout the chapter, to enable you to assess your understanding and marketing experience.
- *Headlines*: These usefully divide chapters into easy-to-read sections.
- *Marketing insights*: Marketing anecdotes and observations contextualize learning.
- *Case studies*: Illustrations from hospitality companies around the world are used to illustrate how the theories work in real-world situations.
- *Conclusion*: This condenses the main themes of the chapter enabling you to check your learning and understanding.
- *Review questions*: These appear at the end of each chapter allowing you to test your knowledge and understanding, and to put the theory into practice.

Each chapter contains online sources to help students explore the good examples of hospitality marketing in practice.

Part A

# Introduction

# 1

# Introduction to hospitality marketing

After working through this chapter, you should be able to:

- Define key marketing terms; understand that the role of marketing is to manage demand; and explain the marketing concept
- Describe major environmental influences that impact hospitality businesses and their customers
- Explain the special characteristics of services that influence the practice of hospitality marketing
- Identify the eight elements of the hospitality marketing mix.

## Introduction

In this chapter, you will be introduced to some fundamental principles of marketing. We review several definitions to clarify precisely what we mean by 'marketing'; we define 'the marketing concept' and we show that being 'marketing-oriented' is one of several ways of running a business. We then describe the macro- and micro-environments in which hospitality companies operate, the special attributes of services and the 'hospitality marketing mix'.

Whether we recognize it or not, we are all involved, willingly or unwillingly, passively or actively, in marketing. We encounter marketing practices every day when we are exposed to advertising and product displays, evaluate brands, make buying decisions, shop and consume; we may also

DOI: 10.4324/9781003186342-2

encounter marketing at work even if we don't have a job in marketing. Although marketing has a powerful and pervasive influence in modern life, it is often misrepresented and misunderstood.

Students learning about marketing for the first time can become quite confused because expert definitions of marketing differ from the everyday use of the term. Many people equate marketing to advertising or selling, but it's much more than that. Confusion grows when you consider that marketing is both a business philosophy and a management practice.

---

### ACTIVITY 1.1

Before you read the rest of this chapter:

- Write down what you think 'marketing' means.
- Write down what you think marketers do.
- List job titles that you think involve marketing.

We will review your ideas at the end of this chapter and see whether they have changed!

---

## What is marketing?

### Marketing as a business philosophy

Some experts believe that marketing is primarily a business philosophy that puts the customer first. From this perspective, the primary goal of any hospitality business is to create and retain satisfied customers. Marketers who endorse this 'business philosophy' idea believe that customer focus is not just a marketing responsibility but that everyone in the organization should consider the customer as they make management decisions, whether in operations, finance, human resources or marketing. Adopting this philosophy requires a total management commitment to the customer, and companies that pursue this approach can be described as having a *customer-orientation*.

### Marketing as a management practice

An alternative perspective proposes that marketing is a management practice that aims to manipulate customer demand. After a lifetime devoted to developing marketing theory and promoting the benefits of marketing, the celebrated marketing guru Professor Philip Kotler claimed that 'marketing's central purpose is demand management' and marketers need 'to manage the level, timing and the composition of demand'.[1] This perspective on marketing explains most accurately what marketing managers do day to day. Marketing management practice is part art and part science. Marketing is art in the way it uses creativity and innovation to stimulate consumers' imaginations and arouse intentions that ultimately translate into demand. It is also a science in the way that it uses data and customer insight to guide its use of the demand management toolkit known as the 'marketing mix', about which we have more to say later in this chapter.

### Transactional and relationship marketing

Marketers work in a variety of contexts that require different demand-management responses. At one extreme, the challenge is to make a one-off sale; at the other, the challenge is to build a long-term relationship with the customer that delivers many transactions over time. These are respectively known as transactional and relationship marketing.

- *Transactional marketing* is associated with hospitality businesses that serve transient or temporary markets. For example, independent food and beverage businesses operating in day-tripper destinations aim to generate sales from customers who are unlikely ever to return. These businesses provide products and services that are mutually rewarding for both parties, generating profit for the seller and satisfaction for the buyer.
- *Relationship marketing* is associated with businesses that have repeated transactions with customers over time. Relationship marketing involves the development of mutually beneficial long-term relationships between suppliers and customers; relationship marketers recognize that the lifetime value of a retained customer can be high, even though the value of each transaction may be relatively low. The major hotel groups stress relationship marketing when striving to build repeat business from guests. Offering added value to these high-value guests is a component of these companies' loyalty or reward programmes.

### Institutional definitions of marketing

Two important professional bodies for marketers are the American Marketing Association (AMA) and the UK-based Chartered Institute of Marketing (CIM). They offer these definitions of marketing:

> *'Marketing is the activity, set of institutions, and processes for creating, communicating, delivering, and exchanging offerings that have value for customers, clients, partners, and society at large.'*
>
> (AMA)[2]

> *'Marketing is the management process responsible for identifying, anticipating and satisfying customer requirements profitably.'*
>
> (CIM)[3]

The AMA definition stresses the importance of value creation. Customers experience value when they use or consume a product or service. This is known as 'value-in-use'. A restaurant meal or a guest room has no value until such time as customers use or consume them. The CIM definition stresses the importance of satisfying customer requirements. To integrate both definitions we can say that every customer's broad requirement is to experience value. If the customer does not experience value from a hospitality company's products or services then they will not be satisfied; on the other hand, once value is experienced then customer satisfaction is more likely.

These definitions also stress the importance of bringing the voice of the customer into the business. The CIM definition notes the importance of identifying customer requirements. The AMA definition stresses the activities and processes that enable businesses to create offerings that have value for customers. Taken together, these mean that businesses have to monitor markets, customers and competitors for shifts in customer requirements and expectations, and continually adapt offerings to ensure that customers experience value. These monitoring and forward-looking processes mean that the voice of the customer continues to be heard in the business, and that the business is externally oriented towards customers. Marketers become ambassadors or spokespersons for customers and ensure that the organization is always focused on the value-in-use expectations of customers.

### The marketing concept

Companies that place a customer at the centre of their thinking, and organize their operations and communications around the value requirements of customers, are said to have adopted the marketing concept. In competitive markets, these companies accept that to achieve their goals, they must be more effective than competitors at creating, delivering and communicating value to their chosen customers. Companies that adopt the marketing concept are said to be 'marketing-orientated'.

### What is a market?

Originally, a market was a meeting place where people could buy and sell produce; of course, this type of market still exists today. In modern societies where people connect online, markets can be much more complex, but they still reflect the core principle of bringing together buyers and sellers with common interests. This modern concept of the market is based on groups of people who have similar needs and wants (potential consumers and actual customers), and companies that aim to satisfy those needs and wants better than their competitors (an industry).

*Needs* can range from the basic requirements for survival – food, shelter, safety – to much more complex social needs, such as belonging and recognition. *Wants* are how different people choose to satisfy their needs; wants are shaped by culture, traditional and social media, and personality. People with similar needs, for example, the need to travel for a family event and stay overnight, can have different wants – some will want to stay with relatives while others may want to have the independence of staying in a hotel.

A major limitation on how people can satisfy their wants is the amount they can afford to pay. Consumers have to make buying choices based on their own resources or buying power. Consumers will often buy the best bundle of value-creating benefits provided by a product for the price that can be afforded. The aggregated purchase decisions of *all* the individuals buying a product (or service) are expressed as *market demand*. Market demand is normally measured using two criteria:

1  The number of units sold; this is called the volume.
2  How much people have paid for the product; this is called the value.

Individuals can satisfy similar needs in many different ways. Not everyone wants the same bundle of benefits, and this creates sub-markets, or market segments, within the overall market. In hospitality markets, deluxe, luxury, mid-market, economy and budget market segments represent different bundles of benefits sought by different groups of customers. Over a period of time, the volume and the value of market segments can increase or decrease depending on a wide range of factors.

Market supply can also be measured and this is called the *industry capacity*. In the hotel market, the number of hotels and rooms in an area is called the *market capacity*. If the number of hotels and rooms is increasing, because new hotels or room extensions have been built, then the market capacity increases. In the hospitality industry, market supply is often categorized under the same headings as market demand segments; thus, the luxury, deluxe, mid-market, economy and budget classifications are also used to describe the different types of operations serving those market segments. Other ways of categorizing hospitality market supply include:

- Purpose of travel (e.g. business; leisure)
- Niche markets (e.g. ethnic restaurants; vegetarian restaurants)

- Tourist board, motoring or other organization ratings for hotels and restaurants (e.g. the American Automobile Association – AAA Diamond rating classifications for hotels or the Michelin Guide star ratings for restaurants).

The level of market demand and the amount of industry capacity are crucial factors underpinning the profitability of hospitality firms:

- When market demand is high and industry capacity is low, hospitality businesses should enjoy high sales volume and profitability.
- When market demand falls (e.g. in an economic downturn or recession) but industry capacity remains high, sales and profitability will normally fall.

## Marketing as demand management

We have suggested that one way to think about marketing is to view it as the art and science of managing customer demand. Because demand states vary, so does the task of marketing. Table 1.1 provides a list of eight categories of demand and the marketing response. When demand states 1–4 occur, actual demand is lower than the business's desired level of demand and the hospitality marketer is primarily interested in facilitating and stimulating more demand. Negative demand exists when consumers dislike a product – for example, an unpopular food or drink product. The marketing response is to encourage demand by educating consumers about the positive features of, or benefits from, the product (or by educating operations people in their business to change the product so it does satisfy customers!). You can often witness free tastings of food and drink products in supermarkets and wine outlets, which enable potential customers to see, taste and maybe buy the product.

When there is no demand, the marketing task is to create demand. Raising awareness by outbound communications such as advertising and public relations to demonstrate a product's positive attributes may help to educate consumers and encourage them to try the product.

Latent demand means that demand would exist if there were a suitable product/service. The development of domestic short breaks as a hotel product was originally based on consumers' increasing affluence and available leisure time. When demand is falling, the marketing challenge is to revitalize demand. This situation can occur when a product/service is beginning to lose its appeal. Marketers need to research the reasons why the product no longer

Table 1.1  Demand management[4]

|   | Category of demand | Marketing task |
|---|---|---|
| 1 | Negative demand | Encourage demand |
| 2 | No demand | Create demand |
| 3 | Latent demand | Develop demand |
| 4 | Falling demand | Revitalize demand |
| 5 | Irregular demand | Synchronize demand |
| 6 | Full demand | Maintain demand |
| 7 | Overfull demand | Reduce demand |
| 8 | Unwholesome demand | Destroy demand |

satisfies customers, reformulate the offer and re-launch it to refresh interest and revitalize demand.

Irregular demand is widespread in hospitality; it takes the form of seasonal demand. In these situations, companies strive to develop marketing strategies and tactics to synchronize demand over the high and low seasons, often using price-led promotions. Full demand occurs when actual demand matches the available capacity. Here, the marketing task is to maintain the current level of demand. In hospitality markets, full demand rarely occurs since competitors are likely to enter attractive markets and disturb the equilibrium.

If there is too much (or overfull) demand, the hospitality operation will not be able to cope and there is likely to be considerable customer dissatisfaction. Hospitality marketers respond by reducing demand either by increasing prices or by managing the booking/queuing process to prevent overfull demand. A long-term solution to overfull demand is to increase capacity by building more rooms or extending the seating area in a restaurant, but managers need to be confident that overfull demand will be sustained.

Unwholesome demand can occur when prohibited activities such as drug dealing, gambling or prostitution are taking place on the hospitality premises. Management clearly has a legal and ethical duty to try and inhibit or destroy unwholesome demand; however, this can be a difficult situation when customers are willingly involved.

## *Market demand in hospitality*

Market demand in hospitality falls into four broad categories:

1 Business travel demand includes all those trips business-people take to meet customers and suppliers, or attend conferences, exhibitions and seminars. Business travel does not include the daily trips people make when commuting to and from work.
2 Leisure travel demand includes trips that people take away from home for amusement, entertainment or relaxation – for example, vacations, weekend breaks or same-day visits. A major component of leisure travel is visiting friends and relatives, and this is described using the acronym 'VFR'.
3 Domestic travel demand includes all the travel generated within a country by people living in that country – so, for example, the domestic demand for business travel in the USA is all business trips taken in the USA by people living in the USA.
4 International travel demand includes all the trips taken to a country from people living in other countries. France is the world's most popular tourist destination and attracts international visitors from all over the world.

Some types of travel do not fit easily into these broad categories, for example people who combine business and vacations in the same trip, but these are convenient descriptions that tourist and hospitality organizations use to broadly categorize the major markets – see Table 1.2.

Table 1.2 Categories of demand in hospitality

| Purpose of travel | Domestic | International |
|---|---|---|
| Business | Domestic business demand | International business demand |
| Leisure | Domestic leisure demand | International leisure demand |

## Management orientations

Not every company is 'marketing-oriented'. Five different management philosophies, or orientations, have been identified in developed economies. Some of these orientations have been linked to specific economic conditions or to certain periods in economic history. Hospitality organizations, like other businesses, could adopt any one of the following orientations, regardless of the economic circumstances.

### Product or service orientation

Companies adopting a product orientation believe that their customers can *only* be satisfied with a particular type of product or service and that the foundation of corporate success is product or service excellence. Management may concentrate on developing better versions of the *existing* product, but fail to recognize that customers could be satisfied better by different *types* of products. For example, hospitality companies with a product orientation include the famous restaurants with celebrity chefs, who serve what they think customers should want regardless of what the customers actually want! Product-oriented management is inward looking. Although a company can prosper with a product orientation, changes in consumer tastes and fashion can quickly undermine a product-oriented company as businesses lose touch with changes in customer preferences. Theodore Levitt's famous article[5] 'Marketing myopia' warned companies that a product orientation could lead to failure.

### Operations or production orientation

Originally developed by the automobile entrepreneur Henry Ford in the early twentieth century, a production orientation is appropriate when there is a rising demand for strong, innovative products. If demand exceeds supply, management concentrates on producing volume to satisfy the growing demand. Improved technologies generate economies of scale, which allows management to reduce prices further and grow the market.

Production orientation is a good fit for businesses servicing customers who have a narrow range of expectations, and who expect low prices and consistent product quality. This leads to an inward-looking focus as management strives to control costs, standardize quality, enhance efficiency and increase volume. Critically, from a marketing perspective, the needs and wants of customers can be subordinated to the pursuit of operational efficiency. If customers are satisfied with a low-cost, mass-produced product, then a production orientation is appropriate.

There are many examples of product innovation generating strong demand in the fast-food industry. When American quick service restaurants entered the major cities of countries such as China and Russia, they generated high demand for what was considered an innovative foreign food product. This meant that McDonald's adopted a production orientation. McDonald's management's main focus was on achieving operational efficiency by improving their food supply chain and training staff to service the high demand. Airline, contract and welfare food service operations also have a production focus because of the mass markets they serve.

There are also examples of hospitality organizations using a production orientation ineffectively. Sometimes, the standard operations manuals in the large hotel corporations that detail rules and procedures for every aspect of the hotel operation can stifle employee initiatives in customer care. This bureaucratic approach inhibits innovation, making hospitality managers focus on the systems and processes instead of customers. Smaller companies can also neglect customers by adopting an operations focus. Simplifying the production process for operational convenience can lead to limited customer choice – for example, small sandwich shops can easily limit the choice of fillings to reduce waste and thereby lose customers by not offering sufficient choice.

### Selling or sales orientation

Companies adopt the selling orientation when their products are competing in markets where supply exceeds demand, and market growth is flat-lining or declining. A critical issue for many hospitality firms is surplus industry capacity combined with a high fixed capital investment in buildings and plants. This combination can force management to focus on achieving high sales volume and adopt aggressive sales promotions to make a reasonable return on investment. Companies with a selling orientation tend to accept every possible sale or booking, regardless of its suitability for the business or other customers. By mixing incompatible customer segments, hospitality companies can fail to deliver customer satisfaction, which is ultimately self-defeating. Long-term, profitable relationships with existing customers can be damaged in the pursuit of short-term sales generation.

The sales orientation is endemic in the hospitality industry, as many marketing programmes are really only sales promotions aimed at filling rooms, bars and restaurants – regardless of customers' needs and wants.

Although selling is a vital element of hospitality marketing, sales strategies should be integrated into marketing plans and should be consistent with a marketing orientation.

### Marketing orientation

Marketing-oriented businesses have adopted the marketing concept and put customer focus at the heart of the business. It is an alternative to the selling orientation and designed to cope with similar economic conditions (i.e., surplus capacity leading to a fiercely competitive environment). Companies adopting a marketing orientation recognize that customers have considerable choice. Marketing-oriented businesses accept that to maintain long-term profitability they need to understand and serve customers better than their competitors.

Marketing-oriented businesses carry out marketing research and develop an integrated approach to marketing, ensuring that all marketing activities are coordinated and contribute to the delivery of customer satisfaction. A marketing orientation is an outward-looking management philosophy, which responds to changes in the business environment and considers the business from a customer perspective. As customers' needs and wants change, so the business adapts accordingly.

The advantage of a marketing orientation is that the business focus is on developing mutually beneficial, often long-term, relationships with customers, based on an intimate understanding of their needs and wants and the market-satisfying capabilities of competitors. The adoption of a marketing orientation suggests that companies are seeking long-term profits, as opposed to increasing profits in the short term at the expense of long-term customer satisfaction.

At its most advanced level, a marketing orientation becomes focused on the satisfaction of individual customers, either organizations or people. Companies that tailor their offer to meet the needs of individual customers are said to be practicing one-to-one marketing. In hospitality, databases containing customer-related data such as guest history, demographics, contact details and preferences increasingly enable hotel companies to personalize services and communications to satisfy individual customers.

### *Societal (sustainable) marketing orientation*

The marketing orientation has been criticized for its narrow focus on customers and its lack of concern for environmental and social issues. The societal marketing orientation is a response to these criticisms and recognizes that commercial organizations have a wider responsibility than simply looking after customers. A societal marketing orientation suggests that companies should become proactive in the community, adopting a 'good neighbour' policy and being attentive to environmental, social and cultural considerations, whilst running a sustainable business.

Recently, consumers' concern for environmental and social issues such as animal welfare, climate change, diversity, equity, inclusion and ethical food sourcing has generated considerable interest in companies' sustainable business practices. Marketing responses to environmental and social concerns are often described as eco-marketing, green marketing or socially responsible marketing. There are several examples of smaller hospitality organizations founded by eco-minded and/or socially responsible entrepreneurs who strive to operate on a sustainable and socially responsible basis. The larger hospitality corporations have adopted the concept of 'responsible business' as an umbrella term to reflect their response to broader societal concerns and enhance their credentials as good 'corporate citizens'. These corporations have introduced a range of policies to reduce their carbon footprint and food and water wastage; create more energy-efficient properties, value diversity and equity; and be more inclusive. Many produce annual corporate responsibility reports to explain to their corporate customers, shareholders, the media, environmental lobby groups and grassroots organizations their progress towards sustainability and social responsibility practices. In Activity 1.2, you can explore the webpages of both large hospitality corporations and smaller hotel businesses to compare their different approaches.

---

**ACTIVITY 1.2**

Compare the sustainability and social responsibility credentials of these two international hotel groups and two hotels on their webpages:

1  Hilton Hotels at www.hilton.com/en/corporate/ under 'About Us'

2  Accor Hotels at https://all.accor.com/usa/index.en.shtml under 'Sustainable development'

3  Kandalama Eco Hotel, Sri Lanka, at www.heritancehotels.com under 'Sustainability'

4  Chaa Creek, Belize, at www.chaacreek.com/ under 'About Chaa Creek'

List the sustainability and social responsibility policies of each company and identify any similarities and differences.

---

A number of hospitality organizations have genuinely adopted a societal marketing approach. One example is 1 Hotels (see Case Study 1.1). Other organizations may claim to adopt a societal marketing approach, but in reality are only putting a 'sustainability spin' on, or 'greenwashing', their otherwise routine management practices. The distinction between a genuine societal marketing approach and a superficial approach lies in the value-driven practices of the organization. If the organizational culture is clearly committed to a sustainable and socially responsible business model and demonstrates this in all its activities, then it has adopted a societal marketing approach.

A company's orientation may be formally embedded in a written mission statement, informally agreed by the management team or simply implied in the way the business is run. Many hospitality companies may not even be aware of their business orientation. Opinions differ on whether a specific orientation is appropriate for any given economic situation. Some experts maintain that a marketing orientation is the only appropriate orientation, whilst others suggest that competitive and economic circumstances should determine which orientation to adopt. Companies often adopt different orientations at different stages of their growth, and global companies can adopt different orientations depending on which country they are operating in.

## CASE STUDY 1.1

### 1 Hotels

1 Hotels is a nature-inspired luxury lifestyle hotel brand that utilizes sustainable design and architecture to make the buildings environmentally friendly and sustainable while offering extraordinary comfort and an unrivalled level of service. SH Hotels & Resorts, an affiliate of global private investment firm Starwood Capital Group, is the hotel brand management company that operates 1 Hotels.

The 1 Hotels brand was launched in 2015 with the opening of exclusive properties in Miami's South Beach and Manhattan's Central Park. Later, new properties were opened in Brooklyn, West Hollywood, Cabo and Haitang Bay in Hainan Island, China. The company plans to open new properties in Hawaii, London, Melbourne, San Diego, Nashville, Paris, San Francisco and Toronto.

The 1 Hotels concept was inspired by a simple idea that those who travel the world should also care about it; it is, after all, 1 world. As stated by Barry Sternlicht, Chairman, Starwood Capital Group, 'I wanted to capture the beauty of nature in a hotel and commit to safeguarding it as best I can, a responsibility that I believe we all share. It's 1 world. But 1 is more than a hotel – it's a philosophy and a platform for change.' This is clearly reflected in the vision statement of 1 Hotels: 'The future of the world and the future of hospitality are one and the same. 1 Hotels aspires to be a platform to spark conversations, between innovators and guests, that transform the industry and our lives.' 1 Hotels upholds this vision by channelling nature through design and culinary partnerships, while connecting with the local community and taking sustainable steps to make a big difference.

All of 1 Hotels' design, construction and operational decisions aim to ensure successful environmental, social and economic sustainability while providing extraordinary hospitality experiences to customers. In order to minimize its negative impacts on the environment, 1 Hotels has implemented a wide range of energy, water and environmental design strategies to keep their footprint small. In fact, all of the 1 Hotels properties operating across the USA are now certified carbon neutral hotels. The guest loyalty programme offered by SH Hotels & Resorts, the hotel brand management company that operates 1 Hotels, allows guests to direct their loyalty credits to efforts to offset carbon emissions around the planet. Guests can earn rewards worth as much as 4 per cent of the money spent at the company's luxury hotels. The earned credits can then be used to fund forest preservation in the US, wind power projects in India and other environmental protection initiatives. This eco-minded and carbon offsetting focused loyalty programme is a collaboration between SH Hotels and CarbonClick, a company founded to help businesses and customers tackle climate change. In addition to funding various environmental projects, the programme can also help you calculate your 'flightprint', the carbon emissions from your flight, before travelling. So, you'll have some sense for how much 'offsetting' you'll need to undertake to achieve carbon neutrality.

1 Hotels also offers a number of programmes to improve the social wellbeing of its various stakeholders such as employees, customers, suppliers and anyone else who is affected by the operations of 1 Hotels. 1 Hotels human resource management practices are better than most in their sector, including competitive pay and very good promotion prospects. 1 Hotels has ambitious sustainability targets to reduce the business's impact on the environment and is proactive in charity support for various causes. 1 Hotels' advocacy, education and engagement programme aims to initiate conversations about the environment and its role in protecting it. The company organizes volunteer activities and offers paid volunteer days for their teams' advocacy and educational pursuits. The company's focus on human health and wellbeing and food and beverage responsibility initiatives suggest that 1 Hotels is committed to offering environmentally friendly, sustainable and extraordinary hospitality experiences to their customers.

1 Hotels' management orientation is clearly based on a societal marketing approach, and continued expansion and recognitions suggests that its mission works. Due to their sustainability initiatives and implementations, 1 Hotel South Beach was awarded #1 in the top 10 Hotels in Miami in the 2019 Conde Nast Traveler reader's Choice Awards. 1 Hotel Central Park and 1 Hotel Brooklyn Bridge claimed the number 5 and number 8 spots respectively in the Top 50 Hotels in New York City.

*Source*: 1 Hotels – look at 1 Hotels' website for more details, www.1hotels.com/

## The marketing environment

Since marketing is an outward-looking business philosophy, marketers in hospitality companies need to understand and adapt to changes in the marketing environment. Macro- and micro- environmental factors influence consumers, customers and businesses, which in turn influence the practice of marketing. Figure 1.1 provides an overview of the marketing environment in which hospitality organizations operate.

### The macro-environment

The macro-environment includes all the political, economic, socio-cultural, technological and environmental (PESTE) forces that impact on its customers and operations. Hospitality companies have limited, if any, control over PESTE influences, but major changes in even one PESTE factor can have a significant impact on the business, either for better or worse. PESTE factors are constantly changing. These changes affect consumers, drive market demand and influence the competitive environment.

### Political

The political direction of a country determines how consumers and commercial organizations can act. The political philosophy of government can either stimulate or stifle economic, social

Figure 1.1 The marketing environment

and technological development. Although Western nations generally foster an open economy, encourage tourism and create a positive climate for hospitality businesses, some countries – for example North Korea – restrict international access and inhibit the development of tourism and hospitality businesses. Political and governmental decisions are constantly changing the environment in which we live and work, and impact on hospitality marketing activity in a variety of ways.

For Americans, the political environment includes the federal government as well as their state and local governments. The federal government only has those powers granted to it in the Constitution while a state government has inherent powers allowing it to act unless limited by a provision of the state or national constitution. For Europeans, the political environment includes the European Union as well as their own national and local governments. Decisions about the Single European Market and the euro currency are examples of European political regulation.

The political environment includes the legal/regulatory environment, which covers any legislation that influences the marketplace. Examples include the following:

- Employment laws and regulations. The U.S. Department of Labor (DOL) administers and enforces more than 180 federal laws, which cover many workplace activities for about 150 million workers and 10 million workplaces.
- Planning regulations (permission for building hotel, restaurant and leisure extensions or developing new properties), which alter the industry capacity.
- Licensing laws, which regulate the opening times of licensed premises.
- Local, regional or national government taxes that impact on prices (taxes on general

merchandise and services like Value Added Tax and the General Sales Tax; taxes on hospital-ity and tourism services like lodging tax, excise duty on alcoholic drinks and taxes like the Airline Passenger Duty on airline travel). The rate of taxation can significantly influence the demand for hospitality and tourism products – generally, higher taxes have a negative influ-ence on demand.

- Regulation of marketing communications. Different countries have a variety of regulations for online and offline customer communications such as tracking customers' online activi-ties, advertising, sales promotion, sharing customer information, and direct and database marketing. One important concern is the protection of customer privacy, especially the on-line privacy in the age of data economy.

## Economic

The economic environment includes all influences on the wealth and income of the population. Examples of economic influences are

- State of the economy from rapid growth though to recession
- Employment levels and associated wages
- Rate of inflation
- Exchange rate.

These factors combine to influence business and consumer confidence, consumers' disposable income and purchasing power, and business investment, which all play a significant role in changing the supply of, and demand for, hospitality services. When business and consumer confidence is high, hospitality markets thrive; when business and consumer confidence is low, hospitality markets decline and firms are prone to failure.

### THE BUSINESS CYCLE

Business cycles have a major impact on demand. Hospitality firms need to understand the busi-ness cycle and modify their operations accordingly. Although hospitality businesses all trade at the same stage of the business cycle, firms will respond differently according to their financial and marketing strengths, and their leadership. The stages of the hospitality business cycle (see Figure 1.2) are as follows.

- *Growth*: Occupancy and room rates increase in response to growing demand. There is a strong positive cash flow, which means that capital is available for further investment; prop-erty values increase and hoteliers have high business confidence.
- *Peak*: Occupancy and room rates remain strong, and funds are still available for investment; however, customer demand tends to slow.
- *Decline*: Occupancy begins to decrease. If the decrease is gradual, room rates are only in-creased in line with inflation. If the decrease in demand is dramatic, then investors sense the higher risk in declining occupancy and seek more attractive returns before agreeing to invest in hotel businesses. Property values begin to fall. As the rate of decline becomes more rapid, occupancy falls further, price competition becomes more intense and revenue per available room (RevPAR) falls; if decline becomes faster the industry moves toward recession.

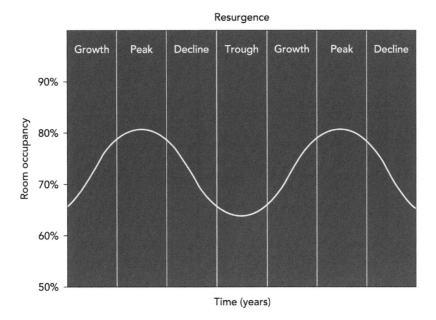

Figure 1.2 Typical hotel industry cycle

- *Trough*: There is a large imbalance of supply and demand during a recession; low occupancy, low room rates and low RevPAR create a slump in hospitality property values meaning that highly geared (over-borrowed) companies are put into receivership. There is a bottoming out period as demand gradually stabilizes and then slowly begins to increase.
- *Resurgence*: There is a gradual resurgence, and the cycle starts all over again.

A major recurring problem for the hospitality industry is that hotel development projects are funded in the growth and peak stages of the business cycle but, because of the time lag between gaining investment funds and planning permission, many hotels open for business after the cycle peaks. Hence, additional new build capacity is added to the stock just as demand falls, creating further problems for the industry. Capacity does not diminish quickly during periods of declining and low demand. From a hospitality marketing perspective, companies' response to the business cycle during a downturn period and a recession is problematic. Companies engage in major cost-cutting activities; marketing positions and expenditures are often significantly reduced; and financially weaker brands are vulnerable to takeover. During resurgent and growth periods, marketing activity increases as companies respond to the growth in hospitality demand. Although nobody can accurately predict the precise timing of a turning point in the business cycle, it is vital for hospitality managers and owners to understand the implications of each stage.

### Socio-cultural

The socio-cultural environment influences consumers' purchase and consumption behaviour. A country's socio-cultural environment is a complex product of its geography, climate, history, religion and ethnic make-up. We are all influenced by the values of our own culture, even though we may not be aware of this. Indeed, cultural differences between regions and countries provide hospitality marketers with some of the greatest challenges when developing global brands.

A person's eating and drinking habits are significantly influenced by culture. Each country and region has developed its own cuisine based on factors such as climate, which dictates what produce is available, and religion, which proscribes what foods and beverages may be consumed. The growth of international travel has widened people's cultural knowledge and encouraged the development of new food and beverage concepts.

Demographic changes (changes in the composition of a population) also make a significant impact on market demand in hospitality. Examples include the following:

- The number of older people living in Western countries is growing, changing vacation preferences, expectations and requirements.
- The increase in the number of single people (caused by people marrying later and more people divorcing) has changed the demand characteristics for eating out.

Hospitality marketers need to be aware of socio-cultural and demographic trends to ensure their companies adapt to changes in markets and remain competitive.

### Technological

The technological environment in hospitality is closely associated with innovation and developments in information and communications technology (ICT) and especially the Internet and mobile platforms. Changes in the technological environment influencing consumers and the hospitality industry include the following:

- The rapid adoption of the Internet and mobile technology by consumers searching for and booking hospitality and travel products
- The use of online comparison sites by consumers before making a hotel or restaurant reservation
- Customers' use of social media to share their hospitality experiences with family, friends and their online social networks
- The utilization of inter-connected artificial intelligence powered property management systems, computerized reservation systems, global distribution systems and networks (GDS), the Internet and mobile technologies to facilitate online booking
- The utilization of artificial intelligence powered applications to monitor and reduce energy consumption and improve in-room comfort and security for guests
- Improvements in kitchen equipment which have enhanced food production techniques
- Increasing utilization of artificially intelligent devices in delivery of customer experiences and customer services.

Since the development of the Internet in the early 1990s the practice of hospitality marketing has been revolutionized by technological change, though the core principles of marketing remain the same. Disruptive technologies can cause rapid and dramatic change in the marketing environment. Airbnb was founded in 2008 and describes itself as an online/mobile community and marketplace that connects travellers with hosts all around the world in a sharing economy. Sharing economy platforms such as Airbnb and Couchsurfing have completely revolutionized the hospitality industry by creating a new form of competition or by offering value-added services that are not provided by conventional hospitality companies. For example, Airbnb has become a major competitor for hotel owners. Hosts offer travellers accommodation in their homes and travellers book directly through the Airbnb website. In less than 15 years, Airbnb has signed up more than 4 million hosts (units) over 220 countries and looked after more than 900 million guests. You can read more about Airbnb in Case Study 4.3 later in the book. The current and predicted rate of technological change is super-fast, and new developments are constantly altering the technological environment.

### Environmental

Environmental factors have become more important in all parts of the world as people recognize the impact tourism businesses have on the planet. In particular, mass tourism has become controversial. The tourism and hospitality industry is accused of:

- Encouraging inappropriate new hotel and leisure developments
- Eroding natural habitats
- Threatening the integrity of indigenous cultures
- Using scarce resources which local people need
- Generating air, noise and carbon pollution
- Creating waste disposal problems
- Introducing undesirable activities to local communities.

The concept of sustainable tourism is much publicized. Environmental groups lobby government and hospitality companies to improve the industry's environmental policies.

As travellers explore more widely, they become exposed to many different conditions, not all of them welcome. The COVID-19 pandemic, for example, had a significant influence on the hospitality industry due to large-scale shutdown of social activities, lockdowns, stay-at-home orders and travel restrictions.[6] According to U.S. Travel Association reports,[7] travel spending in the U.S. was down by 42 per cent in 2020 compared to 2019. Due to international travel restrictions imposed by many countries, international travel was one of the hardest hit segments of the industry, as it decreased by 76 per cent in 2020 compared to 2019. Meanwhile domestic travel declined by 34 per cent. Business travel was down by 70 per cent, and leisure travel was down by 27 per cent.

### Interaction of PESTE factors

Each PESTE element can influence other elements. For example, demographic changes and migration trends are forecast to become a major influence on economic, social and political factors later in the century. National population changes affect a country's economy. Global and national changes in population affect socio-cultural forces and influence the composition and character of travel markets. Countries react politically to migration pressures, especially from economic and political refugees, and demographic changes also stimulate the creation of pressure groups that lobby government on behalf of their interests. Diversity, inclusion and equity movements for a better future are reshaping the hiring, marketing and business practices of all companies. Thus, one driver of change influences several PESTE factors, and each of the PESTE factors interacts with the others.

### The micro-environment

The micro-environment includes the people and organizations that a business interacts with in its everyday operations. These include customers, employees, suppliers, intermediaries, competitors and various other 'publics' such as traditional and social media influencers and regulatory bodies. Unlike the PESTE framework for the macro-environment, there is no recognized mnemonic to help you remember the components of the micro-environment.

### Customers

Hospitality companies typically target a broad mix of customers, including business and leisure hotel guests; non-resident diners; and convention, meeting and event participants. Managing the customer mix to ensure that all the different types of customers are satisfied or delighted is one of the major challenges for marketing. Over time, customers' needs and wants are likely to change, so companies have to monitor and respond to these changes. Since many consumers share their hospitality experiences with their personal networks through social media platforms, companies also need to monitor and manage their presence online.

### Employees

For most hospitality organizations, the local labour market is a key resource. The availability and quality of skilled employees who have been educated and can be easily trained is an important factor in delivering a quality service. Like customers, many current and former employees share their work experiences with a company on social media. Since negative comments about a company's human resources practices can significantly shrink their potential labour workforce, employers, like customers, also need to monitor and manage their social media presence. Because employees interact with customers, they have a major influence on customer experience and satisfaction.

### Suppliers

The hospitality company's performance is significantly dependent on its suppliers, for example for delivery of foodstuffs to the kitchen. Although marketers are not directly involved in operational purchase decisions, marketing should have an input in setting quality standards and specifications. The hospitality marketer will certainly be responsible for handling relationships with external marketing communication and marketing research agencies.

### Intermediaries

Intermediaries, also called distributors, are those companies who advise, influence and make bookings for customers. They include entities like search engines, travel agents, tour operators, conference placement agencies and specialist online retailers who are known as TPI (third-party intermediaries). Intermediaries are important links in the distribution channel from the customer to the hospitality outlets. Marketing managers need to cultivate good relationships with actual and potential intermediaries.

### Competitors

There are several kinds of competitor:

- Direct competitors are businesses offering a similar product or service aimed at the same customer group. Direct competitors operate in the same geographic location and in the same (or adjacent) product category. A three-star provincial business hotel could have a local competitor set including all three-star hotels and possibly some two- and four-star hotels within a 10-mile radius or 15-minute travel time. Watching, knowing and anticipating what your competitors are doing is vital for hospitality marketing success.
- Competitors offering substitute products – these are offers that potential consumers can choose instead of a hospitality product. These competitors satisfy the same need, but in other ways. For example, someone might choose to stay at home and cook a convenience meal instead of going out to a restaurant.
- Indirect competition – this includes all those companies and non-profit organizations that are competing for consumers' disposable income e.g. choosing between buying a new car or going on an exotic holiday.

The competitive environment in many hospitality markets has become more intense in recent years. The actions and reactions of competitors including their level of technology adoption, social media presence and management capabilities have radically changed market structures, influenced consumer behaviour and altered market demand.

### Publics

The location of hospitality premises and the size/scale of the company will determine the various publics with which the organization interacts. These publics may include:

- Local government authorities that enforce health and safety, hygiene and planning regulations
- Businesses and people who live or work in the neighbourhood, some of whom may also be customers
- Community, educational, religious, social and voluntary institutions
- Leisure, sporting and tourism organizations
- Media owners and publishers
- Social media and social media influencers.

Local publics can exert considerable influence on a hospitality business. Developing effective public relations and fostering good relationships with local publics is part of the marketing task. Monitoring and managing social media is critical for the success of any hospitality companies these days since most customers pay close attention to social media posts and reviews posted to sites like Tripadvisor.

## Special characteristics of services marketing

Because the hospitality industry is just one of many service sector industries (for example, financial services, distribution services, retailing) we use services marketing principles to underpin our explorations of marketing practice in the hospitality industry. Services such as those provided by hospitality organizations possess a number of special characteristics that present challenges to marketing practitioners. These special characteristics are seasonality, intangibility, perishability, inseparability, variability, interdependence, supply exceeding demand and high fixed costs. You can use the mnemonic SIPIVISH to remember the characteristics.

## Seasonality

Seasonality refers to the fluctuations and demand in any given period. In hospitality operations, the impact of seasonality can be felt at different times of the year, month, week or even day.

The demand for business accommodation is highest during the middle of the week and outside the peak holiday periods of religious festivals and summer. Hotels that mainly serve leisure travellers can have a poor mid-week business but achieve high occupancies at the weekends, when hotels that mainly target business travellers can be quiet. Restaurants can be full of customers on a busy Saturday night and empty on Monday lunchtime or evening. Over time seasonality patterns may change in line with consumer trends. For example, many city hotels have recently seen busier weekends due to an increase in weekend conference demand and better marketing of city leisure breaks. Case Study 1.2 illustrates a seasonal business – the Eden Project.

The under- or over-utilization of capacity creates operational difficulties. Sudden unexpected increases in customers can lead to production problems, unacceptable waiting times, negative posts on social media and review sites, and dissatisfied customers. The profitability of hospitality companies suffers during low season periods creating a marketing challenge to increase demand by deflecting over demand from peak periods to the low season.

## CASE STUDY 1.2

### Seasonality at the Eden Project, Cornwall, England[8]

The Eden Project is a unique environmental visitor attraction. The iconic build began in Cornwall in the UK in 1998 in what had previously been an open cast mine for china clay. The attraction officially opened on March 2001 and provides three climatic zones – Temperate, Mediterranean and Tropical – referred to as Biomes. The latter two Biomes are maintained in a greenhouse setting. The Tropical Biome is the largest display greenhouse in the world.

The Eden Project mission is to promote the understanding and responsible management of the vital relationship between plants, people and resources, leading to a sustainable future for all. Therefore, Eden aims to entertain and communicate important environmental messages, provide a memorable day out and inspire visitors. Apart from the natural plant domains, there are a wide range of activities all year round including art and music events and a summer programme for families. The site and seasonal events attract over 1 million visitors annually.

The Eden Project is open every day of the year except the 24th and 25th December. Visitor numbers can range from 300 on a weekday in winter to 14,500 on the busiest day in the summer. Visitor flow is predictable and driven by traditional holiday periods;

approximately 70 per cent of visitors visit between the Easter holidays and the October school half term. Although a sophisticated planning system accurately forecasts the number of visitors on a weekly basis, visitor flow through the week (day by day) is less predictable. During the peak summer period of the school holidays, many tourists take a week-long break travelling from home to Cornwall and back at the weekends, resulting in busy days Monday to Thursday. However, due to the vagaries of the British weather, it is much more difficult to forecast daily visitor numbers more than a week in advance. If the weather is warm and sunny, holidaymakers will stay at the beach, but if it rains, then they look for indoor attractions like the Eden Project. For example, on a sunny week in summer, the forecast might be for an average of 6,000 visitors per day between Monday and Thursday, but if there are days of heavy rain an extra 4,000 to 6,000 visitors will suddenly arrive at Eden on each rainy day. From a catering perspective, nearly all these extra visitors will combine a visit to the Biomes with the need to eat and drink.

The Eden Project provides several cafés and restaurants with the focus on fresh, local and tasty food. All the cafés and restaurants are Eden managed, and there are no franchised outlets. Menus cater for omnivore, vegetarian, vegan and gluten-free consumers. Wherever possible, food is freshly prepared – for example, all the sandwiches are made fresh each day. In Jo's Café, customers can learn about the food they eat and its impact on their own health as well as the environment. Organic and fair-trade products are sourced wherever possible and more than 80 per cent of catering produce is sourced from local suppliers. There are four priorities when sourcing food products – quality, price, seasonality and Cornishness. Eden's interpretation of the 'triple bottom line' is to ensure that products are environmentally sound, socially acceptable and economically viable. Indeed, Eden spends around £10 million each year with approximately 2,000 local suppliers.

So, how does the Eden Project team cope on these busy days? If there are more visitors than expected, then many of the catering and front-of-house employees will be helped by other employees who do not normally work in operations. The behind-the-scenes employees will receive an email asking for their assistance at short notice. Predictable busy days are classed as 'tricky days'. At the start of the season, each back-of-house employee has to select five tricky days out of a list of 30 potentially busy days when they will be available to support their front-of-house colleagues. Additionally, because of the proximity and strong relationship of their local suppliers, if Eden suddenly requires extra food produce, the suppliers will readily help out.

If the team has over-estimated visitor numbers, then any produce that cannot hygienically be used the next day is composted in a closed aerobic food compost system. Indeed, annually 64 per cent of all waste across the site is recycled, of which 9 per cent is food based. Of that food waste, the vast majority is what is left on consumer plates or peelings from food preparation.

The Eden Project is another good example of a societal marketing approach with a strong focus on environmental and sustainable values.

*Source*: The Eden Project (www.edenproject.com/)

## Intangibility

Almost everything that is marketed comprises a mix of tangible and intangible components. If you were to buy a car (which is clearly tangible), it comes with a service warranty (which is intangible). If you buy a take-away meal, the burger, bun and fries are tangible, but someone would have prepared the food and provided the counter service, which is intangible. Services are intangible-dominant products, that is, they are principally made up of intangible components. Since services are intangible-dominant, it means that they cannot be experienced – they cannot normally be heard, seen, smelt, tasted or touched – prior to being consumed. Unlike shopping for a laptop computer or buying a motorcar, hospitality consumers cannot really examine competing hotel, restaurant or leisure services without entering into a purchase contract and experiencing the product. For example, they cannot stay overnight in a hotel and test out the rooms without being expected to pay first.

Since there is no tangible product to take home except for souvenirs, pictures and receipts in most cases, marketing intangibles create difficulties for the service provider. Customers often sense a higher level of risk and find it more difficult to assess the quality of intangibles. Customers need to be provided with information to help them choose an appropriate hospitality outlet to satisfy their particular needs and wants. The challenge for marketers is how to provide such information in a way that will encourage customers to choose *their* offer – without raising customer expectations too high and then failing to deliver customer satisfaction. The role of marketing communications to generate appropriate bookings whilst managing customer expectations is crucial.

When they sense risk and uncertainty purchasing an intangible hospitality experience, consumers often turn to online review sites such as Tripadvisor, online micro-blogging sites (Twitter, etc.), online picture sharing sites (Instagram, Flickr, etc.) and online social networking sites such as Facebook. An increasing number of hospitality customers read reviews posted by other consumers before making their final hotel or restaurant selection decisions. This increasing reliance on those sites makes it extremely important for marketers to monitor and manage their business's online presence and image.

## Perishability

Everyone working in hospitality knows that you cannot sell last night's empty bedroom tonight. Hotels and restaurants have a fixed number of rooms and seats available each day or night. Unlike manufactured products, which can be stored in warehouses, services cannot be stored; this feature of service industries is called 'perishability'. The difficulty for hospitality companies is how to manage their capacity (the inventory) with a fluctuating demand pattern.

Hospitality managers recognize that managing demand for the inventory is a critical issue in optimizing customer satisfaction, sales and profitability. The key marketing principle is to ensure that the price at peak demand times is set to deliver the maximum return to the company, provided it is compatible with customer satisfaction. In low season periods, the aim is to generate additional sales by developing attractive promotions, whilst still making a contribution to cover operating and some of the fixed costs. Managing the booking process to ensure that the business achieves this balance is essential. Larger hospitality businesses use computerized revenue management applications to maximize sales and reduce unsold inventory (see Chapter 7 for more information); smaller hospitality businesses have to rely on the experience of the owner, manager or reception team.

## Inseparability

Hospitality services are produced as they are consumed – production and consumption are insepa-rable. The simultaneous production and consumption of services mean that hospitality employees are an important part of the hospitality experience. When you check into most hotels, the recep-tionist produces that check-in service at the same time that you consume it. Customer service staff do not produce service unless there is a customer for whom to produce service. Customers have to be present to consume hospitality services and because they are present and sometimes interact with employees and other customers, they become co-creator of their own and other customers' experiences. Customers can exert significant influence on their own and other customers' experi-ence of the hospitality product during the co-creation process, either by enhancing or spoiling the experience for the other customers. These factors mean that customer interaction and their participation in the co-creation process with hospitality staff and other hospitality guests provide a variety of opportunities to influence customer satisfaction positively or negatively.

Ways to manage the problems of inseparability include the following:

- Ensuring that customer segments are compatible
- Utilizing technology to optimize operational efficiency in line with customer expectations
- Ensuring that the operations system is suitable for the projected market demand
- Adopting appropriate booking policies
- Organizing effective queuing systems
- Training staff effectively.

## Variability

Partly as a result of inseparability, hospitality operations suffer from considerable fluctuations in the standards of delivery of the service. This is called variability or heterogeneity. Variability is influenced by service inputs such as people, products and technologies. Services comprise a high element of interaction between customers and staff; indeed, every service performance can be described as a unique event. Human interaction cannot be standardized, and consequently it is impossible for service companies to deliver a totally non-variable customer experience. Inputs such as fresh produce vary in availability and quality, making consistent food production a challenge. Furthermore, technologies sometimes malfunction.

All this means that customer experience and service quality perceptions can vary considerably. Imagine that the same customers order the same meal that is cooked by the same chef and served by the same staff, in the same restaurant, at the same time of the week, on two succes-sive weeks. The resulting meal experience could be very different from one week (possibly per-fect) to the next (possibly disastrous). Some customers are highly knowledgeable about food and wine. These 'expert' customers, with their more refined understanding of service and qual-ity, can be more critical of a meal experience than less knowledgeable customers who might have really enjoyed the occasion. Companies respond to this problem of variability by trying to standardize their operations and training their staff to perform according to the company's standard operating procedures.

## Interdependence

Tourists make a variety of travel purchase decisions in one trip, and their overall satisfaction with a visit is based on a complex set of evaluations of different elements, including the travel arrangements, accommodation, attractions and facilities of a destination. The choice of hospitality products is only one decision the consumer makes. Hotel accommodation decisions in particular are influenced by the consumer's choice of other tourism products. Most significant is the tourist's choice of destination. Visitors may base their decision to travel to a particular destination on the range of attractions; the ease and accessibility of transport to and from the area; the image of the destination; the price; word-of-mouth recommendations made by family, friends and associates; and online review comments posted by other travellers. This means that the generation of demand for some hospitality operations is directly connected to the demand for complementary tourism products – so this type of demand is interdependent.

The response to interdependency is that individual businesses, regardless of the tourism sector they operate in, their size or ownership, must cooperate in the promotion of their destination. Destination marketing organizations (DMO's) bring together hospitality and tourism organizations, and local government agencies to promote demand for tourism. Every business can benefit when these collaborations succeed.

### Supply exceeds demand

The hospitality industry is a fragmented industry. While the entry barriers are high for some sectors of the hospitality industry such as the lodging sector, barriers to entry are low in some other sectors such as the restaurants, bars, cafés, teashops, etc. Thus, many hospitality companies are small and medium sized businesses. Indeed, many of today's famous brands (Hilton, Marriott and McDonald's) were originally small companies developed by visionary entrepreneurs.

Although regulations vary in different countries, governments have generally welcomed the development of tourism. The current trend of massive investment in new resorts, hotels, restaurants, cruise ships, leisure facilities and casino operations is continuing and therefore most sectors of the industry in many (though not all) parts of the world suffer from excess capacity. In good economic times, record numbers of people travel for business and leisure purposes, but the growth in hospitality capacity has not always been matched by a sufficient growth in demand. When supply exceeds demand, the competitive environment becomes more intense and price competition can affect all firms' profitability.

### High fixed costs

The cost structure of hospitality firms has a major influence on marketing practices. Hospitality businesses are capital, labour and energy intensive. Hospitality firms typically have high property costs and also employ large numbers of staff, many of whom are full-time, permanent employees. These costs do not change; they are 'fixed' regardless of the number of customers using the premises. During periods of low demand, high fixed costs erode the profitability of the business. High fixed costs encourage hospitality firms to become sales orientated; they will welcome any sale that makes a contribution towards the fixed costs. The marketing response to high fixed costs is to design new offerings and attractively priced promotions to stimulate sales in the low season.

## Service-dominant logic: co-creation and co-production

Vargo and Lusch have proposed that all entities offered to customers, whether conventionally called goods or services, produce service.[9] A microwave meal bought from a supermarket renders a service: not only does it provide you with nutrition and energy, but it also provides a food-preparation service for you. The manufacturers have done the food prep; you don't need to. When you buy a can of beans from the supermarket, other people have planted the crop, harvested it, processed it, canned it and distributed it. These are services provided by farmers, canners and others, so that you don't have to do so yourself. Vargo and Lusch have coined the term service-dominant logic (SDL) to describe this way of thinking.[9] Supporters of SDL claim that all firms are service firms; all markets are centred on the exchange of services, and all economies and societies are service-based. SDL embraces concepts of the value-in-use and co-creation of value. In other words, a good or a service has no value whatsoever until a consumer uses or engages with it; and the consumer is an active participant in value co-creation. Take the microwave meal. If the consumer fails to follow correct heating procedures the meal could be disastrous. By intelligently following printed instructions the consumer is co-creating a meal experience that can be enjoyed. Similarly, value is co-created by customers when they co-produce service in collaboration with employees of the service firm. The information that a customer provides to a guest service agent and their subsequent interaction allows the hospitality firm to identify and satisfy the customer's requirements. In SDL, customers are viewed as a co-production resource and their effective participation can help hospitality organizations to both reduce costs and enhance customer experience. You can read more about SDL here: www.sdlogic.net.

## The role of marketing management in hospitality

The marketing manager's tasks include research, planning, implementation and control of all activities that impact on the customer experience, including:

1  research and analysis of the needs and wants of current customers and selected target markets, changes in the PESTE environment and actions of competitors.

2  planning and budgeting marketing strategies to achieve agreed marketing objectives that may include sales revenues, profits, occupancy, RevPAR, food and beverage revenues, new customer acquisition, customer retention and market share growth.

3  Implementing marketing strategies by designing, developing and rolling out new product concepts; setting brand standards; and designing and executing online and integrated marketing communication campaigns. Many of these activities are accomplished through the marketing mix, which we introduce later in this chapter.

4  monitoring and controlling marketing strategies by ensuring that marketing objectives are being achieved; ensuring that marketing activities are carried out within the agreed budget; understanding the reasons why there are any variances between targeted performance and actual performance, and commissioning marketing research to evaluate marketing performance.

5  influencing other departments to become more focused on the customer, including influencing operations departments to make or buy what customers want to experience, and human resources departments to recruit the right type of people for customer-contact positions.

Some of these marketing activities will be carried out in-house by the company's own marketing personnel; other activities will be delegated to specialist marketing and publicity agencies. We explore all these marketing activities in later chapters.

## The hospitality marketing mix

The term *marketing mix* is used to describe the tools that the marketer uses to influence demand. The marketing mix is a core concept in marketing. The hospitality marketing mix adopted in this text is based on the eight marketing activities shown in Figure 1.3.

Figure 1.3 The hospitality marketing mix

### Product/service offer

Hospitality products and services are primarily designed to satisfy the needs and wants of business and leisure travellers. Examples include the following:

- Accommodation – a bed, bedroom, cabin or suite, in a hotel, inn, chalet, apartment, house, timeshare, cruise ship, hospital
- Food and beverage – a drink, sandwich, fast food, family meal or gourmet dinner, in a bar, café, cafeteria, coffee-shop, hotel, restaurant, tea-house, service station, roadhouse or ship, at an attraction or leisure centre
- Business services – a meeting, conference or trade show, in a hotel or conference centre
- Leisure – a short break, domestic holiday or international vacation, in a hotel, resort, self-catering accommodation, camping and caravan site or a cruise
- Event – a wedding, birthday party or anniversary, in a hotel, restaurant, bar or dedicated venue.

Marketing, working with operations, should play a role in developing product and service offers to ensure that the needs of customers are the focus of product development.

## Location

Finding a suitable location to offer the chosen service is absolutely critical for a hospitality organization. Location decisions focus on where the hospitality business should build, buy, franchise or rent the site(s) from which it operates.

## Price

The pricing decisions a hospitality organization makes include the following:

- Setting prices for all the different products to ensure that objectives (usually profit) are achieved
- Agreeing the level of discounts for key accounts
- Pricing bundled packages such as conferences, events, leisure breaks and vacation packages
- Developing special priced promotions to increase sales during low season periods.

Price influences demand. Price is crucial in driving profitability, and plays an important role in presenting the 'image' which the hospitality firm wants to project to customers and other stakeholders.

## Distribution

Distribution in hospitality is concerned with how a company can make it convenient for a potential customer to book or buy hospitality products directly from the hospitality company or through intermediaries. The impact of Information and Communication Technology (ICT), the Internet and mobile apps has radically transformed hospitality distribution channels and will continue to change relationships between hospitality providers and travel agents, tour operators, conference placement houses and incentive houses.

## Marketing communication

Marketing communication covers all the tools that hospitality firms can use to communicate with customers, employees and other stakeholders. It is also known as promotion and is popularly described as 'marcom'. Marcom decisions allow two-way communication between customers and the hospitality firm, or between customers, for example in social media. Communication is a core activity of most marketing and sales departments. The key elements of marketing communications in hospitality are

- Brand/corporate identity
- Online marketing (website and mobile design; search engine marketing; advertising; social media; and affiliate marketing)
- Personal selling (the sales team)
- Print and publicity material (e.g. brochures)
- Advertising
- Direct marketing
- Sales promotion
- Publicity

- Merchandising
- Sponsorship.

### Physical environment

The physical environment consists of the tangible features of the hospitality offer – the external appearance of the premises (the landscaping, lighting and signage), the internal layout (decor, furniture and furnishings), and the dress and physical appearance of staff. The physical environment can influence what customers believe and feel about the service, and how they behave. The ambience or atmosphere of a property is significantly influenced by conditions in its physical environment. Innovative hospitality companies can adopt the techniques of sensory marketing to create distinctive smells, sounds, sights, tastes and touches to enhance the ambience in a unit. The physical environment can also impact on service operations staff.

### Process

Because of the simultaneous production and consumption of hospitality services, the processes through which customers buy and consume hospitality products are of critical importance to marketers. Important processes include booking, checking in and checking out, queuing systems, and food and beverage service operations. Marketers need to ensure that the organization's service delivery processes are efficient, customer friendly and competitive.

### People

In the hospitality marketing mix, 'people' includes both employees and other customers. We have already discussed how hospitality customers interact with each other whilst on the premises – indeed, in certain hotel and destination environments, a good rapport between customers is an essential ingredient of a successful customer experience. Managing the customer mix and ensuring that target markets are compatible play a key role in delivering customer satisfaction. Being a service, the interaction between customers and hospitality employees is a critical element of the customer experience. Therefore, marketing needs to have an input into human resources aspects of the operation, and this is called *internal marketing*.

## Hospitality brands and the integrated marketing mix

Brands are central to the marketing of multi-unit hospitality businesses. Hospitality companies develop branded concepts and then blend the elements of the marketing mix to provide target customers with a better brand offer than their competitors (see Case Study 1.3). It is crucial that each element of the marketing mix is consistent with all the other elements. For example, a luxury hotel brand cannot be successfully located in a 'down market' area, and a cheap and cheerful restaurant cannot successfully promote gourmet dining. Those hospitality companies that do not provide a consistent service experience confuse customers by sending out mixed messages.

Thinking independently about each element of the marketing mix helps you to understand the complexity of the marketing offer. However, it should be remembered that customers form opinions based on their overall impression of the offer, and this can be influenced by 'minor items' such as the comfort of the pillow or the price of a drink, as well as by overarching considerations such as the general quality of service. If you reflect on all the different elements of the marketing mix, it becomes clear that marketers need to work closely with operations (on product, process and physical environment decisions), with finance (on pricing and marketing communication budget decisions) and with human resources (on staff recruitment, training and retention).

In smaller, single-unit operations, where the owner/manager is close to the business and is responsible for all the marketing mix decisions, the integration of marketing with other departments is easier. In large-scale, multi-unit national and international operations, such cooperation is much more difficult to achieve. Effective marketing is dependent on all the departments in a hospitality business working closely together.

### Experiential marketing

Marketers sometimes use what is known as experiential marketing to attract and retain customers. Experiential marketing is a particular patterning of marketing mix elements that involves the activation of multiple senses to create an innovative, memorable encounter that aims to 'wow' or delight customers. The distinctive patterning becomes associated with the brand. Hospitality sectors that have embraced experiential marketing include boutique hotels, cruises, adventure holidays, trade shows, music festivals and gastronomic restaurants. Consumers get to see, feel, hear, taste and even smell a hospitality experience that differentiates the brand from its competitors, and they can enjoy benefits that are physical, social, emotional or intellectual. Experiences that stand out from the routine are often the subject of everyday conversation; customers who've had a delightful and memorable experience will inject positive word-of-mouth into their conversations, spreading the good news online and offline, influencing others to become customers. Experiential marketing is used in both transactional and relationship contexts. Dining outdoors in the moonlit desert outside Dubai city is, for most customers, a one-off transaction that will never be repeated, and is most certainly a multi-sensory customer experience. Taking a short overnight cruise along the coast, however, is a multi-sensory experience that may entice a customer into a relationship that entails many subsequent longer cruises, each of which offers different locations and experiences. The Eden Project case study provides a good example of experiential marketing.

## So what do marketers actually do?

Most hospitality marketers are employees in sales, sales promotion, print and publicity, direct marketing, advertising, public relations, guest relations, marketing research, loyalty or frequent guest programmes, web operations, social media content management, search engine optimization and database management. However, many of those who work in marketing, especially in smaller operations, are focused on increasing sales using different forms of promotional activity such as online and offline advertising, sales promotion and publicity.

### CASE STUDY 1.3

**Premier Inn, UK – an integrated approach to marketing**[10]

In the 1980s, market demand for better-quality, low-cost accommodation in the United Kingdom grew significantly and Travelodge (the original developer of the concept) expanded rapidly. In 1987, Whitbread developed a competitor concept, called Travel Inn, which imitated the market leader in most aspects. By the late 1990s and despite intense competition from Accor, Days Inn and Holiday Inn Express, Travel Inn overtook Travelodge to become the market leader. In 2004, Travel Inn acquired Premier Lodge for over £500 million and increased the number of hotels by approximately 130 – the new brand was initially badged as Premier Travel Inn to reflect both brand names. In 2007, the Premier Inn brand was created following extensive consumer and customer market research. A new brand identity was created, which retained the equity of the previous incarnation. A new strapline was developed: 'Everything's Premier but the Price' and the brand experience was refreshed through significant investment in the product offer and a multi-million pound advertising campaign. By 2021, Premier Inn's continuous expansion resulted in over 800 units across the UK, the Middle East and Europe, which made Premier Inn the largest hotel brand in the United Kingdom. The Premier Inn marketing mix comprises:

- *Product* – low-cost, mid-market accommodation standards, with standardized bedrooms. Each room has an en-suite bathroom, king-size Hypnos beds (Hypnos also make beds for Queen Elizabeth II), high-quality Fogarty duvets, a choice of firm or soft pillows, flat screen digital TVs and Wi-Fi access. There are self-check-in kiosks at many sites to speed up arrivals, and every site has a bar/restaurant serving an 'all you can eat' cooked breakfast, all day snacks and lunch/dinner menu. During the COVID-19 pandemic, the chain has introduced 'Premier Inn CleanProtect' – an enhanced cleaning regime to ensure the safety and wellbeing of their guests and team members.

- *Location* – there are over 800 sites in the United Kingdom, and internationally there are hotels in the Arabian Gulf and Germany. In the UK, Premier Inn has developed a sophisticated approach to site selection using an in-house computer model with an extensive database of 1,600 British cities and their catchment areas (see Case Study 6.1 for more detail on Premier Inn's location strategy). All sites are either located adjacent to Whitbread branded restaurants such as Beefeater, Table Table, Brewers Fayre, Taybarns and Thyme or on occasions, alongside franchise partners.

- *Price* – Premier Inn moved from a fixed price strategy to dynamic pricing to boost RevPAR.

- *Distribution* – Premier Inn utilizes a combination of direct sales, sales through online travel agencies and third parties, affiliate marketing and sales through bricks-and-mortar travel agencies. Premier Inn also utilizes the Premier In Mobile App for bookings and customer service and customer relationship management.

- *Marketing communication* – the brand identity uses a strong, vibrant purple as the brand colour, which respondents in the focus groups suggested implied high quality. There is considerable investment in point-of-sale material to promote offers in the lobby and the front desk area, bedrooms and bar/restaurants. Premier Inn has been heavily utilizing online advertising, email marketing, PR, direct marketing and social media campaigns in recent years. However, due to the COVID-19 pandemic and its influence on the hospitality industry, Premier Inn has been ramping up marketing efforts in expectation of an improved post-pandemic travel environment. For the first time in more than three years, Premier Inn has returned to television with a 'Rest Easy' message designed to reassure wary travellers it's safe and comfortable as lockdown restrictions ease. This new marketing campaign also aims to revamp Premier Inn's visual identity as it looks to 'humanize' its communications. The new-look brand focus attempts to highlight the emotional benefits of travel and persuade guests to stay at one of the chain's 800+ hotels.

- *Physical evidence* – the external signage is consistent with the brand identity, and an extensive internal maintenance programme is designed to keep product standards consistent. Each room is refurbished every three years to maintain high levels of comfort and decor.

- *Process* – Premier Inn provides customers with the option of managing their accounts and bookings online or through a mobile app using a basic My Premier Account facility. The brand is a simple product with simple operating processes that prides itself on offering quality customer service levels with outstanding levels of housekeeping. The safety and wellbeing of Premier Inn's guests and teams has always been important to the company. Premier Inn recognizes that every guest and team member rightly expect a safe, clean and protected environment. The coronavirus crisis brought this into sharp focus. As a result, Premier Inn launched a new rigorous, daily cleaning regime called 'Premier Inn CleanProtect'. The CleanProtect was developed in partnership with Diversey, a global leading cleaning and hygiene product supplier for the healthcare and hospitality industries. The CleanProtect is Premier Inn's promise to give each customer extra peace of mind so they can book and stay with confidence. The food operation is predominantly managed by Whitbread branded restaurants either within or adjacent to the hotel.

- *People* – Premier Inn aims to recruit local, friendly staff who know the area; a key service performance metric is friendly service. As clearly expressed in the company culture statement 'We are proud to be a family of ambitious people and brands. We work hard for each other, succeed together and know we are part of something special – putting the customer at the heart of everything we do,' Premier Inn places heavy emphasis on employees' well-being and success.

Continuous investment in the Premier Inn brand has been rewarded by continued growth, increased brand awareness, many awards for marketing excellence and most importantly a good profit. The well-established 100 per cent money-back Good Night Guarantee, which promises comfortable surroundings, quality rooms and friendly staff, was a first in the UK market and continues to be a key differentiator. Premier Inn's integration of all the elements of the marketing mix provides a consistent marketing offer, which is customer focused and financially successful.

Visit the Premier Inn website at www.premierinn.com.

*Source*: Premier Inn

## The three marketing mixes

Because of the perishability and inseparability of hospitality products, marketers need to produce three marketing mixes, each aimed to influence demand at different stages of the customer journey.

Before the customer experiences the accommodation, food and beverage or entertainment, the marketer is faced with identifying and influencing customer expectations and trying to generate a first-time purchase. The first marketing mix is therefore called the *pre-encounter marketing mix*, because it happens before the customer has the service encounter.

The second marketing mix occurs on the premises at the time of consumption and is, therefore, called the *encounter marketing mix*. The task of this marketing mix is to produce a service encounter that meets or exceeds the customer's expectations, produces customer satisfaction and promotes positive word-of-mouth.

The third marketing mix is known as the *post-encounter marketing mix*, because it is designed to influence customers after the service encounter, with a view to creating long-term relationships.

Different parts of the eight-element marketing mix are important at each stage – before, during and after the encounter. Before the encounter, marketing communications such as website content, social media posts, customer reviews, advertising, selling, pricing and brochures influence expectations. Marketers may conduct research to understand the product/service expectations of customers as they design offers for the selected customers. They must also make products easy to buy by establishing appropriate distribution channels.

During the encounter, customers come in contact with the people element of the marketing mix (employees and other customers), processes and physical evidence at locations where the service is produced and consumed.

After the encounter, hospitality marketers will want to communicate with customers to find out what they thought of the experience, to identify and resolve customer complaints; to encourage the customer to come back; and to encourage customers to share their positive experiences through social media, review sites and with their friends and relatives. Therefore, marketing communications are used to build future demand from existing customers. Table 1.3 summarizes what is important at each stage of the customer relationship with the firm.

Table 1.3 Marketing before, during and after the encounter

| Marketing mix | Pre-encounter marketing mix | Encounter marketing mix | Post-encounter marketing mix |
|---|---|---|---|
| Product/service offer | √ | √ | |
| Location | √ | √ | |
| Price | √ | √ | |
| Distribution | √ | | |
| Marketing communications | √ | √ | √ |
| Physical environment | √ | √ | |
| Process | √ | √ | √ |
| People | | √ | |

The symbol '√' indicates which element is important in a particular marketing mix.

## Conclusion

A popular misconception is that marketing is the same as selling and advertising. This chapter has shown you that there is much more to marketing than this. Indeed, effective marketing encompasses virtually every aspect of the hospitality organization.

In this chapter, we have explained that:

- Marketing is a business philosophy that places the customer at the centre of the hospitality organization.
- The essential purpose of marketing is to manage demand.
- Marketing oriented companies seek to satisfy customers better than competitors.
- Marketers need to scan the PESTE and micro-environment to understand changes in the marketplace.
- Hospitality marketers need to respond to the challenges presented by service-related characteristics (SIPIVISH).
- The hospitality marketing mix comprises eight variables that need to be integrated and consistent to ensure brand integrity.
- Marketers work to influence demand before, during and after the service encounter.

---

### ACTIVITY 1.3

Look back to Activity 1.1

- Compare what you wrote about the meaning of 'marketing' with the definitions we have presented in this chapter. How different are the academic definitions to popular ideas about marketing?
- Reflect on what you think marketers do: have you changed your original ideas since reading his chapter?
- Can you now list more of the employment opportunities in marketing?

---

### REVIEW QUESTIONS

Now check your understanding of this chapter by answering the following questions:

1 Discuss the definitions of marketing, and explain the differences between transactional marketing and relationship marketing.
2 Discuss the advantages and disadvantages of each management orientation. Provide examples of each management orientation from your own experience of the hospitality industry (either as a customer or as an employee).
3 Discuss the macro- and micro-environmental factors that might influence a hospitality organization you know.
4 Evaluate the special characteristics of hospitality and services marketing.
5 Describe briefly the role of each element of the hospitality marketing mix.

## References

1. Kotler, P. (1999). *Kotler on Marketing*. New York, NY: Simon and Schuster.
2. American Marketing Association [Internet]. *What Is Marketing*. [cited September 8, 2021]. Available from: www.ama.org/the-definition-of-marketing-what-is-marketing/
3. Chartered Institute of Marketing. (2015). *Marketing and the 7Ps: A Brief Summary of Marketing and How It Works*. [cited September 8, 2021]. Available from: www.cim.co.uk/media/4772/7ps.pdf
4. Kotler, P., & Keller, K. (2016). *Marketing Management*. 15th ed. Upper Saddle River, NJ: Pearson Prentice Hall.
5. Levitt, T. (1960). Marketing myopia. *Harvard Business Review, 38*, 45–56.
6. Gursoy, D., & Chi, C. G. (2020). Effects of COVID-19 pandemic on hospitality industry: Review of the current situations and a research agenda. *Journal of Hospitality Marketing & Management, 29*(5), 527–529.
7. U.S. Travel Association [Internet]. *Travel Facts and Figures*. [cited September 8, 2021]. Available from: www.ustravel.org/research/travel-facts-and-figures
8. The Eden Project [Internet]. [cited September 8, 2021]. Available from: www.edenproject.com/
9. Vargo, S. L., & Lusch, R. F. (2004). Evolving to a new dominant logic for marketing. *Journal of Marketing, 68*(1), 1–17.
10. Premier Inn [Internet]. [cited September 8, 2021]. Available from: www.premierinn.com/gb/en/home.html

Part B

# Pre-encounter marketing

DOI: 10.4324/9781003186342-3

Pre-encounter marketing is how hospitality companies attract target customers. If pre-encounter marketing strategies are not effective, then the hospitality business will not have sufficient appeal to its target markets and sales/profit objectives may not be achieved. A key focus of pre-encounter marketing is to ensure that all the different marketing mix elements are integrated into a coherent and appealing offer to encourage the target customer to purchase your hospitality products and services, not the competition's hospitality products and services.

Chapter 2 introduces the basics of marketing research that produces the insight that should underpin marketing decision-making; Chapter 3 explains how to segment markets and select target customers; and Chapter 4 presents strategies to compete effectively. For new ventures, all of these activities take place before the hospitality concept is developed; for existing operations these activities should take place as part of the annual research for writing the marketing plan.

Chapters 5, 6 and 7 explain how the hospitality experience is developed; why location strategies are important; and how to price the offer in an increasingly transparent, competitive environment. Chapter 8 discusses distribution strategy, and particularly how hospitality organizations work with intermediaries to attract customers. Chapter 9 explores the many different ways that hospitality firms communicate with target audiences.

Chapter **2**

# Marketing research

After working through this chapter, you should be able to:

- Explain the role marketing research plays in decision-making in the hospitality industry
- Identify sources of marketing information available to hospitality organizations
- Distinguish between secondary and primary data
- Understand how hospitality researchers conduct online marketing research
- Explain the differences between qualitative and quantitative research methods
- Recognize how bias and sampling errors can distort marketing research findings.

## Introduction

Research is the foundation of successful marketing. Research needs to be undertaken before a new hospitality concept is developed or new markets are explored. Research also provides the information that underpins the annual marketing plan (see Chapter 15). This chapter explains how marketing research provides the foundation for effective marketing decision-making. We introduce the concept of the 'marketing information system' and then review the wide range of internal and external information sources available to hospitality managers. Both secondary and primary data collection techniques, and qualitative and quantitative data, are discussed with relevant examples. We discuss how to conduct secondary online research and, finally, we explain the marketing research process.

DOI: 10.4324/9781003186342-4

You are probably aware of marketing research in general terms. You may have been interviewed or even carried out some primary research, and you will certainly know about surveys and opinion polls from stories in the media. In fact, marketing research is a major industry that impacts on our everyday lives.

---

### ACTIVITY 2.1

Before reading the rest of the chapter, try to think about the role of marketing research.

- Why do you think hospitality companies carry out marketing research?
- What do you think are the main uses of marketing research in the hospitality sector?
- List the marketing research activities you have heard about.
- List the sources of information you can access for marketing research.

---

When you have completed the chapter, carry out this activity again and then compare your answers.

## Marketing research

Managers are paid to make decisions. The purpose of marketing research is to inform and improve their decision-making by reducing uncertainty. Marketing research can be defined as the systematic gathering and analysis of data to provide relevant information that aids marketing decision-making.

As the preceding definition states, marketing research is systematic; that is, it follows a sequence of logical steps. Initially, research objectives need to be agreed and information sources identified. Quantitative and/or qualitative data are collected using a number of scientific methods, and these data are analyzed. The data are then evaluated and interpreted to provide useful information to aid decision-making. However, marketing research cannot eliminate all risk in management decision-making.

You may have noticed that the term *marketing research* has been used – not *market research*. There is a difference.

- *Market research* is the term used to describe the investigation of consumer and organizational markets – the size and structure of a market, its consumption patterns and the demographic profile of consumers, for example.
- *Marketing research* has a much wider application, including research into all the marketing mix variables and the macro- (PESTE) and micro-environments.

Professional marketers use the term *marketing research* to cover all aspects of research activity, including consumer and market behaviour.

## Marketing information systems

Hospitality managers need relevant, accurate, timely and usable information to be able to make effective decisions that will influence the future of their businesses. Small, single-unit, owner-

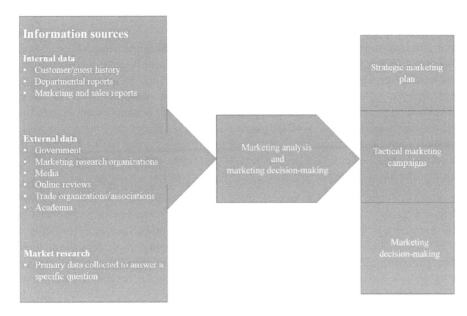

Figure 2.1 The hospitality marketing information system

operated companies normally rely on informal approaches to data collection and interpretation. Owner-managers can easily talk to customers and read customers' comments posted to third party review sites or social media to judge levels of customer satisfaction and intention to return or to obtain clues about how to improve performance. They can also read comments posted by customers of their competitors to determine strengths and weaknesses of their competitors and use this information to identify opportunities and threats to their and their competitors' businesses. Owner-managers can also read about consumer and industry trends in the hospitality media and adapt their marketing offer in response to changes in the external environment.

Larger organizations need to develop more sophisticated *marketing information systems* to ensure that corporate executives understand the more complex environments in which they are operating (see Figure 2.1). This is because marketing managers in larger companies are separated geographically, and sometimes culturally, from the markets they serve. A marketing information system helps marketers identify trends and plan for the future, utilizing:

- Existing data from *internal* company sources (accounts and sales, guest history and customer satisfaction)
- Data collected from *external* sources (government, media, marketing research associations, trade associations, etc.)
- Commissioned marketing research studies (brand perceptions, consumer trends, customer review comments, customer sentiments, competitor innovations and corporate reputation).

## Sources of information

There are three sources of information marketers use to make decisions: internal information sources, external information sources and commissioned marketing research studies.

### Internal information

Internal information is information that is sourced from inside the organization. Sometimes this may be sufficient to answer a marketing research question. Internal information is available from many departments – sales, marketing, operations and banqueting. While in some small businesses, each department maintains its own records, with the increasing use of customer relationship management (CRM) systems, most small businesses are able to create a centralized database of customer-related information. This brings together and standardizes information across departments so that anyone in the business can have a complete view of the customer's relationship with the business – purchases, contracts, contacts, responses to marketing campaigns, issues or complaints, and loyalty scheme activity.

Some accommodation businesses such as hotels or cruise ships are required by law to obtain customers' personal details; other businesses have to find ways to motivate customers to supply this information, for example, when they sign up for a competition or a newsletter. Cash-based businesses such as cafés and bars do not normally hold contact details on customers; however, the electronic point of sale (EPOS) computer systems used in chain operations enable them to monitor customer preferences and purchase patterns. A sample of the internal data available in accommodation outlets is given in Table 2.1.

Table 2.1 Internal data for accommodation outlets

| | |
|---|---|
| Customer records | Hotel guest registration details. In most countries it is a legal requirement to record the name, address and length of stay of all guests. |
| Guest history | *Source of booking*: direct, call/contact centre, mobile app, website, third party Internet, travel agent, local company |
| | *Method of reservation*: Internet, Intranet, email, call, walk-in |
| | *Type and number of guests*: corporate, private, tour operator |
| Departmental reports | Weekly/monthly accounts recording actual performance against budget, for sales, occupancy, RevPAR; non-residential sales – food and beverage, banquet sales, conference, leisure outlets |
| Marketing and sales reports | In-house customer satisfaction questionnaires and surveys; customers' compliments and complaints; sales force information from key accounts and intermediaries; loyalty club activity; mystery customer surveys; brand conformance audits; brand performance surveys |

### External information

Most researchers faced with the need to access data from external sources search online. Appropriate search terms help to focus the area of research; however, Internet research can still be very time-consuming and, if the search term is too broad, thousands, if not millions, of possible sources can be generated. You can try this yourself. Go online and use a search engine such as Google, Bing or Baidu to search for information on hotel chains in a particular country. Searching for 'hotel chains in Ghana' will generate well over a million results. Examples of organizations that provide useful online data for hospitality researchers include:

- International and national government organizations such as the World Tourism Organization, International Monetary Fund, United Nations and World Travel & Tourism Council

(WTTC) publish a wide variety of useful marketing data and analysis. However, you should be aware that direct comparisons of key statistics between different countries are not always accurate due to cultural, sampling or respondent bias.

- Governmental publications such as the National Travel and Tourism Office (NTTO), which functions as the U.S. federal tourism office, European Travel Commission and VisitBritain (Britain's tourist authority).

- Marketing research organizations such as Mintel, Keynote and the Economist Intelligence Unit; management consultancies such as BDRC Continental, Deloitte, KPMG and PKF, which produce commercial market reports on major sectors of the hospitality industry (e.g., hotels and holidays).

- Trade associations, such as the American Hotel & Lodging Association (AH&LA), the American Hotel Sales and Marketing Association, the National Restaurant Association (NRA) and the U.S. Travel Association, which provide market information and services for members; sometimes these reports are also made available to the public.

- Publicly listed companies publish annual accounts for shareholders, which are also available to the public; annual accounts provide essential information about companies' marketing strengths and strategies; often the chief executive officer's (CEO) report will contain information about the future outlook for the business.

- Useful company and market information is found in the industry's trade press (*Food and Beverage Magazine, Caterer, Hotels Magazine*), the financial press (*Financial Times, Wall Street Journal, New York Times*) and surveys on media expenditure by companies such as Nielsen.

- Universities and academic publishers produce journals reporting current academic research; the journals discuss academic theory and provide insights into current industry practice, e.g. *Journal of Hospitality Marketing & Management, International Journal of Hospitality Management, Journal of Destination Marketing & Management* and *Journal of Vacation Marketing*.

- Competitors' websites and online booking/comparison sites, e.g. booking.com and Tripadvisor, provide current product/pricing data and customer feedback/rankings.

- Travel guides such as *Lonely Planet, Rick Steves, Frommer's, Fodor's* and *Rough Guides* provide details of destinations' tourist attractions, cultural issues and popular hospitality outlets.

- Online review sites such as Tripadvisor, Booking.com, Google and trivago, and social media such as Facebook, Instagram and YouTube provide information about customer experiences, customer sentiments, customer complaints and satisfaction levels.

Marketers analyze data collected from the marketing information system and use the information as a basis for developing and refining marketing strategies and tactics.

### Commissioned marketing research studies

The major hospitality companies have invested significant capital in developing computerized databases, linked to guest history, to track customer behaviour and identify emerging trends. In recent years, large hospitality companies have also introduced artificial intelligence powered data mining and analysis software and systems to harvest, monitor and analyze information shared by consumers on review sites and social media. Because larger companies routinely monitor their marketing environments, most of this marketing information is collected on a scheduled, regular basis. However, there are occasions when there is a requirement for specific marketing information. On these occasions, a dedicated marketing research project needs to be commissioned to answer a specific question. Commissioned research can help marketers to better understand specific market segments wants, needs, behaviour, purchase behaviour, and other characteristics. It helps them understand and compare their products and services with their competitors and industry standards. Hospitality businesses also commission marketing research to understand the behaviour of their customers towards newly launched products and services. Marketing research is also used to explore potential markets and market segments, and the needs and wants of customers in those potential markets.

Hospitality managers will use information from marketing research studies to help them make decisions on questions such as the following:

- Should the restaurant increase the number of vegetarian items on the menu? A review of eating preferences is needed.
- Should the company open a new retail fast-food unit in an airport? A feasibility study will need to be undertaken.
- Should the company invest in a new brand concept? Research into consumer needs and wants, potential market demand, competitors, and an audit of company capabilities, is needed.
- Should the company invest in artificially intelligent devices to provide some of the back of the house and front of the house services?

## Types of data

Marketing researchers distinguish between two types of data: secondary and primary.

### Secondary (or desk) data

Secondary data are data that have already been collected. Externally sourced data provided in UNWTO international visitor arrivals and Mintel reports are examples of secondary data. It is relatively easy to obtain secondary data since the information has already been published. Some organizations provide this data for free; however, commercial companies make a charge that can range up to several thousand dollars. However, this may be good value compared to the cost of setting up an independent research project to collect the same data.

There are limitations to secondary data. First, the data have been collected and analyzed by another organization that will have had its own – maybe very different – reasons for carrying out the research. This means that the information may not be sufficiently detailed, accurate or relevant. Some organizations, including government bodies and pressure groups, may deliberately present findings that support their own agendas. Other organizations may have inadvertently introduced bias or error into their data due to poor research methods. Another limitation of desk research is that the information is generally also available to other organizations, including competitors, the media and pressure groups, and so offers little by way of competitive advantage. Finally, secondary data and analysis can often be dated because of the long time between carrying out the research and publishing the findings. When carrying out secondary research, it is essential to check the date of the research, verify the credibility of the source of the material and validate the research methods employed.

Despite these limitations, secondary research is usually the starting point for a research project and provides useful background information cost-effectively.

### Primary data

Primary data consist of original information collected by an organization for a specific purpose. The data have not been published before. The organization conducting or commissioning the research determines the research objectives and research questions. The data are collected directly to provide answers to those questions.

Primary research is usually more costly than secondary research. However, the advantages of primary research include the following:

● There is an ability to frame the research questions to the needs of the organization.
● Results are current and not dated.
● The research is confidential to the commissioning organization.

Primary data can enable a hospitality company to gain a competitive advantage if its rivals are not carrying out similar research.

---

**MARKETING INSIGHT 2.1**

**Closed and open questions**

There are two major types of questions used in survey research: closed-ended questions and open-ended questions.

*Closed-ended questions* provide a number of alternative answers from which the respondent chooses one answer. Examples include questions about the respondent's age, sex, employment, income or about the frequency with which the respondent visits a restaurant, drinks coffee or takes a holiday. Closed-ended questions use a structured format, and this creates a data set that can be easily analyzed using statistical methods. The research findings are described as 'hard' data and provide numerical information. If the research uses a quantitative approach, then closed questions are essential.

*Open-ended questions* allow respondents to provide their own answers, without any guidance. Examples of open questions include: 'Where would you stay tonight if this hotel was fully booked?' and 'What do you feel about the quality of service?' The response to an open question allows the respondent to use their own words to describe their experience, feelings and opinions. The research findings provide 'rich' data that are used in qualitative research. Analysis of answers to open-ended questions is enabled by text analytics software which converts unstructured responses into structured data.

Researchers can ask a combination of closed-ended and open-ended questions, and analyze the findings using both qualitative and quantitative methods.

---

## Qualitative and quantitative data

### Qualitative data

Qualitative research aims to provide a deep understanding of people's contextualized behaviour. It aims to explain how and why people behave as they do. As such, it examines beliefs, perceptions, motives, attitudes and opinions. This type of research can provide deep insights into consumers' responses to an organization, its products, services, brands and image. Qualitative researchers use observation, in-depth interviews, focus groups (also known as group discussions), online customer reviews and user-generated content (UGC), as well as embedding qualitative questions in surveys.

*Observation* is a powerful research tool. Simply sitting in a reception lobby (or quietly observing the service at an event) and watching the customer/employee interaction can provide insights into the efficiency of the service operation, the friendliness of the service staff and the level of customer satisfaction.

*In-depth interviewing* enables a researcher to ask respondents open-ended questions, often in a semi-structured format. A semi-structured format typically involves the researcher creating a research protocol (a list of topic areas and ideal question running order) in advance of the interviews and then asking questions in an informal, conversational way. The interviews can take place face-to-face, by telephone, VoIP (Voice Over Internet Protocol) service such as WhatsApp, Messenger, chat, email, or over a video conferencing application such as ZOOM, Microsoft Teams, Skype or Webex. Face-to-face or video-enabled interviews enable the researcher to note and react to the interviewee's body language and to probe the respondent with more searching questions in order to obtain more complete, detailed responses.

*Focus group* discussions use group dynamics to explore important marketing issues. The researcher invites a number of people (usually less than 10) to participate in the discussion, which is normally held in a neutral environment. Depending on the purpose of the discussion, the invitees may be consumers, existing customers, potential customers, former customers or employees. A small reward is often offered for participation. A moderator hosts the discussion, which is conducted in a friendly, informal, even 'chatty' way. Focus groups start by discussing broad issues and then begin to focus on the core topic of the research. The researcher asks the participants' permission to film or record the session to enable further analysis. The group dynamics enable a skilled moderator to draw out different perspectives from each member of the group, as well as the group's collective views.

*User-generated content (UGC)* refers to any form of content, such as reviews of hospitality experiences, images of food and videos of hotel facilities that has been posted by users on online platforms such as third party review sites, social media and wikis. The content is created by consumers who are willing to share and disseminate information and opinions about their experiences with a product or a service. Hospitality companies harvest the most applicable UGC and then analyze using content/text mining analysis. This may be done for a wide variety of reasons including identifying customer sentiments toward their offerings and competitors' offerings, assessing customer satisfaction, identifying problem areas in service delivery, identifying their own and competitors' strengths and weaknesses, online reputation management, problem processing, advertising and much more.

*Questionnaires* often include open-ended questions that generate qualitative data. Participants in qualitative survey-based research – or focus groups – may not be truly representative of the population they are intended to represent. Many hospitality customers are too busy, or not sufficiently interested, to give up their valuable time to participate. The inducements to participate – if any – are modest. Although qualitative findings may be insightful, they cannot be generalized, and other forms of quantitative marketing research need to be used to further test or validate the findings.

Sometimes, qualitative research is performed after quantitative research. This happens when quantitative research has discovered interesting information that needs further investigation. For example, a customer satisfaction survey may indicate that a high percentage of customers do not like the menu options in a restaurant. Qualitative research can explore the reasons behind the statistic.

### Quantitative data

Quantitative researchers use a wide range of methods to obtain and analyze numerical data. Quantitative research counts numbers, in terms of either volume or value. For example, the number of customers, passengers, residents, diners, room-nights, room occupancy; a restaurant unit's sales; or a hotel chain's room sales. If data are numeric, then the research is quantitative. Quantitative research techniques are founded upon statistical theory.

### Sources of error in quantitative research

Hospitality marketers may feel more confident making decisions based on quantitative data but need to be aware that errors may still exist: there are four main forms of error in quantitative marketing research.

#### SAMPLING ERROR

This is when sampling procedures introduce error into the results. The most common form of sampling error is sample bias. To be valid, the research has to be based on a representative sample of the population of interest to the researcher. Random sampling depends on the availability of a relevant sampling frame – a list of the population of interest. If the list is dated, contains omissions or duplications, or other errors such as missing contact details, then this introduces sampling error.

#### RESPONDENT ERROR

Participants in surveys might introduce error in their responses to questions. Some people may give answers that they think are the 'right' or socially acceptable answers, rather than being honest, stating the facts or giving their true opinion. Consumer surveys of alcohol consumption are notorious for underestimating true consumption!

#### INVESTIGATOR ERROR

Researchers can accidentally make errors by entering the data inaccurately. This type of recording error can easily happen when inexperienced researchers are not trained thoroughly. Sometimes interviewers may subconsciously choose to interview people who are similar to themselves.

#### ADMINISTRATIVE ERROR

This error is associated with the method and timing (the administration) of data collection processes. A survey that is only conducted by email misses out on segments of the population who are not online. Responses to questionnaires vary according to the day of week and the weather. For example, on a rainy or oppressively hot day more hotel guests remain in the property. On a pleasant day, in-hotel surveys will therefore have fewer guests to interview.

In large surveys, statistical software packages are used to process the quantitative research data. Optical scanners can also be used to read completed questionnaires and provide detailed data analysis.

There is a variety of survey methods used in quantitative marketing research. The methods commonly used in hospitality organizations include exit surveys; mystery customer audits; face-to-face, email, app and telephone surveys; and omnibus surveys.

*Exit surveys* are questionnaires that guests complete immediately, or soon, after their hospitality experience. All the major hotel chains, and many independent hotels, use exit surveys. A common administrative method is to leave questionnaires in the rooms for guests to complete, or to email the guest a link to an online questionnaire after checking out. Questions typically seek feedback on the quality of accommodation, food, service and value for money. These customer satisfaction surveys are important tools for evaluating how a unit is performing, but they suffer from a low response rate and normally attract either the extremely dissatisfied or the highly delighted customer.

The example in Figure 2.2 shows the Belmont Hotel's exit survey, which has both closed and open questions asking customers to comment in detail on every department in the hotel. Companies such as Malmaison do not ask any questions, but simply allow customers to write what they feel (see Figure 2.3).

*Mystery customer audits* are used by multiple-unit branded operators to assess how individual units are performing. Researchers posing as customers check whether a unit is conforming to the brand standards and evaluate the operation from a customer perspective. Each aspect of the operation is marked, and an overall score is recorded. Unit managers and employees do not know who the 'mystery customer' is, but later receive a copy of the report, which highlights brand and operational compliance and deficiencies.

Surveys can be administered in many ways, including *face-to-face*, *email*, *app*, *mobile device* and *telephone*. Computer-aided telephone interviews (CATI) can be conducted by a human interviewer, or completely automated, with interviewees responding by voice or keystrokes to questions. Telephone-administered questionnaires can be cost-effective for researching certain segments, e.g. the conference market. Key accounts and conference placement agencies can be contacted to ascertain their purchasing intentions or changing requirements.

*Omnibus surveys* involve several companies sharing the costs of the research. Essentially, each client pays for a number of questions to appear in the survey, and to receive a customized analysis. Costs vary according to the number of questions and types of analysis required. The survey is carried out by an independent marketing research agency, collecting data from a common sample. An omnibus survey, which is a form of syndicated research, is a major research exercise. Syndicated research is conducted by market research companies and sold to a number (syndicate) of clients. Omnibus surveys are relatively expensive to carry out because of the large sample size but can be very cost-effective when costs are shared between multiple clients. The BVA BDRC omnibus hotel guest survey is carried out in over 90 different countries[1]; most of the leading hotel brands participate in the survey and are able to benchmark their performance against previous years and competitors. Brands can also add their own specific questions to the survey for an additional fee – the responses to these specific questions are confidential.

---

### ACTIVITY 2.2

Compare the questionnaires in Figures 2.2 and 2.3.

- What is the main difference between the Belmont and Malmaison's approach to soliciting customer feedback?
- What types of questions are used?
- How will the data be analyzed?

---

A company can either carry out its own marketing research, which is called 'in-house' research, or contract out the work to a marketing research agency. Although marketing research agencies can be more expensive, as specialists in their field they will have the expertise, experience, qualified staff, connections and appropriate technologies to carry out the research professionally.

**Dear Guest**

I hope you are enjoying your stay. Our aim as a team is to welcome you back and we continually strive to maintain and improve the service standards and facilities of the hotel. We would very much appreciate your view regarding your present visit and the facilities you used.

Name _____  Room number _____  Date of stay _____

Email address _____

What influenced your stay at the Belmont Hotel? _____

How did you make your booking?              _____

Do any of our staff deserve a special mention?    _____

|  | Excellent | Good | Satisfactory | Poor |
|---|---|---|---|---|
| **RECEPTION** | | | | |
| Your reservation | ☐ | ☐ | ☐ | ☐ |
| Your check-in | ☐ | ☐ | ☐ | ☐ |
| Warmth of welcome | ☐ | ☐ | ☐ | ☐ |
| **ACCOMMODATION** | | | | |
| Cleanliness of room | ☐ | ☐ | ☐ | ☐ |
| Standard of facilities | ☐ | ☐ | ☐ | ☐ |
| Room Information | ☐ | ☐ | ☐ | ☐ |
| **JAMIES BAR** | | | | |
| Greeting | ☐ | ☐ | ☐ | ☐ |
| Quality of food | ☐ | ☐ | ☐ | ☐ |
| Quality of service | ☐ | ☐ | ☐ | ☐ |

| | Excellent | | Good | | Satisfactory | | Poor | |
|---|---|---|---|---|---|---|---|---|
| **WINDOWS ON NEW WALK** | Breakfast | Dinner | Breakfast | Dinner | Breakfast | Dinner | Breakfast | Dinner |
| Greeting | ☐ | ☐ | ☐ | ☐ | ☐ | ☐ | ☐ | ☐ |
| Quality of the service | ☐ | ☐ | ☐ | ☐ | ☐ | ☐ | ☐ | ☐ |
| Quality of the food | ☐ | ☐ | ☐ | ☐ | ☐ | ☐ | ☐ | ☐ |
| Menu Choice | ☐ | ☐ | ☐ | ☐ | ☐ | ☐ | ☐ | ☐ |

Do you have any further comments regarding any aspect of the hotel?

_____
_____

(Please continue overleaf if necessary)

Thank you very much for taking the time to complete this questionnaire, please hand it to Reception on leaving, or leave in your bedroom to be collected. We look forward to welcoming you back to The Belmont.

If you do not wish to receive any information about the Belmont Hotel please tick the box ☐

**Eloic Montagnier, General Manager**

Figure 2.2  The Belmont Hotel guest questionnaire

Malmaison

COMMENT CARD

Name: ............................................... Date of stay: .......................... Room No: .................

Comments

Figure 2.3 Malmaison open-ended customer questionnaire

The decision to use an agency or do the work in-house will depend on the type of research undertaken and the budget available. Observation, customer satisfaction and exit surveys are normally handled in-house. Focus groups, in-depth interviewing, mystery customer, competitor surveys and omnibus surveys are more often conducted by specialist marketing research agencies.

## The marketing research process

Marketing research follows a sequence of logical stages as described next.

1 *Formulation of research objectives*. The aims, scope and limitations of the research project need to be established at the beginning. Clearly identifying the research problem, deciding the desired research outcomes and defining the research objectives at the beginning save time and money later. Establishing the available budget is essential, since budget constraints will determine what type of marketing research is undertaken and whether the activity is carried out in-house or by an agency. Research objectives are largely determined by the marketing decisions that are to be made.

2 *Development of a research plan*. Each stage of the research process needs to be carefully planned, with provisional actions, costs, people requirements and deadlines set out. An evaluation of which research methods are most appropriate needs to be based on the research objectives and budget.

3 *Data collection*. There are two major components to this phase of the process: first, identifying sources of information (who has the information and where is it?), and second, deciding how to collect the information from those sources. Data collection usually starts with a review of secondary sources. This desk research enables the researcher to understand what is already known about the research question, and the data collection methods that have been used. A good understanding of secondary sources provides the researcher with a solid foundation before embarking on any primary research. Indeed, some research projects can be completed with secondary data alone. If primary research is required, a pilot study to test the research instrument or method is essential. Changes can then be made to the research instrument before the full-scale marketing research study is rolled out.

4 *Data analysis*. There is a wide range of statistical tools available to aid marketing data analysis, including:

- *univariate* techniques, which present analyses of single variables such as the value of restaurant receipts or the number of complaints per month
- *bivariate* techniques, which analyze two variables simultaneously and establish whether there is a strong, weak or non-existent correlation between them – for example, the correlation between the number of employee training hours and restaurant customer satisfaction
- *multivariate* techniques, which analyze three or more variables simultaneously to establish what, if any, link exists between them – an example might be all the complex factors that influence hotel customer loyalty.

5 *Assess the reliability and validity of data*. Responsible researchers recognize that marketing research has limitations and that it is important to identify any possible error or bias in the data prior to interpretation. Professional marketing researchers are particularly concerned with the issues of reliability and validity of data. If you want to measure customer satisfaction, it would be invalid to use a questionnaire designed to measure service quality perceptions. Valid measures are free from the sources of error described earlier: respondent error, investigator error, sampling error and administrative error. A reliable measure is one that is consistent and does not vary over time. Data from research have to be placed within the context of the PESTE environment at the time of the research, since research findings in the hospitality industry are influenced by different periods of economic prosperity and recession. So, it is important to always check the date when the research was carried out to see how current the data are. Finally, some organizations deliberately manipulate or distort information, but it is not always easy to determine what data have been misrepresented.

6 *Presentation of findings*. Finally, the researcher has to present the findings. Normally, there will be large amounts of data and analysis, which need to be presented in an accessible and useable manner. Key findings should be provided in an executive summary. The main report should contain an explanation of the methodology and detailed discussion of the findings. Any research limitations and source of error or bias should be explained. The raw data can be presented either in the appendices or in a separate document.

## Internet research

Online marketing research is rapidly growing because there can be significant cost savings in the design and administration of questionnaires, and it can be conveniently and cost-effectively used to survey existing or lapsed customers. Generating a representative sample is just as important in online marketing research as offline. Businesses wanting to investigate guests' service quality perceptions and satisfaction may incentivize their participation by including them in free prize draws with attractive rewards. Larger hospitality companies can mine their frequent guest programmes to identify a sample to research a specific aspect of their operations and can obtain thousands of responses. Many hospitality firms use online applications such as SurveyMonkey to conduct their own online research – see Marketing Insight 2.2.

An increasing number of hospitality companies have been using blogs and offering various incentives to entice customers to comment on their customer experiences, or employing social media marketing tools and technologies to harvest customer comments and user-generated content posted to various sites including third party review sites (i.e., Tripadvisor), social media sites (i.e., Facebook, Instagram), and online booking sites (i.e., Expedia.com, Booking.com, Agoda. com) and price comparison sites (trivago.com, KAYAK.com, Google travel). After harvesting and identifying the most applicable comments to their research question, those companies employ content/text mining and sentiment analyses to analyze those comments to explore issues like customers sentiments, service quality, problem areas and customer satisfaction.

## International marketing research

The international reach of major hospitality companies means they need to carry out research in various national markets. This presents a range of problems due to the cultural, language and technological differences between countries.

---

### MARKETING INSIGHT 2.2

**SurveyMonkey**[2]

SurveyMonkey is a company that provides online cloud-based survey services to individuals and companies in 16 different languages. Individuals can design their own basic questionnaire with a combination of closed and open questions, post it online and, when respondents have completed the survey, the results are analyzed for free. Commercial organizations are charged for these services. The surveys can be designed to investigate branding issues, consumer behaviour, customer satisfaction and future trends. SurveyMonkey provides sample surveys, sample questions and analytical reports on the sample selection, bias elimination and data analysis.

If you want to explore SurveyMonkey and design a questionnaire, go to www.survey-monkey.com. You could adapt some of the questions from the Belmont Hotel's guest satisfaction questionnaire (Figure 2.2) to input into your own survey.

*Source*: SurveyMonkey

---

Issues include the following:

- *Translation difficulties* – when English-speaking researchers are conducting survey research in another country or a region of their own country that has a large proportion of non-English speakers, they initially compile their questionnaires in English and have a native speaker translate the questions into the local language. Another native English speaker then back-translates the questionnaire into English. This process checks whether translation has changed the meaning of any questions.

- *Difficulties in obtaining comparable samples* – some countries are unable to provide reliable lists of the population. Even if they can provide a reliable list, classification criteria used for assigning individuals into specific groups may vary. For example, definitions of middle class and education level may vary.

- *Different cultural responses to research* – in some cultures, women are discouraged from participating in surveys, and some types of question are regarded as too intrusive.

- *Differences in the infrastructure that supports research* – some countries have poor postal systems, and not all research participants have access to the Internet or electronic devices such as tablets, cell-phones or even landlines.

Companies carrying out international marketing research need to be aware of these difficulties and should employ specialist local research agencies to provide appropriate in-country advice. Case Study 2.1 provides an example of global marketing research.

## CASE STUDY 2.1

### Global Marketing Research at IHG[3]

InterContinental Hotels Group (IHG) conducted one of the largest and most comprehensive research projects ever undertaken by an organization within the hospitality industry. IHG needed to review the strategic position and juxtaposition of its portfolio of brands to fit the needs of contemporary consumers. The company also recognized that its largest and most established brand, Holiday Inn, was in need of rejuvenation.

IHG combined qualitative and quantitative research including focus groups, in-depth interviews and quantitative surveys with regular hotel users and non-users, including people who stayed with family and friends or in hostel accommodation. Over 18,000 consumers from the USA, Canada, China, Germany and the UK participated in the research. The central objective was to understand how consumers viewed and selected the hotels they used, whether it was for business or leisure purposes. The focus was on the customer journey – from selection and booking, in-hotel experience to check-out and even post-stay communications. The research benchmarked IHG brands and competitors on current and desired brand attributes.

The results enabled IHG to develop detailed consumer profiles for each segment of the hotel and lodging market. Matrices were developed to plot the IHG hotel portfolio against competitor brands in detail, such that the marketing team could clearly visualize the relationship among current brand attributes, consumer segments and competitor offers. This visualization helped IHG to map the future desired position for each of their brands and identified gaps in the market where new brands, such as Hotel Indigo, a branded boutique concept, might be developed. Most importantly, the research helped the brand managers of Holiday Inn and Holiday Inn Express to focus on improving brand conformance across the world and provided a strategic direction to reinvigorate these brands.

The two-year research project culminated in a detailed plan to enhance the guest experience at Holiday Inn and Express and to improve the consistency of that experience. The findings also drove product enhancements such as improved food and beverage, public area design and pillow menus. In the past, only a few luxury hotel brands offered a choice of pillow, but Holiday Inn and Express introduced a choice of pillow as an in-room requirement for the brand standards. As part of the relaunch, the iconic Holiday Inn logo, unchanged since 1952, was given a refreshed look, which helped hotel owners, management, employees and consumers to more closely identify with the rebranding.

Since Holiday Inn and Express is a franchise, IHG needed to obtain the support of the hotel owners (the franchisees) to invest in these improvements. Crucially, the original research played a major role in helping to inform and convince the franchisees about the need to invest in the hotels to improve brand performance. Before an existing franchisee was allowed to participate in the relaunch programme, a Holiday Inn or Express had to pass more than 50 quality thresholds to ensure that the property quality and unit management was serious about the commitment to new brand standards.

IHG recognizes that marketing research is critical in developing an appropriate marketing offer to hospitality consumers. Research is an ongoing company activity to ensure that IHG remains competitive. While some of the research is conducted in-house, IHG also partners with other companies to conduct joint research. For example, IHG partnered with a global travel technology group, Amadeus, to commission a study to identify drivers shaping the future of the hospitality industry. The research that was conducted with 7,500 consumers worldwide and industry experts identified three trends that the hospitality sector must respond to to meet the needs of consumers of the future. **The Beginning of the End for Room Types** was a key trend identified. Hotel accommodation, which has traditionally been bought in a standard and uniform way, will need to adapt as 61 per cent of global travellers state a preference for hotels to be priced in a way that allows them to add-on bespoke options. This will see the emergence of attribute-based booking, where guests pick and choose the individual components of their room, marking a challenge to traditional room types. New selling models will become more mainstream too, with guests able to book a room for a length that suits their needs rather than a traditional overnight stay.

The second trend identified was **the Rise of Tech-Augmented Hospitality**: hospitality providers will need to serve guests in a significantly more connected way, striking the right balance between automated solutions and human interaction. The study suggests that technology needs to support human interaction, not replace it, as the majority of guests (67 per cent) say they prefer to interact with a person for the emotional experience.

The third trend identified was **Achieving Cult Status at Scale**: the kind of status usually reserved for luxury or boutique hotels will be available for all, if they can build a loyal following of fans who feel an emotional connection. In the competition for guest loyalty, hospitality providers need to identify how to offer value through delivering memorable, shareable experiences. To do this, hotels must understand individual guest needs on each trip, and offer a host of unique and unexpected surprises. In fact, 70 per cent of global travellers would like hotels to provide more advice and tips about unique things to do, with only 20 per cent saying they currently get ideas from the hotel.

*Source*: IHG

## Criticisms of marketing research

Academics and practitioners have criticized modern marketing research for a number of reasons, including the following:

- Lack of relevance – marketing researchers are professionals who get tempted into collecting large volumes of data and performing advanced statistical analysis that does not provide new insights for the business or improve decision-making.
- Flawed marketing research methodologies can introduce unacceptable levels of bias or error.
- An over-emphasis on research stifles creativity in marketing.

Despite these criticisms, major hospitality companies recognize the importance of marketing research and carry out extensive customer and competitor research on a continuous basis.

## Conclusion

You now know that marketing research is based on scientific principles and provides hospitality marketers with essential information to help decision-making. Managers use marketing research to confirm or reject their own intuitions about a decision. Marketing research is a tool that managers use in developing, implementing and controlling marketing strategies and tactics, but no amount of marketing research can actually make decisions for the hospitality manager. It is the manager's task to make decisions based on the information available.

In this chapter, we have explained:

- The purpose of marketing research
- The role of a marketing information system
- How hospitality organizations can utilize internal information for marketing research purposes
- Where to find external sources of information
- The differences between secondary and primary data
- The differences between qualitative and quantitative research
- The marketing research process
- How hospitality organizations can conduct online research
- The issues faced by international market researchers
- Criticisms of marketing research.

### ACTIVITY 2.3

Carry out Activity 2.1 again and compare your answers.

- Do you know why hospitality companies carry out research?
- Do you understand what is researched in the hospitality sector?
- List the marketing research activities you have learned in this chapter.

### REVIEW QUESTIONS

Now check your understanding of this chapter by answering the following questions:

1 Discuss the components and the role of a marketing information system for a major hospitality organization.

2 Review the different sources of information which researchers can use to collect data. Which sources are appropriate for:

- a review of a restaurant's operational performance?
- a hospitality competitor survey?
- a market entry strategy for an international hotel brand?

3  Evaluate the relevance of secondary and primary data for:

- owner-managed hospitality units
- branded retail hospitality units
- international branded hotel chains.

4  Describe the differences between qualitative and quantitative data in hospitality marketing.

5  Design your own questionnaire to include three demographic questions, three service quality and/or customer satisfaction questions, and an open-ended question.

## References

1. BVA BDRC [Internet]. *Business Opinion Omnibus.* [cited September 8, 2021]. Available from: www.premierinn.com/gb/en/home.html omnibus
2. SurveyMonkey [Internet]. [cited September 8, 2021]. Available from: www.surveymonkey.com
3. IHG Hotels & Resorts [Internet]. *IHG Research Centre.* [cited September 8, 2021]. Available from: www.ihgplc.com/en/news-and-media/research-centre

Chapter **3**

# Understanding and segmenting customers

After working through this chapter, you should be able to:

- Understand the core principles that explain hospitality consumer and organizational customers' behaviour
- Discuss the role of customer expectations
- Identify the factors that influence the hospitality consumer, buyer and organizational customer decision-making process
- Explain the principles of segmenting customers for hospitality markets
- Describe hospitality market segmentation variables
- Evaluate the characteristics of hospitality target markets.

## Introduction

In this chapter, we review the topics of consumer and organizational buying behaviour, and we explore the principles and practice of market segmentation and target marketing. Segmentation and targeting are fundamental marketing disciplines that underpin all marketing strategies and tactics. Segmentation recognizes that hospitality customers are enormously varied, but they can nonetheless be clustered into groups with similar needs, wants, expectations and requirements. Targeting is based on the premise that hospitality organizations cannot hope to satisfy all potential customers, but must choose to focus their efforts on particular clusters that

DOI: 10.4324/9781003186342-5

share broadly similar needs and wants. By targeting specific markets or market segments, the company is much better placed to design, brand and deliver their services in a way that delivers enhanced customer satisfaction to the targeted customers, and compete more effectively against other providers.

---

**ACTIVITY 3.1**

Before reading the rest of the chapter, think about how you make buying decisions. What influences (or would influence) your decision to purchase a:

- Drink in a local café?
- Short vacation in your own country?
- Long vacation in a country on the other side of the world?

When you have completed the chapter, carry out this activity again and then compare your answers.

---

## Consumer behaviour

In Chapter 1, we established that the main task of marketers is to manage customer demand. Marketers study consumer behaviour to try to understand the processes that consumers go through when they make buying decisions, and the factors or conditions that influence those decisions. Our understanding of consumer behaviour is derived from research in a wide range of social science disciplines, including psychology, social psychology, sociology, anthropology, philosophy, economics and marketing. Each discipline takes a different perspective in seeking to understand consumer behaviour. We will now discuss influences on consumer behaviour and hospitality buyer decision-making processes.

## Influences on consumer buyer behaviour

A significant influence on consumer buyer behaviour is the amount of disposable income available to consumers. This tends to vary according to environmental conditions. When economies are growing and there are many employment opportunities, consumers are more optimistic about the future. These factors create the conditions where consumers can enjoy real increases in disposable income. Consumer confidence is higher, and they are likely to spend more on hospitality products. When the reverse happens and the economies slow or go into recession, unemployment increases, consumers become concerned about the future and disposable income falls. Consumer confidence is lower, and they are less likely to spend on hospitality products. In developed countries, consumer confidence is tracked on a regular basis to measure this 'feel-good' factor. In market economies, consumers have choice; they can choose to spend their disposable income as they want. In this sense, hospitality competes against other product categories such as automobiles or clothing for the consumers' disposable income. A young, newly married couple may have to choose between buying items for their home and going on vacation.

Naturally, individual consumers choose to buy different products for different reasons at different times. Much research has been carried out to identify influences on consumer purchase behaviours. The major influences on individual consumer buyer behaviour can be categorized into three broad headings: socio-cultural influences, individual differences and contextual circumstances. Socio-cultural influences include culture, reference groups, family and social class. Individual differences include personality, lifestyle, gender, age, income and education. Contextual circumstances include perception of risk and involvement (see Figure 3.1).

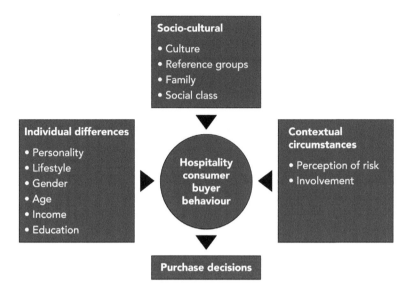

Figure 3.1 Influences on individual hospitality consumers

## Socio-cultural influences

We now discuss how culture, family, reference groups and social class influence consumer behaviour.

### Culture

All of us are born into a culture. Culture can be thought of as the shared values, beliefs and practices that help individuals to function in society. These values and beliefs provide individuals with guidelines for behaviour. Culture is passed from generation to generation as a part of the socialization process we undergo when growing up, and is expressed in and reinforced by learned behaviours. Some of the factors that help to shape culture also influence our shared values:

| | | |
|---|---|---|
| Human needs | Family relationships | Social organization |
| Ethnicity | Political systems | Religious beliefs |
| Language | Education | History, customs and habits |

People from different cultures behave differently. In hospitality, culture is particularly evident in the food choices that guests make. When hospitality employees look after foreign customers they notice significant differences in consumer behaviour that can clearly be attributed to culture.

However, although culture is deeply rooted, it can and does change slowly. You may be aware of the debate about 'globalization' in today's international marketplace and how globalization influences consumer behaviour. Levitt[1], a famous American academic, wrote a seminal article suggesting that cultural differences are being eroded as consumer markets become more global. Advocates of this 'convergence' theory propose that the combination of powerful multinational corporations, global distribution channels, new technologies, Internet, and social media tools and channels that enable companies to communicate messages worldwide are driving the homogenization of global consumer needs and wants. Convergence theory is predicated on the *similarities* that international consumers share. The rapid growth of international business and leisure travel means that hospitality organizations cater for an increasing number of visitors from all parts of the world. If global hospitality consumers have similar needs and wants, then companies can provide a more standardized marketing offer, which is more cost-effective.

However, critics of convergence theory suggest that contemporary consumers have diverse consumption patterns mixing local and global products and services. Thus, a thorough understanding of local culture is critical in understanding consumer choice in those markets. If hospitality consumers in different country markets have different needs and wants, then companies should adapt their global products and services to local cultural requirements. Quick service restaurants such as KFC and McDonald's adapt their menus to ensure a good fit with local food preferences, which are significantly influenced by cultural tradition. This local adaptation of the hospitality offer should provide enhanced customer satisfaction but may not be as cost-effective as standardizing the marketing offer.

## Family

Families have a significant influence on consumer behaviour. Adult preferences for food, beverage and leisure activities are largely products of childhood influences. The family unit of a working father, stay-at-home mother and two children that used to be a stereotypical family is no longer dominant. Today, families comprise a wide range of different combinations, including dual-earning couples with no children, single working parents, same-sex partners, extended families and traditional nuclear family groups. The composition of a household affects the amount of disposable income. Typically, higher disposable income leads to higher household expenditure on hospitality and tourism services. While, in African, Arabic and Asian countries, the extended family plays a much greater role, and many consumer decisions are discussed collectively, the extended family has little or no influence on consumer decisions in Western societies.

## Reference groups

Individual consumer behaviour is also influenced by identification with, or membership of, groups. A distinction is made between primary and secondary groups. Primary groups are those in which we interact face-to-face or online with other members – for example, family, friends and classmates. Secondary groups, being larger or dispersed, do not experience the same, regular interaction. They include cultural and nationality groupings, business associations and alumni. Reference groups can be classified in three useful ways:

1  *Membership groups*: These are groups to which you belong. Your choice of a vacation destination may be influenced by membership groups such as family, friends, fraternities and sororities, social clubs or by the online social networks of which you are member – Facebook and Instagram, for example.

2  *Aspirational groups*: An aspirational group is a group to which you do not belong, but with which you aspire to be associated. For example, you might aspire to work for a specific

hospitality company, or join an elite hospitality business or professional organization with strict membership requirements.

3  *Disassociative groups*: A disassociative group is a group you do not wish to be a member of. In contemporary culture, there are a variety of fashions and fads that appeal to different subsets of young people. Although some groups might appeal to you, there are probably some groups you really want to avoid so you do not wear 'their' clothes, listen to 'their' music or stay in 'their' hotels.

Reference groups perform two functions: they set and enforce standards, and they act as points of reference for individuals to compare their behaviours. Within peer groups and communities, individuals whose opinions are most respected influence others. These people are described as 'opinion leaders'. In hospitality and tourism, food critics and travel writers have been critical opinion leaders, whose positive or negative comments in local and national media can boost or destroy demand for destinations, events, hotels and restaurants. There will also be opinion leaders within your own social networks, too; these will be friends, family members or social media influencers whose opinion you value and who you turn to for advice.

## Socio-economic class

All countries have social class systems (also known as social grading or socio-economic classifications), although some are more formal than others. Class systems can have significant influences on consumer behaviour. Social class is linked to education, occupation and income, and provides a widely adopted customer classification system for market segmentation. In the United Kingdom, the socio-economic classification system created by the Joint Industry Committee for National Readership Surveys is widely used as a descriptor of consumer groups by marketing researchers, by hospitality managers working on new product development and by media owners who are profiling their audiences for advertisers. The descriptors of social structure in Anglo-American countries (Australia, Canada, New Zealand and the United States) are broadly similar, which usually include lower class, working class, lower middle class, upper middle class and upper class.[2] In some countries, like India, the caste system provides a highly formalized social classification system. In other countries, like Norway and Sweden, social class is regarded as less important. However, social class is not a perfect predictor of consumer decisions, because social strata are not strictly homogeneous and there are wide differences in the attitudes, interests, opinions and, therefore, purchase behaviour of individuals within the same stratum.

## Individual differences

Individual differences that influence buyer behaviour are discussed under the headings of age and gender, education and income, personality and lifestyle.

### AGE AND GENDER

A person's age clearly influences needs and wants. Young adults have very different interests, tastes and income levels than their parents and grandparents. Older people may think of a 'good meal out' as a formal dining occasion, whereas younger people tend to look for a more informal dining experience. However, many people aged between 50 and 75 tend to think and act much younger than previous older generations. Marketers realize that there is a difference between chronological age (reflected in the passage of years) and cognitive age (what we think and how we act).

Women and men can have different needs and wants, and gender can, therefore, influence an individual's purchase behaviour. Often, women feel less safe and secure than men when travelling and staying in hotels, whereas men have a different approach to consuming food and beverages (in terms of taste and portion size) compared with women.

### EDUCATION AND INCOME

Education influences employment opportunities and income, and also shapes our values, beliefs, attitudes, interests, activities and lifestyle. College students meet a variety of different people, often from foreign countries. They develop their analytical and intellectual competences and learn a wide range of transferable skills, as well as studying a subject in greater depth. Their education also provides them with enhanced employment prospects. This enables graduates eventually to earn higher salaries in their workplace. Normally, but not always, people with lower education have fewer career opportunities and earn lower salaries.

The level of income helps to determine the amount of consumer disposable income available for discretionary purchases. People with higher income levels spend proportionately less on household necessities and, therefore, have more disposable income. This has considerable influence on travel and dining out expenditure patterns.

### PERSONALITY

An individual's personality can influence behaviour and the type of products purchased. Researchers have identified five key dimensions of personality: neuroticism, extraversion, openness to experience, agreeableness and conscientiousness.[3] Each of these broad dimensions is composed of several sub-dimensions that can be used to research consumer behaviour. People in the same family can, because of their different personalities, have different purchase and consumption habits – especially in more individualistic societies.

### LIFESTYLE

An individual's lifestyle can have a powerful influence on the purchase of discretionary products like travel and dining out. Lifestyle is a reflection of an individual's personality and social influences. Lifestyle can be described in terms of a person's activities, interests and opinions (AIO), as follows:

* *Activities* include work, sport and entertainment, hobbies and travel.
* *Interests* include family, the home and community, watching TV or YouTube, sport, food and fashion.
* *Opinions* about our own culture, other cultures, ourselves, social and political issues, business and economics and even about the future.

Activities, interests and opinions cross cultural, social and demographic divides – for example, there are supporters of Seattle Seahawks and Manchester United Football Club of both sexes, from every continent, socio-economic class and age groups. A person's passion for sport, music or birdwatching will influence how that person spends his or her time and money. Lifestyle has become an increasingly important concept in understanding consumer behaviour and predicting consumer purchasing.

## Contextual circumstances

Sometimes, contextual circumstances are more important than socio-cultural factors and individual differences in influencing our behaviour, as illustrated in Marketing Insight 3.1. Two concepts that are helpful for understanding the role of context are perception of risk and involvement.

---

### MARKETING INSIGHT 3.1

#### Effect of the COVID-19 pandemic on hospitality consumer behaviour[4,5]

The sudden outbreak of the COVID-19 pandemic had both short- and long-term negative effects on hospitality businesses. The pandemic confronted the hospitality industry with unprecedented challenges. Initiatives and actions taken to flatten the COVID-19 curve such as community lockdowns, social distancing, stay-at-home orders, and travel and mobility restrictions resulted in temporary closure of many hospitality businesses and significantly decreased the demand for businesses that were allowed to continue to operate. Almost all hospitality businesses were asked to limit their operations. Restrictions placed on travel and stay-at-home orders issued by the authorities led to sharp decline in hotel and restaurant revenues.

Many people around the world have died from COVID-19 infections. As a result, consumers grew to fear the pandemic, which significantly impacted their purchasing behaviours. The highly infectious nature of the COVID-19 virus and the perceived health risks resulting from the fear of getting infected with the COVID-19 virus made many consumers nervous and uncomfortable. This is especially true for hospitality consumers since most hospitality services are consumed in a social setting. Even after the reopening of hospitality businesses, a large portion of hospitality customers were not willing to dine out or travel due to fear of infection and resulting anxiety. Hospitality businesses around the world were forced to take active measures to mitigate the negative effects of the pandemic on their sales and revenues.

Hospitality businesses made substantial changes to their operations in order to ensure employees' and customers' health and safety, and enhance customers' willingness to patronize their business. Many businesses adopted new business practices to lower customers' fears. They initiated cleaning procedures that showcased visible sanitizing efforts (such as hand sanitizers at the entry, staff wearing masks and gloves). They also implemented social distancing guidelines, limited the number of customers served, practised more rigorous and frequent cleaning of high-touch surfaces in common areas, and provided employee training of health and safety protocols. An increasing number of hospitality businesses also adopted new technologies to decrease human contact in service delivery. Some of the new technologies include the use of service robots in service delivery, contactless payment such as Apple Pay or contactless bank cards, digital menus that can be viewed on personal mobile devices via QR codes, contactless digital payments, keyless entry and touchless elevators, etc.

*Source*: Gursoy and Chi[4,5]

#### PERCEIVED RISK

A consumer's perception of the risk associated with buying a hospitality product may influence the purchase decision. Perceived risk exists when the consumer is uncertain about the consequences of a purchase or about the decision itself. Perceived risk is higher when a consumer has little experience or knowledge about the product, has low self-confidence about making a purchase decision or faces significant long-term consequences as a result of buying the product. There are different types of perceived risk, including financial, social, psychological, and health and safety risk:

- *Financial risk* occurs when there is a significant amount of money at stake. It is linked to major hospitality purchases – organizing a wedding day or planning the worldwide travel arrangements for a gap year. The greater the amount of money involved, the greater is the perceived financial risk.
- *Social risk* is linked to product symbolism and may be experienced when hospitality products have a deep social significance for the consumer. Your choice of where to have dinner sends social signals to other diners.
- *Psychological risk* occurs when consumers perceive a threat to their self-image or self-esteem. In Asian societies, the concept of 'face' is very important, so consumers are very concerned about making the correct hospitality purchase decisions to avoid losing face in front of their family and friends.
- *Health and safety risk* refers to hazards that can lead to the harm, injury, death or illness of a hospitality customer or worker. As discussed in the Marketing Insight 3.1, health and safety risks posed by consumption of hospitality experience due to the COVID-19 pandemic had significant impact on hospitality consumer behaviour.

#### INVOLVEMENT

Consumers vary regarding the level of involvement they have in purchasing decisions. A high-involvement purchase decision is one that is personally significant and relevant for a consumer. Older married couples choosing the venue for a golden wedding anniversary are making a high-involvement decision, whereas the choice of a coffee shop when shopping with friends is a low-involvement decision. Involvement tends to vary between individuals (some people are highly involved in many decisions), products (some products are more involving than others) and context (the level of involvement can vary across purchasing contexts); for example, the choice of a restaurant for a lunch break may be low involvement, but when a business guest is invited, it becomes a high-involvement decision.

Involvement is an important idea to understand because the buying process varies according to whether the decision is high or low involvement. High-involvement decisions like planning a honeymoon (Table 3.1) or organizing a conference are more complex than low-involvement decisions (planning where to meet friends at the weekend). A high-involvement decision will involve much more pre-purchase search for information about alternatives and a post-purchase evaluation of whether the decision was successful.

## Buyer decision-making processes

If marketers are to influence customer demand, they need to understand how customers make buying decisions.

Table 3.1 Hospitality consumer decision-making process for a high-involvement or high-perceived risk product

| Process | Example |
| --- | --- |
| Problem recognition | Engaged couple planning a honeymoon |
| Information search | Search the Internet, read customer reviews, ask family and friends for advice on alternative honeymoon holidays in various destinations |
| Evaluation of alternatives | Agree 'decision criteria' – these include the budget, number of days on the honeymoon, where to go (domestic, short haul, long haul), what type of destination |
| Purchase | Make the decision and buy the honeymoon |
| Post-purchase evaluation | On returning home, evaluate the consumption experience, which will inform future anniversary holiday decisions and whether to recommend the destination and accommodation to family, friends and social networks |

The starting point for decision-making is when a consumer recognizes that he or she has a problem that is not solved or a need that is not being satisfied. The need may be caused by internal conditions (feeling hungry) or motivated by external stimuli (seeing an advertisement). If the decision involves a low-involvement product, the consumer's response is more likely to be a routinized buying decision: feeling hungry at lunchtime and visiting the local sandwich shop, for example. If the decision involves a high-involvement product, consumers are more likely to go through an extended problem-solving process, particularly when faced with making a first-time decision. That extended process starts when the consumer recognizes the problem or need. This is followed by actively searching for information, evaluating the alternatives and then making the purchase decision. Highly involved decisions use more evaluative criteria than low involvement decisions, access more information sources, and assess the importance and reliability of accessed information. Involved consumers want to know the strengths and weaknesses of possible alternatives in more detail.

This search process can be internal or external. An internal search uses our memory to recall previous experiences (or information) to provide a satisfactory solution. If the internal search does not provide a solution, then the consumer has to engage in an external search.

Consumers evaluate alternative ways of solving the problem, weighing the alternatives against their own set of criteria. In hospitality, some of the criteria used by consumers include location, price, quality, convenience, reputation and availability. Consumers frequently refer to reviews posted to social media and user-generated content sites about their experiences with hospitality products and services. This is known as electronic word-of-mouth (eWOM). Since consumers view these reviews as more trustworthy than other corporate communications, they tend to have more influence on consumers' decision-making.

After evaluating options, the consumer makes a buying decision – assuming that the price is affordable and the time to purchase and consume the hospitality product is available. After the transaction has been completed, the consumer assesses whether the product actually satisfied their relevant needs and this post-purchase evaluation influences the consumer's propensity to repeat purchase and to recommend positively (or negatively) the hospitality product. If a customer who is not satisfied complains and the company is able to recover the situation and retain the customer, the customer will be more likely to repeat purchase and speak positively about

Part B

their experience. However, if the complaint is not handled effectively, the unhappy customer is likely to tell many more people about a bad experience than a good experience (see Chapter 13 for more information about customer satisfaction and complaints handling).

## Understanding customer expectations

An important concept for marketers is *customer expectation*. Customers have expectations of hospitality encounters, which marketers must meet if customers are to be satisfied.

### Customer beliefs

Customers form beliefs about what a hospitality experience will be like. Customers' beliefs are formed by a combination of different influences, including culture; reference groups; education; word-of-mouth; previous experience; marketing communication; various media including Internet, the social media and review sites; and individual personal characteristics. An individual customer's beliefs can be idiosyncratic (such customers are often called eccentric because of their unusual behaviour), and different national cultures have a strong influence on customers' belief systems, which in turn influence customer expectations. For example, international tourists who come from high service cultures (such as Japan and Thailand) have higher expectations when travelling abroad and staying in hotels, while the expectations of travellers from countries with a limited-service culture (like some of the East European countries) have lower expectations.

### Zone of tolerance

There have been a number of attempts to understand and classify expectations. One scheme suggests that there are four different types of expectation:

1   the *ideal level* – 'what can be'
2   the *desired level* – 'what should be' (this is the level that customers think is appropriate, given what they have invested in finding and buying the product)
3   the *predicted level* – 'what will be'
4   the *minimum tolerable* – 'what must be'.

In seminal research, Zeithaml, Berry and Parasuraman suggested that customer expectations lie within a *zone of tolerance* ranging from 'what must be' (minimum tolerable) to 'what can be' (ideal level). It is also suggested that customers are willing to accept a level of performance that falls within a *zone of indifference*.[6] This zone ranges around the customer's judgement of what is a reasonable expectation of the particular supplier.

During and after service performance, customers compare their expectations with their perceptions of the service they are receiving or have received. However, in the hospitality industry the quality of service can fluctuate. Customers who are knowledgeable about the variability in hospitality service can have greater tolerance for the variations in a service performance (i.e. a wider zone of tolerance), while other customers who are less knowledgeable might be much less sympathetic and have a lower tolerance to service fluctuations. This range of tolerance represents a customer's propensity to accept variable service standards.

A number of factors influence the customer's zone of tolerance, including the customer's personality and current circumstances, the importance of the purchase occasion and the characteristics of the product and the price paid. The levels of perceived risk and involvement can explain variations in the zone of tolerance. Clearly, customers have different zones of tolerance at different times. As individuals, we can all have mood swings and hence sometimes we feel more tolerant and relaxed about service quality, whilst on other occasions we can be less tolerant. Customers who have a time constraint are less tolerant of service failure.

## Organizational markets

Although individual consumers represent a significant proportion of hospitality customers, especially for smaller hospitality companies, the larger hospitality firms cater for the needs of organizational customers. These include business organizations generating corporate travel and corporate meetings; professional and trade associations; conventions, exhibitions and trade fairs; tour groups; aircrew; and other miscellaneous types of volume bookings. In tourism and hospitality, some of these activities are clustered into a category known as the Meetings, Incentives, Conference and Exhibitions (MICE) market.

Organizations have a different approach to the buying process compared with individual consumers. These differences include the following:

* The number of participants involved in the purchase decisions tends to be greater.
* The users are not always the buyers.
* The complexity of the arrangements – coordinating hundreds or thousands of people's travel, accommodation, catering and entertainment needs is not a simple task.
* The technical requirements, involving conference and banqueting arrangements, audio-visual and stage facilities, major event planning and exhibition stand details, are complex.

Buyer behaviour researchers have identified several roles in organizational purchase decisions: users, influencers, deciders, buyers and gatekeepers. These roles are collectively known as the 'decision-making unit' (DMU), and hospitality marketers will need to communicate with them about different issues, in different ways, at different times.

* *Users* are the customers who consume hospitality products.
* *Influencers* are the people who influence any part of the decision, such as the location or venue.
* *Deciders* are the people who make the purchase decisions – the manager, executive or director.
* *Buyers* are the people who make and pay for the booking.
* *Gatekeepers* are people who control the flow of information to other members of the DMU – administrators or personal assistants often play a key role as gatekeepers in their organizations.

The buying process in organizations is more formalized, with varying degrees of bureaucratic and/or committee reporting structures. A professional approach is required when discussing or negotiating bookings with these types of organizations. The value and volume of organizational bookings vary, but for many of the major hospitality companies the MICE market represents a key element in their business.

## Market segmentation

Understanding individual consumer behaviour and organizational buyer behaviour helps hospitality organizations to understand customer expectations. Marketers use this information to identify potential customers who have similar needs and wants. Once they become the focus for marketing strategies and tactics they become known as *target markets*. This process of identifying subsets of consumers who have distinct, homogeneous demand characteristics is called market segmentation. Segmentation is the starting point for developing effective marketing strategies because:

- Trying to target all consumers is not cost-effective; some consumers may never want to buy your hospitality product.
- Identifying the characteristics of target markets enables a company to design and develop the hospitality offer to satisfy customer needs more effectively.
- Concentrating a company's limited marketing resources on the most profitable target markets leads to a more focused and cost-effective marketing strategy.
- Segmentation improves profitability by maximizing customer satisfaction and generating repeat and recommended sales.

However, there are difficulties for hospitality firms trying to establish effective segmentation strategies due to:

- The costs of carrying out marketing research into segmentation opportunities
- The complexity of constantly changing consumer needs and wants
- The lack of flexibility in many hospitality products (the physical characteristics and location of a property may make it unsuitable for some target markets.)
- The additional costs of developing and communicating separate offers for different target markets
- The problem of targeting different and often incompatible target markets who use the premises at the same time.

The key point is that market segments are inherently unstable. Their membership, size and value change in response to changes in the PESTE environment.

### The segmentation process

There is a logical sequence that can be followed during market segmentation. The stages of the segmentation process outlined in Table 3.2 are discussed here in more detail.

Table 3.2 The segmentation process

| |
| --- |
| 1 Specify the market |
| 2 Establish segmentation criteria |
| 3 Generate segmentation variables |
| 4 Develop market segment profiles based on segmentation variables |
| 5 Evaluate fit with company's competences |

1 *Specification*: The market to be researched and segmented must be clearly identified, for example, the market for business lunches.
2 *Establish segmentation criteria*: A set of criteria needs to be developed against which the various segmentation opportunities can be evaluated. Segmented markets should be:

- *Discrete* – can the segment be described as having a unique set of shared requirements and expectations requiring a specific marketing program?
- *Measurable* – can the market size be measured in terms of value and/or volume, growth rates and market share of current providers?
- *Profitable* – does the segment have sufficient profit potential to justify the investment? By careful analysis, companies can often identify smaller, more profitable 'niche' markets within larger market segments. For single-unit hospitality companies, the market will primarily be focused on the company's micro-environment and depend on the local characteristics of demand and existing/potential competitors. For the major international hospitality corporations, the market might include many countries with consumers from a variety of cultures and a very broad range of competitors.
- *Accessible* – can the segment be reached via distribution and marketing communication channels? There is no point in targeting a segment if the company cannot communicate cost-effectively with potential consumers.
- *Compatible* – marketers should ensure that any new target markets are compatible with existing target markets.

3  *Generate segmentation variables*: Segmentation variables provide the basis for classifying consumers into different market segments. Hospitality segmentation variables include purpose of visit; geo-demographics; buyer, user and lifestyle characteristics; price; and time. In hospitality, a wide number of variables are used to build a more detailed profile of the target markets. The more detailed the segmentation data, the deeper the understanding of potential customers.

4  *Develop market segment profiles based on segmentation variables*: Specific market segment profiles include the size of the market in terms of value and volume, customer purchase behaviours (frequency of visit, customer spend and number in party), consumer characteristics (benefits sought, price sensitivity) and accessibility/responsiveness to marketing programmes.

5  *Evaluate fit with the company's competences*: The hospitality company needs to ensure that it has the competences and resources to serve and satisfy the segment's needs and wants profitably.

This approach suggests that there is a precision in the analysis of market segments, but this is not always true. Many hospitality markets are fragmented, and it is difficult to calculate the volume and value of a market segment accurately. Market share can be even more difficult to ascertain accurately. However, an important benefit of using segmentation analysis in hospitality operations is to identify consumer trends to establish which market segments will become attractive in the future and which market segments are becoming less attractive now.

### Hospitality segmentation variables

Segmentation variables are the basis for classifying consumers into different market segments. Some of these segmentation variables have already been discussed in the consumer behaviour and customer expectations sections of this chapter. The segmentation variables form the building blocks in developing target market profiles of customer expectations.

The primary segmentation variable used by virtually all hospitality companies is *purpose of travel*. The three main categories are business, non-business (variously defined as leisure, vacation, personal or social) and visiting friends and relatives (VFR). The business and leisure categories can be further subdivided into several distinct market segments (see Figure 3.2), but a key point to remember is that the *same person* can have *different* needs and wants depending on whether the customer's purpose of travel is business, leisure or VFR. Each micro-segment has

Part B

| Tourist accommodation market | Purpose of visit | Segments | Price | Geographic | | Demographic & family unit | Party size | User status |
|---|---|---|---|---|---|---|---|---|
| Business | FIT<br>Corporate<br>Local company<br>Meeting<br>Conference<br>Exhibition | {Management<br>{Sales<br>{Training<br>]------{Recruitment<br>{Professional advisors<br>{Boards | Luxury<br>Mid-market<br>Budget | Domestic<br><br>International | Cities<br>Countries<br>States<br>Regions<br>American<br>British<br>Chinese<br>Japanese | Age: 18–24<br>25–34<br>35–54<br>55–65 | Single<br>2–4<br>Small group<br>Large group | Non-user<br>Potential<br>First-time<br>Light<br>Medium<br>Heavy<br>Lapsed |
| Leisure | Overnight stopover<br>Family holiday<br>Honeymoon<br>Package holiday<br>Leisure break<br>Exotic holiday<br>Go-as-you-please<br>Fly-drive<br>Incentive | {Destination<br>{Activity<br>{Cultural<br>{Event<br>]------{Relaxation<br>{Sight-seeing<br>{Sand, sea, sun | Luxury<br>Mid-market<br>Budget | Domestic<br><br>International | Cities<br>Countries<br>States<br>Regions<br>American<br>British<br>Chinese<br>Japanese | Age: Under 18<br>18–24<br>25–34<br>35–54<br>55–70<br>70+<br>Family cycle:<br>Young single<br>Young couple<br>Couple & children<br>Older couple<br>Old single | Single<br>Couple<br>2–6<br>Small group<br>Large group | Non-user<br>Potential<br>First-time<br>Light<br>Medium<br>Heavy<br>Lapsed |

Figure 3.2 Hospitality market segments

its own characteristics, with implications for hospitality providers (see Figure 3.2 for a summary of accommodation market segments).

## Business

Compared to leisure travellers, hotel guests travelling for business tend to be:

- Less price sensitive, since the employer generally covers hospitality and travel expenses
- More likely to stay for one night, or only a few, on each trip
- More frequent, or regular, users of hotel accommodation
- Less seasonal – business travel patterns are less dependent on weather and holiday schedules, and
- Stay at establishments that are within a reasonable (up to 30 minutes) travel time of their place of work – hence the higher demand for business accommodation close to commercial, industrial and retail areas.

The business travel segment includes business trips that are unavoidable, like sales meetings with customers and technical visits to factories by engineers. Other trips are more discretionary – for example, attending a conference or exhibition.

## Leisure

Hotel guests travelling for leisure tend to be:

- Much more price sensitive than business travellers, since they are paying for the accommodation out of their own after-tax income
- More likely to stay longer on each trip – short breaks are normally at least a couple of days, two-week vacations are common and longer vacation periods are usual
- Less frequent users of hotel accommodations (unless they are also business travellers)
- Much more seasonal, both in terms of climate and the time of year, and
- More likely to stay at establishments that are close to leisure amenities and tourist attractions – hence the demand for cultural, rural, mountain and beach resort hotels.

There are some business and leisure travel markets that overlap. For example, international conferences and exhibitions often include an element of free time to be enjoyed as a leisure period. The incentive travel sector uses the appeal of free, and often luxurious or adventurous, leisure travel to motivate and reward performance in business markets.

## Visiting friends and relatives

From an accommodation demand perspective, this segment does not generate significant volumes of business for hotels, because people tend to stay in the homes of their friends and relatives. This market is more important to tourism establishments in the day-visitor attraction sectors, and to restaurants and bars.

## Geographic

The geographic origin of a customer is a widely used segmentation variable. Origin is associated with a customer's home address, post-code (zip-code) and/or nationality. National governments often require hotels to collect passport details from international visitors, and these data provide important marketing information about the types of international markets being served. Geographic segmentation variables within a country's domestic market include the cities, counties, states and regions of customer origin.

The benefits of segmenting consumers using geographic variables include the following:

- Nationality is a universally recognized method of categorizing visitors in international tourism marketing.
- The special needs and wants of consumers from particular regions can be researched, and products can be specifically developed to satisfy those needs and wants.
- Media owners often profile their audiences using geographic variables, making it relatively simple for hospitality marketers to choose a geographically appropriate medium to deliver their marketing messaging.
- Customer registration data make it easy to identify customers' addresses.

United States Census Bureau offers publicly available, free, tools that can be used for segmenting and evaluating markets. ZIP Codes Tabulation Areas (ZCTAs) is one such geo-demographic (mix of geography and demography) segmentation tool.[7] ZCTAs are generalized areal representations of United States Postal Service (USPS) ZIP Code service areas. United States Census Bureau provide a wealth of geographical and socio-demographic data about the people and businesses located in each ZIP Code Tabulation Area.

### Demographic

Demography is the study of population characteristics. Much demographic information is collected during government censuses of population. Market research companies in developed countries use the census data to develop consumer profiles. Since changes in birth, survival rates, education, income levels and household composition can have significant impact on demand for hospitality experiences, hospitality marketers are keenly interested in these changes.

Demographic variables include age, gender, family size and structure, ethnic origin, religion, nationality and socio-economic class.

### AGE

Hospitality companies use age as a critical segmentation variable when planning product concepts, especially in the activity, dining and leisure markets. There are considerable differences in consumer needs and wants between, and within, age groups. In the eating-out market, the needs of young families with babies (special dietary requirements and changing facilities) are different from the needs of unmarried teenagers.

Although this division based on age is somewhat arbitrary, it does help when evaluating the different needs and wants of the sub-segments of market. For example, people older than 80 years are less interested in participating in sporting activities, whereas people aged between 55 and 75 years are still relatively active and interested in participating in leisure and sporting activities. The disposable income of people older than 55 years is higher than that of the general population, because they have fewer financial outgoings on matters such as raising a family or paying off a mortgage. This provides older people with more money to spend on leisure purchases. One of the characteristics of the current older generation is that they are more educated, sophisticated and well-travelled than previous generations, and they, therefore, have higher expectations when staying in hotels and dining out. The special needs and wants of the older generation staying in hotels include quieter rooms with safety features like bath rails and non-slip shower mats, good porterage facilities to help with luggage, early evening dining options and smaller food portions.

## GENDER

Some hospitality products are specifically geared to the needs of male or female consumers. Hotel companies have responded to the expectations of female travellers by providing greater security measures in rooms, feminizing the room decor and offering healthier menu options in restaurants. However, gender segmentation is not always precise – male consumers can notice and prefer greater security measures, more feminine decor and healthy menus. Gay and lesbian markets, often described as the 'pink market', are regarded as affluent and mobile consumers. Their expectations cross gender boundary borders when it comes to hospitality experiences.

## FAMILY SIZE AND STRUCTURE

In Western cultures, the average number of children in a family is just below two; in China, the one-child-per-couple rule restricted the size of the family between 1980 and 2016; however, in African and Arabic countries, large families are the norm. The size of the family influences the disposable income available for hospitality and leisure purposes. Family size also influences the design of hospitality products, such as family accommodation and dining units. The hotel facilities that individuals and couples without children find acceptable are often not suitable for families with children, and vice versa. The growth in the number of people living alone, especially through divorce, has created a market for singles clubs and organizations that provide opportunities for single people to meet, travel and socialize.

## ETHNIC ORIGIN, RELIGION AND NATIONALITY

Ethnic origin, religion and nationality are important demographic variables that are closely linked to each other and to culture. One consequence of these cultural influences is our very different attitudes to food. Kosher cuisine is one of the well-known religious food disciplines for orthodox Jews, whilst fasting during Ramadan is equally important for Muslims. International hotels operating in Asia recognize the taste preferences of both Eastern and Western guests when they provide both styles of cuisine at breakfast, lunch and dinner. Although restaurants are typically described by the nationality of their cuisine – American, Chinese, English, French, Turkish, Indian, Italian, Japanese or Thai – this does not mean that their customers are clustered according to nationality.

## SOCIO-ECONOMIC CLASS

Hospitality companies may not state explicitly which socio-economic class they target, but this is often implicit in their marketing strategies. The low-cost family holiday camp market clearly targets specific socio-economic groups. The hospitality offer varies but typically includes basic accommodation, with a choice of half-board or self-catering options, a range of bar and food outlets (often with popular quick-service restaurant (QSR) franchises such as Burger King and Pizza Hut), various activities, swimming, live entertainment and a nightclub. This offer caters for the needs of the parents and children of lower income families.

Part B

**ACTIVITY 3.2**

- Log on to the United States Census Bureau website at www.census.gov/.
- Explore the site and review the available data.
- Click on the 'Access Local Data' button (www.census.gov/quickfacts/fact/table/US/PST045219).
- Enter state, county, city, town or zip code to the box located in upper left corner. After that, select the information you would like to view from the 'select a fact' box.
- Discuss how this information can help hospitality marketers.

### Buyer needs and benefits

The idea of segmenting markets according to the benefits sought from products is well established. Examples of benefits that buyers look for in hospitality products include the following:

- Rest and relaxation – associated with quiet rooms and spa facilities
- Convenience – this is often linked to location and speed of service
- Luxury – this is naturally associated with high levels of service and high price
- Family-friendliness – families travelling have specific needs (like informal, child-friendly dining facilities)
- Healthfulness – spa resorts offer exercise and dietary regimens for the benefit of their health-oriented patrons. This is becoming an important feature for all hospitality businesses.

A number of different 'benefits' can be combined together to provide the total solution to a customer's set of problems. All-inclusive resort hotels not only provide the accommodation and food elements but also all the sporting activities, excursions, leisure and entertainment facilities, and even alcoholic drinks, in a safe environment. This process of creating product/price benefit bundles should be based on a deep understanding of customer needs.

### Price sensitivity

Price sensitivity is a crucial segmentation variable in hospitality markets. Each hospitality market segment has its own specific pricing dynamics that need to be understood. Research and analysis should determine what consumers are willing to pay. The price consumers are willing to pay plays a key role in determining the design, facilities and amenities, and the standard of decor, fixtures and furniture in planning a new product concept.

In hospitality, the link between price and quality in different product classes is strong. Consumers looking to be pampered in a luxurious environment expect to pay higher prices, while consumers of basic products expect to pay lower prices. Whilst the price/quality difference between product class extremes (e.g., the expensive, gourmet restaurant versus the inexpensive and cheerful café) is clearly apparent to consumers, the difference between adjacent product classes (e.g. a four-star conference hotel/venue and a three-star conference hotel/venue) can be virtually indistinguishable. This can lead to customer confusion, as the relative value for money between competing offers is not transparent.

Many hospitality chains develop their accommodation options with a particular price point in mind – for example, a $100 per night accommodation price.

Many hotel companies describe their accommodation market segments in terms of product. Examples include conference; convention/exhibition; and leisure break. The flexing of rates is discussed in Chapter 7, where we introduce the topic of revenue management.

### Current user characteristics

Identifying the characteristics of current customers provides operators with insight into their served markets. These customer profiles can then be used to identify attractive market segments for targeting purposes. There are a number of user characteristics that are important to hospitality operators, and these are described here.

#### USAGE STATUS

This characteristic categorizes consumers into non-users, potential users, first-time users and regular users, who in turn can be light, medium or heavy users (see Figure 3.3). Marketing communication campaigns can be developed to target different user categories, to encourage first-time visits, regular patronage or repeat visits after lapsed patronage. Understanding the different usage patterns enables marketing communication campaigns to be designed to influence the category of user.

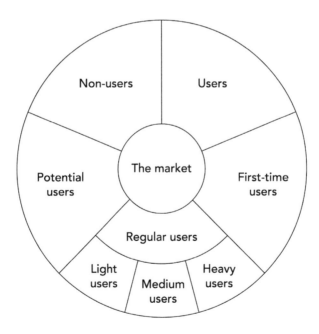

Figure 3.3  Guest usage status[8]

*Source:* Osman[8]

#### FREQUENCY

In accommodation markets, frequent business travellers – people who stay away from home on business travel for 15 or more trips per year – are a highly attractive segment, because their lifetime value is high. Hotels strive to encourage regular and repeat customers, and over time hoteliers can build strong, long-lasting, special relationships with their 'regulars'. Frequent guest promotions, often linked to loyalty programmes, are designed to reward frequent guests for their patronage (see Chapter 14).

Given the lower frequency of leisure trips, a regular customer might return to a favourite leisure hotel less frequently. A distinction needs to be drawn here between those hotels catering for extended-stay, long-haul vacations and those catering for short leisure breaks within a couple of hours' driving time from the customer's home. The long-haul guest might only return once per year, if that – indeed, a highly satisfied customer may only return once every five years – whereas the short-break leisure guest might return to a favourite hotel three or four times per year. One consequence of this user profile is that the hotels targeting leisure customers need to allocate a higher promotional spend to attract a wider customer base or distribute their product via tour operators and travel agents.

## BRAND LOYALTY

A key objective of frequent guest or visitor programmes is to build loyalty amongst those travellers who are heavy users. Consumers' loyalty to hospitality brands varies. There has been considerable research into customer loyalty. Customers have become more promiscuous in their shopping habits; indeed, promiscuous consumers might be members of many different hotel loyalty programmes. However, the investment in loyalty programmes by airlines, hotels, rental car firms and supermarkets suggests that businesses do believe consumers are influenced by these programmes (see Chapter 14).

## PURCHASE OCCASION

The type of purchase occasion influences the consumers' needs and wants. Many hospitality banqueting, restaurant and event products are aimed at the special family occasions that mark every important event in our lives – birth, coming of age parties, weddings, special birthdays, retirement functions, wedding anniversaries and funerals.

## SIZE OF PARTY

Party size has a considerable influence on the needs and wants of hospitality consumers. Clearly, group travellers have different check-in, check-out, dining, drinking, meeting and entertainment requirements from individual travellers. Companies that specialize in volume hospitality operations develop the facilities and skills necessary to cater for large-scale events. Sensible smaller outlets should avoid taking bookings from larger parties – which they know they cannot cater effectively – to avoid alienating their regular customers.

## LIFESTYLE (OR PSYCHOGRAPHICS)

Psychographic segmentation classifies consumers according to their personality traits and lifestyle. It is based on detailed marketing research into the AIO (activities, interests, opinions) of consumers and is linked to geo-demographic variables to provide consumer profiles. Marketing research analysts combine individual responses to questions about a person's AIO with details about his or her geo-demographic characteristics, and then cluster consumers into groups with similar responses to form psychographic profiles of market segments. The data characterizing each psychographic segment provide a detailed picture of where consumers live; what education, occupation and income they enjoy; their AIO; the media they consume; and the products they purchase. For example, Hilton uses psychographic segmentation to target ambitious individuals who would like to express their perceived high status and achievement by staying in five-star rooms offered by the company at premium prices.

Proponents believe that psychographic segmentation:

- Is a good predictor of consumer behaviour
- Enables companies to design products better to meet consumer needs
- Provides the opportunity to develop cost-effective marketing campaigns for selected target markets.

Critics contend that psychographic segmentation:

- Develops lifestyle segments that are not strictly homogeneous
- Is very expensive – research costs are high because of the detailed interviewing and complex analysis necessary to reveal AIO
- Is not effective, because people change occupation and move homes frequently.

### TIME

There are two aspects concerning the role of time as a market segmentation variable. First, from a seasonality perspective, hospitality operators need to understand why consumers patronize their outlets during quieter periods in order to develop effective marketing campaigns to increase sales during low and shoulder season periods. Some older people, who do not live with children and have flexible vacationing arrangements, enjoy relaxing in a quiet, peaceful environment, and can be considered a potential target market for destinations and hotels in low or shoulder seasons.

The second aspect of time refers to how far in advance customers make their bookings – the time between the customer booking and then actually consuming the hospitality product. This time period is an important segmentation variable, because the length, whether it is a couple of hours in advance or several years away, influences the design of the marketing programme aimed at capturing the customer. The marketing programme targeting a convention planner who is booking an international conference to be held in three years' time will be different to the marketing programme targeting an impulse diner who wants to eat out this evening.

## Hospitality target markets

Major hospitality firms planning to market their products in a new geographic market invest in detailed marketing research to evaluate the attractiveness of competing cities or suburbs before deciding which to enter (see Chapters 2 and 6). The smaller operator adopts a much less formal process, which is often based more on intuition than marketing research. Once selected, the market segment is defined as a 'target market' for which the company designs an appropriate marketing programme. Target markets are groups of consumers, with similar needs and wants, for whom a marketing programme is specifically developed.

Hospitality companies target several different market segments at the same time, but each target market should have its own marketing programme. Heavy users, for example, frequent guests in hotels, are a very attractive target market offering considerable profit potential. However, they are also going to be attractive to the competitors and, therefore, highly sought after, and difficult to recruit and retain.

We now turn to a discussion of the two broad classes of target market: consumer markets and organizational markets. Each requires a different marketing approach because buyer behaviour differs between individuals and organizations.

## Consumer target markets

Consumer markets can be defined as travellers and local people who consume hospitality products as individuals, couples, families or small groups of people, for business or leisure purposes (see Figure 3.4). Consumers tend to choose their own hospitality provider, set their own budget and pay from their own after-tax resources. Examples of consumer target markets include international travellers, families, seniors, wellness travellers and the gay/lesbian market.

---

### MARKETING INSIGHT 3.2

#### International outbound market – China

Since 1993, there has been a significant growth in Chinese outbound tourism – indeed, the number of Chinese travelling abroad increased from 3.7 million in 1993 to 169.2 million in 2019. Even though the number of Chinese travelling abroad decreased significantly in 2020 due to the global COVID-19 pandemic, the Chinese outbound travel market is expected to recover quicker than other source markets. However, Chinese outbound travellers' post-COVID-19 travel behaviour is significantly different compared to pre-COVID 19 behaviours. They seek new, less crowded and friendly destinations that offer quality experiences customized to meet their specific needs and wants.

The drivers for this remarkable increase in the number of Chinese outbound travellers are the rapidly growing Chinese economy and resulting increases in disposable incomes, growing urban upper/middle and very affluent classes in China. Since consumption of lifestyle products such as travel and eating out is regarded as an indicator of social esteem and success, visiting outbound destinations such as the USA or Europe become very popular among affluent Chinese.

However, most Chinese outbound travellers choose outbound destinations that are located in countries that have a friendly relationship with China; are in close proximity (e.g. South-East Asian countries like Thailand); and based on word-of-mouth recommendation from friends, family and social networks. Both business and leisure markets use package tours organized with host-speaking tour guides. The main problems for host countries catering for Chinese travellers are confusion about accommodation quality expectations due to differences in hotel classification systems; language; dissatisfaction with food, especially breakfast; disappointment with local restaurants – Chinese restaurants in Western countries adapt their cuisine for local markets, which then disappoint mainland Chinese diners. The number of independent Chinese travellers has been growing rapidly during the last few years and is forecast to continue growing. Many young, modern, urban Chinese delay marriage, and rearing children, to enjoy a contemporary lifestyle – which includes travelling abroad. An emerging issue for some popular international tourism destinations is the volume of Chinese visitors, which is forecast to continue exponential growth and might create tensions between mass tourists from one culture, other international visitors and the local host population.

Hospitality companies targeting international markets, like the Chinese market, need to adapt their offers to ensure that guests from significant source markets are satisfied. Adaptations include the following:

* Multilingual front desk operatives and food/beverage managers

* Hotel/restaurant information and safety notices in multiple languages

* International food options (restaurant, in-room service).

## THE SENIORS MARKET

SAGA is a well-established Britain-based company that targets the over-50s mature market and originally focused on travel, but now also provides complementary health, insurance and financial services. SAGA offers package holiday and travel services to major tourist destinations in every continent. The product, which is carefully designed for people aged over 50, concentrates on safe travelling. Many of the customers' grateful comments stress how the SAGA staff solved minor travel problems. The focus is on companionship, excursions with cultural/historic sightseeing and shopping, educational trips – one vacation is called 'Art Treasures in Italy' – and good quality, comfortable hotels. Consumer concerns about help for disabled and elderly people travelling (e.g. porters to carry the luggage at airports and hotels) are answered on the frequently asked questions (FAQs) pages on the SAGA website. The language in the publicity material and on the Internet is mature and very sympathetic to the needs of older people. Photographs show groups of older people dressed in smart/casual clothes quietly enjoying attractive views of scenic areas. Hotels are selected for comfort and quality and are unlikely to be very noisy late at night.

## GAY/LESBIAN AND WOMEN-ONLY HOTELS

There is a distinction between hotels that are gay/lesbian friendly, but primarily target other markets, and hotels that only target gays/lesbians. The five-star designer Hotel Skt Petri, Copenhagen, which targets multiple markets, describes itself as gay-friendly. A women-only hotel such as the Luthan Hotel & Spa in Riyadh, Saudi Arabia, is an example of a service targeted at straight female travellers. Rainbow Tourism, an Australian-based gay/lesbian travel operator with an international scope, developed their own accommodation accreditation scheme (Rainbow Tourism Accredited) and identify gay/lesbian owned and operated hotels in over 20 different countries. However, homosexuality is still a crime in over 70 countries and many countries would not allow a gay/lesbian hotel to operate.

## EATING OUT AND ENTERTAINMENT

Apart from a small number of high-profile outstanding eating and entertainment establishments (these become known as 'destination' restaurants, because their reputation is so high that customers are prepared to travel a long distance), customer markets for local hospitality units are focused on locally defined areas. Market variations occur according to whether the unit is sited in a city centre, the suburbs or a rural location and are determined by the different geo-demographic characteristics of the neighbourhoods. The characteristics of these target markets are also defined using gender, income and benefit segmentation criteria like service/ quality, price/value and time/convenience.

## Enjoy some excellent music breaks with Best Western Hotels

If you love attending concerts and would like to visit some of Britain's leading venues, this will be music to your ears.

Wherever you stay you will enjoy the unique combination that Best Western can offer you. Because every hotel is individually owned and managed each one has its own unique atmosphere and personality. And because they're all Best Western hotels, you are guaranteed the highest standards of hospitality.

So wherever you want to hear some of the finest music in Britain, you can be sure you'll enjoy accommodation to match.

### ROYAL OPERA HOUSE, CONVENT GARDEN, LONDON
The world-famous home to The Royal Ballet and The Royal Opera has a year round programme of performances.
Ticket office: 0207 304 4000   Website: www.royalopera.org

> Stay at – Best Western Shaftesbury Hotel, Piccadilly, London
> Stay right in the heart of central London in this recently refurbished hotel.

### THE GRAND THEATRE, LEEDS
The main leeds home of the acclaimed Opera North company. Autumn highlights include productions of Tosca and Der Rosenkavalier.
Ticket office: 0113 222 6222   Website: www.leeds.gov.uk/grandtheatre

> Stay at – Best Western Guide Post Hotel, Leeds/Bradford
> A modern hotel in a peaceful village location close to both Leeds and Bradford.
> The Yorkshire Dales are also just a short drive away

### BIRMINGHAM SYMPHONY HALL, BIRMINGHAM
Right in the heart of Birmingham city center, this is home to the Birmingham Symphony Orchestra. Since it was opened in 1991 the Hall's superb acoustics have earned it the reputation as one of the world's finest music venues.
Ticket office: 0121 212 3333   Website: www.necgroup.co.uk

> Stay at – Best Westren Lea Marston Hotel and Leisure Complex, Birmingham
> A modern, friendly hotel situated in a rural environment, just 15 minutes' drive from Birmingham city centre.

### USHER HALL, EDINBURGH
In a city famous for its performance spaces Usher Hall is one of Edinburgh's best known, housing the Royal Scottish National Orchestra and the Scottish Chamber Orchestra
Ticket office: 0121 212 3333   Website: www.necgroup.co.uk

> Stay at – Best Western Bruntsfield Hotel, Edinburgh
> Its center, yet peaceful, location overlooking an attractive park means you'll enjoy the best of the city with a really relaxing place to stay.

### BRIDGEWATER HALL, MANCHESTER
This £42 million concert hall is one of the architectural highlights of the regenerated Manchester city centre and is the home of the famous Halle orchestra
Ticket office: 0161 907 9000   Website: www.bridgewater-hall.co.uk

> Stay at – Best Western Willowbank Hotel, Manchester
> Five minutes drive from the city center, the Willowbank has been recently refurbished throughout to create the perfect base for any visit to Manchester.

There are over 300 individual Best Western hotels throughout the UK.
Call **0845 072 0700** now to arrange your refreshingly different stay quoting MBBC or visit www.bestwestern.co.uk

**Best Western**

Figure 3.4  Best Western advert targeting classical music lovers

*Source*: Best Western Hotels

Research consistently demonstrates that diners look for quality of food, quality of service, value for money, friendly staff and cleanliness. Different target markets will rate the importance of these criteria according to their own needs. For example, price/value and time/convenience are rated more highly by the family eating-out segment, because of the costs of taking a family out and the need to dine quickly to avoid restless children becoming disruptive. Adults dining out without children can afford the time and money to have a more sophisticated eating out experience. Because the geo-demographic characteristics of an area are the prime influence on potential dining out target markets, hospitality providers need to choose the sites of their operations with great care to ensure that they target appropriate customer markets.

## Organizational target markets

Organizational target markets are groups of travellers who consume hospitality products for business and leisure purposes. Individual customers who are travelling as part of a group of travellers have less influence (or none) over the choice of hospitality provider and will sometimes have to pay for all or some parts of the service out of their own resources. If the organization is a corporate business, then the company (not the individual) will pay and will normally set expenditure limits. Examples of hospitality organizational target markets include corporate travel, MICE markets, aircrew, tour groups and a miscellaneous category called SMERFE (social, military, educational, religious, fraternal and ethnic).

### CORPORATE TRAVEL

Corporate travel is a major expense item for national and international companies. Corporations regard the purchase of hotel accommodation the same as the purchase of any other business necessity. Companies are aware of their own purchasing power and expect discounted rates. Most hotel groups and larger independent hotels offer a standard corporate rate with a minimum 10 per cent discount off the accommodation rack rate and those companies booking larger volumes of nights negotiate higher discounts. However, if the agreed volume of business is not achieved and the contract is not sufficiently specific, there can be problems between hoteliers and corporate clients.

There is an image of business executives enjoying the most luxurious travel and hotel accommodation, dining out in the finest restaurants and conspicuously consuming the best wines with 'no expense spared'. This might be true for a small number of senior executives but is certainly not the case for all business travellers. Corporate organizations are usually hierarchical in design, and most companies set expense limits according to the position of employees within the hierarchy of the company. Business travel allowances depend on the corporate culture of individual organizations, which will vary immensely.

## MICE

The MICE (Meetings, Incentive, Conference and Exhibition) market is often discussed in homogeneous terms, but in fact each element of the MICE market has its own distinctive needs and wants.

### MEETINGS

The meetings market can be divided into two distinct categories – corporate and association.

### CORPORATE MEETINGS

The meetings market includes company management meetings, planning, recruitment and sales meetings, and training events in locations that are not company-owned. The number of delegates attending a meeting can range from only two to over a thousand. This market is a major source of revenue for hotel operations and includes both day meetings and meetings requiring overnight accommodation. Delegates attending such meetings are required to attend. The company organizing (and paying for) the event needs to achieve its own specific organizational goals for the meeting to be a success. Organizers and delegates who attend corporate meetings have high service expectations. Prior to the meeting, the hospitality venue has to work with the meeting organizer to plan the event and ensure that all the details are carefully agreed. In recent years, the major hotel brands have developed guaranteed conference packages to satisfy the needs and wants of meeting organizers and their delegates.

### Association meetings

In addition to corporate meetings, there is a large number of professional and trade organizations/associations that hold regular meetings for members. These voluntary meetings are normally held during the weekends and summer months. While small association meetings may not generate significant amounts of accommodation, food or beverage revenue, mid-size and large association meetings can generate significant amounts of accommodation, food and beverage revenues. Most local associations and/or local chapters also hold functions such as annual dinners and fundraising events, which can generate significant food and beverage revenues for local hospitality businesses. Examples of such organizations include the Lions, Masonic Lodges, Rotary Club and Round Table.

### Incentive

Companies use travel or food and beverage as an incentive to improve company performance (often sales) or to reward and recognize successful employees. The incentive packages usually are all-inclusive packages that include everything from travel to/from the destination to accommodation, food and beverage and entertainment. Incentive travel often features exotic or extraordinary destinations combined with atypical (adventure) activities or luxurious pampering. Hospitality companies targeting the incentive market need to provide exceptional customer experiences to ensure that the customers are wowed. Incentive trips are normally short, expensive trips that offer extraordinary hospitality experiences. Dedicated incentive travel intermediaries broker destination/hospitality/activity packages to corporate buyers who want to incentivize employees or customers.

### Conventions, exhibitions and trade fairs

The lead (or booking) time for major national and international events involving hundreds or thousands of delegates ranges from two to more than 10 years. Very few venues are capable of hosting these major events. Major convention and exhibition centres are often built by local, state or central governments. Cities like Chicago (USA), New York (USA) and Birmingham (UK), and city-states like Singapore have dedicated facilities that attract major national and international events.

Key issues for event organizers include the following:

- An effective transportation infrastructure (e.g. good airport and road connections)
- Provision of modern convention and exhibition facilities of sufficient size
- Availability of a wide range of quality hospitality facilities
- Resort, leisure and recreational amenities.

For international events, climate, the relative cost of travelling to and from, and travel distances are additional factors that can influence the decision about which venue to book. There is considerable international competition between the venues, which has led to the emergence of convention or visitor bureaus linked to tourist information centres co-funded by local government and business. The role of the visitor bureau is primarily to promote the area as a whole to convention, exhibition and trade fair organizers and act as an information provider. These events may last from a few days to a week or more as in the case of mega-events like FIFA World Cup or Olympic Games.

Venue selection for events is usually made by a small group of people in the organization that hosts the event. Individual companies and visitors are responsible for making their own travel and hotel arrangements. Individual visitors may see the event as an opportunity to combine work activities with some leisure, relaxation, sporting or sightseeing activities, which explains the appeal of more exotic locations for international events. Examples of organizations booking exhibitions and conferences include professional and trade bodies, and political parties.

### Aircrew

A market segment that hotels target in 'gateway' locations is that of airline employees, and specifically airline crew. The high volume of intercontinental, regional and international flights, coupled with the need for aircrew to have proper rest periods between flights, has created a specialized group market for hotels within approximately 15–45 minutes' travel time of major airports. Aircrew have special needs and wants, including:

- Efficient 24-hour check-in and check-out procedures
- Rooms that are available immediately upon arrival and check-in
- Quiet and dark rooms, preferably with blackout blinds, to facilitate sleeping at any time of the day or night
- 24-hour food and beverage service, at a reasonable price, since airline crews have limited expense allowances
- Transportation from and to the airport.

### Tour groups

The growth of global tourism has increased the demand for international group travel that is organized by tour operators. These groups of travellers are provided with inclusive travel and accommodation products and, depending upon the location, food service. Since this is a very high-volume business, hotels that are interested in this market have to offer low, competitive prices to win the business. Groups need:

- Dedicated, efficient group check-in and check-out procedures and concierge/porters' services
- Good-sized lobby/lounge areas, where members of the tour group can conveniently meet
- Efficient food service, because they are often on a strict schedule and do not want to run late.

Sometimes, hotel employees treat tour group customers as the least important of all clients, but, in volume terms, tour groups represent a significant market, especially in major tourist destinations.

### SMERFE

SMERFE is a North American expression that stands for 'social, military, educational, religious, fraternal and ethnic', and it is a convenient heading to discuss all the group market segments not already discussed.

This segment is generally very price sensitive. SMERFE organizations are usually non-profit organizations and members/family pay for their event out of after-tax income. Consequently, the organizers of SMERFE bookings are inclined to take advantage of low or shoulder season bargain rates. Although the room rates offered have to be low to attract SMERFE bookings, there can be a significant food and beverage revenue from these events. An exception in the SMERFE market is the family special occasion, like weddings and wedding anniversaries, which can range in price from the very modest budget to the most extreme, extravagant budget.

## Intermediaries

The complexity of efficiently arranging group travel has created a role for speciality intermediaries, to act on behalf of organizations in their negotiations with hospitality and travel providers. These intermediaries have become target markets for hospitality companies in their own right. Key intermediaries who book volume business and expect competitive rates, include:

- Conference and meetings planners
- Travel agents
- Wholesalers and tour operators
- Incentive travel houses.

The role of intermediaries is discussed in detail in Chapter 8.

## Mixing market segments

A key issue for all hospitality operations is to ensure that the various target markets are compatible. Mixing incompatible market segments leads to customer dissatisfaction and can generate serious customer complaint. Filling rooms during low and shoulder seasons can motivate reservation and yield managers to accept bookings from customers whose needs and wants are not compatible with prime target markets. Examples of incompatible segments include elderly tour groups and families with children, and mixing them with airline crew segment. Similar problems can arise when hotels cater for banquets, and guests are disturbed by large, noisy, late-night functions with music and dancing. The principle of separating segments with incompatible needs is the answer to this problem.

## Conclusion

Understanding consumer behaviour and customer expectations is essential if hospitality managers are to succeed in delivering customer satisfaction. Segmenting markets is the starting point for effective marketing. Marketers need to identify attractive market segments and then develop appropriate marketing strategies to win and keep customers from those segments. We will discuss how to develop the marketing strategies in the later chapters, but the process should always start with identification of the needs and wants of target markets.

In this chapter, we have explained:

- The factors that influence hospitality consumer behaviour
- Customer expectations and the 'zone of tolerance'
- The hospitality buyer decision-making process
- The importance of segmentation in developing effective marketing strategies
- The market segmentation process
- Key hospitality market segmentation variables
- How to evaluate potential hospitality target markets
- The characteristics of hospitality consumer and organizational target markets.

---

### ACTIVITY 3.3

Look at your answers to Activity 3.1.

What influences (or would influence) your decision to purchase a:

- Drink in a local café?
- Short vacation in your own country?
- Long vacation in a country on the other side of the world?

Can you now explain your decisions, using consumer behaviour theory to help you?

---

### REVIEW QUESTIONS

Now check your understanding of this chapter by answering the following questions:

1 Discuss the factors that influence hospitality consumer behaviour. Provide examples to illustrate your answer.

2 Evaluate customer expectations and the concept of the 'zone of tolerance'. How does this model help explain customer behaviour?

3 Discuss the consumer decision-making process for hospitality products.

4 Describe the segmentation variables that hospitality companies can use to categorize potential customers.

5 Evaluate the characteristics of hospitality customer and organizational target markets.

## References

1. Levitt, T. (1983). The globalization of markets. *Harvard Business Review, 38*, 45–56.
2. Thompson, W., & Hickey, J. (2005). *Society in Focus*. Boston, MA: Pearson.
3. Judge, T. A., Higgins, C. A., Thoresen, C. J., & Barrick, M. R. (1999). The big five personality traits, general mental ability, and career success across the life span. *Personnel Psychology, 52*, 3.
4. Gursoy, D., & Chi, C. G. (2020). Effects of COVID-19 pandemic on hospitality industry: Review of the current situations and a research agenda. *Journal of Hospitality Marketing & Management, 29*(5), 527–529.

5.  Gursoy, D., & Chi, C. G. (2021). Celebrating 30 years of excellence amid the COVID-19 pandemic – An update on the effects of COVID-19 pandemic and COVID-19 vaccines on hospitality industry: Overview of the current situation and a research agenda. *Journal of Hospitality Marketing & Management, 30*(3), 277–281.
6.  Zeithaml, V. A., Berry, L. L., & Parasuraman, A. (1993). The nature and determinants of customer expectations of service. *Journal of the Academy of Marketing Science, 21*, 1–12.
7.  United States Census Bureau [Internet]. *ZIP Codes Tabulation Areas (ZCTAs).* [cited September 8, 2021]. Available from: www.census.gov/programs-surveys/geography/guidance/geo-areas/zctas.html
8.  Osman, H. (2001). Practice of relationship marketing in hotels. *PhD thesis.* Oxford, UK: Oxford Brookes University.

Chapter **4**

# Competitive strategies

After working through this chapter, you should be able to:

- Describe how hospitality organizations vary in their segmentation, positioning and differentiation strategies
- Understand the characteristics of hospitality firms that impact on marketing practice
- Carry out a competitive analysis using Michael Porter's 'five forces' model
- Evaluate the role of branding in hospitality organizations
- Evaluate the international significance of major players in the hospitality industry.

## Introduction

The hospitality industry continues to grow rapidly as the largest firms continue their international expansion in emerging markets and new players enter more established and mature country markets. Since there is more supply than demand in most market segments, the industry's competitive environment is dynamic, intense and turbulent. Competition can be fierce, and knowing your competitors is of crucial importance to hospitality marketers. In this chapter, we examine how companies develop and implement their segmentation, positioning and differentiation strategies to compete for customers. We then explore the characteristics of hospitality firms – especially the differences between large-scale companies and smaller independent operators – as they influence competitive strategies. We next introduce the 'five forces' model

DOI: 10.4324/9781003186342-6

that is widely used to analyze the hospitality industry's competitive environment. Finally, we explain the critical role of branding, especially for international hotel and restaurant firms.

---

### ACTIVITY 4.1

Before reading the rest of the chapter, think about the major international hotel brands:

- Can you name three different hotel brands?
- Which market segments does each of these brands compete in?
- Which company owns each of these brands?

When you have completed the chapter, carry out this activity again and then compare your answers.

---

## Segmentation strategies

In Chapter 3, we discussed hospitality market segmentation variables and target markets in detail. There are significant differences between the segmentation strategies of large hospitality organizations with multiple properties and brands, and those of independent, single-unit operators. For larger organizations, there are three alternative segmentation strategies: mass marketing, differentiated marketing and focused marketing (see Figure 4.1).

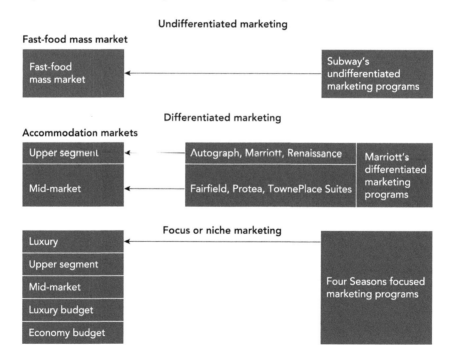

Figure 4.1 Segmentation strategies in marketing

### *Mass marketing*

Companies that adopt a mass marketing or an undifferentiated segmentation strategy recognize the similarities of all customers' needs and wants. They develop a single brand or product offer to satisfy these customers. In doing so, these companies can benefit from economies of scale by standardizing operations, menus, staffing, purchasing and promotion. However, in today's fiercely competitive business environment, it is almost impossible for hospitality companies to adopt a mass marketing or an undifferentiated segmentation strategy and survive.

### Differentiated marketing

Companies that adopt a differentiated segmentation strategy recognize that there are differences between the needs and wants of different market segments. They therefore develop different offers to better satisfy these different segments. The key advantage of this segmentation strategy is the potential to increase sales and market share by providing options that satisfy the needs and wants of the chosen segments. Large international hotel firms often adopt this approach and offer different hotel options at different price points and for different usage occasions, often in a single location. For example, Accor has 68 hotels in and around London that include Sofitel, Novotel, Savoy, Lord Milner, Mercure, Ibis Styles, Draycott, Ibis, Ibis Budget and Pullman brands. Marriot has around 45 hotels in and around New York city that include Marriott, Renaissance, Sheraton, Four Points by Sheraton, Fairfield Inn & Suites, TownePlace Suites, Aloft, SpringHill Suites, Residence Inn, Courtyard, Element and the MC Hotel. Sometimes hotel firms develop brands for specific country markets, such as the HUALUXE Hotel and Resort brand developed by IHG specifically for Chinese travellers. These different brands meet the needs of different segments better than a mass marketing approach, thereby satisfying customers and generating higher numbers of repeat customers and recommendations. As these firms are less dependent on any single market sector, their financial risks are reduced. However, these firms do incur higher costs in developing and operating multiple brands, and from customized purchasing, specialized staffing and developing brand-specific promotion and communication strategies and tactics.

### Focused, concentrated or niche marketing

Hospitality firms that concentrate their marketing programmes on a single market segment adopt what is alternatively known as a 'focused', 'concentrated' or 'niche' marketing strategy. These firms can either focus on a specific market segment, such as the luxury leisure market or adopt a geographic concentration where all the firm's outlets are located within a specific geographic region. The focus on a single market segment enables these firms to deeply understand the needs and wants of customers within that segment and develop appropriate offers. Firms that adopt this strategy build up expertise and develop operational efficiency. They are also better able to satisfy customers and potentially enhance profitability as a result. The main disadvantage with this strategy is that over-reliance on one market segment can make the firm extremely vulnerable to any decline in the size of the segment or the segment's purchasing power. Sandals, a company with 15 luxury resorts in the Caribbean, is an example of a firm that adopts a focused or niche strategy. As this firm is located within one specific geographic area, it is also vulnerable to any instability in the area, which could impact on travel and customer demand.

### Single-unit businesses

The segmentation strategy adopted by individually owned and managed hotels is linked to the property's character, location, catchment area and competition. While individually owned and managed hotels usually have smaller marking budgets compared to multi-unit, franchised chain hotels, individually owned and managed hotels tend to have a better knowledge of their local markets. In reality, most hotel properties, including chain-affiliated branded properties, need to target several different market segments to ensure the operation trades profitably. The seasonality of hospitality markets and the variability of demand from different segments mean that operators have to target different segments at different times of the day, week, month or year. Typically, hotels will target business market segments for midweek occupancy and leisure market segments for the weekend. Even independent leisure destination hotels and resorts will normally target several segments of the market.

## Targeting, positioning and differentiation

The selection of target markets provides a focus for firms to develop their positioning and differentiation strategies. Consumers are inundated with messages from both commercial and non-commercial organizations and from other consumers via traditional and social media. Therefore, hospitality firms try to differentiate themselves from their competition in order to stand out and be noticed by their target markets. The problem is that for many hospitality operators there are rarely significant differences between the core products offered by their direct competitors. The tangible elements of a hospitality experience – a bed, a meal, a drink – are so similar that they can be considered as commodities, making it extremely difficult to provide a significantly differentiated product offer. The intense competition in the hospitality industry makes it even more difficult for firms to differentiate themselves. Innovations introduced to create differentiation are often easily copied or imitated by competitors. For example, when Pizza Hut first introduced the 'stuffed crust' innovation, it was not long before supermarket chains introduced these to their store-branded pizzas.

However, hospitality consumers do recognize that some products and companies have very distinct images compared to their rivals. The design and maintenance of a distinctive position in the minds of target markets relative to competitors is the focus of a positioning strategy. The purpose of positioning is to ensure that target markets clearly understand what the product, service or brand stands for in the marketplace. Figure 4.2 demonstrates the link between segmentation, targeting and positioning.

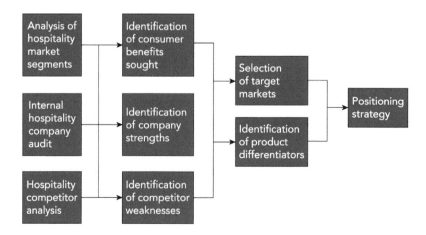

Figure 4.2  The segmentation, targeting and positioning process in hospitality

Marketing research should provide an understanding of what customers want, expect and are willing to pay. An internal audit should identify hospitality company strengths that could possibly be developed into differentiators. A competitor analysis will identify competitors' weaknesses and possibilities for effective differentiation. The marketer then evaluates these three analyses, with the aim of establishing a match between the benefits sought by consumers, the strengths of the company and the weaknesses of competitors. The process culminates in the articulation of the company's desired position in the marketplace, which is designed to produce competitive advantage.

Hospitality marketers use product and service differentiators as part of the positioning process. Product and service differentiation helps to distinguish tangible and/or intangible elements of the hospitality offer from competitors within the same product class. Again, the purpose is to create a competitive position attractive to selected target markets. Elements of the product or service offer that firms use to differentiate themselves include location, quality, price, range of facilities and services, safety/security and reward programmes. These product or service differentiators may only be minor in nature, but when articulated effectively over a period of time they can help a brand to stand out from the competition in the mind of the target markets. One key differentiator that is more difficult for competitors to imitate is the brand and company image. Well-established brands or hotels are increasingly capitalizing on their brand image to demonstrate their history of quality service. For example, the Historic Davenport Hotel in Spokane, Washington actively promotes the glamour and luxury experienced in this 100 years old property that has been expertly reinvented for the twenty-first century.

---

**ACTIVITY 4.2**

Visit the Historic Davenport Hotel Website and explore the hotel's history at: www.davenporthotelcollection.com/the-historic-davenport-hotel/

Examine where and how this hotel emphasizes its history and heritage.

---

There are two approaches to positioning: objective and subjective, as explained next.

### Objective positioning

Objective positioning makes reference to the tangible, real or physical attributes that a hotel or restaurant offers to its customers. Attributes like the size of rooms, a beachfront location, the facilities and amenities in the bathrooms of luxury hotels, and the menu on a quick-service restaurant, are objective. In objective positioning, these tangible attributes are used as the main differentiators to distinguish the hospitality offer from those of competitors. However, positioning that is based on these tangible product attributes can often be easily copied or imitated by competitors. For this reason, objective positioning is not considered sustainable. Nonetheless, many independent and international chain hotels and restaurants seem to favour objective positioning judging by the images used in their promotional campaigns. Unfortunately, managers sometimes fail to understand that pictures of rooms and restaurants look the same as thousands of others and therefore do not differentiate their hotel or restaurant from the competition.

### Subjective positioning

Subjective positioning focuses on intangible aspects of the hospitality offer. Subjective positioning offers hospitality operators more opportunity to position their company or brand effectively because intangible claims are more difficult for competitors to imitate.

There are two approaches to subjective positioning, according to whether the hospitality product is more tangible-dominant or intangible-dominant. When hospitality products are more tangible-dominant – for example, budget hotels – and there is little difference between competitor offers, marketers differentiate their products by stressing the intangible attributes. While this is not an easy task, Whitbread's economy brand Premier Inn has been successful in stressing the 'quietness' of their hotel bedrooms, so that 'a good night's sleep' could be guaranteed.

The second approach to subjective positioning is more often associated with intangible-dominant products. Intangible attributes that support positioning strategy include the service, the atmosphere, the reputation, the history and the image of the offer. Being intangible, marketers need to be highly creative to position these positively in the minds of targeted consumers. One way to do so is to 'tangibilize the intangible' by finding or creating tangible evidence that supports the positioning of the company. Four Seasons Hotels and Resorts has always positioned itself as a luxury offering with exceptional quality and service. However, in face of the growing competition in the luxury hotel and resort segment, it introduced its luxury jet service to transport customers to its resort locations. The luxury jet 'tangibilizes the intangible' by implying exceptional quality and service.

### Positioning strategies

Positioning strategies are designed to answer two basic questions:

1  Against whom should a brand position? These are usually other brands in the same competitive set. For example, Holiday Inn Express competes against Hampton Inns (a Hilton brand) and Domino's Pizza competes against Papa John's Pizza. They are direct competitors in the same product class.

2  How should a brand position? The answer to this question provides the basis for a brand's competitive efforts since the goal of positioning is to be differentiated from your competition. Subway is the market leader among sandwich chains. In fact, it has more locations than McDonald's. Customers choose the ingredients that are in front of them for their sandwiches while a 'sandwich artist' builds the sandwich for the customer per the customer's instructions. The customer selects the bread and fillings and decides if they want it toasted or not. 'Eat Fresh' has been the core positioning strategy for Subway. A number of brands has been trying to emulate Subway's success by imitating their positioning strategy. A good example is Quiznos. The brand that once owned more than 5,000 stores declared bankruptcy in 2018 and was sold to venture capitalists High Bluff Capital Partners. As of 2021, there were fewer than 500 Quiznos stores. Quiznos' failure is attributed to its positioning, which was not unique.

Several specific positioning strategies can be identified in hospitality companies:

• *Product or other special features*: This strategy focuses on a tangible attribute. For example, an extended stay hotel brand may position itself on the spacious and ergonomic workspace in bedrooms.

• *Price/quality*: This positioning strategy can be applied to both luxury and budget brands. For a luxury brand, the positioning would focus on high quality, relatively high price and an exclusive image like Ritz Carlton. For a budget property like Motel 6, the focus is on standard quality for a lower price and a value-for-money image within the product class.

- *Customer benefits*: This type of positioning emphasizes the brand's ability to solve customer problems. For example, Club Med is positioned as a place to be happy. It was designed to offer an experience that freed people from their daily constraints so they could rediscover themselves and recharge their batteries through contact with nature, sports and like-minded people.

- *Use or usage*: This positioning strategy focuses on the reasons why the customers use the product. The Fantasy Land Hotel in the West Edmonton Mall in Canada is positioned as a place when fun and adventure are on your doorstep. The hotel has developed a recommended itinerary so that guests can take advantage of the leisure activities and shopping available within the mall.

- *User*: This positioning strategy often focuses on the type or class of user of a brand, the family market, or younger or older segments of the population. For example, Walt Disney World designs all its theme park experiences and rides to target families with children, while Sandals Resorts offers all-inclusive luxury Caribbean experiences just for couples.

Each of these positioning strategies focuses on the type of experience offered to guests, albeit in different ways. A well-executed positioning strategy will provide a customer experience that is different from that of competitors.

### Positioning new hospitality ventures

In new hospitality ventures, there is likely to be a strong focus on the positioning strategy as part of the venture development process. Large multi-branded organizations will want to ensure that any new brand is distinct from the other brands in their portfolio, and from competitor offers. Smaller organizations will need to demonstrate to any financial backers that they have a clear and well-formulated positioning strategy in place. New ventures provide the hospitality firm with the opportunity to use marketing research to plan the new concept and position their offer more effectively.

## CASE STUDY 4.1

### Country Inn & Suites by Radisson[1]

Country Inn & Suites by Radisson, formerly Country Inn & Suites by Carlson is a hotel chain of the Radisson Hotel Group (former Carlson Hotels). It was established by Carlson Companies in 1986 as a 'middle-class' brand. The sister brand, Radisson Hotels, is classified as full-service, upscale brand of the group. In January 2018, two years after Carlson sold Carlson Rezidor Hotel group to HNA Group, the chain was rebranded into 'Country Inn & Suites by Radisson' in order to leverage the global recognition and strength of the Radisson brand. Country Inn & Suites by Radisson is a part of Carlson Rezidor Hotel Group, which also includes Quorvus Collection, Radisson Blu, Radisson, Radisson RED, Park Plaza and Park Inn by Radisson.

When Carlson first developed its Country Inn & Suites hotel brand in the USA, they wanted to make sure that it stood out from the many other midmarket brands in the country. They decided to target the domestic 'road weary' business travellers, those travellers who were frequently away from home on business. They positioned the brand therefore as a place where these travellers could feel at home while away from home and designed features into the brand to deliver this experience. The original brand had a reception area that looked more like a living room, so that when guests arrived they felt like they were returning home. There were 'free' warm cookies in Reception that guests could help themselves to at any time. In the evening, the fire was lit in the living room so guests could relax in a warm and cosy environment. Although the original brand design has been updated and the chain was rebranded into 'Country Inn & Suites by Radisson' in 2018, the positioning remains consistent. The brand continues to offer warm, personal service and amenities that make for a comfortable stay at every guest touchpoint. Signature brand experiences include social spaces that are open, friendly and inviting, where guests can feel at ease, enjoy, relax and work in comfort. The brand still offers guests a living room with relaxed seating, a den where guests can work or read, a servery where guests can help themselves to snacks and a veranda where guests can mingle, just like they would at home.

*Source*: www.radissonhotels.com/

## Repositioning

It is not unusual for hospitality marketers to re-examine their current positioning strategy and decide to reposition their brand or their property. The reasons for repositioning include:

- Falling sales (perhaps a symptom of customer dissatisfaction or a change in the demographics of the catchment area)
- An opportunity to target an emerging (and possibly growing) market segment
- Competition eroding market share.

The process for developing a repositioning strategy is similar to that of developing a positioning strategy for new hospitality ventures or brands, with one caveat. In trying to reposition a hospitality property, there is the danger of sending out confusing signals to existing and potential target markets. If existing customers are alienated and do not like the changes, they might abandon the property. If these customers are not replaced with new ones quickly, the business can rapidly lose sales and profitability. In addition, there are often high costs associated with repositioning, including capital expenditure to alter the physical product, the development of new marketing collateral and marketing campaigns to promote the new positioning, changes in food-service operations, and changes in staff or new staff training to implement the new positioning strategy. Repositioning can be a risky strategy, but the alternatives are either to continue trading in a deteriorating, downward spiral or to dispose of the property.

### CASE STUDY 4.2

#### Repositioning at The Breakers, Palm Beach, Florida, USA[2]

*Property profile*: The Breakers was originally constructed in 1896 by Henry Morrison Flagler, a Standard Oil Company magnate who also opened up Florida's east coast for tourism by building railways and several hotels in the late nineteenth and early twentieth centuries. The Breakers, completely rebuilt in 1926 following a hotel fire, is a luxury oceanfront resort hotel created in the Italian Renaissance architectural style. The AAA Five Diamond Hotel comprises 538 rooms, including 68 suites; extensive dining, leisure and sports facilities, including 10 restaurants, two 18-hole championship golf courses, 6,000 square-foot indoor/outdoor oceanfront fitness centre, 20,000-square-foot indoor/outdoor spa, Mediterranean-style beach club overlooking one-half mile of private beach, four swimming pools, five whirlpool spas, luxury poolside bungalows, variety of water sports, 10 lighted tennis courts, an extensive programme of family and children's activities, as well as 11 on-site boutiques with distinctive merchandise. The Breakers is still privately owned by Flagler's heirs, and an average of US$25 million is invested annually to preserve the landmark property and to ensure that the property matches the needs of contemporary customers. The Breakers employs more than 2,200 associates to deliver outstanding luxury experiences.

*The positioning challenge*: As an iconic hotel with more than 100 years of brand history and its roots in American high society, research identified not only many positive attributes in The Breakers' current position but also some consumer perceptions that the feel of the hotel was too formal and the customer experience overly predictable. The hotel's management team needed to redefine the position of The Breakers, to match contemporary needs whilst retaining its high quality and quintessentially American heritage.

*The key idea*: To embed the concept of 'New American Glamour' as the foundation for the new positioning strategy. Although the phrase 'New American Glamour' is not mentioned in any promotional material to customers or employees, the idea underpins three core components in the hotel's operations: the physical refurbishment, the service delivery and the organizational culture which is the intangible, critical element of The Breakers – its 'DNA'. Each of these core operational areas developed a range of initiatives to implement the 'New American Glamour' concept and create a feeling of informal elegance, connecting with customers emotionally and delivering 'delightful surprises'. This repositioning provides a coherent brand strategy, which has enabled The Breakers to evolve and enhance the customer experience whilst retaining its historic roots.

*Source*: The Breakers

## Positioning maps

Positioning maps, also called perceptual maps, are tools used by marketers to plot consumer evaluations of competing hospitality products or brands using two or more attributes. The attributes used to map competitors should be those that are important to target markets and can include price, quality, location, reputation, value for money and types of facilities offered. Marketers can undertake qualitative research with focus groups of hotel or restaurant users to gather data and plot competitors on the map. In addition, they can also make effective use of the Internet to gather quantitative data on price, location, star rating, types of facilities offered and consumer reviews to gather qualitative and quantitative data on perceptions of quality and value for money.

Maps can be as simple as two-dimensional. For example, mapping price against quality. For three-dimensional and more complex maps marketers can use statistical software packages that reproduce brand positions in n-dimensional space. These maps help marketers to identify where their property or brand 'sits' on the map in relation to the competition and identify the 'perceived' strengths and weaknesses of the properties in the competitive set. Figure 4.3 provides an illustration of a positioning map using quality (as measured by star rating and consumer data) and price (from budget to luxury properties). Note the relationship between quality and price, where luxury hotels charge higher prices than budget hotels. Normally a hotel must stay within its price/quality product class, indicated by the dotted lines on the map. If hotels charge more than the price/quality norm, customers might accuse them of having a 'rip-off' strategy, unless other factors compensate for the higher price. For example, a hotel having a monopoly at a busy airport terminal would be able to command higher prices due to its advantageous location. In contrast, if a hotel is offering higher quality at too low a price, the strategy is unsustainable in the long run. A three-star hotel property truly offering the quality and standards of a five-star hotel would not be profitable over the long term.

Positioning maps are useful tools for tracking changing competition positions over time, as the marketing environment does not remain static and consumers' perceptions will change in response to competitor offers. Hotels constantly battling for competitive advantage continue to adapt their offer and their positioning strategies.

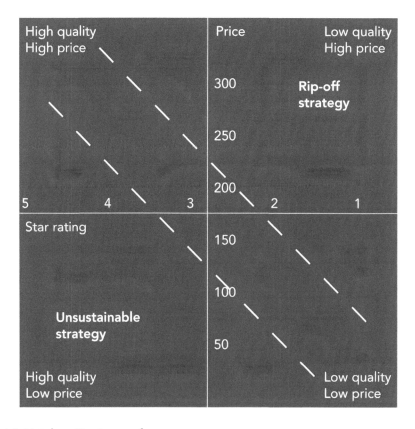

Figure 4.3 Hotel positioning map[3]

*Source:* Adapted from Lovelock and Wright

---

**ACTIVITY 4.3**

Identify five hotels in your local area that represent luxury, upscale, midmarket (full service), midmarket (rooms only) and budget offers.

- Check the price of a room for each property on the same date.
- Identify the star rating of the hotel and look up the quality rating on Tripadvisor or Booking.com.
- Use this information to plot each hotel's price and quality ranking (using both the stars and the consumer-driven scores to help you plot quality more accurately).
- Evaluate your findings.

---

## Characteristics of hospitality firms

We now discuss a number of characteristics of hospitality firms that impact on their competitive strategies. These include ownership and size, ownership and affiliation, and hotel classification schemes.

## Ownership and size

Many hospitality firms started as single-unit enterprises – often termed 'Mom and Pop operations' – and have remained single-unit businesses throughout their commercial life. The characteristics of small, single-site hospitality firms include the following:

- Owners manage the business
- Owners interact with customers
- Owners tend to be entrepreneurial and innovative in responding quickly to changes in the PESTE and micro-environments
- Focus on operations and the immediate issues facing the business; if planning is undertaken, it is normally restricted to a short-term time frame
- Limited access to financial capital.

The major hotel groups do not own or operate small hotels, because small hotels do not deliver the required revenue and profitability. Hence, bed and breakfasts, guesthouses and small budget hotels tend to be privately owned, although there are some exceptions for budget chains like Accor's Ibis Budget brand or Motel 6. The three-star market generally incorporates both privately owned hotels and midmarket chains, whilst larger upscale and luxury units tend to be owned by or affiliated with larger organizations, although there are numerous independent large luxury hotels and resorts located around the globe.

Firms that grow are said to have a life cycle, as they develop from a single-site owner-managed business operating in a familiar environment to multi-site business units with hierarchical corporate organizations, operating in a complex environment. As these businesses grow, marketing decision-making often becomes removed from those interacting with the customers. The corporate office tends to be responsible for strategic marketing decisions, while operational marketing decisions are made at the unit level. The characteristics of larger hospitality firms include the following:

- Ownership is normally diffused across a large number of shareholders, although institutions such as pension funds and banks may hold larger stakes in the business.
- Separation of ownership and management – if general managers and directors of a hospitality corporation have an equity stake in the firm, it will normally be a minor shareholding or option.
- Multiple-site operations – the largest hospitality corporations comprise thousands of geographically dispersed units, across dozens of countries on many continents, using a complex array of brands, targeting a variety of markets, using a range of business formats (ownership, franchising and management contract) and employing hundreds of thousands of employees.
- Employment of professionals to manage at the unit level, regional level and at head office – these professionals have developed considerable expertise in hospitality operations management, as well as the functional disciplines of finance, revenue, human resources and marketing management.

Large firms enjoy significant advantages in terms of:

- Economies of scale, giving cost savings through bulk purchase discounts
- Economies of scope, giving cost savings through sharing centralized functions (e.g. production, finance, marketing)
- Economies of experience (comprising the accumulated managerial experience that large companies enjoy)
- Access to financial markets, which provide capital for investment
- Powerful and well-known brands
- Access to the best global distribution systems
- Access to specialist resources such as financial consultants, design consultants and advertising and public relations agencies
- Focus on long-term strategic planning

but

- Management procedures tend to be more formalized and bureaucratic
- Management is removed from interaction with the customer and therefore may be slower to recognize and respond to market changes.

Although smaller, single-site, owner-managed hospitality units can give regular customers a much more personalized service, in the past it has been more difficult to attract travellers to stay in an unknown property, especially when consumers do not have the assurance of good service quality. However, social media and consumer reviews on websites like Tripadvisor, booking sites like hotels.com and travel search engines like KAYAK.com enable customers to compare prices and have altered the competitive playing field. So too, has the advent of the sharing economy and the growth of firms like Airbnb, which offers guests the opportunity to rent accommodation in privately owned properties. While powerful hotel brands still provide reassurance for some customers, many consumers are now seeking to book a different kind of travel experience (see Case Study 4.3).

---

### CASE STUDY 4.3

#### Airbnb[4]

In 2007, when hotels in San Francisco were completely sold out due to a large conference, Joe Gebbia and Brian Chesky decided to rent out three air mattresses on the floor of their apartment to desperate conference delegates. Deciding to serve breakfast as well, they created a website, www.airbedandbreakfast.com, and within a week they had bookings from three guests who were willing to pay $80 each night. Recognizing the potential of their venture, the entrepreneurs founded Airbnb in 2008. They identified cities around the USA where conferences or conventions were planned and invited anyone who had a spare room to rent, to list their accommodation on their website. They discovered that private homeowners across the USA were happy to rent out their spare rooms. Unfortunately, the original venture was not profitable. However, the founders were successful in obtaining financial backing, adapting their business plan and technological systems to ensure they could take commission on bookings. The pace of growth for Airbnb has been phenomenal. Airbnb now has more than 5.6 million accommodation listings in over 100,000 cities and 220 countries. Over 150 million worldwide users have booked over 800 million stays through Airbnb, staying in a wide range of accommodation options at different price points and which include spare rooms, caves, boats, treehouses, castles and private islands.

Airbnb is considered as a major disruptor and one of the most successful pioneers of the sharing economy, transforming the hospitality industry around the world. Airbnb has significantly disrupted the hospitality business by offering alternatives to hotels, putting considerable pressure on room rates and forcing hoteliers to become more creative with their offerings. This pressure resulted in the creation of affordable hotel brands and development of restaurants, bars and lobbies that channel the local vibe. In order to stay competitive and to address evolving customer needs, Airbnb has started diversifying its offerings by adding services like Airbnb Experiences, Airbnb Adventures, Airbnb Plus and Airbnb Lux.

## Ownership and affiliation

Within the hospitality industry, firms use a range of different market entry modes, business formats or models. In the hotel industry, the current trend for many large corporate players is towards more 'asset-light' models. In this section we will explore the different market entry modes that hospitality firms employ and the implications of choosing different modes.

### Owned and operated

A company, partnership or individual can own the business and its freehold property, giving them control of both the physical asset (e.g. the hotel or restaurant) and its management. Owners are therefore free to develop their business, subject to any financial or legal constraints. Historically, many large hotel chains have owned and operated their hotel properties. These firms grew their portfolios of hotels through greenfield development, where hotels were built from scratch or through merging or acquiring (M&A) individual hotels or branded chains of hotels. However, as ownership of the freehold property ties up capital, many larger chains now opt for different business formats that are 'asset-light' and which enable them to expand more rapidly. For example, IHG, one of the largest hotel companies in the world, owns less than 1 per cent of its hotel properties.

### Leasehold

Hospitality firms can lease their property from the property-owning landlord and pay commercial rents. The physical asset therefore remains in the ownership of the landlord, but the hotel or restaurant operator maintains full control over the daily operation of the brand. While the sale-leaseback concept has been widely applied in the non-hotel property sector for decades, it is only recently that it has been adopted in the hotel sector. In recent years, many hotel firms that have acquired branded chains have then sold the physical assets on to another firm and then leased them back in a process known as sale-and-leaseback. For example, Club Med is one of the larger users of the sale-and-leaseback model. Club Med operates seven resorts in the Caribbean, five in Mexico and two in South America. Three of their resorts that are located in Ixtapa, Cancun and Turks & Caicos are currently under the sale-and-leaseback structure. This model provides immediate opportunities for unlocking equity in the hotel and generating liquidity that can be used to pay off debt, cover costs and invest in profitable new ventures.

### Management agreement or contract

A management agreement is a contractual agreement between a hotel owner and a hotel management company. A management agreement is asset-light as the ownership of the hotel is separate from its management, although sometimes the hotel management firm will take an equity stake in the property. The first recorded hotel management agreement was between Hilton Hotels Corporation and the Puerto Rican government in 1967, when the latter wanted to develop their tourism industry but did not have the expertise to manage hotels. Management agreements were popular in the development of the hotel industry in many Asian Pacific countries.

Today, the largest hotel management company in the US is Aimbridge Hospitality, with 182,000+ guestrooms and 1,400+ hotels in their portfolio. Aimbridge's hotels are mostly Marriott, Hilton and Hyatt branded properties in US and Caribbean markets. The second largest hotel management company is Hyatt Hotels. Unlike many other chain hotel brands, Hyatt actually manages about ⅔ of all Hyatt properties, with 61,217 guestrooms and 372 hotels under corporate management. The third largest hotel management company is the InterContinental Hotels Group (IHG). IHG takes an asset-light approach and only manages a small percentage of their 5,800+ hotels worldwide, which include brands like Crowne Plaza and Holiday Inn.[5]

In these agreements, the hotel management firm's role is to provide a brand name, reservation and distribution systems, technical support, design and operational management. It must also provide the hotel owners with a sufficient return on their investment in the hotel as an asset. As competition has intensified in the hotel industry, the nature of the management agreement has changed. Contracts between hotel owners and managers tend to be shorter in length, and hotel owners have started to demand more say in operational decisions, sometimes having an asset manager located within a hotel. As a result, hotel management firms lose some of the control they have over their physical assets and their hotel operations. Some hotels operate within 'three party' agreements, where the hotel owner, the brand owner and the hotel brand manager are different firms. While this type of arrangement increases the complexity of operating a hotel and making decisions, hotel management agreements continue to be popular, as hotel brand managers can focus on their core business of managing hotels.

### Franchise agreements

Franchise agreements are another type of 'asset-light' model. Franchising, and business format franchising in particular, has long been popular in the hospitality industry. In business format franchising, a franchisor develops a business concept that franchisees replicate and operate on the franchisor's behalf. The franchisee buys the right to use the franchisor's brand name, trademark, operating system, and technical and marketing support for a contractually determined period of time. The franchisee pays an upfront fee for the franchised unit, ongoing marketing fees and royalty fees based on a percentage of gross sales. Franchisors benefit from this market entry mode as franchisees provide the financial and human capital required for expansion and franchisees gain access to an established brand and a 'ready-made' operating system. However, there are frequently tensions, as franchisees want autonomy to respond to local demand whilst franchisors want to maintain strict control to maintain uniform brand standards. Nonetheless, business format franchising is extensively used within the quick-service restaurant (QSR) sector. The original QSR franchisor is often said to be Ray Kroc, who began franchising McDonald's. Although its historical roots are within North America, business format franchising has been growing in popularity globally, and within hotel chains particularly in the budget and midmarket sectors. Choice Hotels of the USA operates its entire portfolio of over 7,000 hotels under franchise agreement. There are, however, many different variations of franchise contracts used within hospitality and tourism, as you'll find out in Activity 4.4.

---

**ACTIVITY 4.4**

### Wyndham Hotels & Resorts – the world's largest hotel franchisor

Wyndham Hotels & Resorts is reported to be the world's largest franchisor of hotels. In 2021, the company operates a portfolio of 21 hotel brands. They have over 8,900 hotels and nearly 813,000 rooms in more than 95 countries.[6]

● Log on to the Wyndham Hotel Group website, www.wyndhamhotels.com/, and read about hotel brand franchising opportunities.

● Log on to Jimmy John's at www.jimmyjohns.com/ and read about their franchising opportunities and requirements.

● Can you identify the differences between these two companies franchising opportunities?

---

### Hybrid organizations

The term 'hybrid organization' refers to companies that combine both company owned and operated units with franchised units. This hybrid model has long been popular within the QSR sector. For example, 93 per cent of McDonald's 38,000 restaurants are franchised and the balance are company owned.[7] The hybrid model enables a franchisor to both expand their footprint while fine tuning their processes such as training, and new product development and testing. Franchisors are more likely to open company owned and operated stores in flagship locations and in prominent areas. Company owned and operated stores can serve as model stores of the brand.

Franchisors who also own and operate company-owned stores can keep a close eye on evolving customer needs and wants. They can use these company owned and operated stores for new product development in response to customers' evolving needs and wants and market test new products in these stores to maintain control over the growth of the brand and brand standards. Franchisees who are close to customers can also come up with new innovative product ideas. In fact, it was a McDonald's franchisee who first suggested putting a breakfast sandwich on menus in response to the needs of his local customers. However, the Egg McMuffin was tried and tested in corporate owned units before it was added to menus across the franchise network.

### Consortia

Consortia are groups of independently owned and operated hotels that join forces to achieve the benefits of economies of scale and scope of larger hotel chains. Each individual hotel retains its autonomy and control of its operations, but generally must meet a defined quality standard to belong to a particular consortium. Benefits of belonging to a consortium include:

- Access to a central reservation system
- Referred bookings from other consortium members
- A recognized brand name
- Participation in national or international marketing campaigns
- Economies of scale through the consortium's bulk purchasing power
- Economies of scope through centralized marketing and distribution services
- Access to management and marketing expertise through other consortium members.

There are numerous hotel consortia, including the Preferred Hotel Group, Small Luxury Hotels of the World and Supranational Hotels. Activity 4.5 identifies one of the largest consortia in the hotel industry.

### Implications of ownership and affiliation

As the previous section indicates, different market entry modes or business formats give rise to different types of ownership or affiliation with hotel chains. They also yield different degrees of control, both over the physical asset and the management of the brand. The greatest control is available to owner-operated models, although this business format ties up capital and can limit further expansion. In many parts of the world, independent operators typically own or lease their hotel properties.

---

**ACTIVITY 4.5**

**Hotusa Hotels – one of the largest consortia**

Hotusa Hotels of Spain has around 2,604 hotels and 235,000 rooms within its consortium.[8]

- Log on to the Hotusa Hotels website, www.hotusagroup.com/.
- Identify the benefits of becoming a Hotusa member.
- Identify the requirements of becoming a Hotusa member.

In contrast, asset-light models such as franchising and management agreements can help accelerate organizational growth by reducing the capital required for expansion. However, these firms yield an element of control to the property owner and, in the case of franchising, to the franchisee as the operator. Franchisees can behave opportunistically and shirk their obligations or 'free ride' on the franchisor name by not delivering the brand standards. Franchisors, in turn, can extract significant revenues from franchisees, making it difficult for the franchisee to turn a profit. These practices have a negative impact on brand reputation and therefore all franchisees in a network.

In reality, many restaurant chains employ a hybrid form and maintain a portfolio of owned and operated and franchised units to balance these (often conflicting) demands. Hotel chains also employ hybrid forms. It is common for some of the larger hotel chains to own and operate some properties, operate others under management agreements with varying degrees of equity investment, and some as franchised hotels. Accor, for example, operates 37 per cent of its hotels under franchise agreements, 59 per cent under management contracts and 4 per cent are either owned or leased. This means that hotels within a chain can be diversely affiliated with the corporate headquarters. Hotel chain affiliation is popular in many countries, including China, Canada, the USA, France and Spain. For example, in the USA 60 per cent, in Croatia 26 per cent and in Spain 34 per cent of hotel room capacity is chain-affiliated. In emerging markets in the Middle East, Africa and Latin America, most hotel supply growth is through chain-affiliated hotels.

## Hotel management companies

There are many firms that specialize purely in hotel management. These firms operate hotels on behalf of themselves, independent hotel owners and the owners of many well-known brands. Plateno Hotels Group, founded in China, is one of the larger hotel management companies, operating over 6,300 (mostly independent) hotels in Asia Pacific. In contrast, Westmount Hospitality Group, although smaller in size, operates hotel brands belonging to Hilton, IHG, Fairmont, Starwood and Wyndham across North America, Europe and Asia.

### Hotel classification schemes

In most countries, the quality of hotels is rated on a five-star system. These rating systems are developed either by national tourism associations or other professional bodies. For example, the rating systems in the USA and Canada are run by the national automobile associations (AAA and CAA), but a diamond rating system is used for both hotels and restaurants. The rating system in UK is operated by the National Tourist Boards and the Automobile Association. Because these systems are developed nationally, there is some variation between countries' star-rating classifications. In Europe, efforts have been made to harmonize different country ratings through the European Hospitality and Quality (EHQ) scheme that offers accreditation to national inspection bodies for hotel rating. The EHQ scheme is based on five stars and a Superior mark to indicate extra facilities at each star level. The scheme is based on 21 criteria with 270 different elements.[9] While some individual hotel properties have promoted themselves as having seven stars (the Burj Al Arab in Dubai and the Emirates Palace Hotel in Abu Dhabi), the five-star system is the most commonly accepted and generally reflects the criteria listed next.

In addition to these ratings, private organizations assess the quality of hospitality services. Many travellers these days access the quality reviews available at online travel agents (OTAs)

| One star | A budget hotel with limited facilities, offering bed, breakfast and possibly an evening meal, and characterized by informal standards of service to residents |
| --- | --- |
| Two star | An economy hotel with limited facilities, normally offering more extensive dining facilities, and characterized by informal standards of service to residents |
| Three star | A midmarket hotel with more extensive facilities, offering a full range of dining and bar services, with professional standards of service, to residents and non-residents |
| Four star | An upscale hotel offering extensive facilities and services to residents and non-residents, and higher-quality service standards often through higher staffing levels |
| Five star | A luxury hotel offering impeccable service standards, with professional multilingual staff, dedicated 24-hour service and a full range of facilities of the highest quality |

and customer review sites, such as Tripadvisor. At Tripadvisor, guests rate hotel location, sleep quality, rooms, service, value for money and cleanliness on a scale of one to five, which is then amalgamated to give an overall rating for the hotel. Visitors to the website can also see the number of guests who have rated a hotel, as well as the individual ratings and comments. Booking.com provides an overall numerical rating out of 10 for hotels based on customer feedback. There are also quality-rating services for restaurants. For example, the Michelin Guide offers extensive critiques for restaurants around the world using Bib Gourmand, knife and fork and star-level rankings. Travellers around the world can access these ratings through the Michelin app which will identify the nearest Michelin-rated restaurants and provide directions.

## Understanding the competition

As we've already mentioned, competition within the hospitality industry is intense. The internationalization of many hotel and restaurant brands has only added to this intensity. Nonetheless, some hospitality operators insist that their hotel or restaurant is so unique that they do not have any competitors. Unfortunately, this is a foolish assumption and the reality is that all hospitality businesses face a variety of different types or levels of competition. Although there are different ways to categorize these levels of competition, one simple way to do so is to distinguish between macro- and micro-competitors.

### Macro-competition

At the macro level, hospitality businesses compete for consumers' disposable income with firms in many different industry sectors. Consumers make decisions on what to spend their disposable income on, and sometimes have to choose between spending in different commercial sectors and between substitute products. For example, they may choose between:

- A luxury holiday or a new car
- A trip to the spa or a trip to the theatre
- A take-away meal from a restaurant or a pre-packed meal from the supermarket.

### Analyzing competition at the macro level

Michael Porter's 'five forces' model[10] continues to be one of the most popular tools for hospitality marketers to understand the forces that influence competition at the macro level. This model has had a significant influence on both practitioners and academics alike. Porter identified five forces that drive competition and the profitability of businesses, as follows.

1   *The bargaining power of customers (buyers)*: This force reflects the strength of the bargaining position that customers have over suppliers, particularly in relation to price. Customers who purchase large volumes of room-nights and who have low switching costs (i.e., it is easy and inexpensive to switch suppliers) have strong bargaining power. For example, large corporations like Amazon, Microsoft, IBM and Deloitte who book thousands of hotel rooms annually have a strong bargaining position and can demand lower prices from hotel operators. Similarly, tour operators who also book a very large volume of hotel rooms annually have a strong bargaining position and can demand lower prices from hotel operators. Many tour operators who run direct flights to tourist destinations have strong bargaining power since they also have some control over the number of tourists arriving to a destination. When hotel capacity is high and demand is variable, customers have strong bargaining power. Conversely, increasing demand in destinations where the hotel capacity is low decreases customers bargaining power. As such, individual customers who book and consume hospitality products have limited bargaining power.

2   *The bargaining power of suppliers (including employees)*: Suppliers can influence the attractiveness and profitability of an industry through their ability to control the supply and price of input goods and services, and employees. Powerful suppliers are those organizations that have a monopoly over goods and services, such as electricity, gas, water or the Internet, within a country or region. Trade unions that can negotiate pay and employment conditions are also powerful suppliers. For example, UNITE HERE is the international union representing over 300,000 workers in the hotel, food service, airport and gaming industries throughout Canada and the USA. Some local chapters are much stronger than others.

3   *The threat of new entrants*: The threat of new entrants or new competitors is dependent on the barriers to entry. Barriers include the capital required to establish a business, access to distribution channels, the opportunities to differentiate products and services from competitors, and the ability to generate economies of scale. While barriers to entry are high in some hospitality sectors such as hotels and resorts, within many hospitality sectors such as restaurants and coffee shops the barriers to entry are low and therefore the threat of new entrants is high. Within the hotel industry, potential new entrants can be identified through 'pipeline' reports that are available from hospitality consultancy firms. The hotel pipeline is the projected supply growth for any given location or market.

4   *The threat of substitutes*: Substitute industries provide competing product offers that perform the same function or offer the same benefit to consumers. For example, consumers can receive the benefit of convenience from a microwavable meal purchased from their local supermarket or a take-away for a neighbourhood restaurant. Similarly, consumers travelling in Vietnam could choose to stay in a branded hotel chain or in a growing number of 'homestay' accommodation options. With the advent of the sharing economy and the demand for 'local experiences', there have been a growing number of substitute products, particularly in the accommodation and travel sectors. During the COVID-19 pandemic working from home and use of video conferencing to interact with colleagues and customers became more common. Teleconferencing, web conferencing and video conferencing

also replaced business travel. Some tourist destinations and attractions started offering virtual experiences and tours. While virtual experiences may never replace traditional travel, they still offer intriguing possibilities. If the technology becomes sophisticated enough, these virtual travel experiences can have significant impact on the demand for hospitality products and services.

5  *The intensity of rivalry between competitors*: This force is associated with rivalry between different industries and between different sectors of the same industry. Rivalry is characterized by the level of conflict (efforts to destroy competitors), coexistence (rivals allow each other to operate in different segments), cooperation (rivals cooperate to compete, for example, in marketing campaigns for destinations) and collusion (illegal cooperation to fix prices and produce a managed market). Rivalry is dependent on the number of competitors and their dominance, the level of profitability, levels of demand and capacity, and on the personalities of competitors. This information is often available commercially. For example, STR Global produces profitability reports with information on revenues, costs and profits on selected hotel samples. Within hospitality and tourism, while competition is intense, cooperative efforts between hotels and restaurants are common.

Porter concluded that when these five forces are at high levels of intensity, industry profitability is low. As owners want to make a return on their investment in any hospitality business, it is important that they understand the environmental dynamics that might impact on their return and influence the profitability of the business.

The first step in using the five forces model is to identify the specific market sector that the business will operate in so that the parameters for analysis can be determined. For example, the market sector could be the QSR market in Seattle, the budget hotel market in Winnipeg or the luxury hotel market in Europe. Geographic parameters can change depending on the nature of the industry sector and it is important to understand these parameters so that each of the five forces can be evaluated. For example, if buyer power is high and there is an intense price-based rivalry between firms, the prospects for a new venture may not be favourable. Used alongside the PESTE analysis, managers can assess the potential for a hospitality offering. Figure 4.4 illustrates the five forces model using a midmarket hotel example.

### Competitive environments analysis

In addition to the five forces model, Porter developed another framework for analyzing the competitive environment.[10] This framework distinguishes between four types of competitive environment: fragmented, niche, volume and stalemate.

#### FRAGMENTED

In a fragmented competitive environment, no firm has a significant market share. A fragmented market comprises a large number of small and medium-sized enterprises (SMEs). There are low barriers to entry and low economies of scale; in some hospitality contexts there is high product differentiation because of the personality and panache of the owner-operators, and in other contexts there is low product differentiation, where competitors simply imitate each other. Profitability is unrelated to size, and larger firms are therefore not necessarily more profitable than SMEs. The restaurant market is a good example of a fragmented industry, given the dominance of privately owned and operated restaurants.

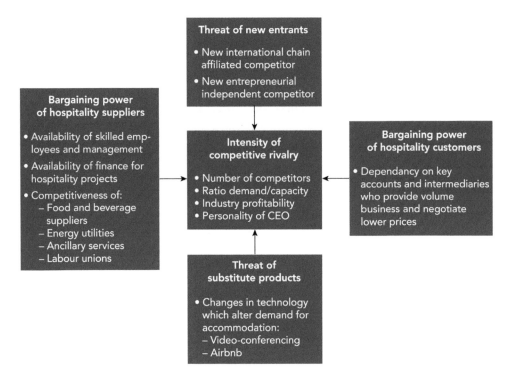

Figure 4.4  Five forces analysis[10]

*Source:* Porter

## SPECIALIZED OR NICHE

In this type of competitive environment, there are different ways of achieving competitive advantage. Firms focus on serving a specific market sector and may be able to charge a premium price for doing so.

A niche market is a focused and targetable segment of a larger market that has unique demands, needs and wants, which are not served by mainstream providers. Companies that target those niche markets develop and offer specialized products or services that can satisfy the unique needs and wants of those markets. Targeting a niche market with specialized products or services can produce significant competitive advantage. Image, quality and service are important factors in specialized or niche environments.

A number of well-known hotel companies utilize niche marketing successfully. For example, both Motel 6 and Ritz Carlton target completely different niche markets, While Motel 6 targets a niche segment of travellers who are on a limited budget and need a room for one night, Ritz Carlton targets a niche segment of travellers and customers who are willing to pay for excellent experience and personalized service. Motel 6 offers clean and comfortable rooms that are easily accessible from highways at an inexpensive price. On the other hand, Ritz Carlton offers luxury accommodations with a wide range of customized services for sophisticated customers including excellent locations and magnificent room views, architectural style with national flavour, great restaurants, fine cuisine, luxurious lobbies, swimming pools, gyms, technical perfection of rooms, various hotel services, and large and well-trained staff.

## VOLUME

In a volume competitive environment, large players serve mass markets. As there are a limited number of ways to achieve competitive advantage, the control of costs is key to success in this type of environment. A key objective for firms is to be the cost and volume leader, and therefore economies of scale, expertise and technology are important. A good example of a volume environment is the QSR burger market in the USA. This market generates annual sales in excess of $126 billion and is dominated by four firms: McDonald's, with approximately $40.4 billion U.S. sales; Burger King, $10.2 billion U.S. sales; Wendy's, $9.8 billion U.S. sales; and Sonic Drive Ins, $4.7 billion U.S. sales in 2019.[11]

## STALEMATE

The stalemate competitive environment is characteristic of mature or declining industries where there are limited opportunities for differentiation. This competitive environment is normally dominated by a small number of large players that focus on large-scale operations and improving productivity to remain profitable. Stalemate industries suffer from excess capacity, limited innovation and high barriers to entry. The drive-in restaurant industry, where diners sat in their cars to eat their meals served by carhops, were very popular in the USA in the 1950s and 1960s. However, by the 1970s, the large number of restaurants, a lack of innovation and the growing costs of the land where these restaurants were situated helped to create a stalemate situation. Very few of these restaurants exist today.

## Micro-competition

In contrast to macro-competition described earlier, micro-competitors offer:

- The same or similar products and services
- At the same or similar prices
- To the same or similar customer markets
- In the same location.

These competitors are therefore referred to as 'direct' or 'product form' competition. Examples include:

- Costa Coffee and Starbucks
- Burger King and McDonald's
- Four Seasons and Fairmont Hotels & Resorts.

Micro-competitors are most frequently located in the same geographic area. For example, a Costa Coffee and a Starbucks located within the same shopping mall will be direct competitors. However, sometimes direct competitors are more geographically dispersed. For example, the top destination spa resort the Cal-a-Vie in California is a direct competitor of the Mii Amo in Arizona. Understanding the competition at the micro level is extremely important in the hospitality industry.

## ANALYZING COMPETITION AT THE MICRO LEVEL

The first step in undertaking a competitor analysis at the micro level is identifying the competitor set. For hotels, a simple way to do this is to ask customers where they would have stayed if they had not booked into your hotel. The Marriott County Hotel in London adopted this approach. Once the competitor set is identified, a visit to competitor properties is an effective way of fully understanding their offerings. Companies also monitor and analyze customer review comments posted to review sites, booking sites and social media about competitors' products and services to fully understand competitors' offerings and customer experiences at competing properties. Companies first harvest those review comments using a specialized harvesting software and then analyze them utilizing content and sentiment analysis approaches. Through visits to competitor properties and analysis of customer review comments, companies can fully understand competitors' offerings, their weaknesses and strengths in delivering satisfactory customer experiences by examining:

- The size, quality, decor and facilities in guestrooms and public areas
- The food and beverage facilities, menus and quality
- The staff and their approach to, and quality of, service
- The price and value offer
- The marketing communications and the service promise promoted
- The image projected by brand signage and the physical appearance of the property
- The reputation of the brand.

Keeping up to date with competitor activity is a key activity for firms. The development of an annual marketing plan provides a clear-cut opportunity to revisit competitors to experience or analyze their offers, as we explain further in Chapter 15. By analyzing competitor offers, hospitality marketers can understand their competitive strengths and weaknesses. However, it is very important when analyzing competitor offers to have a clear understanding of the elements that are the most important to the target markets. For example, do customers place more value on the quality of the food and beverage or on the size of the hotel guestrooms and the amenities on offer?

### International competitor sets

International hotel chains and their brands compete at both local and international levels. Given the differences in star ratings around the world, different types of classifications are employed for competitor sets. STR Global uses the following chain-scale classifications for the competitors listed:

- Luxury chains: Four Seasons, Jumeriah, Ritz Carlton, Rosewood, Shangri-La, Taj
- Upper upscale chains: Corinthia, Dusit Thani, Hilton, Hyatt, Malmaison, New World, Westin
- Upscale chains: citizenM, Coast Hotels, Hilton Garden Inns, Jin Jiang, Melia, Park Plaza
- Upper midscale chains: Ashok, Barcelo, Holiday Inn, Jurys Inn, Penta, Sunspree Resorts
- Midscale chains: Best Western, Campanile, Corus, Grupotel, La Quinta, Ramada, Wingate
- Economy chains: Balladins, easyHotel, Formule 1, Howard Johnson, Motel 6, Premier Inn
- Independents.

As can be seen from the preceding list, this competition is grouped at the brand level. For example, Hilton's core brand is an upper upscale brand, whereas the Hilton Garden Inn is listed in the upscale chain category. Brands within the same sector or chain scale are direct competitors. However, these brands not only compete with each other on an international or global basis, but they also compete with independent domestic hotels in the same categories in each location around the world.

## Sustainable competitive advantage

Given the number and intensity of competitors, hospitality companies must continuously strive to compete effectively. However, not all factors are equally influential for firms to achieve competitive success. Some factors or criteria can be regarded as more important to achieve competitive advantage and these are called 'critical success factors' (CSFs). Companies should identify their CSFs so that they can ensure they deliver hospitality experiences that meet and exceed the expectations of target markets better than the competition, providing exceptional value to target customers. The process of identifying critical success factors includes:

- Researching customer expectations (e.g., consistent service quality)
- Identifying the key components of the offer that create value for customers (this is often an intangible element that creates memorable customer experiences)
- Identifying four to six potential CSFs that impact on satisfying these expectations (e.g. recruiting and retaining empathetic, enthusiastic and skilled employees; close relationships with suppliers of fresh produce)
- Analyzing company competences that underpin the key factors identified (often linked to inspiring leadership and effective financial/human resource and marketing expertise)
- Scrutinizing the list of CSFs to ensure that superior performance will deliver a competitive advantage
- Specifying the performance standards that need to be achieved to outperform competitors
- Assessing the ability, competences and resources of the company to achieve the required performance standards
- Assessing the ability of competitors to imitate and improve performance on the same CSFs.

Examples of CSFs in the hospitality sector include the following:

- Lowest cost base and extensive geographic coverage for budget hotels chains
- High service quality for exclusive hospitality events
- Highly regarded brand reputation and high brand awareness for international hotel chains
- Technical superiority in food production and delivery processes for QSR chains
- Easy-to-find locations and secure parking facilities for provincial business hotels competing in urban locations.

Although the most successful hospitality companies have clearly defined competences and understand their CSFs, many hotels and restaurants are not so aware. These companies often fail to understand their own competitive strengths and do not identify competitor weaknesses, and thus they fail to develop a competitive advantage.

Competitive advantages that are easily copied have limited value. Sometimes, companies engage in a process called 'amenity creep' by offering additional product enhancements to customers in an attempt to gain competitive advantage. For example, a hotel chain may start to offer additional complimentary in-room amenities (bed turn-down service in the evening, more luxurious toiletry products) or increase the reward benefits on a frequent guest programme to try and increase customer loyalty and repeat business. Since each added amenity is easily copied by competitors and increases costs, chains using this tactic are unable to develop a genuine sustainable competitive advantage. Amenity creep can also inadvertently alter the positioning of the brand and lead to inappropriate pricing policies that erode the original market position.

For hospitality companies, the reputation and image of a business is built up over many years, and a distinctive brand can become a focus for sustainable competitive advantage. Hotel chains like Marriott and Hilton and restaurants like McDonald's have developed strong and sustainable competitive advantages, based on a deep understanding of key factors for success in their market segments. Success factors change over time. New competitors can seize a competitive advantage by recognizing – earlier than their established competitors – environmental factors that alter the structural dimensions of the market and therefore consumer demand. Kemmons Wilson recognized the growth of car ownership and family leisure travel in the USA when developing the Holiday Inn brand. He gained a competitive advantage over long-established city-centre hotels by providing convenient locations with parking on access roads to cities, free accommodation for children sharing their parents' room and a pool to keep the family entertained.

## Measuring competitive success

For publicly traded hospitality firms, key measures of success are the financial and operational metrics that underpin shareholder value: sales revenue, operating profit, net profit, average daily rate (ADR), revenue per available room (RevPAR) and room occupancy. Market share is another key indicator of competitive success. It is important for hospitality firms to understand how they perform compared to the competition.

---

### MARKETING INSIGHT 4.1

**Luxury hotel market**[12]

The size of the global luxury hotel market was estimated to be around US$93 billion in 2020. The luxury hotels witnessed a negative demand shock across all regions due to the COVID-19 pandemic. Demand for luxury hotels was down by 60.82 per cent in 2020. The market demand and growth in this segment is expected to return to the pre-pandemic levels once the pandemic is over. The luxury hotel market is expected to reach US$238.49 billion by 2028 due to rising demand expectation post-COVID-19 world for premium hospitality services. Backed by a high spending potential of North American consumers, North America is expected to dominate the luxury hotel market share in the near future. The North American market size was US$30.66 billion in 2020. The luxury market in Europe is also expected to have a period of sustained growth due to forecasted increases in the number of tourists visiting Europe. Asia Pacific regions will also experience a significant growth as the number of international luxury hotel chains hoping to establish their presence in countries such as India, China and Indonesia keep increasing due to rapidly growing upper-middle-class and middle-class populations in the region.

*Source*: Fortune Business Insights[12]

---

Sometimes competing local hotels will share their operating performance data so that they can understand their own competitive performance. However, there are now a number of different hospitality consultancy firms that provide actual operating performance data for hotels so that firms can 'benchmark' their performance against that of their key competitors. Typical operating performance data include room occupancy, RevPAR and ADR. Firms can then benchmark or compare their performance against the performance of their competitor set. Firms select which competitors they want to include within their competitor set for comparative purpose and are provided with analytical reports on a weekly or monthly basis. The Smith Travel Accommodation Report (STAR) report, produced by STR is an example of such a report (see Case Study 4.4).

## CASE STUDY 4.4

### STR[13]

STR was formed in 1985 with a mission to provide one standardized, worldwide premium data benchmarking, analytics and marketplace insight reports for global hospitality sectors. STR was acquired in October 2019 as a division of CoStar Group, Inc. (NASDAQ: CSGP), the leading provider of commercial real estate information, analytics and online marketplaces. Since its inception, STR Global has grown through established and emerging markets including Europe, the Middle East, Africa and Central and South America. STR Global tracks supply and demand data for the hotel industry, providing market share analysis at the international, regional and local level. STR obtains performance data from over 68,000 hotels across 180 countries. Hotel firms can use STAR reports to compare their performance against members of their competitive set. Performance data on occupancy, ADR and RevPAR is submitted by 75 per cent of US hotels and 55 per cent of hotels in other countries around the world, including 90 per cent of chain hotels. STR Global uses these data to produce the STAR reports. Subscribers are not able to see the performance data of individual competitors, but can measure their performance against the set as a whole. Hotels can select up to four different competitor sets. STAR reports are available on a monthly, weekly and daily basis by annual subscription.

STR Global also provides a range of different market reports that are used by hotel operators, owners, investors, destination management companies, local and national governments, suppliers, financial advisors and academics. These reports deliver critical market information on supply and demand in different locations and on the 'pipeline' of hotels that are under development in different global locations. This information is essential for identifying the current and future level of competition within specific local, regional and national markets and thus the potential outcome of investing or developing in these markets. Log on to the STR Global website at https://str.com/:

- Identify the different types of reports available.
- Identify the different types of customers who would use these different reports.
- If you were a hotel general manager, how would you use the information from a STAR report?
- What qualifications are available for students who want to improve their understanding of hotel analytics?

When all the hotels in the competitor set experience an increase or fall in business the change can be attributed to factors in the PESTE or micro-environment, but if one hotel's performance is consistently better (or worse) than its competitors', this indicates that competitor factors (as opposed to the external environmental factors) are responsible for the difference in performance. Thus, performance needs to be placed within the context of the micro- and macro-environments, and reasons for inferior or superior performance need to be identified. The benchmarking process enables the marketing team to identify and correct important weaknesses compared with the competitor set, and ultimately to improve customer satisfaction.

Other comparative brand performance measures for the hotel chains include brand awareness and brand reputation on important attributes. BVA BDRC provides the leading hotel companies in Europe with confidential, customized research, benchmarking each brand's performance on measures relevant to customers in their market sector across different countries. Hotel and restaurant chains also track the performance of their advertising campaigns using specialist media expenditure analysts such as Nielsen to monitor spending by all leading companies in their sector. Market leaders want to know what competitors are spending on advertising relative to their own spend – this is called 'share of voice'. McDonald's and Burger King's advertising campaigns across the world are carefully monitored to measure the share of voice.

## Branding

While the segmentation, targeting and positioning (STP) process identifies target markets, differentiates and positions the offering against competitors, it is the brand that is the most overt manifestation of STP strategy. Successful marketing, STP and service delivery processes should enable hospitality companies to establish a strong brand image among consumers that enables consumers to immediately distinguish a hospitality brand's offerings from its competitors. Brands can help customers to understand what a company or product stands for and this in turn, has benefits for the hospitality firm. Branding is therefore a core focus in hospitality marketing.

As the hospitality industry became more international and competitive and hospitality products became more diversified (e.g., budget, extended stay, boutique, resort and spa product concepts in the accommodation sector), marketers recognized the importance of having a branded hospitality product. National hotel companies in the US operated over 170 different brands in 2021. Branding is most prolific within large, multi-unit chain operations. However, as we will see next, many of the principles of brand management can be applied to individual properties.

### Defining the brand

According to marketing guru Philip Kotler, 'a brand is a name, symbol, logo, design or image, or any combination of these, which is designed to identify the product or service'.[14] The key function of a brand is to identify the product or service in such a way that consumers perceive relevant, unique or sustained value that matches their needs. Brands offer a number of benefits or advantages to hospitality firms as well as to consumers.

### Advantages of branding

For a hospitality firm, key advantages of branding include:

● A brand is a marketing asset that can be legally protected. Legal protection of the brand name, logo and design is a defence against imitation. Competitor firms can be prosecuted for infringements.

- Differentiation from competitors offers a distinct image which can help the brand to stand out in a highly competitive marketplace.
- Ability to charge a price premium. Consumers who perceive that one brand offers superior value over another are willing to pay more to use that brand.
- Enhanced profitability. Brands with high awareness and a high brand reputation are likely to capture greater market share and achieve higher profit levels.

For consumers, the key advantages of branding include:

- Ease of making purchase decisions as a brand helps to differentiate the offer.
- Risk reduction. Purchasing a known brand gives consumers confidence that their expectations will be met as the brand provides a type of 'unwritten contract'. The brand name and visual identity also provide customers with a degree of quality assurance.
- Intangible benefits and added value. Purchasing certain brands can provide consumers with a range of intangible benefits, such as 'status' from staying in a luxury hotel or 'moral conscience' from staying in a resort run as a social enterprise.

### Challenges of branding

Despite the potential benefits from branding, there are a number of challenges that hospitality firms face when developing brands. These include:

- *Cost*. The cost of developing a new brand with a distinctive image and creating associated brand awareness should not be underestimated. Growing the brand internationally and attracting both consumers and investors is even more costly.
- *Time*. Brand development is a lengthy process; it takes time to develop and establish a distinctive image and create awareness.
- *Brand distinctiveness*. In today's crowded, competitive environment it is becoming harder to create a truly distinctive brand.
- *Brand consistency*. Customers develop certain expectations of a brand. While firms try to ensure that these are met by developing brand operational and quality standards, ensuring these are met in properties around the world is both difficult and costly. A poor customer experience in one hotel or restaurant can have a negative impact across an entire branded portfolio.
- *Brand reputation*. The reputation of a brand is strongly influenced by consumers. The growth of social media and the development of online brand communities who share their experiences and opinions of the brand have increased the potential impact (both positive and negative) of consumers on brand reputation. A positive impact results in greater consumer commitment to, and trust in, the brand.

In order to realize the advantages and overcome the challenges of branding, it is important for hospitality firms to ensure that the brands they develop are as distinct as possible by considering each of the core elements of the brand. If they do not, they may not be successful. Of the 75 US hotel brands introduced between 1980 and 1988, 35 went out of business or were bought out and rebranded within the same decade.

## Core elements of a brand

A brand can be considered a combination of five core elements:

1 *An effective product/service.* Successful hospitality brands meet the target customers' needs, taking into account what the customer is willing to pay. In 1962, Paul Green and William Becker recognized the growing cost of staying in traditional motels in the USA and decided to develop a 'no frills' hotel brand, selling rooms for $6 per night in their first branded Motel 6 property in California. Motel 6's estimated annual revenue is currently around $1.1 billion.

2 *A distinctive identity.* The brand name and trademark or logo makes a substantial contribution to the creation of a distinctive brand identity. Hospitality marketers must consider how a brand name is vocalized and whether the name is easy to pronounce, whether it is distinct and suggestive of the benefits offered to customers. The Extended Stay Hotels brand clearly indicates the product class of the brand and suggests to consumers it is suitable for those having to stay in a hotel for extended periods of time. Marriott's BVLGARI brand is reflective of the quality of the Italian luxury goods retailer of the same name. The Red Lobster brand is clearly indicative of what Red Lobster restaurants serve – a variety of seafood including lobsters in New England-themed restaurants. For international brands, marketers must also consider whether brand names and associated positioning statements have the same meaning in new country markets as they do in the home country. When KFC entered China, their slogan, 'Finger-lickin' good', unfortunately translated into 'Eat your fingers off'. The brand's trademark and logo must also be capable of legal protection in all countries of operation. Table 4.1 presents a typology of brand names.

3 *Added value.* A brand enables consumers to experience three types of benefits. *Functional* benefits are provided through the product and service features of the brand. For example, a 24-hour gym offers functional benefits to hotel guests. *Emotional* benefits are provided through the intangible elements of the brand, such as pampering and relaxation in the spas offered by Six Senses Hotels & Resorts or the luxury and prestige of butler service in Ritz Carlton. Finally, brands can provide *symbolic* benefits to consumers by offering them something beyond hospitality that they care about. For example, Banyan Tree Resorts prides itself on their ecological, sustainable and culturally sensitive hotels and resorts. They encourage guests to get involved in their 'Stay for Good' initiative, making contributions which are matched by Banyan Tree and used to support social and environmental efforts in their local communities.

4 *Personality.* A brand's personality is defined by the brand's traits. These are very much like the personality traits you would use to describe people. You were introduced earlier in this chapter to the Country Inn & Suites by Radisson brand (Case Study 4.1). The personality of this brand could be described as relaxed and homely.

5 *Positioning.* As we saw earlier, positioning is consumers' perception of the brand relative to that of the competition and is of vital importance in distinguishing one brand from another in a competitive environment. Country Inn & Suites by Radisson is positioned as a 'home away from home' for the road-weary traveller. It is clear, therefore, that the brand's relaxed and homely personality helps to contribute to this positioning.

## Brand congruence

A critical issue for hospitality brands is to ensure that all the different elements of the marketing mix contribute to the overall customer experience in a brand-congruent manner. Brand standards

Table 4.1  A typology of hotel brand names

| Brand type | Examples |
| --- | --- |
| Founder | Hilton, Marriott |
| Geographic description | Best Western, Intercontinental, Scandic |
| Price | Budget Inns, Econolodge |
| Functional | Sleep Inn, Travel Inn |
| Symbolic | Burj Al Arab |
| Experiential | Extreme |
| Acronym | IHG, AC, HE1 |
| Lifestyle | Arcadian, Romantic |
| Market Segment | Budget, Grand, Luxury Collection |
| Architectural/heritage | National Trust Historic Hotels of America, Artotel |
| Animals, birds, insects, flowers | Red Lion, Swallow, Butterfly, White Rose |
| Colours | Green Tree, Orange |
| Letters | W, M-Hotels |
| Numbers | Motel 6, H10 |
| Location and brand name | New York Marriott Downtown, New York Marriott East Side |
| Wacky! | YOTEL |

provide the guidelines for individual units to deliver the operational and communication strategies, and they are set out on the company Intranet, websites and in brand manuals. Brand standards are checked and enforced in a number of ways, including formal property/service audits and mystery shopper visits. Indeed, in some hospitality companies, the corporate executives enforcing brand standards are (unofficially) called the brand police. Units that consistently underperform on brand standards are vulnerable – managers may be replaced, franchisees may have their contracts terminated, and ultimately a property may be disposed of, if senior management recognizes that the unit will never be able to deliver the required brand standards.

## CASE STUDY 4.5

### Westin Hotels & Resorts[15]

Marriott's Westin Hotels & Resorts brand is an example of a congruent brand. When you take apart the brand and identify all the different component parts listed next, you will see that they complement each other in a way that delivers value for the customer.

*Functional benefits*: Heavenly beds, Heavenly baths, Heavenly Spa, Heavenly dog bed, Service Express, SuperFoodsRx™ dishes, Westin Fresh by The Juicery, Westin WORKOUT Studio, Sensory elements on arrival, Marriott Bonvoy Preferred Guest Program

*Emotional benefits*: innovation and rejuvenation, Westin wellbeing

*Symbolic benefits*: committed to environmental renewal, sustainability, and wellbeing of guests and associates

*Personality*: savvy, sophisticated and wellness-oriented traveller

*Positioning*: upper upscale brand that focuses on guests' wellbeing

*Source*: Westin Hotels & Resorts[15]

### Harder or softer hospitality brands

Hospitality brands have often been categorized as being harder or softer. Harder brands tend to have a higher degree of standardization across all elements of the marketing mix including brand name, menu or facilities, decor, location, distribution channels, pricing, marketing communications and collateral, staffing and service levels. The delivery of a hospitality customer experience that is consistent and meets uniform standards is difficult due to:

- Inconsistency and variability in service staff and customer behaviour
- Differences in demand due to seasonality and location
- Different planning and legislative requirements, meaning that the building designs, opening hours, menus and service styles may vary across locations
- Variation in refurbishment schedules across branded chains, so the units that are newly refurbished can vary immensely compared to others.

In reality, however, there are no completely hard or soft brands within the hospitality industry; rather, there are different degrees of standardization. Budget hotel brands tend to be harder brands. Brands like Travelodge or hotelF1 in France are purpose-built properties using standardized designs, decor and service systems and styles. Brands like Starbucks, Subway and KFC are also harder brands, with most elements of the marketing mix standardized even across international locations, although there are adaptations made for menu items in different countries where required.

Softer brands place less emphasis on standardization, particularly the tangible elements of the product. For example, hotel consortia like Best Western or Relais & Châteaux are softer brands. The hotels are owned by different businesses and their size, decor and facilities vary immensely. However, they are standardized to the extent that they offer an approved level of service consistent with the brand, a certain level or range of facilities, some standardized marketing collateral, and can be booked through the same distribution channels. Many of the large multi-branded hotel corporations have started to add softer brand collections to their portfolios. For instance, Marriott launched Autograph Collection in 2010. Each Autograph Collection Hotel has its own personality that reflects its individual founder's vision. Later, Marriott added the Luxury Collection to their brand portfolio through the merger with Starwood.

### ACTIVITY 4.6

**Comparison of harder and softer brands**

Research two Relais & Châteaux and two Ibis hotels in two different countries of your choice. Compare the hotels using the following criteria:

- Location
- Architectural style

- Number of rooms
- Restaurant/banqueting facilities
- Business and leisure facilities
- Prices.

Which brand provides a more consistent offer and should be marketed as a harder brand?

When should a softer brand strategy be adopted?

### Brand awareness and brand reputation

Two key measures used to assess the effectiveness of brands are brand awareness and brand reputation. Public and target market awareness of a brand can be measured using marketing research. Surveys tend to ask respondents to name brands they know within a certain sector (e.g. hotels or restaurants) so that marketers can measure unprompted top-of-the-mind brand awareness. They may also ask survey participants to identify the names of any brands that they recognize from a list, so that prompted brand awareness can be measured. High brand awareness means that a brand is well known. Brand awareness is one of the 'success' measures tracked by hotel and restaurant chains. Brand reputation can range from excellent to poor. A brand's reputation is generally good when it delivers what it promises.

In Figure 4.5, brand awareness and brand reputation are plotted on a matrix. A brand's position in one of the four quadrants on this matrix is indicative of its future success or longevity.

Figure 4.5  Brand awareness and brand reputation

- Brands that have low awareness and a poor reputation are fortunate that their reputation is not well known. There is therefore the opportunity to improve performance. If no action is taken, it is likely the brand will gradually become unprofitable and fail.

- Brands with low awareness and an excellent reputation are brands with the potential to grow. Efforts should be made to create greater awareness while maintaining the reputation of the brand.

- Brands with high awareness and an excellent reputation are successful brands that need to be protected and nurtured.

- Brands with a poor reputation and a high awareness are in a difficult situation. If action is not taken immediately to improve the reputation of the brand, it is possible that the brand will die relatively quickly.

### Multiple branding

The history of many of the large, international corporate chains can be traced to their entrepreneurial founders who followed a traditional brand development pathway. Conrad Hilton, J.W. Marriott and Charles Forte are all entrepreneurs who gave their name to their company and their original brand. These entrepreneurs, like many others in the industry, started with one brand often targeted at a specific market segment in their domestic markets. Investor pressure for continued growth and the need to reduce the risk from relying on a single market segment led the many hospitality organizations to develop multiple brands targeting a wider range of market segments. Many of the larger international hotel chains, like Accor and Wyndham, operate a range of brands in different market sectors or chain scales.

Hospitality firms adopt multiple branding strategies to try to increase market share by offering different brands for different customer segments at different price points. For example, IHG boasts a portfolio of 16 brands promoting 'a hotel for every occasion' and Hilton comprises 18 brands for business and leisure customers at a range of different prices. Interestingly, many of these chains also consider their loyalty programmes as one of their brands. Marriott lists its Marriott Bonvoy loyalty programme on its brand website and IHG similarly lists its IHG Rewards alongside its other brands. The advantages of multiple branding include:

- Increased market share
- Less dependency on the volatility of a single-market segment.

The main danger of multiple branding is the risk of 'cannibalizing' the company's sales by encouraging the company's existing customers to trade down and stay at a cheaper brand of lodging facilities also owned by the same company. This criticism is particularly directed at corporations who have retained one family name for the entire range of lodging brands by adopting a branded house strategy (described next). This strategy enables lower graded accommodation to benefit from the brand reputation of a more upscale offering. Some firms therefore continue to operate as a single brand. For example, Four Seasons Hotels & Resorts continues to operate a single luxury brand in a niche market, although they have recently expanded their offer to include luxury jet travel to some of their resort locations. Omni Hotels also continues to operate a single brand.

### Brand strategies

Corporate chains that have developed multiple brands adopt one of three different brand strategies:

• *House of brands strategy*. These hotel companies have a group or collection of brands that have no clear connection. For example, there is no clear connection between the Shangri La, Traders Hotels, Kerry Hotels and Hotel Jen, all owned by Shangri La Hotels and Resorts. Similarly, there is no clear connection between Accor's hotelF1, Ibis, Jo&Joe, Mercure, Novotel and Sofitel brands. Chains adopt this strategy to avoid any 'cannibalization' across their brands. In the restaurant sector, Yum adopts this strategy for their fast-food brands Taco Bell, KFC and Pizza Hut.

• *Branded house strategy*. In this strategy, hotel companies use a single brand name or the corporate name to cover a series of different brands. This strategy is often used for brand extensions. For example, Best Western adopted this approach when it expanded its brand offering to include Best Western Premier (upscale), Best Western Plus (upper midscale) and Best Western (midscale).

• *Hybrid strategy*. In this strategy, firms adopt a mixture of house of brands and branded house strategies. For example, Marriott includes the Marriott name for its Residence Inn Courtyard, Marriott, JW Marriott, Fairfield Inns and Suites and Vacation Club, but does not include the Marriott name next to the Ritz Carlton, BVLGARI and Edition hotel brands. Hotel chains with multiple brands, extending from the budget to the luxury end of the market, often keep their corporate name removed from the luxury brands to avoid any association with brands within lower market scale segments.

Table 4.2 provides an example of some of the largest hotel corporations and their hotel brands. You will see from this table that different firms adopt different brand strategies. They also classify their brands in different ways. Be aware that this ownership and brand information is constantly changing – you should check the company's website for current data. For example, Marriott bought Starwood in a US$13.6 billion deal in 2016, which made Marriott the largest hotel chain in the world.

Table 4.2  Major international hotel corporations and their lodging brands

| Corporate brand | Product brands | No. of hotels | No. of bedrooms (000) | No. of countries |
|---|---|---|---|---|
| Marriott International | Marriott Hotels & Resorts, JW Marriott Hotels & Resorts, The Ritz-Carlton, St. Regis, Ritz-Carlton Reserve, The Luxury Collection, W Hotels, Edition, Sheraton, Marriott Vacation Club, Delta Hotels, Le Meridien, Westin, Renaissance Hotels, Gaylord Hotels, Courtyards Hotels, Four Points, SpringHill Suites, Protea Hotels, Fairfield Inn & Suites, AC Hotels, Aloft Hotels, Moxy Hotels, Marriott Executive Apartments, | 7,642 | 1.420,000 | 110+ |

*(Continued)*

COMPETITIVE STRATEGIES   119

| Corporate brand | Product brands | No. of hotels | No. of bedrooms (000) | No. of countries |
|---|---|---|---|---|
| | Residence Inn, TownePlace Suites, Element, Home & Villas by Marriot International, Autograph Collection Hotels, Design Hotels, Tribute Portfolio | | | |
| Hilton | Waldorf Astoria, LXR Hotels and Resorts, Conrad Hotels and Resorts, Canopy, Signia, Hilton Hotels and Resorts, Curio Collection, DoubleTree, Tapestry Collection, Embassy Suites, Tempo, Motto, Hilton Garden Inn, Hampton, Tru, Homewood Suites, Home2 Suites, Hilton Grand Vacations | 6,500 | 1,020,000 | 119 |
| IHG | Intercontinental Hotels and Resorts, Crowne Plaza, Hotel Indigo, Holiday Inn Hotels and Resorts, Holiday Inn Express, Staybridge Suites, Candlewood Suites, Six Senses, Regent, Kimpton Hotels and Restaurants, Voco, Hualuxe, Even Hotels, Avid, Atwell Suites, Holiday Inn Club Vacations | 5,959 | 883,819 | 100+ |
| Wyndham | Wyndham, Wyndham Grand, Days Inn, Hawthorne Suites, Howard Johnson, AmericInn, Microtel, Ramada, Super 8 Motel, Travelodge, Wingate, Dolce Hotels & Resorts, Tryp, Esplendor, Dazzler, TM Trademark, La Quinta, Wyhndham Garden, Baymont | 9,000+ | 813,000 | 90+ |
| Accor | Raffles, Banyan Tree, Orient Express, Delano, Sofitel Legend, Fairmont, SLS, SO/Hotels & Resorts, Sofitel, Onefinestay, The House of Originals, Rixos Hotels, Mantis, M Gallery Hotel Collection, Mondrian, 21c Museum Hotels, Pullman, Swissotel, Angsana, 25h twenty five hours hotel, Art Series, Hyde Hotels, Resorts & Residences, Movenpic, Peppers, The Sebel, Grand Mercure, Adagio Aparthotel premium, Matra, Novotel, Mercure Hotels, Adagio Aparthotel Mama Shelter, Tribe, BreakFre, Ibis, Ibis Styles, Ibis Budget, Jo&Joe, Greet, HotelF1, Thalassa Sea & Spa, Huazhu Hotels Group, Adagio | 5,100+ | 704,000 | 110+ |

*(Continued)*

Table 4.2 Continued

| Corporate brand | Product brands | No. of hotels | No. of bedrooms (000) | No. of countries |
|---|---|---|---|---|
| Choice | Comfort Hotels, Cabria Hotels, Ascend Hotel Collection, Quality Inn, Sleep Inn, Clarion, Clarion Pointe, MainStay Suites, WoodSpring Suites, Suburban Extended Stay Hotel, Econo Lodge, Rodeway Inn | 7,000 | 570,000 | 40 |

*Source*: Individual hotel company websites, June 2021

## International hotel and restaurant chain expansion

The major hotel groups now operate in a large number of countries around the world. The trend towards internationalization in the hospitality industry began in the latter decades of the twentieth century in both the restaurant and hotel sectors. The largest international restaurant chains, predominantly originating in the USA, began their international expansion after saturating the home country market. Examples include:

- McDonald's, with over 39,000 restaurants in 119 countries serving 69 million customers a day
- KFC, with over 25,000 restaurants in 145 countries
- Subway, with 41,600 restaurants (more than any other competitor) in 110 countries
- Starbucks, with 32,660 restaurants in 78 countries.

With some notable exceptions, many hotel firms also spread throughout their home country prior to expanding into overseas markets. For example, Marriott Hotels developed throughout the USA prior to their international expansion. Accor developed rapidly in France before expanding to Switzerland and then further afield. In contrast, the InterContinental Hotel brand opened its first property outside its original home country of the USA in 1946 and is therefore considered to be a 'born global' brand. International expansion also gave rise to merger and acquisition activity between hotel brands.

### Horizontal integration

Today's major hospitality organizations have evolved by taking over or merging with competitors in the same sector (horizontal integration), and/or by taking over or merging with distribution channels, customers or suppliers (vertical integration). We return to this issue in Chapter 8.

The largest hotel companies have all grown by acquiring competitor brands. Companies such as Marriott, Accor, Hilton, IHG, Sol Melia and Wyndham have all bought brands to grow the business and sold brands to focus on key strategic areas. Marriott has a long history of acquiring brands, including Residence Inn and Fairfield Inn in 1987, to expand into the extended stay sector in the USA; the South African Protea brand, to speed its expansion into Africa in 2015; and the entire Starwood portfolio of brands in 2016, which made Marriott the largest hotel chain in the world. French hotel giant Accor adopted a similar strategy to enter the North American luxury market when it acquired Fairmont. The largest hotel group in China, Jin Jiang International Hotel Group, has acquired a number of hotel groups like Groupe du Louvre in 2015, Plateno Group in 2017, Vienna Hotels Group in 2015 and Radisson Hotels & Resorts in 2019 to expand its brand portfolio, market share and market reach.

When a major player buys a brand, a decision has to be made whether to integrate the acquired hotels into one of their existing brands or to retain the newly acquired brand (as in the Groupe du Louvre and Radisson Hotels & Resorts acquisitions by the Jin Jiang International Hotel Group example earlier). Acquired hotels are carefully evaluated to see whether their property profile fits with the requirements of an existing brand's standards. Hotels that conform to brand standards are re-'flagged', and hotels that do not are sold off. If the newly acquired brand is retained, as in the case of Radisson Hotels & Resorts, then existing hotels in the acquirer's portfolio may be rebranded under the new brand name. These mega-corporations are continuously evolving and will continue to expand given the benefits realized, or else they risk being acquired by a competitor or new entrant to the international hotel market. The process of horizontal integration leads to consolidation – this means a smaller number of larger players. However, the dynamic characteristics of the hotel industry mean that there are always entrepreneurs developing new businesses. In addition, the large players often have several hotel properties 'in the pipeline' of development in new and emerging markets and locations. At the same time, they will lose individual properties to new management companies and other franchisors. The rate of churn (hotel properties moving from one brand to another) in the industry is high. As such, the size and extent of any one company's hotel portfolio is continually changing.

## Managing international hotel and restaurant chains

The international expansion pattern and the home country of a hospitality firm can have a major influence on the way that the company is organized and operated. Firms that have developed in the home country market prior to international expansion will have been influenced by the home country culture, and this may influence the approach adopted in its international operations. While current thinking suggests that international companies must adapt their approach for international operations, historically this has not always been the case. One way of classifying the approach to managing international operations is according to the centricity of the firm. *Centricity* (or centric orientation) was a term first developed by Perlmutter and his colleagues back in late 1960s.[16] Four distinct orientations are discussed next.

### ETHNOCENTRIC ORIENTATION

Firms that adopt this orientation generally use the home-country approach in international markets. They consider that what has worked in the home country will work in host country markets and there is limited need for change. Decision-making tends to be centralized within the home country. This approach can be successful if the target markets in the host country are customers from the home country. For example, outside of the USA, Marriott originally targeted US customers who were travelling overseas and tried to ensure that these customers received the same experience as they would at home. An ethnocentric approach was therefore considered appropriate. When Disney first opened in Japan, they adopted an ethnocentric approach because Japanese customers wanted to buy the 'authentic' US theme park experience.

However, generally when customers are drawn from the host country or from mixed country markets, the ethnocentric approach is not appropriate. Disney discovered to their cost that an ethnocentric approach is not always appropriate when it entered France.

### POLYCENTRIC ORIENTATION

Firms that adopt this approach consider that operations, marketing and human resource management practices should be customized in each country based on the business practices and culture of each country. This orientation therefore is considered a host-country orientation. Decision-making is generally decentralized to the host country, which is deemed to know best. When firms are targeting the customers from domestic markets, this approach can be appropriate. Many hotel brands that operate as consortia adopt this approach. For example, Best Western is typically polycentric – each country has considerable autonomy in developing marketing campaigns and each hotel has the autonomy to develop its own operational practices.

### REGIO-CENTRIC ORIENTATION

Closely related to the polycentric approach, the regio-centric orientation reflects the development of approaches to managing the firm across regions that are broadly similar in terms of economic development and customer requirements. For example, this orientation was appropriate for Scandic hotels when their properties were located only in Scandinavian countries.

### GEOCENTRIC ORIENTATION

Firms that adopt a geocentric orientation recognize the need to compete at both global and local levels. Firms that adopt this orientation are therefore referred to as 'glocal'. These firms are fully aware of the marketing and economic advantages of standardizing brands and practices where possible, and adapting these where necessary to reflect local demand, culture, legislation or economic circumstance. Brands like InterContinental that were 'born global' often adopt a geocentric orientation, believing that this approach provides the best of both worlds when operating across international markets.

## Conclusion

Segmenting markets to identify profitable target markets, developing a differentiated offer to deliver enhanced customer satisfaction and positioning the hospitality brand against competitors are essential components in the development of marketing strategies to compete effectively.

In this chapter, we have explained:

- Three segmentation strategies – mass, differentiated and niche
- Difficulties of differentiating the hospitality product
- Criteria for successfully positioning a hospitality offer
- Porter's five forces competitive analysis
- Four industry competitive environments – fragmented, niche, volume and stalemate
- Different forms of ownership and affiliation, including ownership, lease, management contract, franchising, consortia and hybrid organizations
- The benefits and key elements of branding in the hospitality industry
- International firm growth trajectories and competition in the hotel industry.

## ACTIVITY 4.7

**Carry out Activity 4.1 again and compare your answers:**

- Can you name three different hotel brands?
- Which market segments does each of these brands belong to?
- Which company owns each of these brands?

## REVIEW QUESTIONS

Now check your understanding of this chapter by undertaking the following tasks:

1 Analyze a hospitality industry competitive environment using Porter's five forces model.

2 Discuss differentiation and positioning strategies in the hospitality industry using two different hotel or restaurant brands.

3 Discuss the advantages and disadvantages of branding in hospitality:

- from a customer's perspective
- from a company's perspective.

## References

1. Country Inn & Suites by Radisson [Internet]. [cited September 8, 2021]. Available from: www.radissonhotels.com/en-us/corporate/about-us
2. The Breakers Palm Beach [Internet]. *About The Breakers Palm Beach.* [cited September 8, 2021]. Available from: www.thebreakers.com/about-breakers/
3. Wirtz, J., & Lovelock, C. (2016). *Services Marketing: People, Technology, Strategy*, 8th ed. Upper Saddle River, NJ: Pearson Education.
4. Airbnb [Internet]. *The Airbnb Story.* [cited September 8, 2021]. Available from: https://news.airbnb.com/about-us/
5. Hotel Tech Report. (2021). Hotel management: A complete industry overview. *Story.* [cited September 8, 2021]. Available from: https://hoteltechreport.com/news/hotel-management
6. Wyndham Hotels & Resorts [Internet]. *About Wyndham Hotels & Resorts.* [cited September 8, 2021]. Available from: www.wyndhamhotels.com/about-us
7. McDonald's [Internet]. *Our Company.* [cited September 8, 2021]. Available from: https://corporate.mcdonalds.com/corpmcd/home.html
8. Hotusa Group [Internet]. *About Hotusa.* [cited September 8, 2021]. Available from: www.hotusagroup.com/
9. Hotrec Hospitality Europe [Internet]. *European Hospitality Quality: Description and Criteria.* [cited September 8, 2021]. Available from: www.hotrec.eu/wp-content/uploads/2018/04/EHQ_description_and_criteria.pdf
10. Porter, M. E. (1980). *Competitive Strategy: Techniques for Analyzing Industries and Competitors.* New York: Free Press.
11. QSR Magazine. (2020). *The QSR 50 Burger Segment.* [cited September 8, 2021]. Available from: www.qsrmagazine.com/content/qsr50-2020-burger-segment
12. Fortune Business Insights. (2021). *The Luxury Hotel Market Is Projected to Grow from $119.55 Billion in 2021 to $238.49 Billion in 2028 at a CAGR of 10.4% in the Forecast Period [2021–2028].* [cited September 8, 2021]. Available from: www.fortunebusinessinsights.com/luxury-hotel-market-104408

13. STR [Internet]. *About STR*. [cited September 8, 2021]. Available from: https://str.com/about
14. Kotler, P., & Keller, K. (2015). *Marketing Management*, 15th ed. Upper Saddle River, NJ: Pearson Prentice Hall.
15. Westin Hotels & Resorts [Internet]. *Westin Hotels & Resorts*. [cited September 8, 2021]. Available from: https://westin.marriott.com/
16. Perlmutter, H. V. (1969). The tortuous evolution of the multi-national corporation. *Columbia Journal of World Business, 4*, 9–18.

Chapter **5**

# Developing the hospitality experience

**CHAPTER OBJECTIVES**

After working through this chapter, you should be able to:

- Identify the core, tangible and extended product in hospitality operations
- Evaluate the function of product/benefit bundles in hospitality markets
- Explain the characteristics of standardized and adapted product concepts in branded hospitality chains
- Identify all stages in the product life cycle and explain their marketing implications.

## Introduction

Hospitality experience is a function of a set of interactions between a customer and a company, the company's offerings, and other customers. Customers experience hospitality offerings through immersing physically and mentally in five components of experience. These five components are SENSE, FEEL, THINK, ACT and RELATE. SENSE refers to sensory experiences including sight, sound, taste, touch and smell. FEEL involves customers' internal feelings and emotions. THINK represents a customer's cognitive thinking process, with their curiosity and creativity being aroused. ACT embraces all actions and behaviours related to consumption. RELATE reflects the fulfilment of individuals' social needs or values such as connecting with others. Even though these five components have their own objectives, inner structures and principles, there are also strong interrelationships among them. The hospitality product is usually the core component of customer experience and the marketing mix. All other interactions

DOI: 10.4324/9781003186342-7

usually take place around the core hospitality product. Sometimes marketers develop offerings to be delivered at a particular price point, but in the majority of cases marketers first try to construct an experience offering that will satisfy the targeted market segment.

In this chapter, we will explore the components of the hospitality experience including the hospitality product, product/benefit bundles, the standardization versus adaptation debate and the product life cycle (PLC). The hospitality experience is a complex combination of tangible and intangible elements. While all core hospitality products deliver basic functional solutions to consumers' needs and wants, both tangible and intangible components of the overall hospitality experience offerings must be configured to deliver customer satisfaction to specified target markets better than competitors in order to succeed in the marketplace.

We can consider the hospitality experience from two perspectives – first from the customer's perspective as a bundle of benefits that will solve their problems, and second from the firm's perspective as a complex mix of carefully selected, modelled and congruent tangible and intangible elements offered to the customer. It is important to note that the hospitality product that marketers strive to create and deliver may be quite different from the hospitality actually experienced by the customer. In any service encounter, unplanned events can dramatically enhance or upset the customers' experience. Disruptions (e.g., rowdy customers) tend to lead to customer dissatisfaction, but some unplanned acts or events can lead to customer delight. An unexpected gift delivered to a customer's room when the front desk clerk learns of a birthday celebration can delight guests and create a highly memorable customer experience.

## Defining the experience

The hospitality experience is a combination of tangible (e.g., food and beverage) and intangible (e.g., service and atmosphere) elements. Another way of conceptualizing the hospitality experience is to think of it as a combination of a core product, a tangible product and an augmented or extended product.[1] Figure 5.1 provides an example of each component of the hospitality experience for a destination resort.

### Core product

The core product of any hospitality firm is the basic benefit that customers are buying. For example, at the most basic level, a hotel offers a place to sleep; a restaurant offers a place to eat; a conference centre provides a venue for an event. It is the customer who determines the hospitality provider's core product. All hospitality products, whether branded or not, offer functional benefits of some description. If a customer seeks the basic benefit of a good night's sleep, then that is the core product for that customer. However, as Figure 5.1 indicates, customers generally demand more than the core product alone, and hospitality organizations therefore have to offer more than just the core product in order to attract and keep customers in a competitive marketplace.

### Tangible product

The tangible product is composed of the physical elements that are necessary for the core product (benefits) to be experienced by the customer. For a hotel, the tangible product includes product features such as the size of the bedroom, quality of mattress and the range of amenities in the bathroom. Companies can differentiate their offer through the tangible product. For example, extended stay hotels try to differentiate their offer through larger bedrooms with well-designed areas where travellers can work, and in-room kitchen facilities. As you read in Chapter 4, differentiation through tangible features is easy for competitors to copy, thereby eliminating any competitive advantage that might have been enjoyed.

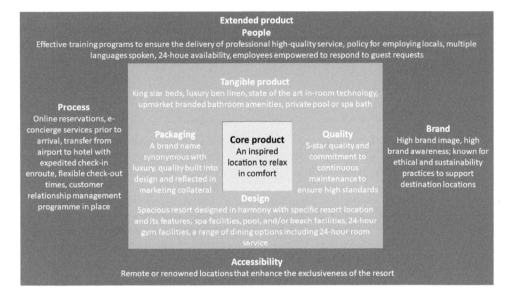

Figure 5.1 A destination resort's core, tangible and extended product offer

## Extended product

The extended product includes intangible elements of the product that can enable the customer to experience enhanced value or additional benefits. The extended product includes the following:

- Accessibility – this includes location characteristics and opening times
- Employee attentiveness and responsiveness – the quality of interaction with customers
- Atmospherics – this important sensory element of the hospitality experience includes sight (the visual design), sound (the style and volume of music), smell (the aroma), taste (the flavour and texture of food) and touch (the feel of fabrics)
- Brand reputation and corporate ethics
- After-sales service including customer billing procedures, complaint handling and post-encounter direct marketing activities.

In service industries, it is the extended product that delivers the distinctively different customer experience – and this is where competitors in the same product class really attempt to differentiate. Delivering a memorable hospitality experience consistently is a major challenge for hospitality organizations. Because experiences are usually short-lived moments in time, excellent hospitality organizations strive for their customers to have a series of delightful experiences that can be translated into memories. Fairmont Hotels & Resorts actively promotes the experience element of their guests' stays and how they help to turn moments into memories. To support this campaign, Fairmont has asked guests to film their experiences with Fairmont and share them online as part of a competition to demonstrate how their brand can create memories.

As competition within the hospitality industry increased, firms began developing a range of different product concepts aimed at specific target markets. A product concept is a package or bundle of core, tangible and extended product elements designed to deliver a particular customer experience. Tables 5.1 and 5.2 provide examples of different hotel and restaurant product concepts.

Table 5.1  Hotel product concepts

| Concept | Examples |
| --- | --- |
| Exclusive luxury hotels | Hotels in this product category are designed to provide the ultimate service experience to the most discerning guests. The Rosewood Hotel near Covent Garden in London is an example of this type of hotel concept. Guests enter the hotel (converted from an historic building) through an archway that leads them to a tranquil Edwardian courtyard. Accommodation is provided through a range of different rooms, suites and signature suites, with state-of-the-art audio and visual equipment, upmarket in-room amenities and butler service. Guests can choose from a number of dining and bar options within the hotel and make use of the spa and fitness facilities. |
| Boutique hotels | These are exclusive hotels that focus on contemporary design with local flavours as the key factor in delivering customer satisfaction. They are typically smaller and more personal than other upmarket brands, although many corporate chains have introduced their own boutique brands in their portfolios. Blakes Hotel in London is frequently credited as being the first boutique hotel. The Delano in Miami Beach is an example of an independent boutique hotel, and W Hotels is the boutique brand of Marriott International. |
| Eco hotels and resorts | There are many hotels and resorts around the world that have been designed as eco hotels or resorts. These properties provide accommodation designed to be sustainable and eco-friendly. Visit https://greenglobaltravel.com/eco-lodges-eco-resorts-eco-hotels/ to learn what is an eco-lodge and to see the Green Global Travel list of Top 20 eco resorts and eco hotels in the world, properties that are considered to lead the way in achieving sustainability goals. See also Activity 1.2 about the Heritance Hotel at Kandalama, Sri Lanka. |
| Large convention, entertainment and gambling complexes | Orlando's Orange County Convention Center (OCCC) is the second largest convention centre in the United States. The two convention halls, connected by a pedestrian skywalk host more than 230 events annually, with approximately 1,400,000 attendees who contribute $2.4 billion to the local economy. The facilities comprise 2.1 million sq. ft. of exhibition space, a 2,643-seat theatre, multipurpose rooms, 74 meeting rooms and eight food courts. Over 46,000 hotel rooms are located near the centre. OCCC has its own mobile app to enable conference attendees to find their way around easily and access local transportation. Some guests use a Segway in order to get around the convention centre. |

*(Continued)*

| Concept | Examples |
|---------|----------|
| Extended stay hotels | These hotels are designed to target business travellers who need to stay in one location for an extended period of time. They combine a hotel room with a workspace and usually some type of kitchen facilities, like a fridge and a microwave. Staybridge Suites is an example of an all-suite extended stay brand with properties in 275 locations worldwide. The brand offers guests the opportunity to meet with other guests socially over drinks and a meal. It also offers rates that are priced according to the length of stay. |
| Capsule hotels | Capsule hotels originated in Japan and comprise prefabricated plastic or fibreglass capsules, stacked in rows with one unit on top of another, and designed for solo occupancy. There are no en-suite facilities. Some Japanese capsule hotels are mixed, but with separate areas for males and females; others are men or women only. Examples include the Capsule Hotel Askausa River Side, Tokyo and the Nine Hours Kyoto Teramachi. |
| | A Western adaption of the capsule concept is YOTEL. Its design copies the space limitations from luxury airline travel to provide cabin-style accommodation for one or two people with en-suite (monsoon showers) facilities, free Wi-Fi, wired Internet access and a techno wall entertainment system. While the original design included windowless cabins in airports, there is now a range of cabins available through three brands (YOTEL, YOTELAIR and YOTELPAD) in a number of locations. However, there is still a limited food service offer that helps to keep costs down. |
| No-frills budget hotels | Budget hotels offer guests basic accommodation with minimal service levels and few if any additional facilities at a low price. An example of a budget hotel that describes itself as practical, simple and economical is hotelF1, Accor's chain of over 170 budget hotels in France. The hotel offers five types of rooms at a reasonable price: 'Cabrio' room (with a double bed and a bathroom equipped with a shower and WC, for travellers who want privacy and superior comfort), 'Combi' room (this large capacity room has six single bunk beds with reading lights, a table and chairs, as well as two sinks and six individual lockers), 'Tandem' room (for couples, this room has a double bed and a sink), 'Sidecar' room (adapted to pairs of friends or colleagues, the room is equipped with two single beds and a sink) and 'Break' bedroom (with three single bunk beds with reading lights and washbasin are suitable for small groups. |
| | The shared rooms are sold by the bed at a rate of around 15 euros. There is also an 'all you can eat breakfast' available for an additional fee. |

---

### ACTIVITY 5.1

Access the following websites and explore details of the hospitality product offer. For each of the products, identify the core, functional and extended products using Figure 5.1 to help you.

**Hotels**

• Burj Al Arab, Dubai at www.jumeirah.com/en/stay/dubai/burj-al-arab-jumeirah

• The easyHotel in Dubai at www.easyhotel.com/hotels/united-arab-emirates/dubai/dubai.

---

**Restaurants**

● The Ivy in London, UK, at www.the-ivy.co.uk/

● The Hard Rock Café in Hyderabad, India, at www.hardrockcafe.com/location/hyder-abad/.

---

Table 5.2  Restaurant product concepts

| Restaurant concept | Example |
| --- | --- |
| Molecular gastronomy | The chefs in these restaurants use innovative cooking techniques known as molecular gastronomy to produce individual and distinctive dishes and menus. They are fine dining restaurants where customers go to enjoy a gastronomic experience. Reservations are required, and customers must book a long time in advance to secure a table. A famous example is the Fat Duck in Bray, England, the brainchild of the celebrity chef and owner, Heston Blumenthal. This three Michelin star restaurant not only serves up unique culinary creations such as snail porridge and hot and cold tea (in one glass), but also offers menu items customized to consumers' tastes. Visit The Fat Duck at www.thefatduck.co.uk/. |
| Michelin starred (traditional) | Many other restaurants that have a Michelin star rating are far more traditional fine dining restaurants that offer formal, professional service with high-quality cuisines. French company Michelin has been awarding one (very good), two (excellent cooking, worth a detour) and three stars (exceptional cuisine worth a special journey) since 1926. There are Michelin starred restaurants in cities all around the world. The Arpège in Paris, France is a three Michelin stars restaurant. Log on to their website to see their offer at www.alain-passard.com/en/. |
| Upmarket dining | Restaurants in this category offer a range of less formal but high-quality dining experiences for a much larger number of customers. D&D's fashionable and stylish restaurants fit within this product category – restaurants include the Issho in Leeds, Alcazar in Paris, Sartoria in London and Guastavino's in New York City. |
| Casual restaurant | These restaurants tend to offer modern and comfortable dining experiences at moderate prices. They provide table service. They often have a separate bar area. There are both independent and large chains of casual restaurants. International chains that fit within this product category include Chilis Grill and Bar, TGI Fridays, Applebee's and the Hard Rock Café. |
| Quick service restaurant (QSR) | The QSRs have average food, offer limited menus and rarely provide table service. QSR menus are limited, and usually the food is available as takeout, though seating may be provided. The ambiance is essentially functional – lots of plastic seating and tabletops, fluorescent lighting and the chain's branded graphics. The top four fast-food restaurants in the United States (ranked by size) are Subway, McDonald's, Starbucks and KFC. |

*(Continued)*

| Restaurant concept | Example |
| --- | --- |
| Fast casual restaurant | Fast casual restaurants are hybrid restaurants that offer a blend of fast-food dining and casual dining. Fast casual borrows a little from fast food and a little from casual dining. Fast casual typically has no table service; orders are placed and paid for, and customers are then directed to an assembly area where their food is ready and waiting for them to take to a table. Some chains use a slight variant – they will take your order, let you proceed to your table, and a food runner will bring your meal to you. The ambiance is more upscale compared to QSRs, with soothing interior designs ranging from soft pastel colours to fireplaces. |
| | Fast casual industry leaders include Panera Bread, Five Guys Burger and Fries, Jimmy Johns Gourmet Sandwich Shop and Chipotle Mexican Grill. Fast casual establishments feature a more upscale and diverse menu selection, as can be seen at Chipotle Mexican Grill (www.chipotle.com/). |
| Themed or novelty | There are numerous examples of themed or novelty restaurants around the world. For example, The Rainforest Café is an environment concept café that offers customers a rainforest themed dining experience complete with special effects including mist, thunderstorms and lightning in North America, Europe and Asia Pacific (www.rainforestcafe.com/). |
| | Dans le Noir is a French restaurant concept where diners eat completely in the dark. The waiting staff are blind, although the kitchen staff are sighted. The idea behind this concept is to challenge guests to use their other senses (rather than sight) in order to have a different dining experience. There are Dans le Noir restaurants in London, UK, Paris, Bordeaux, France, Brussels, Belgium, Madrid, Spain, Cairo, Egypt, and Auckland, New Zealand. See www.danslenoir.com for more details. |
| Single fast-food concepts | These fast-food restaurants tend to offer a menu based around one core ingredient. They tend to offer counter service with clean, but basic decor at affordable prices. Many of these concepts are privately owned establishments that might serve burgers, pizza, fried chicken or fish. There are also branded chain single food concepts such as Potatotopia (potatoes), Flex Mussels (mussels) and The Nugget Spot (chicken nuggets). However, given the closure of many of these single item chains within their first year of operation, industry experts have questioned their ability to survive in the long term. |
| Organic restaurants | Restaurants in this concept might serve menus that include organic meat products, although many are strictly vegetarian. They promote themselves as serving menus made from food raised or grown sustainably and in a way that promotes ecological balance, and that are (mostly) free from chemicals and preservatives. The Daylight Kitchen in Tokyo is an example of an organic restaurant that promotes itself as serving simple, honest and handmade foods crafted from the finest raw, local ingredients they can get their hands on. Menus evolve with the season, include both meat and vegetarian options. See www.daylightkitchen.jp/ for more details. |

### Product benefit bundles

Consumers rarely look at one single feature of a hospitality product when making purchase decisions. They generally look for a combination of features that deliver the benefits they are seeking. Hospitality businesses can provide these benefits either independently or in partnership with other organizations. We call these combinations 'product benefit bundles'. Buying a bundle is advantageous to customers, as it makes the purchase decision more convenient. For example, instead of a tourist making many separate decisions and purchase transactions about travel, accommodation and food and beverages, the customer can make a simple, single decision about the purchase of a package. For the hospitality business, the advantages are economies in selling (for example, sell one package rather than three separate components) and increased value of a sale. Within hospitality, examples include:

- Bed and breakfast; dinner, bed and breakfast; full board (accommodation with breakfast, lunch and dinner)
- Themed accommodation packages – like murder mystery weekends that combine accommodation, entertainment and meals
- Restaurant, or function menus with drink packages (inclusive of starter, main course, dessert, coffee and relevant taxes) – for religious festivals or wedding receptions
- 24-hour conference packages including accommodation, all meals, tea and coffee and hire of meeting rooms
- Themed party events with inclusive menus, live entertainment, dancing and activities – for example, New Year's Eve parties or other special events.

In addition, hospitality businesses can work with external organizations – such as local leisure and sporting attractions – to offer inclusive product bundles. For example, hotels might bundle accommodation and meals with theatre tickets or tickets for popular sporting events.

The accommodation, food and drink products offered by hospitality businesses form part of the larger tourism product, either formally when bundled together by a third party such as a tour operator and an online travel agency such as expedia.com, or informally, when the customer independently visits various hospitality businesses at the tourist destination. Tour operators and online travel agencies can combine all the essential elements, such as flights, transfers, rooms and food (and frequently drinks for all-inclusive resorts), excursions and offer a combined product in one inclusive package. Tourists buying these packages regard the hospitality product simply as one component of the entire package, not as an independent product, and customer satisfaction with the hospitality product cannot easily be separated from satisfaction with the other elements of the travel package. While uncontrollable external factors, such as the weather or an unhappy retail experience, can also affect the customer experience and satisfaction, hospitality businesses often collaborate with other organizations to create an effective marketing strategy that ensures repeat and referral business. This collaboration can take different forms:

- Individual hospitality operations formulate, develop, promote and deliver their product as a part of the total tourist offer of the destination.
- At the destination, hospitality operators work with official tourist organizations who formulate and develop tourism products based on the destination attributes and promote them to target markets.
- Tour operators coordinate the products offered by hospitality firms and other suppliers, and then formulate them into a single offer (package) which is promoted to target markets.

---

**ACTIVITY 5.2**

Access details of a conference or wedding package from a conference venue, event company or hotel website and review the different product combinations and prices.

What are the advantages of product bundles for:

● The customer?

● The hotel?

Are there any disadvantages? If so, make a list of these and determine whether the advantages outweigh the disadvantages.

---

## Service delivery concepts and the product

Understanding customer needs, within a given price band, is fundamental to creating successful products that match customer expectations. One of the most important product decisions facing multi-unit organizations is determining how much of the product should be standardized and how much should be adapted for different locations or outlets. When hospitality organizations standardize a product, their objective is to provide the same experience to all customers in every unit. An adapted hospitality product deliberately offers a modified product, which means that the customer experience varies between units. There are clear arguments for and against standardization, particularly when hospitality companies operate internationally.

### Standardized products

In domestic markets, QSR chains provide many examples of standardized hospitality products. They offer the following features in their restaurants:

● The same menu
● At the same price
● Created using the same kitchen production process
● With the same service delivery process
● The same staff recruitment, training and service standards
● In a unit having the same layout, seating and internal decor, and
● The same external frontage, signage and brand.

There are advantages to both the consumer and the organization from a standardized product. Customers receive a consistent, reliable product that meets their brand expectations. Companies gain significant economies of scale and experience through fully preconfigured design concepts, volume purchasing, reduction in stock levels, lower employee skills requirements and easier staff training procedures. Service processes can also be blueprinted. Essentially, a blueprint is a flowchart or map that sets out the various tasks that have to be performed for a service to be delivered to a customer. Blueprints can also identify who is to perform the task and the required performance standards (see Chapter 11 for more information). There are also opportunities to grow brand awareness through marketing communication campaigns that promote the same, standardized product formula. The consistency of product and service delivery across different locations can also enhance brand reputation.

A precondition for developing a genuinely consistent standardized product in hospitality operations is to build new developments instead of adapting existing buildings and structures that inevitably create brand inconsistencies. Budget hotel chains are more likely to have a standardized product if the accommodation is factory-built, with prefabricated bedroom units erected on the building site. As we saw in Chapter 4, hospitality brands offering a standardized product can be described as 'harder' brands. Companies with successful standardized offers can expand more easily – every time a new unit is opened, all product decisions have already been tried, tested and agreed. This has enabled a small number of standardized hospitality branded products to grow rapidly throughout the world. The standardized product concept is either loved or loathed by consumers!

### Adapted products

The alternative approach to standardization for a branded chain operation is to adapt the product to suit local market conditions and consumer expectations. In other words, hospitality firms deliberately adapt their product offer to compete more effectively in different markets. The types of adaptations hospitality chains might make include the following:

- Individually designed hotels in different sites, often built in different historical periods, offering a different range of services and facilities in different locations – for example, the Malmaison brand has grown through converting unique historical buildings.
- Different decor and different types of furniture – hotel and restaurant chains frequently adapt interiors to incorporate local materials and artefacts.
- Restaurants with different menu items reflecting local ingredients and culinary customs – for example, while Pizza Hut in China serve pizza, their menu also includes special items like durian pizza, bacon wrapped quail eggs with abalone mushroom and warm corn juice.
- Staff trained to unit standards of operation, instead of group standards of operation.

The adapted approach provides consumers with different experiences in different unit locations, and appeals to customers who are tired of standardized product offers and want to experience something different or local. Other advantages include the possibility of lower costs by sourcing locally, and the opportunity to enable managers to respond to local consumer/competitor requirements. Disadvantages of an adapted approach include higher hospitality product development costs, since there are fewer opportunities for economies of scale. Hospitality brands offering an adapted product are 'softer' brands.

### International product decisions

Decisions about standardization or adaptation are even more complex for international hospitality chains. The international hospitality product needs to take into account different country conditions, cultural differences and competitor offers to compete effectively. In essence, companies must decide what adaptations must be made to meet macro-environmental conditions (e.g., planning, legislation, economic conditions) and what adaptations should be made to gain local consumer acceptance. Identifying target markets and developing a thorough understanding of the macro- and micro-environments is therefore crucial when developing international products.

If the target market is primarily from the home country, then the product can be standardized using the home country culture. The family-run, British-based tour operator Ski Olympic provides a British skiing holiday product for British customers in the French Alps. The product includes British-style food (porridge and cooked English breakfast, Tetley teabags, afternoon tea, and evening meals complete with an after-dinner cheeseboard), British beers, British television (especially sport and soap operas), British and Commonwealth staff and management, and even British ski instructors. This British product in France is deemed suitable because the customers are all British and this is what they want.

If the target market is primarily people from the host country, the product must be adapted to local tastes, cultural values and spending power. Even 'hard' QSR chains make local menu adaptations to suit local cultures and tastes. When KFC expanded into China, the menu was adapted to include fried dough sticks, shrimp burgers, egg tarts and soya milk drinks. Newer menu adaptations include the bright-pink rose cheese chicken leg roasted burger, congee (rice porridge), the 'Dragon Twister' (a wrap that includes fried chicken, cucumbers, scallions, and duck sauce, similar in preparation to Peking duck) and the black diamond bacon spicy chicken leg burger. Rice is also provided as an alternative to French fries. Along with food items, local tastes and cultures also determine whether alcohol is served. McDonald's first began serving alcohol in Munich, Germany, in 1971 and continues to do so in other European countries. In the Middle East, however, all menu products served are halal, in keeping with religious conventions. Local economic conditions and competitor offers can bring about adaptation of prices too. In addition, local legislation can restrict trading hours and/or trading on certain religious or national holidays. Planning regulations can force companies to make design adaptions, as was the case when Accor entered Germany. The company was forced to redesign its prefabricated Formule1 hotel brand so that the roof of hotels met planning requirements. Eventually Accor recognized that its Formule1 brand offer did not meet the needs of international markets and was withdrawn from Germany and other European countries; the brand was renamed hotelF1 and now has over 170 units, all located in France.

## ACTIVITY 5.3

Visit the website of IHG at www.ihg.com. Select two different country locations and investigate the hotel offer for the InterContinental Hotel brand in these two locations. Identify which elements of the hotel product offer are standardized in the two country locations and which are adapted.

Visit the website of Kentucky Fried Chicken: www.kfc.com. Select two different country locations. Identify which elements of the restaurant product offer are standardized in the two country locations and which are adapted.

In reality, for most international hospitality groups the decision is not a choice between total standardization or total adaptation. Instead, the decision is about the degree of standardization and the degree of adaptation that is best suited to different country or regional markets. Hospitality firms want to standardize where possible to achieve cost and operational advantages, but adapt where necessary to compete effectively. For hotel companies, accommodation, the range of facilities offered and service standards tend to be easier to standardize, whilst decor, design, staff uniforms and some elements of the food and beverages offer tend to be adapted to reflect the local culture and cuisine. Hotels must also price products according to local market conditions. In Chapter 4, you were introduced to the concept of glocalization, the process of providing international product standards with local adaptations. For international hotel and restaurant firms, the glocal approach is considered to combine the best of both approaches effectively.

## Product life cycle

All products experience a life cycle, which charts their sales and profit behaviour from birth, through various stages, to decline and extinction (see Figure 5.2). The product life cycle (PLC) is one of the most widely known concepts in marketing, and hospitality managers should be aware of its importance when developing marketing strategies for their businesses. PLC concepts apply to every type of product: an item on the menu or in the bar, a sales outlet within a hotel (the restaurant, banqueting or lobby bar), an individual property or unit, a brand or chain of outlets or even a destination. The global hospitality industry comprises hundreds of thousands of 'products', all at different stages of their life cycles.

Although a product's life cycle can vary from a very short period of only a few months to a very long period lasting several generations and even hundreds of years, the typical PLC includes the following stages (see Figure 5.3):

- *Product development*. During this period, the new product concept is conceived, researched, assessed and, in some cases, test-marketed prior to launch in the marketplace. Many new product concepts fail to demonstrate at this stage that they will perform well in the market and, as a result, they are never actually launched.
- *Introduction*. This is the launch period, when the new hospitality product is introduced to the market – for example, the opening of a new restaurant or introducing a new menu item. Some new products survive, but never really take off. If they do grow, they enter the next stage.
- *Growth*. This is the period when the new product becomes more widely accepted by consumers, and sales grow as the product becomes better established.
- *Maturity*. At this stage, the product has reached its potential and growth slows or stagnates.
- *Decline*. Eventually, the product no longer satisfies the needs and wants of its customers, as alternative offers provide better benefits to consumers. Sales fall as the product goes into decline, and management has to decide whether to retain or dispose of the product. A product that is in decline for one company can still be highly profitable for a different company. There are many products in declining markets that are still highly profitable – for example, bed and breakfast establishments in British seaside resorts.

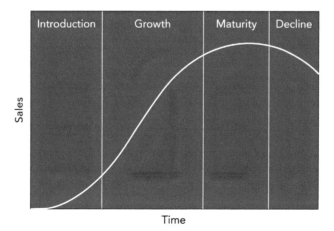

Figure 5.2 The product life cycle

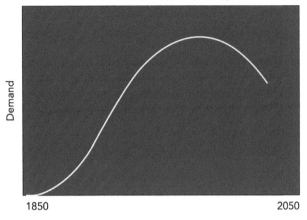

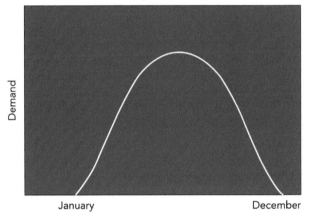

Figure 5.3 Examples of product life cycles

There are a number of criticisms of the PLC. First, it is not always clear where a product is precisely located in its cycle. Second, the PLC is not an accurate forecasting tool, and sales may fall due to an economic downturn or other external causes, rather than a change in customer preferences that typically underlies movements between stages of the PLC. So, if a manager makes a marketing decision based on a faulty analysis of the PLC, then the marketing strategies adopted might be incorrect and damage the business. Whilst accepting these valid criticisms, the simplicity and terminology of the PLC helps us to understand important product management issues explored next.

### New product development concepts

Clearly, many new hospitality products are successful, but the rate of new product failure in hospitality is high – especially in food service. Even successful companies like McDonald's have introduced products that have flopped such as the Hula Burger introduced in the 1960s. Today, independent restaurants and even those opened by celebrity chefs experience some of the highest failure rates. While there is much debate as to the 'true' extent of restaurant closures, the reasons for the high failure rate of new products in hospitality include the following internal and external factors.

*Internal factors* (those that the company has some control over) include:

- Undercapitalization – not having sufficient funds (working capital) to operate the business through the slow introductory period; many new hospitality businesses borrow too much and cannot afford to pay the interest on their loans, so consequently fail
- Higher than expected development costs
- Inexperienced and over-optimistic entrepreneurs
- Poor marketing research
- A flawed product concept
- Inappropriate location
- Inconsistent service delivery
- Poor interior and/or exterior design
- Poor timing (e.g. opening during the decline or recession phase of the business cycle) – although this last factor relates to the external environment, the decision as to when to launch the new product is an internal one
- Poor social media and brand reputation management.

*External factors* (those that the company has little or no control over) include:

- Limited market potential
- Competitors' responses or the extent and type of competition
- Negative publicity from dissatisfied journalists and customers, especially through social media
- Unexpected changes in the macro- or micro-environments (e.g. extended emergency road-works blocking access to a restaurant; natural disasters).

### Innovation

Even when new products make it to the growth phase, it is important for hospitality firms to continuously update and refresh their products or to introduce product replacements to remain competitive. Effective hospitality managers therefore constantly seek to improve customer satisfaction by reviewing their offer. As a result of managers' observations, business performance and customer/staff feedback, monitoring of online customer reviews, product improvements or innovations can be introduced. These can range from minor low-cost enhancements (incremental innovations) to multi-million-dollar new-build developments (major innovations). When the first Banyan Tree Resort opened in Phuket, Thailand in 1987, they were faced with a situation of having rooms without a sea view. As a result, rooms were designed with private swimming pools as an innovative addition. Another incremental innovation was introduced by Hotel Icon in Hong Kong. At this hotel, all guests can make use of the Timeless Lounge to rest, shower and prepare for a meeting after arriving on an overnight flight and being unable to check in to the hotel, or to work or rest when waiting for a late-night departure having checked out of their room. Major innovations in the industry include the global hotel application for use with the iPhone introduced by Choice Hotels. Marriott has developed a virtual reality transporter to give guests a virtual taste of what it would be like to vacation in some of their resorts.

As major hospitality organizations have a large number of products at different stages of the PLC, there is a constant requirement to research and find successful new product concepts to ensure continuous profits. Companies use two different methods to find new concepts: they can either *acquire* products that have been developed by others or they can *develop* their own new products.

## ACQUISITION

The bureaucracy of larger organizations can inhibit creativity, making acquisition attractive. Once a successful entrepreneur has proved the viability of the new product concept, larger hospitality organizations can either imitate the concept or buy out the entrepreneur's company. For example, many resorts now provide private plunge pools following their success at Banyan Tree. New World Hotels acquired the Rosewood Hotels & Resorts brand when it was looking to develop a new luxury brand to add to its hotel portfolio, and later re-named the parent company New World Hotels as Rosewood Hotel Group. Marriott International acquired Starwood Hotels & Resorts creating what J.W. Marriott, Jr., Executive Chairman and Chairman of the Board of Marriott International, calls 'the world's best portfolio of hotel brands, the most comprehensive global footprint, and the most extensive loyalty programs'.[2]

## ORGANIC DEVELOPMENT

The alternative route for both large and small firms is to develop their own new products, although the process undertaken may differ substantially. Smaller, more entrepreneurial organizations are often closer to customers and can generally innovate with much more freedom. In hospitality, there are many examples of people who develop successful new product concepts based on their 'gut' feeling, their intuitive understanding of customer needs and their entrepreneurial flair. Simon Woodroffe, the entrepreneurial founder of YOTEL, explains how his eureka moment arrived when he was thinking how to adapt the Japanese capsule hotel concept for the Western market. He was upgraded to first class on a British Airways flight and, when he woke, he realized the solution was all around him – designing the YOTEL product by imitating the British Airways' cabin. Similarly, Sir Stelios Haji-Ioannou developed the easyHotel brand, believing there would be as much demand for this budget product as for his budget airline.

In larger organizations, an in-house new product development team can be established to generate and evaluate new product concepts formally. The team may be an established part of the organization structure or an *ad hoc* cross-functional group designed to test and guide new products through to implementation. New product teams need marketing input to ensure that the customer's voice is heard. In franchise organizations, this customer voice often comes through franchisees, who make suggestions for new products, which are then refined and tested by product development teams before launching. In recent years, companies also utilize customer comments posted online and social media posts to identify customers' evolving needs and wants and develop products to satisfy those needs. Many so-called new products are actually product modifications, cost reductions or product line extensions, as opposed to original product concepts.

### New product development process

Many companies have a formal new product development (NPD) process that features some or all the following stages:

- *Idea generation*. There are several sources for new product ideas, including managers, employees, customers, social media, suppliers, intermediaries and competitors. Identifying consumer trends early is important.

- *Idea screening*. Ideas need to be screened to ensure that they can be developed further. Some ideas lack potential and are immediately discarded; other ideas might be desirable but do not fit the competences of the company. Screening aims to eliminate bad ideas quickly so that the costlier stages of the NPD process (product development and prototyping) are not required.

- *Concept development and testing*. In this stage, the idea is more fully developed into a new product concept, with carefully formulated core, tangible and extended product elements, creating a detailed, testable proposal. Companies then test prospective consumers' reactions to the new concept, using marketing research techniques such as focus groups.

- *Marketing strategy*. A marketing strategy is developed for the new product that describes the innovation's target market, product positioning and marketing mix. Initial costs, sales and profit projections can then be formulated.

- *Business analysis*. In this stage, the new product is evaluated against company investment and return hurdles. Will the concept deliver the desired return on investment? Investment in new product development is a board-level decision when significant capital sums are involved.

- *Product development*. Finally, the idea starts to become a reality. Large companies sometimes develop a prototype for test marketing. A test market is a limited-scale launch of the product concept to establish the potential for the innovation and the marketing necessary to make it a success. In multi-unit operations, new product concepts can be tested in a small number (maybe one) units to gauge customer reactions before rolling out the concept. Smaller businesses often do not test market new concepts.

- *Commercialization*. The final decision to proceed is based on the results of the test market or the business analysis. Depending on consumer response and the capital investment/profit return calculations, a final decision will be given to proceed or halt the new product development.

Whilst larger companies have a more structured approach to new product development, smaller hospitality companies are generally more entrepreneurial. A restaurant proprietor can introduce new menu items for a trial period before making the decision to add the items permanently or drop them. Failed ideas can be dropped without serious cost consequences.

---

### MARKETING INSIGHT 5.1

#### citizenM hotels[3]

In 2008, citizenM hotels were launched on the platform of innovation and the desire to create hotel rooms that are the 'embodiment of affordable luxury lodging'. The founders of this hotel brand, Rattan Chadha and Michael Levie, recognized a new type or breed of modern, international traveller: those who travel regularly for a wide variety of reasons including both work and leisure purposes, share a respect for different cultures and are young at heart. These travellers were recognized as explorers, trekkers, professionals and shoppers, recognized as independent travellers who are the mobile citizens of the world.

citizenM hotels were designed with the needs of these travellers in mind to offer stylish designs, a comfortable bed, upmarket amenities, entertainment and a sociable atmosphere in a good location without unnecessary or hidden costs. The result is a new style of hotel room that provides all these facilities in much less space than most of their competitors.

The brand promises one-minute check-in and 30-second check-out procedures, free movies and unlimited Wi-Fi, and 24-hour access to food and drink. Public spaces within the hotel include a 'living room' for guests to hang out and socialize in. The brand still promotes itself as offering 'affordable luxury for the people'. The brand that started over a decade ago with one hotel at Schiphol Airport opened its 20th hotel in 2020 and clocked a total of 4,760 rooms on three continents. The brand is planning on extending the number of hotels to 36 and 8,545 rooms in the following three years.

Visit www.citizenm.com to determine the extent of innovation in this new hotel product.

*Source*: www.citizenm.com

## Adoption theory

Some new products become popular very quickly, whilst it can be years before others take off. Some never do! Knowing how customers adopt new products is important to understanding this phenomenon. Researchers have identified a number of different categories of new product adopters, according to whether customers are amongst the first or later groups to buy the product. These categories are as follows:

- *Innovators*. These are the first people to buy a product once it appears on the market. In hospitality, they are the first customers to visit a new restaurant when it opens. They are prepared to experiment and take risks and are an important influence on the behaviours of the next category. They are more likely to share their experiences through social media and post reviews of their experiences with new products and experiences.
- *Early adopters*. These people pay close attention and respond to information shared by innovators about their new product experiences, and the reviews posted by traditional and social media influencers. They are the next group to try the new product. Some early adopters are also opinion leaders and social media influencers, whose messages about, and experiences with, the product can determine whether it will succeed or fail. If the early adopters endorse the product, it will become more established.
- *Early majority*. These people follow the early adopters, whose opinion matters to them. This group consists of people who tend to conform to social trends, are well integrated socially and accept change.
- *Late majority*. This group is slow to purchase new products. They are less responsive to change, are more sceptical and prefer products they know rather than experimenting with new ones.
- *Laggards*. These people are averse to change and reluctant to alter their purchase patterns. They tend to be older, more cautious and conservative, and continue to buy products even when they are no longer fashionable.

### ACTIVITY 5.4

Think about the different categories of adoption – the innovators, the early adopters, the early majority, the late majority and laggards. Which category do you fit into when it comes to trying new restaurants, new hotels or new technology?

### New product launch strategies

The introduction stage for new hospitality products includes new-build openings for hotels, restaurants and bars, new brand launches, and relaunches of tired products that have been refurbished and repositioned in the marketplace. For hotels, the time involved in planning, gaining permissions, constructing and finishing a new-build project can take several years and require substantial capital investment. It is for this very reason that pipeline reports produced by firms like STR identify different stages of hotel readiness. For restaurant and bar concepts, the lead time will generally be shorter and investment costs lower. A common problem is that hospitality new-build and refurbishment programmes are not always completed on time, and often the new hospitality product has to be opened incomplete. As a result, customers might experience a distressingly long list of minor problems, such as incomplete decor finishes, that can take several months to fix.

A typical launch strategy will include a 'soft opening', where invited guests stay and/or dine on a complimentary basis. This opening provides an opportunity to train staff on the job, and test the back-of-house and customer service processes, the food and beverage quality and the equipment before paying customers arrive. Feedback from invited customers and staff helps to identify problems, which can then be resolved prior to the full opening. If problems are not identified and resolved in the soft opening, then (especially with new restaurants) a poor reputation can quickly spread, especially through social media – which is often fatal. The marketing communications challenge during the launch period is to establish the product position and create awareness and interest in order to generate trial purchases. Potential customers therefore need to be persuaded that they will like the new product concept.

During the launch period, sales tend to be relatively low and there can be major fluctuations in demand, causing service problems at crucial times. Start-up costs are high, owing to the uncertain patterns of demand, staff training and recruitment costs, and the promotional spend to raise awareness. The unit is unlikely to be profitable during the introduction stage. However, the launch period is vital for the new hospitality product, because the business needs to generate:

- Satisfied customers
- Positive word-of-mouth
- Positive review comments and social media posts
- Repeat sales.

Smaller companies may never recover from a poor launch, because they may not be able to repair the damage from negative word-of-mouth quickly enough. In contrast, a successful opening means that sales will likely increase and lead to the growth stage of the PLC.

### Growth product strategies

In the growth stage, the hospitality product should be earning a good word-of-mouth and online reputation, as early adopters return and recommend the product to their social networks, who patronize the establishment in growing numbers. Sales grow, but despite this healthy trend there are pitfalls associated with growth. Successful hospitality products are dependent on a consistent product/service offer that delivers the promised customer experience. Sometimes, as the business grows there can be excessive demand at peak periods, resulting in lower service standards and unacceptable waiting times, or even having to turn customers away, which may result in dissatisfied customers posting negative reviews to review sites and sharing their dissatisfactory experiences with their social media networks. Hospitality customers can be fickle, and once they have found another hospitality product that suits them better, they may never return. Management can also inadvertently create problems by raising prices on ancillary products to boost profitability (e.g. on drinks and wines), which might deter repeat customers. Arrogant management, thinking that the business is now a success, may start to overlook customers' special requests and even ignore customer complaints.

Marketing strategies that hospitality companies adopt in the growth stage include the following:

- Relationship marketing to create and build long-term relationships with customers (see Chapter 14 for more information)
- Enhancing the product and service delivery based on feedback from customers and staff
- Setting prices to gradually grow the market; in other words, not raising prices quickly because the establishment has become popular, and in some cases adjusting price downwards
- Targeting new market segments to grow demand, possibly with minor product modifications
- Continuing investment in marketing communications to maintain awareness and build loyalty based on product preference
- Encouraging word-of-mouth recommendation by inviting satisfied customers to refer friends
- Reputation management through monitoring and responding to negative online reviews and social media posts
- Building partnerships with other organizations that can generate a stream of customers, such as theatres or hospitals
- Developing strategies to shift some demand away from peak periods such as early-bird special offers
- Developing capacity management strategies to cope with increased demand such as serving pre-dinner drinks and taking customer orders in the bar to reduce overall waiting times
- Opening additional units in similar geographic and demographic catchment areas to cope with increasing demand.

The growth stage should be increasingly profitable, because fixed costs are spread over a greater number of customers and, as trading patterns become more established, the management becomes more experienced at controlling staff rotas, to enhance customer satisfaction and reduce wage costs.

### Mature product strategies

Many hospitality product concepts operate in the mature stage of the life cycle, which can last for a very long period of time. The market for the product is well established, and the product itself is clearly positioned against its competitors. Sales level off as the business has consistent demand from a loyal customer base. Growth potential is limited and is largely dependent on gaining market share from competitors. The mature hospitality product can suffer from a number of problems, including:

- A dated product concept
- A tired product in need of refurbishment
- Management and staff working in a routine way and no longer 'wowing' customers

- More intense competition from newer product concepts, which cater better for customer needs and wants
- Increased segmentation of the market, ultimately with the risk of market fragmentation.

Effective managers will recognize these symptoms and take action to avoid the product entering the decline stage prematurely. Mature product strategies in hospitality include the following:

- Relationship marketing to nurture and sustain loyal customer segments
- Continuing investment to maintain and enhance service and product quality
- Product modifications/innovations, such as new menus or new recipes, that can revitalize a tired product
- Reformulating the product concept and/or refurbishing the premises to relaunch the product
- Adapting other marketing mix elements – for example, lower prices, increased promotional activity – and targeting new intermediaries to generate additional sales
- Online brand reputation management through monitoring and responding to negative on-line reviews and social media posts.

By careful management of the marketing mix, the mature stage can remain profitable for a very long time. Gradually, profits will begin to decline as increased investment, with heavier promotional costs to maintain market share, coincides with lower prices, driven down by competitors. Even major international brands suffer from competitors eroding their market share. Eventually, the mature stage will enter decline, unless the product has been reformulated and relaunched to start another cycle.

Case Study 5.1 provides an illustration of the PLC.

### Declining product strategies

There is no precise moment when a product or brand enters the decline stage that can happen rapidly or take many years. The decline stage can be caused by changes in consumer tastes, changes in technology, increased competition causing overcapacity, changes in management personnel or changes in ownership. As sales begin to fall, the typical hospitality operator will:

- Aim to cut costs in every facet of the business
- Reduce staffing levels
- Invest only in essential repairs (there will be limited, if any, investment in redecorating or refurbishment)
- Reduce overall product quality by purchasing cheaper food ingredients, bar and housekeeping products
- Take a longer time to pay suppliers.

### CASE STUDY 5.1

#### Little Chef[4]

Little Chef is a roadside diner chain in the United Kingdom, normally open from 7 a.m. until 10 p.m. Since opening in 1958, Little Chef has travelled through all the stages of the PLC, including decline into administration (bankruptcy) and (possible) rejuvenation.

The first unit was opened in Reading in 1958 with 11 covers. It was a British adaptation of an American restaurant diner concept by the entrepreneur Sam Alper. In the introduction stage, growth was modest and the chain increased to 25 units in the first 10 years. In the late 1960s, the British catering sector underwent a period of consolidation and Little Chef became part of the Trust House Forte group, which at that time was one of Britain's larger hotel companies. During the 1970s, 1980s and early 1990s, there was considerable growth in British tourism, and as a brand leader Little Chef expanded rapidly. Indeed, there was little serious competition apart from the Happy Eater brand. Trust House Forte acquired this main rival in 1987 and for 10 years the two brands retained their independent identity under the same ownership.

In 1996, there was a hostile takeover of Trust House Forte by Granada. They merged Happy Eater into the Little Chef brand and bought another competitor, AJ's Family Restaurants, which was also badged with the Little Chef brand. About this time, Little Chef reached its peak with 435 units and the brand was valued at several hundred million pounds.

Granada's mantra was to return value to shareholders and earn the senior management very high bonuses. To deliver this strategy, other stakeholders suffered. Product quality was reduced, prices increased and there was very little meaningful investment in the brand. Gradually, customers drifted away, employees became less motivated and demonstrably unhappy, and Little Chef's reputation declined. From 2000, the brand changed hands in corporate deals a number of times – but new owners failed to invest in Little Chef. Indeed, the 2005 new owners immediately sold or closed 130 of the underperforming restaurants. Unfortunately, these new owners soon went into administration two years later and the value of the brand collapsed.

In 2007, a private equity company, RC Capital, bought the brand and approximately 200 Little Chefs for less than £10 million. There was a serious attempt to rejuvenate Little Chef, including a much-publicized initiative with one of Britain's celebrity chefs, Heston Blumenthal. However, the chief executive suddenly left in April 2010, with the owners saying that the brand had changed too much from its core. The prospects for this well-known brand remained uncertain, but they were listed in the Good Food Guide in 2010 and 2011.

A restructuring exercise in 2012 was undertaken and 67 restaurants were sold so the firm could focus on the 80 profitable restaurants that remained. New menus were launched that focused on locally sourced produce and locally produced ingredients promoted through a 'Wonderfully British' campaign. A take-away concept, Little Chef Express, was relaunched and a partnership was developed with Lavazza Coffee. In 2013, Charlie the mascot was brought back and given a voice on Twitter to try and revitalize the business. In the same year, Little Chef and its 78 remaining restaurants were sold to Kout Food Group. Kout Food Group started revamping the remaining restaurants after the purchase. By 2014 around 14 restaurants had received full renovation. However, Little Chef closed more restaurants in 2014. In February 2017, Kout Food Group sold all Little Chef locations to Euro Garages, though with Kout retaining full rights to Little Chef's intellectual property and franchise control. Euro Garages had started closing down all Little Chefs, replacing them with their other brands such as Starbucks and Greggs. The closure process of Little Chef was scheduled to be complete before the end of 2017 but was postponed until early 2018. Kout Food Group revoked Euro Garage's

Little Chef franchise at the end of January 2018, causing Euro Garages to temporarily rename all Little Chef locations to EG Diner until they could be converted into partner brands. The final EG Diners that were not rebranded closed in October 2018.

*Source*: www.littlechef.co.uk

Disappointed customers, overworked employees and dissatisfied suppliers can combine to generate powerful negative word-of-mouth. Returning customers will notice the poorer standards of product quality (e.g. tired decor and furniture, chipped and faded crockery and cheaper quality in-room amenities) and stop patronizing the hotel or restaurant. Customer complaints and negative review comments posted online unsurprisingly increase and there is little prospect of management being able to encourage the unhappy customers to return. The spiral of decline increases in a deadly no-win situation for all concerned. As sales deteriorate faster, more desperate cost-cutting measures are introduced to try and stem the losses, which in turn reduce customer satisfaction.

For larger firms with several hospitality outlets or brands, the problem of a unit in decline is exacerbated by the negative publicity, which can damage the overall brand reputation of successful units in other stages of the life cycle. In addition, the costs of managing a declining brand are disproportionate to the benefits generated. Owners and managers need to decide whether to keep a declining product and harvest it to maximize profits or to dispose of it. If the product is retained, costs have to be reduced and unprofitable segments eliminated, which further reduces sales.

### Disposal or rejuvenation

At any one time, there are thousands of hospitality businesses that have reached the end of their PLCs. If staff and customers know that the business is for sale, the spiral of decline accelerates even more quickly. Indeed, if a hotel or restaurant is not sold quickly, the business can go bankrupt. The key point to remember is that, when a hospitality product is sold or disposed of, there are two options. First, the new owners can reformulate the product offer, invest in the relaunch of the business and start a new PLC. The second option is that the hospitality product might be bought and converted into other uses – for example, housing and retail outlets, particularly if local market conditions no longer generate sufficient demand for hospitality. Alternatively, the existing owners might decide to rejuvenate the product by closing the existing business, investing in a new product concept and starting the PLC again. However, this particular option requires owners to have sufficient capital to sustain the business during the rejuvenation period.

## Conclusion

In this chapter, we have explored different perspectives on the hospitality product, and emphasized the importance of matching the product to the needs and expectations of target markets. Given the intense competition in the hospitality industry, marketers need to ensure that the product concept is designed to deliver customer satisfaction.

In this chapter, we have explained:

• The complex combination of tangible and intangible elements that comprises the hospitality product

- How products should be designed to cater for the needs and expectations of target markets and to deliver customer satisfaction
- That the hospitality product comprises a core product, a tangible element and an extended element, that are creatively integrated as product concepts
- How hospitality businesses design product–benefit bundles to satisfy a combination of consumer needs and wants
- That multi-unit operations need to decide the degrees of standardization and adaptation in their branded products, particularly in international markets
- The PLC, which charts the sales and profits during the lifetime of every product through the five stages of product development, introduction, growth, maturity and decline
- The high failure rate of new products in hospitality
- The different marketing strategies at each stage of the PLC
- That, when a product reaches the decline stage of the PLC, management needs to decide whether to dispose of, or rejuvenate, the product.

## REVIEW QUESTIONS

Now check your understanding of this chapter by undertaking the following activities:

1 Discuss the core, tangible and extended elements of a hospitality product that you are familiar with.

2 Discuss the advantages and disadvantages of standardizing the product offer for an international branded hospitality chain.

3 Evaluate the effectiveness of the PLC in marketing decision-making. Illustrate your answer by providing examples from the hospitality industry.

## References

1. Kotler, P., & Armstrong, G. (2020). *Principles of Marketing*. New York, NY: Pearson Education.
2. Marriott International. (2016). *Marriott International Completes Acquisition of Starwood Hotels & Resorts Worldwide, Creating World's Largest and Best Hotel Company While Providing Unparalleled Guest Experience*. [cited September 8, 2021]. Available from: https://news.marriott.com/news/2016/09/23/marriott-international-completes-acquisition-of-starwood-hotels-resorts-worldwide-creating-worlds-largest-and-best-hotel-company-while-providing-unparalleled-guest-experience
3. citizenMHotels [Internet]. *Company*. [cited September 8, 2021]. Available from: www.citizenm.com/company/overview
4. Little Chef [Internet]. *Our History*. [cited September 8, 2021]. Available from: www.littlechef.co.uk/history/

Chapter **6**

# Locating the offer

**CHAPTER OBJECTIVES**

After working through this chapter, you should be able to:

- Understand the importance of location as a prerequisite for developing a successful hospitality business
- Identify the main classes of hospitality locations
- Research the characteristics of potential sites using relevant criteria
- Argue a case for the complexity of the destination product
- Evaluate the components of a destination's image
- Understand how hospitality companies work with destination marketing organizations.

## Introduction

When the target markets have been defined and the product concept has been agreed, the next crucial marketing decision is to find the appropriate location(s) for the development of the hospitality business. Finding and occupying suitable locations is a prerequisite for managing a profitable hospitality company. Conrad Hilton, who founded the famous Hilton Hotels brand, is reputed to have said that the three most important factors for success in the hotel business are 'location, location, location'. This remains true today. Ideally, locations are chosen that suit the product concept and its defined target markets. However, hospitality companies often

DOI: 10.4324/9781003186342-8

acquire properties that, of course, have fixed locations, and then have to devise appropriate offerings and find suitable target markets.

We now discuss in detail why the location decision is significant for both a single-site business and for branded multiple-unit operators, and we examine in detail the marketing research task of finding and evaluating appropriate locations. Finally, we will briefly review destination marketing from the hospitality operator's perspective.

## Importance of location

For owners, location choices have major capital investment and long-term financial consequences. When the agreement to buy a site or rent premises is finalized, it is difficult and costly to change the decision – the location is fixed. So, the initial selection of the site is most important. An appropriate site will have the necessary characteristics to ensure strong demand for the business. Although there are many examples of poorly managed hospitality outlets that trade successfully because of an outstanding location, even very good marketing cannot really compensate for a poor location. Clearly, thorough research needs to be undertaken to establish the patterns of demand in potential locations. Major hospitality brands recognize the importance of location and may research a potential location for up to four years in advance. This ensures that a thorough evaluation of the trading area's future growth and economic potential is undertaken before investing in the acquisition of a site.

For the single-site operator, the choice of location is even more important, because the costs of a poor decision cannot be spread among a chain of outlets. Unfortunately, too many individual operators have overly optimistic demand projections and underestimate how long it can take to establish a new hospitality business. This is one of the reasons why so many small hospitality businesses fail in the start-up period. There are, of course, a small number of examples where successful hospitality businesses are located in difficult sites, but this is because of the extraordinary skills of the entrepreneurs involved.

### Developing a network of hospitality units

Multiple-site operators, and in particular the leading branded hospitality chains, have dramatically expanded their network of outlets in the recent past and plan to continue to expand. This expansion is driven by the need to:

* Grow the business (sales and profits) to satisfy shareholders' expectations
* Locate where customers need to stay or dine
* Be where competitors are located.

If your brand is not located where your customer wants to stay or dine, then you might lose that customer forever to one of your competitors.

The theory of location strategy has primarily been developed for multiple retail shopping outlets; however, the principles are equally applicable to hospitality operations. Modelling of location decisions has generally taken the form of spatial interaction models that focus on the flows of passengers or customers between countries, regions, cities or centres. Each hospitality unit's location possesses a bundle of attraction and deterrence factors, which determines the flow of customers to the property. Attraction factors might include a large number of tourist attractions or businesses in the area; deterrence factors might include public safety concerns and inadequate local transportation. The balance of attraction and deterrence factors accounts for variance in customer flows to different hospitality sites. The hospitality brands with multiple units and growth strategies use computerized attraction/deterrence models to aid location decisions.

## Main classes of hospitality locations

Hospitality locations can be categorized in several ways, and these are described here.

### Capital city

Capital cities usually generate strong demand from businesses, government and leisure markets. Capital cities such as Beijing, London, Paris and Washington attract both domestic and international visitors and often have the highest room occupancy, achieved room rate and revenue per available room (RevPAR) in a country.

### Provincial city

Provincial cities are more likely to generate good domestic business demand, with a proportion of international business customers, and limited leisure demand. Provincial cities such as Leicester, Lyons and Stuttgart fall into this category.

### Gateway location

Gateway locations are locations based at convenient destination access points, such as major airport terminals, key shipping ports and railway termini. These sites handle large volumes of travellers, although not all travellers stay in the gateway location. For example, Zurich is a major gateway for visitors taking a skiing holiday in the Alps, but few skiers stay in Zurich. However, Heathrow, as a major international airport and gateway to London, England, the United Kingdom and Europe, generates one of the highest levels of demand for hotels in any location in the United Kingdom.

### Highway location

Highway locations are found on arterial roads, motorways and other major roads and serve the travelling public, whether on business or leisure. Highway stops are normally associated with budget accommodation, and travellers typically stay for only one night. The famous Route 66 from Chicago to Los Angeles has many highway hotels, such as the Vega Motel in Vega, Texas.

### Resort location

Resorts primarily focus on leisure markets but often offer conference facilities to attract the corporate business and meeting markets in shoulder months and low seasons. Many resorts have been developed at coastal and country locations. Many resorts offer accommodation with a wide range of leisure and sporting activities, often but not always on an all-inclusive basis. The One & Only in Cape Town, South Africa, is a resort and spa hotel with non-package pricing, whereas the ClubMed Sandpiper Bay at Port Saint Lucie, Florida, offers couples and families all-inclusive prices.

### Rural location

Country locations also focus on leisure demand and frequently target niche markets, for example, walkers in the English Lake District or climbers in the Swiss Alps.

### Honey-pot destinations

Major tourist destinations are also described as 'honey-pots' because of the large volume of visitors. Examples include Dubai, Las Vegas, Venice and York.

## Researching hospitality locations

Researching suitable sites for a hospitality operation is time-consuming and can involve the collection and analysis of considerable volumes of data. The experience of one independent hotelier who inspected 50 locations over six months before buying a hotel is not uncommon. For international hospitality groups, there is the added complication of deciding which countries to enter.

There are three levels of spatial analysis in researching locations. The research starts with geographic market selection and then focuses on area analysis within the chosen geographic market and, finally, the most attractive sites are identified from the area:

- *Market selection* decisions are based on the geo-demographic and socio-economic characteristics of a geographic region or country; this includes looking at the current situation, examining trends and projecting future conditions.
- *Area analysis* focuses on the characteristics of specific local areas within a region or country.
- *Site evaluation* examines local demographics, traffic flow and accessibility, competitors and the attractiveness of specific sites.

We will now review the criteria used by hospitality companies in country, regional and site selection.

### Country selection

The rapid growth of international hospitality companies has been driven by the globalization of travel markets and intense competition between the major players. As one competitor develops an operation in a new country, other competitors may feel obliged to follow. A PESTE analysis identifying the advantages and disadvantages of specific countries provides the basis for country analysis. Key criteria for evaluating the attractiveness of a country market include political stability, planning risk, foreign exchange risk, development route and market attractiveness.

#### POLITICAL STABILITY

High political stability creates a favourable investment climate. Most Western countries have stable political systems, whereas countries that have considerable political turmoil, such as Afghanistan, Nigeria, Pakistan and Venezuela, are more risky and therefore less attractive to international investors. Countries with high *political stability* generally offer opportunities to purchase freehold properties or negotiate long leasehold agreements. In countries with high *political instability*, the preferred entry option is to franchise the brand to a local company because local organizations understand their own political environment better than foreigners or negotiate an equity-free management contract. Several organizations, such as Transparency International and Coface, conduct research into political stability and corruption, and publish their findings on the Internet. Hospitality companies planning an international investment can purchase more detailed reports about the political stability of countries they are considering.

### PLANNING RISK

Regardless of the stability of a political regime, countries have different approaches to planning controls. This can mean that there are difficulties in obtaining planning consent for building new developments, converting existing properties into hospitality outlets or carrying out major refurbishment programmes to deliver consistent brand standards. Knowledge of the local culture and business/governmental regulations and customs is essential when negotiating planning permissions. A key goal of international marketing is to understand the influence of culture on the way of doing business in a foreign country, but it is much easier to conduct business in a familiar cultural climate.

### FOREIGN EXCHANGE RISK

This is also known as exchange rate risk. This risk can pose significant financial risk to the value of an investment, business's financial performance or financial position due to exchange rate fluctuations. If the currency of the country in which you operate depreciates against your domestic currency, then the value of your investments and any profits your business generates in that foreign country will decrease after being exchanged back into your own currency. Because exchange rates can be hard to predict, this can make protecting your business against this type of risk difficult.

### DEVELOPMENT ROUTE

There are three major expansion options for businesses that develop and own hotels:

1 *Acquisition* – companies buy a group of hotels or restaurants, and/or independent hotels and restaurants, and rebrand these units. This is the most convenient, proven and popular approach, especially if a brand wants to grow rapidly. However, there often are issues of ensuring brand conformity between the newly acquired properties and the company's international brand standards.

2 *Conversion* – companies buy or lease an existing property (e.g. an office block, high-rise flats or warehouse) and convert the property into hotel or restaurant premises. This is much more time-consuming and expensive. Softer hotel and restaurant brands with more flexible approaches to brand standards can convert premises more easily than harder hospitality brands.

3 *New-build development* – companies purchase land and build their own property to their own design specifications or to the design brief of the designated brand (subject to planning controls). For hotels, this can be more time-consuming than acquisition, but the advantage is that the brand standards are delivered from the moment the property opens. For quick service restaurants, a common option is to acquire a site and erect a purpose-built unit constructed from modular components.

The major international hospitality companies have used all three expansion options. The preferred option depends on the target location, the flexibility/rigidity of brand standards, the preferred form of ownership and regulatory planning constraints. Recently, many of the major international hotel corporations have taken a strategic decision to reduce the number of properties they own; instead, they have focused on franchising or managing units – this is a less capital-intensive strategy. We discussed these the asset-light entry modes earlier in Chapter 4.

## Market attractiveness

An attractive market is one with large numbers of potential customers and little effective competition! A comprehensive analysis of market attractiveness enables companies to forecast operating performance in a new country with some degree of accuracy. Useful data include the following:

- Current visitor arrivals, visitor mix (by country), visitor spend and future trends
- Host population size, demographic structure (e.g., age, family size) and future trends
- Economic data including employment and income levels
- Performance of hospitality firms operating in the country.

The attractiveness of a country market will largely depend on potential demand from the selected target markets, the intensity of competitor rivalry and the country's cultural/geographic similarity to the investing firm. The first time a hospitality company decides to develop a unit in a foreign country, there will be increased risk when the target country has a different culture, a different political environment and different forms of customer demand. Because of this added degree of complexity, most companies start their international expansion strategy by either choosing countries which are culturally similar, or which are geographically close – or both. For example, American companies will typically first enter Canada, which is both culturally similar and geographically close, or Mexico, which is less culturally aligned but geographically close. British companies often first enter France and Spain because of the geographical proximity, or English-speaking countries such as Canada and the USA because of cultural proximity. An important consideration for ethnocentric companies is the number of home market visitors travelling to target countries. Some North American hotel companies use the ratio of American visitors to a city as a key criterion for European site selection, because American tourists are likely to stay at the American brands they know and trust.

### Country evaluation

When all the data have been collated, companies input the data to computer models (either developed in-house or bought in) to evaluate the attractiveness of different countries and locations. Figure 6.1 provides an example of the data used in a European development strategy for a major international hotel group. Each criterion is assessed using an internal company grading system. For example, a gateway location might be awarded between 30 and 50 points, whereas a secondary location might be awarded between 10 and 20 points. In the example, London, Paris and Berlin are major capital cities and Heathrow and Charles de Gaulle airports are all gateway locations, so each score very highly, whereas Manchester and Strasbourg are secondary locations, with lower scores. When all the criteria for all the destinations have been assessed, the accumulated scores for each location are computed and a ranking scheme provides a prioritization of the locations. A refinement of this scoring process is to weight some criteria as more important than others. For example, a company may develop a business rule that says they will not invest in a country that has a political stability score of less than 8 on a 10-point scale.

**Part B**

| Geographic | | Location | | Timing | Development route | | | Attactiveness of market segments | | Risk | | Mix home tourists | Score | Ranking |
|---|---|---|---|---|---|---|---|---|---|---|---|---|---|---|
| Country | City | Population | Gateway | Secondary | Urgency | 1 | 2 | 3 | Business | Leisure | Political | Planning | | | |
| UK | London Heathrow | | | | | | | | | | | | | | |
| | Birmingham | | | | | | | | | | | | | | |
| | Manchester | | | | | | | | | | | | | | |
| | Edinburgh | | | | | | | | | | | | | | |
| France | Paris | | | | | | | | | | | | | | |
| | Charles de Gaulle | | | | | | | | | | | | | | |
| | Paris | | | | | | | | | | | | | | |
| | Bordeaux | | | | | | | | | | | | | | |
| | Strasbourg | | | | | | | | | | | | | | |
| Germany | Berlin | | | | | | | | | | | | | | |
| | Hamburg | | | | | | | | | | | | | | |
| | Munich | | | | | | | | | | | | | | |

Figure 6.1  A typical example of the data used in a European development strategy for a major international hotel group

### Region selection

Having selected the country, the next decision is to choose which region, area or city to locate in within the country.

Regional location decisions include the criteria discussed in Figure 6.1, as well as the following factors:

- *Micro-climate* – a detailed examination of regional climates, the hours of sunshine, level of rainfall or snow, temperature and seasonal variations is important for leisure resort operations.
- *Infrastructure* – this establishes access for target markets via air, road, rail and sea connections.
- *Regional demographic characteristics* – within a country there are often wide differences between regions in terms of employment opportunities, disposable income distribution, cost of living and living standards, which impact on domestic and local levels of demand.
- *Competitors* – an evaluation of the locations of major competitors is essential; indeed, locating where your competitors are operating successfully is often a sensible entry strategy.

Expanding hospitality companies need to identify the location gaps with their regional network of units to complete their portfolio of properties. Case Study 6.1 illustrates the importance of site selection.

### Site selection

This decision refers to the process of identifying individual sites that are suitable for acquisition (rent or buy), conversion or development. Hospitality outlets in attractive areas can fail because of poor site selection. Sites can be categorized as follows:

- *Prime*. These sites are the best locations. They are in high demand and can be difficult to acquire (because most are already in the hands of existing operators) and expensive to maintain. An example is the famous Dorchester Hotel on Park Lane, London.
- *Secondary*. These sites are not prominent but are still reasonably accessible. Most hospitality units are in this category.
- *Tertiary*. These sites are less accessible and may have other deterrence factors, for example, being close to a truck stop or an industrial estate (though this can be an attraction factor for some types of hospitality outlets). An example of a hospitality company having successfully developed a low-cost product concept using tertiary sites in France is Accor, with its HotelF1.

### CASE STUDY 6.1

#### Premier Inn site selection strategy[1]

Premier Inn, Britain's largest hotel brand, increased its portfolio from 250 units in 2001 to over 800 units across the UK, the Middle East and Europe in 2021, which made Premier Inn the largest hotel brand in the United Kingdom. Premier Inn's vertically integrated model, which combines the ownership of property with hotel operations, has enabled Premier Inn to grow at a significantly faster pace than competitors, deliver a consistent customer experience and generate a strong return on investment for shareholders over the last 15 years. Premier Inn achieved this rapid and significant growth through developing and utilizing a sophisticated approach to site selection using an in-house computer model with an extensive database of thousands of cities and towns. Demographics, including key data on businesses, the employment profile, tourism visitor statistics, road network and traffic densities, and other relevant hotel demand drivers, have been compiled for each location. These data are then analyzed to identify the characteristics of each city/town according to Premier Inn criteria. Similar cities and towns are clustered into one of the 19 categories, for example, Capital (London), Airport, High Volume Motorway, Major City, Small Town and Seaside Town. Premier's existing property portfolio provides extensive current occupancy and RevPAR data, and the combination of all these data enables the marketing team to identify suitable target locations. This desk-based research is then discussed with the Premier Inn acquisition managers to confirm or challenge the findings, before discussions are entered into with site owners. The data also enable Premier Inn to evaluate the most appropriate size of property (number of bedrooms) and the most suitable restaurant brand to install. Premier Inn has mapped the entire United Kingdom and some other international locations using these data to help the company to achieve its ambitious property network expansion plan.

*Source*: Premier Inn[1]

Factors influencing individual site selection include the following:

- *Local demographics and the characteristics of neighbourhoods*. Village Hotels in UK has explicit site selection criteria to ensure high hotel occupancies and achieve target membership levels for their health and fitness clubs. These clubs target affluent consumers, not families, aged 25–55. To generate a club membership of between 4,000 and 5,000, Village Hotels look for sites with more than 100,000 consumers within a drive time of 20 minutes.
- *Accessibility*, pedestrian and vehicle traffic flows and car parking.
- *Competitors*. The number, size, quality, prices and occupancy of branded and local competitors provide an insight into the local marketplace. Restaurant operators targeting local consumers often cluster together in prime sites, which is an indicator of the attractiveness of the location. Food courts in city centres are an example.
- *Individual site characteristics* – These include the size, landscape, adjacent buildings, aspect (south- or north-facing) and further development potential.

Case Study 6.2 illustrates the importance of site selection.

### CASE STUDY 6.2

### Sophie's Steakhouse and Bar, Fulham Road and Covent Garden, London[2,3]

Sophie Bathgate had always wanted to open her own restaurant, and her friend Rupert Power had always wanted to own his own bar. Both already had extensive restaurant and bar operational experience. Sophie worked for the Mezzanine Group, owners of Smollensky's Restaurants, and had been involved in opening one of their new restaurants. Rupert had worked at Browns and at Quaglino's – a Conran restaurant. On holiday in New York, they ate out in a different type of steakhouse, which really caught their imagination. The concept of Sophie's Steakhouse was born, but both knew that finding the right site was crucial if they were going to launch a successful restaurant business.

The search took 18 months; they looked at hundreds of sales brochures for restaurants on the market. They visited more than 50 sites and asked their architect to draw up plans on five sites that were really promising. Originally, they looked at the West End of London, but property prices were too high; however, they eventually found a site on the Fulham Road in London's inner southwest that fulfilled their criteria. They needed a minimum of 90 covers to make the business viable. Rupert wanted a separate bar area, with its own licence to attract non-diners, and seating for another 20 customers, and they both thought that the production kitchen should be visible to diners. This meant that they needed approximately 2,000 square feet of floor space.

The Fulham Road restaurant was situated in the middle of an affluent cosmopolitan neighbourhood where house prices are high and the socio-economic profile of residents indicates high disposable income. Fulham Road has a wide range of quality shopping, includes professional offices, is close to fashionable Knightsbridge and has lots of passing traffic. It is a busy place, with several other bars and restaurants in the area. The premises are located opposite a cinema and supermarket and only half a mile from a major hospital. Sophie and Rupert believed all these factors would generate strong demand for their midmarket restaurant.

After 18 months of searching, Sophie and Rupert finally agreed to buy the leasehold. They closed for a three-month refurbishment. Finally, two years after starting their search, Sophie's restaurant opened for business. After 12 months had passed, Sophie's 90-cover restaurant was serving 2,000 meals each week. They are open from midday to midnight and can re-lay tables three times on a Saturday night, with a good spend. The cinema, hospital staff and visitors generate demand at normally low season periods, like early Saturday evening.

As the Fulham Road steakhouse became a success, Sophie and Rupert looked for another London site. Rupert was still keen to open a restaurant in the West End because his work experience in this part of London convinced him that the dining out market was strong. However, they did not want to simply replicate the Fulham Road formula in a similar-sized unit; they wanted a much larger space to be able to drive more significant volumes of sales. Rupert remained in touch with the specialist restaurant estate agents, and one day an agent suggested that the owner of a suitable site close to Covent Garden might be interested in selling. The secret negotiations took 18 months, but Rupert was always concerned that another operator might learn about the opportunity and close the deal before they could. However, they finally secured the site and closed for six months to refurbish the premises and reopened.

Covent Garden is in the heart of London's business centre – it is a shopping destination, has many tourist attractions and is surrounded by theatre land. There is a strong demand throughout the year from local business people, domestic and international tourists and theatregoers. The new Sophie's Steakhouse and Bar has seating for 60 customers in the bar, 220 restaurant covers and is open from midday to midnight. On a busy day, tables can be turned over between four and five times, and a record 1,200 customers were served on the busiest day to date.

The long search for the right sites has paid off, and both of Sophie's Steakhouses have become very popular eating houses.

*Source*: Rupert Power[3] and www.sophiessteakhouse.com[2]

### Optimizing location decisions

Clearly, a considerable amount of research is invested in the location decision, and making a correct decision is fundamental to the success of any hospitality business. However, location decisions involve a trade-off between the different characteristics of potential sites and the capital available for investment. Although La Quinta Inns, a brand with more than 900 hotels across North, Central and South America, uses 35 independent variables to predict the profitability of a site, there are four key factors: the purchase price of the site, median income levels for the catchment area, the state population per inn and the location of nearby colleges. Indeed, 51 per cent of the projected profit can be predicted using these four criteria.

The large international hospitality corporations which franchise their brands have well-established location models that determine which sites are suitable; and where a corporation has several brands, the analysis will determine which brand should be located in a potential site. Franchise contracts sometimes give a franchisee exclusive territorial rights that prevent the franchisor from opening another outlet in the same location. This can lead to difficult negotiations if the franchisor wants to open another unit within the territory of an existing franchisee, who might object to possible cannibalization of sales, but franchisors can resolve this by offering the new site to the current franchisee. Sometimes the existing franchisee can benefit from another franchisee opening in the vicinity, as additional brand exposure helps all franchisees. However, as Starbucks has discovered, too many outlets in the same area does lead to cannibalization, and reduced sales per outlet. Franchisors, however, might not feel the pain as they continue to extract franchise fees and royalty payments.

---

### ACTIVITY 6.1

Identify three hospitality units: one in a prime site, one in a secondary site and one in a tertiary site. Carry out some marketing research, both desk research and a site visit if you can, to evaluate the characteristics of each site using the following criteria:

- Local demographics and neighbourhood characteristics
- Accessibility
- Competition
- Individual site characteristics.

---

From a marketing perspective, the crucial factor is the customer appeal of a site. Of course, sites with greater demand potential are much more expensive to acquire. Location theory assumes a high element of rational decision-making, but historically, hospitality companies have expanded opportunistically. So, despite all the research, many location decisions are based on 'gut feelings' and instinct. As Rupert Power, of Sophie's Steakhouse, says: 'You walk into a property and you just know, that gut feeling is really important!'[3]

## Destination marketing from the hospitality perspective

We have discussed the importance of location, and the criteria that hospitality companies use to evaluate the attractiveness of a location. Although chain hospitality operators do have the advantage of access to their own branded distribution systems, the effectiveness of the destination's marketing activities does impact on most units located in that destination. However, destinations are complex products:

- Destinations exist across a wide spectrum of different geographic levels – continents, countries, regions, cities and rural areas.
- Destinations have layers of administrative bodies responsible for the development and promotion of tourism, and roles and responsibilities can be confused, diffused and, in some cases, duplicated.
- Destinations have various zoning, site planning and design requirements, regulations and restrictions.
- Destinations comprise physical characteristics (the natural landscape and climate) that obviously cannot be changed, and the built environment.
- Destinations' culture and history influence the character of local peoples and the visitor experience.
- Destinations incorporate all the components of the tourism product – hospitality operations, transport, travel, intermediaries and attractions.
- There is no single owner of the tourism product in a destination.

Destinations also have a multitude of public and private stakeholders, including the following:

- National tourist organizations, local tourist organizations and public–private partnerships between government and private sectors
- Tourism companies (mainly small and a few larger businesses), their owners, management and employees
- Pro- and anti-tourism lobbies
- Various grassroots organizations that aim to minimize tourism's negative environmental and socio-cultural impacts
- Local inhabitants and visitors.

No single organization has total control over the tourism product and the destination image. This has implications for tourism development, quality control and marketing.

### Destination image

The image of a destination is a crucial consideration in today's competitive tourism market. A destination's image is a mixture of the following:

- Physical attributes
- Built environment
- Cultural and historical heritage

- Reputation and myth
- Local people.

We all have images of a tourism destination, regardless of whether we have visited the place or not. Images that are formed from indirect sources, through the media (online materials, reviews posted on review sites and social media, news reports, television travel programmes, newspapers and advertising) and by word-of-mouth from friends and/or relatives, are *induced images*.

*Organic images* are formed when we visit the destination in person. Our organic perceptions are based on our experiences, enjoyable or otherwise, at the destination. The organic image that we form is more fixed and less likely to be influenced by destination-marketing activities. When we tell family and friends about our impressions of a destination, we are projecting an induced image.

---

### ACTIVITY 6.2

- Identify two tourism destinations – one you have visited, and one you have not.
- Describe the 'induced' image you have formed about the destination you have not visited.
- Describe the 'organic' image of the destination you have visited.
- Compare the image of the destinations. Can you identify any differences between an induced and an organic image?

---

The problem with an induced image is that it may be completely inaccurate, depending on the reliability of the source. Considering that review sites, social media and other online and offline information sources play critical roles in the formation of an induced image of a destination, individuals can form a significantly different induced images of a destination based on where they get their information as presented in Case Study 6.3. For Western tourists, the induced image of a country such as Iran is largely negative, because the popular media portray Iran in a negative way. Interestingly, the organic image of Iran formed by Western tourists visiting the country is largely positive and strongly influenced by the friendliness of the local population.

### CASE STUDY 6.3

**Negative impacts of social media posts on destination image: The case of Jiuzhaigou nature reserve and national park in Sichuan Province, China[4]**

On 8 August 2017, a 7.0-magnitude earthquake hit Jiuzhaigou, a nature reserve and national park located in the north of Sichuan Province in southwestern China, causing serious damage to famous scenic spots, including the Nuo-Ri Lang Waterfall, Sparking Lake and Five-Flower Lake. After the earthquake, in addition to the traditional broadcast and print media news, there were a lot of reports about the damage on social media sites such as TikTok, WeChat, Weibo, etc. Because today's travellers heavily utilize social media and peer-to-peer sharing platforms in their decision-making process, it is not surprising to see that travellers also turn to those sites for information after major events such as natural disasters in addition to traditional media outlets. This is especially true for Chinese travellers since social media are more popular than ever in China. Many potential tourists turned to social media to get the most up-to-date information about the damage to Jiuzhaigou nature reserve and national park, which presented an unprecedented challenge for destination managers. Thus, not only the news and stories about a disaster published in traditional media outlets, but also the news and stories about the disaster and its impact on the Jiuzhaigou nature reserve and national park posted by individuals on social media platforms had significant impacts on individuals' travel intentions to the destination.

While some of the social media posts presented an objective assessment of the situation, some of the information about the damage was deliberately exaggerated by posters in order to get more reads, likes and to increase the number of followers. The exaggerated posts spread the false information quickly that the landscape and natural attractions in Jiuzhaigou nature reserve and national park had been badly damaged and Jiuzhaigou was no longer a place to visit. These posts led to widespread pessimism among social media audiences and greatly damaged the image of Jiuzhaigou. As a result, willingness to visit Jiuzhaigou was decreased significantly. This widespread pessimism had also posed a significant potential threat to its long-term recovery, in addition to slowing down the demand in the short term.

*Source*: Ai, Lv & Gursoy[4]

The world's major tourist cities have powerful images, which are represented by iconic features widely recognized by international tourists. Pictures of a red double-decker bus, the Eiffel Tower, the Golden Gate Bridge and the Opera House immediately suggest London, Paris, San Francisco and Sydney, respectively. Iconic images can be manufactured – the Big Apple and 'I Love New York' campaign is a successful example of a manufactured iconic image supported by an effective marketing communications campaign.

## Image and personal safety

Many tourists are concerned about their personal safety when travelling. Political instability, the presence or threat of war, conflict, terrorist incidents and crime have a major negative impact on the tourist destination image and on visitor arrivals. Throughout the first two decades of the twenty-first century, numerous terrorism incidents have damaged tourist consumer confidence in certain country destinations (Bali, Egypt, Israel, Turkey and Kenya) and cities (London, Madrid, Mumbai, Paris and New York), and this has created a negative impact on the tourism images of these destinations. However, destinations that generate strong domestic demand, like Paris and New York, appear to recover more quickly than countries that mainly rely upon international visitors.

## Destination marketing organizations

Destination marketing organizations (DMOs) can be government funded, a private company or a public – private partnership. Their primary role is to:

- Carry out marketing research and provide market intelligence for stakeholders
- Monitor visitor statistics and trends

- Coordinate marketing campaigns and, in particular, promotional activity
- Build and maintain destination websites and social media sites
- Liaise with intermediaries
- Provide tourist information for visitors before and during visits (this may include booking services)
- Coordinate marketing and sales activities to attract large events, conventions and meetings to the destination
- Manage the brand image of the destination.

Case Study 6.4 illustrates a successful DMO.

We noted earlier that organizations responsible for marketing a destination suffer from limited control of the product and have to resolve the conflicting demands of several stakeholders. Limited resources and unrealistic stakeholder expectations compound these problems. Hospitality companies within a destination work with DMOs in the following ways:

- Companies join the DMO; this normally involves paying a membership fee.
- Companies provide detailed information for DMO websites and social media pages, and printed guide entries; sometimes companies will pay for advertising in destination tourist brochures.
- Companies participate in tourist information and accommodation booking services.
- Companies provide hospitality for familiarization (FAM) visits by travel journalists, conference/exhibition organizers and other key intermediaries visiting the destination.

Proactive hospitality managers join the committees of DMOs and can obtain a degree of competitive advantage by developing good personal relationships with the personnel and management of the DMO.

## CASE STUDY 6.4

### Destination marketing at work – New Zealand[5]

In the late nineteenth century, many famous authors and scientists had visited New Zealand to explore the natural scenery, wildlife and Maori culture; and in 1901, New Zealand was the first country to establish a national tourism organization. By 1903, the country was attracting 5,000 international visitors per year. Today Tourism New Zealand is a government-funded destination marketing organization that advises, coordinates and manages a variety of marketing activities – including extensive research – to support hospitality and tourism in New Zealand. Tourism NZ launched the '100 per cent Pure New Zealand' campaign to promote a single message that focused on the country as a unique destination for the natural environment – hence the 100 per cent 'pure' theme. New Zealand attracts a significant number of adventure tourists who enjoy a wide range of physical outdoor activities. Given the importance of nature to the country's product, Tourism New Zealand also encourages hospitality operators to practise sustainable tourism. The Tourism New Zealand website provides helpful marketing information about their focus, mission and values; the consumer research they conduct;

international visitor arrival statistics; the advertising campaigns they manage; the crucial role of channel management; training and support for in-country tourism operators and responsible tourism in New Zealand.

By 2019, New Zealand was attracting over 3.8 million international visitors per annum. Following the global outbreak of COVID-19, New Zealand's borders were closed from March 2020 to most international visitors to protect New Zealanders from the COVID-19 virus, which had a considerable impact on New Zealand's tourism sector. In April 2020 Tourism New Zealand started developing strategies and action plans to help kick-start domestic tourism in order to help the sector get back on its feet. Tourism New Zealand have also started encouraging future international visitors to experience New Zealand through digital content to keep New Zealand's brand alive internationally not only for when the borders reopen but also for trade and export purposes.

### ACTIVITY 6.3

Log on to www.tourismnewzealand.com. This is the corporate website for New Zealand tourism. It provides a wide range of information about New Zealand as a tourist destination. Click on and explore the Markets & Insights, and Tools for your business; you can also explore the Business Events, Trade and Media webpages at the top of the page.

*Source*: Tourism New Zealand[5]

## Conclusion

Location decisions often involve considerable research, and the consequences are significant. Attractive sites with good demand characteristics have to be balanced against the capital available. Once a location decision has been made, hospitality companies work with DMOs to market the destination.

In this chapter, we have explained the following:

- The location decision is a major investment with long-term financial and operational consequences.
- Thorough research needs to be undertaken to evaluate the potential demand and competition in a location.
- Major hospitality companies use computerized models to evaluate site selection decisions, whereas entrepreneurs may use their 'gut instinct' to choose an appropriate site.
- Location decisions may involve three levels of spatial analysis: country or large geographic market selection, area or region analysis, and site evaluation.
- A wide range of attraction and deterrence criteria is used by hospitality companies to evaluate locations.
- Tourism destinations can be categorized as capital city, provincial city, gateway, highway, resort, rural and honey-pot.
- Destinations are complex products with a host of public and private stakeholders.

Part B

- Destination image has a major impact on tourist destination selection.
- Hospitality organizations work with DMOs to market the destination effectively.

### REVIEW QUESTIONS

Now check your understanding of this chapter by answering the following questions.

1  Why is the location decision an important element of the marketing mix?

2  What are the differences between single-site owners and multiple-unit hospitality operations when making location decisions?

3  Discuss the site selection criteria for locating a hospitality product.

4  Explain the characteristics and relevance of destination image in hospitality marketing.

5  How can hospitality managers work with DMOs?

## References

1. Premier Inn [Internet]. *New Premier Inn Hotels in Great Locations*. [cited September 13, 2021]. Available from: www.premierinn.com/gb/en/why/locations/new-hotels.html
2. Sophie's Steakhouse [Internet]. *Sophie's*. [cited September 13, 2021]. Available from: www.sophiessteakhouse.com/chelsea
3. Power, R. (2016). *Personal Interview*.
4. Ai, J., Lv, X., & Gursoy, D. (2020). Impact of social media posts on travelers' attitudes and behaviors towards a destination after a natural disaster: Moderating role of the source of the post. *Journal of Sustainable Tourism*, 1–19.
5. Tourism New Zealand [Internet]. *About*. [cited September 13, 2021]. Available from: www.tourismnewzealand.com/about/

Chapter **7**

# Pricing the offer and revenue management

After working through this chapter, you should be able to:

- Understand the significance of pricing in the pre-encounter marketing mix
- Identify external and internal factors that influence pricing decisions
- Appreciate how online search and transparency influences contemporary pricing strategies
- Explain quality/pricing strategies in a hospitality context
- Understand how hospitality organizations set prices
- Understand how revenue management can optimize sales revenue
- Describe the role of price promotions to increase revenue in low-demand periods
- Recognize the complexity of pricing in an international context.

## Introduction

In this chapter, we review the significance of pricing in the pre-encounter marketing mix and examine how hospitality companies set prices. We then look at the external and internal factors that influence pricing decisions, including the role of the Internet. We also explore the dynamics of revenue management.

DOI: 10.4324/9781003186342-9

Marketers are keenly interested in pricing decisions. As you know, the role of marketing is to influence the level and timing of customer demand. Price is the one element of the hospitality offer that customers can easily compare before experiencing the product, unlike quality or customer service. Consequently, price considerations often feature very significantly in customer choice. Regrettably, some hospitality companies do not consider marketing- or customer-related issues when they make pricing decisions. We believe this is foolish, because price can not only have a major impact on customer demand, but also position a product in the minds of customers, define the product's competitive set and influence customer expectations. When prices are too high, customers can't find value and don't buy; alternatively, if prices are too low, margins are reduced and business cannot prosper.

Pricing is a strategic component of the marketing mix. Price influences the demand for a product, which in turn determines sales volume and business income. Therefore, setting an appropriate price is one of the most critical factors in demand management and in generating revenue. The Internet, online/mobile technologies and especially comparison-shopping websites provide consumers and hospitality managers with more transparency into the prices of competitors. This has added another layer of complexity to pricing decisions.

Different types and sizes of hospitality business have different approaches to the pricing decision. Smaller accommodation businesses and bar, café and restaurant operations tend to utilize traditional *fixed-price* menus and tariffs. The cruise sector, large conference, event and hotel companies, tour operators with volume travel/accommodation packages, and many large independent hotels use *dynamic pricing* methods to maximize revenues by flexing prices between market segments and across time. This pricing strategy is also called revenue management.

Revenue management is widely adopted in the hotel industry and has the objective of maximizing revenues. The practice relies heavily on the collection of data and the use of analytics to identify booking patterns and forecast demand. Having forecasted demand, computerized Revenue Management Systems (RMS) then optimize prices, product availability and distribution, in order to maximize revenues. Revenue management practices can be applied across all hospitality departments including rooms, food and beverage and laundry services. Larger hospitality businesses are major adopters of computerized RMS.

Many hospitality and tourism businesses also utilize yield management, a similar concept that also relies on forecasting of customer demand for fixed, perishable resources such as rooms in a hotel or cabins on a cruise ship. Yield management is the practice of understanding, anticipating and influencing consumer behaviour in order to maximize yield or profits from that resource. As a specific, inventory-focused branch of revenue management, yield management involves strategic control of inventory to sell to the right customer at the right time for the right price. This process does result in price discrimination, where a firm charges customers different prices for identical goods or services.

In this chapter, we discuss pricing from both perspectives. Table 7.1 defines some of the pricing terms we use and pricing strategies we discuss in this chapter and the rest of the book.

## Significance of pricing in the pre-encounter marketing mix

There is a clear link between the price a customer pays and the customer's quality expectations. The higher the price, the greater the expectations of a high-quality hospitality experience. Price is an indicator and a measure of quality, particularly in the absence of other cues. If a high-quality gourmet restaurant routinely offers discounts, or a five-star hotel continually promotes discounted rooms or packages, customers would become confused and might suspect that the

Table 7.1 Common pricing terminology and pricing strategies used in hospitality

| ADR | Average daily room rate |
| --- | --- |
| BAR | Best available rate |
| RevPAR | Revenue per available room |
| Rack rate | The advertised or normal price of the room – the highest price that can be charged, forming the benchmark for any discounts |
| Revenue management | The practice of forecasting demand and optimizing price, distribution and product availability to maximize revenues. |
| Yield management | A flexible pricing strategy that uses forecasted levels of demand to maximize profits from a fixed and perishable number of resources such as rooms. |
| Dynamic pricing | Pricing strategy which changes prices according to market demand |
| Opaque pricing | Pricing method where unsold capacity (e.g., rooms) is sold at discounted prices, but the customer does not know who the provider is (e.g., the hotel) |
| Price discrimination | Pricing strategy to sell the same product at different prices |
| Transparent pricing | A market where customers and sellers know the price of comparable products |
| Rate parity | Pricing strategy to ensure that all prices are the same regardless of the distribution channel |
| Skim pricing | A pricing strategy that can be used when introducing a new product or a service. The company that introduces a new product or a service charges the highest initial price that customers are willing to pay. As the demand of the first customers is satisfied and competitors start offering similar products or services, the company lowers the price to attract more price-sensitive customers and to stay competitive in the marketplace. |
| Penetration pricing | Pricing strategy aiming to achieve high market share through setting the price of a product or a service initially low. Companies that utilize this pricing strategy assume that customers will switch to the new product because of the lower price. |
| Cost-plus pricing | Cost-plus pricing, sometimes called *gross margin pricing*, is a widely used pricing method because of its simplicity. Managers calculate the cost of producing and delivering a product or a service and add on a percentage (profit) to that price to determine the selling price. |
| Price bundling | The marketer groups a set of products and services for a hospitality or tourism experience such as a vacation or a weekend package and charges a total price that is lower than if those products and services were sold separately. |
| Competitor price matching | Matching the prices of competitors or determining prices based on the prices of market leaders. |
| Marginal cost pricing | The practice of setting the price of a product or service at or slightly above the variable cost to produce it. The final price covers the variable cost and some of the fixed cost. This pricing strategy is justified on the grounds that even a small contribution to fixed cost is better than none since fixed cost will continue to be incurred regardless of the product or service is sold or not. |

quality promised was not genuine. Price also plays an important role in establishing customers' perceptions of a company's or brand's position in the marketplace. Over time, brands often become associated with particular price-points, which serve as reference points in the consumers' perception of that brand.

Although price is the easiest variable to change in the marketing mix, it is also considered the most complex and the least understood variable. In simple terms, price refers to the amount of money that must be paid to acquire or consume a given product or a service. Pricing refers to the decision-making process that establishes the price-point for a product or service. While businesses can utilize a number of pricing strategies to determine prices, the price that is determined during the pricing process is what the customer expects to pay for that product or service.

While the price of a product or a service is expressed in monetary terms, customers make their buying decision based on their assessment of the overall value of and benefits offered by a product or service compared to the financial sacrifice they make to acquire or consume that product or service. In other words, what customers are really interested in is the value, not price. Customer value refers to the customer's assessment of whether the product or service is worth the costs they expect to incur (money, time and effort) for the benefits to be enjoyed (accommodation, food and beverage, service, entertainment, atmosphere and experience). If the cost increases without enhancing the benefits for the customer, then the customer's perception of the value is likely to decrease, which may motivate the customer to purchase a competing product or service that offers a better value.

An important distinction to recognize is that consumers' perception of worth of is strongly linked to their perception of the value/benefits offered by the product or service. For example, the price a customer is willing to pay for dinner at a luxury gourmet restaurant may be at the top end of most consumers' affordability, whilst the price the same customer is willing to pay for a self-service meal, often a convenience purchase, can be at a much lower and affordable price point. Consumers form expectations of what they will have to pay for a gourmet meal and compare competing gourmet restaurant price/product offers. Equally, consumers choosing a self-service restaurant have expectations of what they will have to pay for a self-service meal and compare competing self-service price/product offers.

Consumers tend not to compare the value/price offer between *different* product concepts, whereas they do compare the value/price offer within the *same and adjacent* product classes. In most cases, branded hospitality products can charge a higher price than non-branded products because the regional, national or international brand image provides consumers with a stronger guarantee of service standards than a mom-and-pop or independent business.

## Factors influencing pricing decisions

Factors that influence price decisions can be sorted into two major categories:

1 *external environmental factors* over which companies have little or no control
2 *internal factors* over which companies have a considerable amount of control.

These factors have major influences on pricing decisions.

### External factors

The outer circle of Figure 7.1 mentions five of the external environmental variables that impact pricing decisions – demand and the economy, inflation, industry structure, competition and legal/regulatory factors.

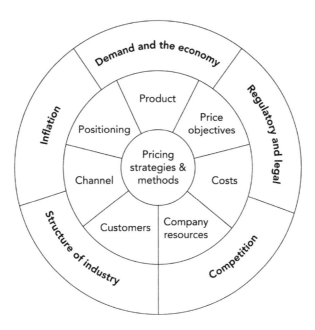

Figure 7.1 Factors that influence pricing decisions

## Demand and the economy

We discussed the importance of macro-economic factors as part of the generic PESTE environment for hospitality services in Chapter 1. In this section, we will review economy and demand-related factors that can influence pricing decisions. These include price elasticity, business and consumer confidence, inflation, exchange rate, as well as the influence of the micro-environment on pricing decisions.

### PRICE ELASTICITY OF DEMAND

Price elasticity of demand is a measurement of the change in demand for a product or service in relation to a change in its price. Price elasticity helps us identify how price sensitive the market is since it tells us the degree to which demand changes based on the changes in the price of a product or service. Price elasticity of demand for a product or service is calculated by dividing percentage change in quantity demanded by percentage change in price.

*Price Elasticity of Demand = % Change in Quantity Demanded/% Change in Price*

Price inelasticity is when a reduction in price does not lift or increase demand for the product or an increase in price does not drop demand. For example, if a hotel increases the room rate by 10 per cent and demand decreases by 5 per cent as a result, then demand is said to be price-inelastic. In other words, the market is not price sensitive. On the other hand, if a 10 per cent increase in room rates results in a 15 per cent decrease in demand, then the demand is price-elastic, meaning that the market is price sensitive. In hospitality, the business traveller segment is traditionally considered to be less price sensitive than leisure travellers since business travellers' expenses are paid by their employer. Thus, demand from the business travellers segment tends to be relatively price-inelastic, whereas demand from leisure travellers is more price-elastic because they are making discretionary, after-tax, purchases they pay for themselves.

---

### ACTIVITY 7.1

Compare the online prices of two different product concepts in the same hospitality sector, for example, compare:

- Dining out – a quick service restaurant and a luxury restaurant
- Accommodation – a budget hotel and a luxury hotel.

Evaluate, from your own perspective as a consumer, the value/price offer between *different* product classes in the same hospitality sector.

Then compare the online prices of two competing hospitality offers in the *same* product class. For example, compare:

- Two quick service restaurants
- Two luxury restaurants
- Two budget hotels
- Two luxury hotels.

Evaluate, from your own perspective as a consumer, the value/price offer for direct competitors in the *same* product class.

---

#### BUSINESS AND CONSUMER CONFIDENCE

We have already discussed the typical hotel industry cycle (see Chapter 1). During periods of economic growth, there is rising confidence and less price sensitivity from businesses and consumers. This means that there is less resistance to price increases. However, during economic downturns or recessions, business and consumer confidence declines significantly reducing demand. Both corporate and individual consumers become much more price sensitive and there is resistance to price increases – indeed, customers may expect price discounts. When business and consumer confidence is higher, businesses' and consumers' tolerance of price increases also rises.

#### INFLATION

Inflation is the rise in the price of goods and services, measured over a period of time. There are several ways in which inflation is reported. There is the overall inflation rate in a country (across a basket of goods and services) as well as various inflation rates for different classes of goods and services. For example, the energy inflation rate and food inflation rate can fluctuate according to supply and demand throughout the year. Also, different countries have different rates of inflation – less developed countries generally experience a higher rate of inflation than more developed countries. A country's domestic inflation rate impacts on the entire national economy and affects businesses and consumers. Companies must factor the rate of inflation into their pricing strategies.

## Exchange rates

An exchange rate is the value of a unit of a nation's currency in terms of another nation's currency, for example, the value of an American dollar in euros. Exchange rate fluctuations present unique pricing difficulties for hospitality operators catering to international travellers. This is especially true if contracts are negotiated in advance of costs being incurred. The price negotiated today must recover costs incurred at some future point in time, as well as return a profit to the service provider. If those costs are subject to exchange rate fluctuation pressures, the negotiated price has to reflect this. Factoring exchange rate fluctuations into the pricing contract, with possible surcharges if the rate moves unfavourably against the hospitality offer, is essential – but often unpopular with customers.

## Micro-environment

Demand for hospitality businesses is often dependent on the local characteristics of the area where the business is located such as the number, scale and buoyancy of local manufacturing and service industries; the image of the area and appeal of local tourism amenities; proximity to major tourist source markets and accessibility; and the density, wealth and purchasing power of the local population. All these factors will influence both franchised and independent hospitality businesses within the area. Popular destinations can charge higher prices and less popular destinations use lower pricing strategies to attract price-sensitive markets.

## Type and structure of industry

Structural factors that influence the pricing dynamics in hospitality include the cost structure, number of players and capacity of the industry.

## Cost structure

Different hospitality sectors have different cost structures, which impact their pricing strategies. A five-star luxury hotel requires a high capital and operating investment in the building, decor, facilities and staffing ratios compared with budget hotels which are constructed with very standardized facilities and rooms, in secondary locations, offering minimal staffing levels and no or few ancillary facilities. The pricing strategies of a five-star hotel must reflect the higher capital investment and operating costs, whereas the pricing strategies of a budget hotel should reflect the relatively lower capital investment and operating costs. Furthermore, sourcing of materials, and produce in remote destinations can also increase the cost structure – for example, hotels in the Seychelles have to air-freight some of the materials and produce that are not available locally in the island, increasing capital and operating costs significantly.

## Number and size of players

If the industry is highly concentrated and dominated by a small number of very large players, the industry's overall profitability is dependent on competitive and pricing strategies utilized by those players. If any of those large players decides to compete using price to gain market share, other players may respond with a similar strategy, which can result in a price war. This price war can force all players to cut their prices to prevent a loss of market share, leading to erosion of the sector's profitability. Thus, companies generally prefer to compete on product or other forms of differentiation rather than price. The rivalry between McDonald's and Burger King in the QSR industry is primarily based on product differentiation and not on price. When there are many players, and no firms are dominant, the opportunity for players to adopt different pricing strategies is greater.

## CAPACITY

The ability of suppliers in an industry to match levels of customer demand has a major influence on price. In the lodging industry supply is restricted and cannot be increased quickly, so firms can charge higher prices when the demand increases. While hotels can charge higher prices during peak seasons when demand is high, they suffer from intense price competition during off peak seasons when the demand is low and there is excess capacity. Because of the relatively low start-up costs, the restaurant industry can easily suffer from excess capacity if there are too many new restaurants in an area and become intensely price competitive.

## COMPETITION

In Chapter 4, we discussed the 'five forces' model driving industry profitability. If the conditions in the five forces are benign, businesses have more flexibility to lift prices, building the sector's profitability. However, if the competitive environment is fierce and the intensity of rivalry is bitter, industry pricing strategies can adversely affect profitability.

### Legal/regulatory

National, regional and local government taxation, health and safety and other regulations influence the prices charged by the hospitality industry and influence consumer behaviour. Examples include value-added tax (VAT), goods and services tax (GST), sales tax, airline passenger taxes, tourist taxes levied in the form of charges on occupied bedrooms and excise duties imposed on alcoholic beverages. Since each government sets its own taxation regime, companies must be aware of their tax obligations in the locations they serve. For example, in France the value-added tax (VAT) for hotels and restaurants is set at 10 per cent, whilst in the UK it is 20 per cent.

Local laws and regulation may also increase the costs of running a business. Hospitality companies are required to comply with local and/or national minimum wage, employee benefits, health and safety laws and regulations in cities and countries they operate. These laws and regulations can have significant impact on the costs of running a business, which may force businesses to charge higher prices to recover the costs of complying with these regulations. For example, the costs of hospitality operators in Mediterranean countries that are members of the European Union have been increasing significantly in recent years due to the European Commission legislations and the euro exchange rate compared to hospitality operators located in Turkey, which is not in the European Union. As a result, Turkish hospitality operators have gained significant price advantages over operators in the European Union.

### Internal factors

The inner circle in Figure 7.1 shows seven internal factors that affect the pricing decision: pricing objectives, costs, company resources, positioning, customers, product, and distribution channels.

## PRICING OBJECTIVES

Companies need to be clear what they are trying to achieve when they set prices; in other words, they need to have clear pricing objectives. A company that is trying to build market share is likely to set very different prices from a company that is trying to achieve a specific profit target. A low price relative to competitors is generally necessary to grow market share; however, this strategy can fail to generate a profit at the end of the financial year. Several pricing strategies can be utilized to accomplish different types of pricing objectives. Those pricing strategies can be profit-oriented, cost-oriented, sales- and marketing-oriented, and competitor-oriented.

### PROFIT-ORIENTATED PRICING STRATEGIES

Most commercial hospitality organizations assess their financial performance against pre-determined profit objectives. An example of a typical profit-orientated pricing objective is 'To achieve a 20 per cent return on investment, per annum, over a five-year period'. Profit-orientated pricing strategies focus on the company's profit expectations and may stress survival, a target return on investment (ROI), optimal current profit, harvesting or skimming.

- *Survival*: A company fighting for survival – for example, during a recession – adopts short-term low prices, designed to attract price-sensitive customers. Sometimes these low prices may not even cover the full cost of the product (fixed cost and variable cost); they may only cover the variable costs and a small portion of the fixed costs. In these situations, companies can use *marginal cost pricing*. The marginal cost is the change in total cost that comes from making or producing one additional unit. In other terms, the marginal cost is the variable cost incurred from making an additional sale – for example, selling an additional room. If a room is unoccupied, there is no marginal cost (variable cost) incurred; if the room is occupied at any rate above the marginal cost, there is a contribution to fixed costs. Thus, marginal cost pricing refers to the practice of setting the price of a product at or slightly above the variable cost to produce it. Marginal cost pricing is justified on the grounds that even a small contribution to fixed costs is better than none since fixed costs will continue to be incurred regardless of the product being sold or not. Covering the variable cost and a small portion of the fixed cost can lower the total amount of loss, which can have significant impact on the bottom line. While this pricing strategy might be beneficial in short-term use, this pricing strategy could have serious consequences if it is used long term.
- *Target return on investment (ROI)*: The selected ROI depends on the type, scale and risk of the investment, the weighted average cost of capital, the forecasted rate of inflation and the company's minimum ROI requirement. Generally, the greater the risk and the costlier the capital (e.g., high interest paid on borrowings), the higher is the target ROI. Prices are calculated to ensure that the target ROI is achieved.
- *Optimal current profit*: Leading players in mature markets generally seek to optimize their profit by setting prices that are consistent with maintaining market share. In mature markets where there is little growth, it is difficult to lift prices, not only because customers have well-established price expectations but also because competitors may fail to follow, because they want to secure a price advantage.
- *Harvesting*: In the late maturity or decline stage of the product life cycle, businesses can 'milk' the remaining revenue stream from a well-established product with a view to investing the cash generated in a newer venture that has greater growth potential. The goal is to maintain a reasonable level of profit as long as possible, by focusing on less price-sensitive customers whilst exiting price-sensitive segments and reducing marketing expense.

- *Skimming*: Skimming involves setting high prices when a new product is introduced and then gradually lowering the price as more competitors enter the market. The objective of price skimming is to maximize profit in the short-term. Price skimming is rare in hospitality, because most companies operate in over-supplied markets with well-established price bands. However, in certain situations like corporate hospitality and at exclusive events (such as during a football weekend in a college town or prestigious sporting events in iconic venues – Wimbledon, for example), a high-price skimming strategy is feasible. Even well-known quick service restaurants have been known to hike prices to patrons attending concerts and sporting events in closed arenas. New product concepts that have little competition are better placed to price-skim, because customers are often prepared to pay a premium price for the new experience. Price-skimming tends to disappear when competitors enter the market.

Profit-orientated pricing objectives are compatible with conventional management performance targets but may fail to take into account the external environment, competitor and customer factors.

## Cost-orientated pricing strategies

Cost-oriented pricing strategies are typically used in catering and food and beverage operations, where the management will set target food/bar cost percentages or profit margins. A typical cost-orientated pricing strategy would be 'to achieve a food operating cost of 30 per cent during the financial period from April to September'. Although cost-orientated strategies are widely used in hospitality operations, they fail to consider external competitor and customer factors.

## Sales- and marketing-orientated pricing strategies

When a company adopts a sales- or marketing-oriented pricing strategy, its goal is usually to achieve a specific sales volume (e.g., number of room-nights), revenue or market share. A typical pricing objective would be 'to achieve $2 million sales within two years' or 'to grow market share from 12 per cent to 15 per cent over three years'. Sales- and marketing-related pricing strategies do vary. They may focus on maximizing sales revenues, targeted sales volumes, achieving market share or building consumer trial. Sales- and marketing-oriented pricing strategies include the following:

- *Maximize sales revenues*: Firms with well-defined, highly differentiated offerings may be able to maximize sales revenue by managing prices upwards over time. For this to be possible, the business must have strong and price-inelastic demand. Firms that are not market leaders and that do not have well-defined, highly differentiated offerings may flex prices downwards or introduce short-term price promotions to increase sales revenues by attracting new customers. However, this strategy may not be very effective in the long term since customers who are attracted to low prices are likely to be price-sensitive, deal seeking customers who may not be loyal to any brand. They may swich providers based on the price of the products or services.
- *Targeted sales volume*: Some hospitality managers set prices that enable them to achieve specific sales volume targets, such as room-nights or occupancy levels. Key intermediaries, such as major tour companies, booking agents and high-volume customers, often negotiate significant discounts from larger hotel companies for a guaranteed sales volume. This negotia-

tion can be one of the most crucial pricing decisions affecting the hotel's profitability for that period.

● *Market share*: Companies that aim to expand their market share may offer lower prices to attract new customers. Hospitality firms that operate in mature markets (e.g., quick service restaurants) can also offer lower prices to maintain and expand their market share. In mature markets, companies can only grow their market share by stealing (winning) their competitors' customers. They may set prices to secure market share growth.

● *Building consumer trial*: Hospitality businesses that aim to enter a new market such as newly opened hotels, resorts and restaurants/bars, or businesses that develop a new product or a service, may utilize a penetration pricing strategy. The pricing objective here is to build sales quickly by offering special lower prices to motivate non-users to try the product or service through lowering the financial risk associated with trial. Unless the location and offer are unique, this is normally achieved by convincing non-users to try the product or service or by attracting competitors' customers.

## COMPETITOR-ORIENTATED PRICING STRATEGIES

It is easy for hospitality companies to find out competitors' prices through a simple online search. Competitors' prices establish a benchmark and price range for players in the same and neighbouring product classes. When market leaders change price, market followers will simply move their prices up or down in line with them to maintain the same price differential as before. The problem with this 'me-too', follow-the-leader strategy is that the cost base of competitors might be very different, and the strategy does not take into account what customers might be prepared to pay.

Whatever the pricing objective, marketers will want to have a say in the final decision. Marketing-orientated organizations try to understand how price influences customers' perception of, and response to, their product offer, and take into account the customer's perspective, asking 'What would our targeted customers be prepared to pay?'

Market leaders in high-quality hospitality markets, such as luxury hotels, gourmet restaurants, first-class travel providers and luxury cruise ships, know that customers expect to pay a high price. They therefore adopt a 'prestige' or premium pricing strategy (i.e., to charge high prices that reflect the top-quality service) and ensure that the customer perception of their service matches the premium prices charged. Hospitality operators striving to offer the 'best value for money' in a given product class will monitor customers' perceptions of their hospitality offer, and scan competitors' prices to ensure that their offer delivers the best perceived value for money.

Organizations often have longer-term strategic price objectives (e.g., build market share next year) and shorter-term tactical price objectives (e.g., fill rooms next week); however, pricing objectives need to be consistent with the other elements of the marketing mix. You cannot have a low price when the product strategy focuses on delivery of a high-quality customer experience, in a costly physical environment.

In some instances, overall corporate objectives very clearly dictate pricing strategies. A corporate objective for a company having financial difficulties might be to maximize cash flow in the short term. This would lead to a pricing strategy of maximizing revenue, regardless of the type or suitability of the sales generated and the possibility that profit may not be generated. Prices would flex accordingly.

## Costs

Another major internal factor influencing the price decision is the cost of producing and marketing the product. There are many types of cost. *Fixed costs* do not vary with sales volume – examples include rent, property taxes, salaries of permanent staff, insurance and depreciation. The key feature of fixed costs, given the seasonality of hospitality products, is that they do not vary and must be paid on a regular monthly, quarterly or annual basis. *Variable costs* vary in proportion to sales – examples include food and beverage purchases, and laundry services. *Semi-fixed costs* vary with, but not in proportion to, sales volume – examples include energy costs (light, heat, air conditioning) and wages of casual employees.

In hospitality businesses, a high proportion of costs are fixed or semi-fixed. This is partly due to the high level of capital invested in buildings, equipment and refurbishment. Although the total capital investment is usually smaller in catering establishments, the predominance of fixed costs is similar.

There are several difficulties associated with the incorporation of cost considerations into pricing decisions. Cost-based pricing techniques are essentially retrospective – that is, prices tend to be based on costs that are known because they have already been incurred. Yet, companies need to recover future costs, which may be quite different. Whatever prices are set they must eventually recover the long-term total costs of being in business.

There is a critical relationship between costs, volume (the number of customers) and profit. Typically, but not always, lower cost operations are associated with higher volumes and lower prices, and higher cost operations with lower volumes at higher prices. Marketers need to be aware of the cost structure of their business and products, and the number of customers required to achieve target profits.

## Company resources

The size and financial assets of a company also influence the pricing decision. International hospitality companies operating strong brands in many countries have easy access to a variety of capital markets and usually develop a strong resource base. They enjoy economies of scale and better purchasing arrangements, which reduce operating costs and improve profitability. Larger companies have more business experience and can afford to experiment with different pricing strategies in selected outlets. They can also tolerate short-term losses during the launch of a new product concept and, if the product concept fails, they can afford to write the investment off and learn from the experience. Single-unit, privately owned operations do not have significant financial resources, and a single pricing error can seriously (perhaps even fatally) damage a small business.

## Positioning

Prices must accurately reflect the business's desired market position, be consistent across the range of products offered and match the target market's expectation of quality and value. There is a close relationship between price and customers' perception of quality. Experienced customers are quick to note a mismatch. Price not only has to cover costs and generate profits but also reflect the quality position that a brand wishes to occupy in consumers' minds. Price should be consistent with the quality of the product or service offered. In planning new hospitality concepts, the price target markets are willing to pay is a key determinant in the sales volume/cost/profit relationship and helps to shape the product format. New hospitality offerings are often designed to match a preconceived price-point.

## DISTRIBUTION CHANNELS

When setting prices, hospitality operators must understand their channels of distribution and factor in the costs of their online and/or offline intermediaries. Traditionally, hospitality products have been distributed both direct-to-customer and through intermediaries such as bricks-and-mortar and online travel agencies, global distribution systems (GDS), chain reservation systems, hotels' 800 numbers, hotels' sales departments, tour operators and online intermediaries such as Booking.com and trivago. These channels can be grouped under three main distribution models in hospitality and tourism: the 'direct selling' model, the 'agency' model and the 'merchant' model. In the direct selling model, the hospitality company sells its products through its website, marketing and sales department, chain reservation system and 800 number. The direct distribution method has seen significant growth over the last decade due to advances in online information communication technologies and its cost advantages. In the agency model, the hospitality company pays a travel agent or an online intermediary a fixed commission for each booking. The minimum commission paid to travel agents is 8 per cent and the norm varies between 10 and 15 per cent, though on certain products (e.g., weekend leisure breaks, special events, etc.) the commission can increase to more than 25 per cent. In the merchant (or wholesaler) model, the intermediary negotiates an allocation of inventory (cabins, rooms, seats) at an agreed rate from the hospitality operator. The discounts for a contract can vary from 15 to 65 per cent off rack rate. Within the contract, there will be a rate parity agreement that prevents the wholesaler from selling the hotel rooms below the same price as the hotel. Rate parity is designed to ensure that all the hotel's distribution channels offer potential customers the same rate for the same product and can offer a 'best rate guarantee'. The merchant/wholesaler then charges customers whatever price they can achieve. If the merchant/wholesaler bundles several components of a vacation/activity into one 'package', then the actual hospitality rate is not public – this is often called opaque pricing and enables the wholesaler to bypass the rate parity agreement. When the merchant is left with unwanted inventory, it can be offloaded online at very low prices using opaque pricing techniques, which might then damage the image and credibility of the hospitality brand.

The transaction charges of online distribution and reservation systems, credit cards and buy-now-pay-later payments incur additional costs, which the business must cover. Credit card commissions can vary from less than 1 per cent for major international companies to over 5 per cent for smaller operators. From a pricing perspective, marketers must understand their distribution costs to ensure that the prices charged do generate a contribution to profit or fixed costs after all distribution costs are met. You can read more about channels of distribution in Chapter 8.

## CUSTOMERS

In Chapter 3, we discussed how hospitality companies may target several different market segments at the same time. Each of the different segments has different price-points – for example, the business traveller segment normally commands a significantly higher price than tour groups. Managing the pricing and volume mix between various segments is critical to achieving target revenue and profits (see Activity 7.2).

Another issue in pricing from a consumer perspective is consideration of customers' response to pricing and value. Customers not only judge the appropriateness of the total bill against their perception of the overall value of the hospitality experience, but they may also judge specific charges for specific products or services. High drink prices or wi-fi charges can generate dissatisfaction, even when the overall bill is regarded favourably.

As part of an effective positioning strategy, business must be aware of the dangers of mixing incompatible market segments. In attempting to maximize sales, hospitality marketers' use of discounted prices can attract and encourage the 'wrong' type of customers. This is especially evident when luxury hotels offer deeply discounted prices through third party online distributors like lastminute.com and attract customers who might not 'fit' with other customers. While the discounted prices paid by those customers may cover variable costs and contribute to fixed costs, reducing profit erosion, incompatibility of those segments with the regular segments may negatively influence the satisfaction level of regular customers who pay higher prices. In the long term, this strategy may lower customers' perception of the value of the hospitality experience offered.

## PRODUCT

Characteristics of the hospitality product that influence pricing strategy include the product class, the stage in the product life cycle, the production and delivery process, and the qualifications, experience and reputation of the people who create and deliver the product or service. Different classes of hospitality products that are sold within different price bands to different target market segments determine the upper and lower price limits for every hospitality business. When a menu item requires a significant amount of prep time and expertise, these costs must be passed on to customers in the form of higher prices. Hospitality companies may experience more freedom in setting prices during the introductory period of a new product's life cycle. If the new product is significantly differentiated from other offerings, the marketer has greater freedom to set a higher price to recover costs of development and launch. Innovators and early adopters (customers who are amongst the first to buy a new-to-market offering) are often prepared to pay more to experience something new and different. As more competition enters the market, prices may fall.

Table 7.3 provides several examples of the pricing objectives, strategies and tactics utilized in a range of hospitality sectors.

---

### ACTIVITY 7.2

Table 7.2 presents the hypothetical operating statistics for a 200-bedroom downtown hotel for June (30 days) using segment, volume mix and rate. The hotel achieved 80 per cent occupancy (4,800 rooms sold of a possible 6,000 rooms), with variable average daily room rates (ADR) for each segment. What actions should the hotel take to improve sales revenue?

---

Table 7.2 Hypothetical operating statistics for a 200-bedroom downtown hotel for June (30 days)

| Segment | Rooms sold | Mix % | ADR | Total revenue |
|---|---|---|---|---|
| Transient travellers | 480 | 10 | 240 | 115,200 |
| Local business | 960 | 20 | 190 | 182,400 |
| Corporate negotiated | 960 | 20 | 180 | 172,800 |
| Conference | 480 | 10 | 180 | 86,400 |
| Leisure break couples/individuals | 480 | 10 | 160 | 76,800 |
| Leisure tour group | 1,440 | 30 | 80 | 115,200 |
| Total | 4,800 | 100 | 175.50 | 748,800 |

Table 7.3 Examples of hospitality price objectives, strategies and tactics

| Price objective category | Hospitality product | Price objective | Price strategy | Price method and pricing tactics |
|---|---|---|---|---|
| Customer: prestige | Five-star international luxury hotel | To charge the premium price for the highest product quality in order to maintain a prestige price positioning; offer for the next five years | • Monitor customers' perceptions of the luxury product offer<br>• Monitor online review comments and social media sites<br>• Monitor local and international competitors' product/service/ price offer<br>• Introduce innovations and constantly refurbish the property to maintain the product quality, whilst always charging premium prices | • Carry out regular customer and consumer marketing research via focus groups to establish whether the luxury product offer justifies the premium price position<br>• Check online non-promotional prices for luxury competitor set<br>• Visit new-build and recently refurbished competitors; evaluate innovations and develop detailed plans to improve product/service constantly |
| Customer: trial purchase | Health and leisure club | • To set a special offer price that will encourage 100 trial purchases of club membership in March | • Research existing and potential club members' attitudes to price sensitivity towards health and leisure clubs to identify price points<br>• Monitor and analyze online review comments posted by existing and potential club members and competitors' members to review sites and social media sites. | • Identify most cost-effective method of reaching members<br>• Draft online questionnaire and run pilot study; adapt questionnaire and carry out main study<br>• Analyze results and set special price offer; test price offer and promotional material with focus groups<br>• Fix price of special offer and launch promotion; monitor results of promotion |
| Financial: volume | International 500-bedroom four-star gateway hotel | • To win a 60-room-per night contract for six months from October to March, | • Research current and potential demand for aircrew room-nights<br>• Research existing and potential hotel supply to major airlines | • Identify major airline operators and the number of flights requiring overnight stopovers for crew, number of crew per flight, length of stopover |

*(Continued)*

Table 7.3 Continued

| Price objective category | Hospitality product | Price objective | Price strategy | Price method and pricing tactics |
|---|---|---|---|---|
| | | from a major airline company, at a rate of $100 per room per night | • Evaluate contract aircrew room rates<br>• Develop a strong relationship with the airline's personnel | • Visit competitor hotels to establish which competitors are catering for which airlines<br>• Establish competitor rates and estimate discount offered to airline companies<br>• Prepare discount rate and confirm with general manager<br>• Contact airline purchasing departments and request opportunity to quote for business<br>• Negotiate competitive market-orientated rates |
| Financial: sales target | 60-bedroom pro-vincial midmarket city hotel | • To increase room sales revenue by 2 per cent above inflation for the 12-month period from October to September | • Scan online and offline environ-ment for potential increases in inflation, consumer demand and hotel room supply during the next 18 months<br>• Review historic and current trad-ing performance<br>• Set price increases | • Carry out detailed research in local and national economy to evaluate forecast industry and general inflation<br>• Identify potential market demand dur-ing period, including seasonal variations<br>• Research competitor prices and any additional accommodation supply<br>• Identify volume (number of bed-nights) and value (achieved room rate) of each market segment<br>• Set room rates to guarantee 2 per cent plus inflation increase across total room revenue |
| Financial: cost-led | Nightclub bar and restaurant | • To achieve a bar cost of 35 per cent for the next finan-cial year | • Utilize a computerized stock-control system to set and moni-tor bar and food costs and | • Carry out a monthly bar and food computerized stock check on all items purchased and selling prices |

| | | | |
|---|---|---|---|
| | • To achieve a food cost of 30 per cent for the next financial year | prices to ensure that the target is achieved | • Monitor the sales mix and ensure that high-volume food and drink products are achieving their required target profit margin |
| Competitor: price followership | Three-star resort hotel | • To undercut the midmarket price leader by 10 per cent on all bedroom rates during the high season | • Monitor competitor price movements and adjust room prices accordingly | • Scan competitor hotels' online offers on a daily basis to check on current room rates<br>• Adapt own hotel's prices accordingly |

## Pricing strategies for leaders, followers and new entrants

Having established the price objectives, hospitality companies need to consider their pricing strategies, which should be linked to the quality standards offered by the operation. The examples below refer to the room-rate strategies hotels can use in certain contexts, but the principles are applicable to all hospitality businesses. In hotels, consumers often associate quality standards with star ratings and there are strong linkages between perceptions of quality and price; these perceptions can be reinforced or challenged by the impact of online reviews – positive reviews can enhance customers' perception of the value of the offer by reinforcing the quality/price relationship, whilst negative reviews can create doubt about the value of the offer. Different pricing strategies are used by market leaders, market followers and new entrants to the market.

### Market leader strategies

Well-established companies with a loyal customer base, a strong brand and high levels of repeat business can adopt *market leader strategies*, where the prices are aligned with the brand's quality positioning. These strategies are suitable for:

- The most exclusive, luxurious, five-star hotels in the world; they deliver the highest quality customer experience and can justify charging premium or prestige prices; prestige pricing appeals to status conscious customers who are normally affluent and enjoy conspicuous consumption
- Traditional midmarket, well-maintained hotels in good locations offering appropriate value for money and competing effectively with a midmarket pricing strategy
- Economy and budget hotels/motels charging relatively low prices for a product offering fewer facilities and delivering value for money.

### Market follower and new entrants to the market strategies

New entrants and less-established hotel brands seeking to build market share can use a penetration pricing or a market follower strategy pricing. Penetration pricing is used to attract customers to a new product or service by offering a lower price during its initial offering. The lower price helps a new product or service to attract customers away from competitors. On the other hand, companies that utilize a market follower strategy offer similar quality but pitch prices lower than the market leader to be more competitive, attract customers and grow market share. These strategies are suitable for:

- High-quality deluxe properties seeking to grow market share by exceptional value pricing
- Midmarket hotels competing against more established properties; or aggressive chains and individual properties seeking to increase room occupancy and build market share by offering exceptional value pricing.

#### COMMON PRICING STRATEGY MISTAKES

Unfortunately, some hotels charge prices that cannot be justified by the quality of products and services they offer. Some of these hotels might have myopic management that unknowingly has allowed their offering to become overpriced. As customers recognize the poor value-for-money, the reputation of the business will rightly suffer. Considering that a large portion of travellers read review comments posted by other travellers before making their booking decisions, the poor value-for-money perception will spread rapidly through review sites and social media posts. Either the company will have to adopt a more appropriate balanced strategy or be forced into either selling or liquidating the business. Examples include the following:

- Old-established, grand three-/four-star hotels that are no longer as luxurious as they used to be and whose facilities no longer match the price charged; these properties are trading on an historic image; as they gradually decline owners will eventually either have to reinvest in their facilities or reduce their prices
- Once glorious now shabby hotels, possibly in good locations, which only generate passing trade but charge high prices; this rip-off value will lead to a poor reputation, and limited – if any – repeat and recommended business
- Midmarket hotels with falling standards but still maintaining a medium pricing strategy, which does not represent value for money
- Budget operations that have gradually increased prices to pay for 'amenity creep'.

Finally, some hotels make the mistake of charging prices that are too low for the quality of products and services they offer. Sometimes, the price they charge may not be able to cover the fixed and variable cost of the product or service offered, which can jeopardize the sustainability of the business:

- High-quality four-/five-star properties charging relatively low, year-round prices due to a decline in the destination's popularity
- Midmarket hotels operating in highly competitive environments and offering budget hotel prices without reducing product/service quality standards
- Hotels that do not manage their cost-base effectively, and do not respond quickly enough to inflationary changes in the external environment.

Companies need to adopt pricing strategies that take into account demand patterns and their quality relative to their competition. There are several companies, such as Booking Expert, MonitorHotels, OTAInsight and eRevMax, who provide price-monitoring services against selected competitors and offer tools and services that can be used to update room rates across online multiple distribution channels in a timely manner.

## Pricing methods

We now briefly review how prices could be set – and sometimes are – in the hospitality industry using a generic marketing-led pricing model.[1] This marketing-led pricing process takes into account pricing objectives, costs, competitors' prices, expectations of channel members and customer willingness to pay. The eight steps in this process are as follows:

1 Determine pricing objectives.
2 Assess the target market's willingness to pay, and their perception of the value of the product offer.
3 Estimate the potential demand.

4 Analyze the demand, cost, volume, price and profit relationships; businesses need to understand their own fixed and variable costs, and factor in distribution costs.

5 Research competitors' price/product offers.

6 Select a pricing strategy. A new entrant can either utilize a penetration pricing or a market skimming pricing strategy depending on the pricing objective.

7 Select appropriate pricing methods (see next).

8 Set specific prices for rooms, food, beverages, conference, and leisure products, and for product bundles.

While companies can utilize any of the pricing approaches described earlier in the chapter, many times they simply determine prices based on costs or competitors' prices. These are known as cost-plus pricing, and competitor-led pricing methods. Here is a summary of the main features of each pricing method.

- *Cost-plus pricing*: Cost-plus pricing is the simplest pricing method. The company calculates the cost of producing and delivering a product or a service and adds on a percentage (profit) to that price to determine the selling price. Sometimes, cost-plus pricing is used to establish the lowest price that a company can charge to remain viable. While this approach ensures a certain percentage of profit, it fails to consider customers and competitors.

- *Competitor-led pricing*: The pricing decision-maker focuses on competitors' prices to establish prices. Companies can price their products and services above or below competitors depending on their objectives and their ability to deliver product or services better than competitors. While companies that have a clear advantage on some non-price components of the marketing mix can price their products or services above competition, companies that aim to gain market share or introduce a new product or a service can charge prices that are below the competitors' prices. While this pricing strategy factors in competitors' prices, it fails to consider customers' willingness to pay, return on investment goals and company costs.

Clearly, marketing-oriented pricing approaches require a considerable amount of consumer, competitor and internal company research and insight. This may present no problems for the major hospitality corporations. However, managers of smaller hospitality companies often adopt a much simpler approach to setting prices, based on a combination of historical factors and the current economic situation. Their approach to setting prices might be as follows:

1 Review last season/year's prices and business performance.

2 Review current and potential cost increases.

3 Consider the general economic situation and factors likely to influence customers' responses to prices.

4 Check competitors' current prices.

5 Set prices by adding a percentage (e.g., 5 per cent on the tariff of each room price) or a fixed amount (add $1 to each à la carte menu item) on to the current prices.

6 Flex prices on the business's website according to need.

Although this process has its own flaws, managers of smaller businesses often set prices using the historic price, plus or minus an additional sum or percentage, because it is simple and easy to adopt.

## Dynamic pricing and revenue management

Dynamic pricing is a flexible pricing approach that allows companies to adjust the prices of identical goods and services based on the availability of those goods and services, forecasted demand levels and customers' willingness to pay. Dynamic pricing is an important component of revenue management. Revenue management involves predicting consumer behaviour and optimizing product supply and pricing in order to maximize total revenues. Revenue management requires an intimate understanding of the price sensitivity of consumers. Methods implemented to maximize total revenue can include product bundling or packaging, variable pricing, discounting, dynamic pricing and yield management.

Maximization of revenues requires price discrimination and is widely used by the airline and lodging industries. Dynamic pricing flexes prices to match forecasted demand with available capacity. Prices change according to the probability of selling the last rooms in a given period and are influenced by the length of time between the date of booking and the date of arrival, customer demand and different customer segments' willingness to pay.

Revenue management systems (RMS) are normally found in large hotels and chain hotels, although some smaller properties can also effectively adopt a revenue management system. A minimum of one year's historic data, including daily occupancy and achieved room rates, is needed – but new hotels, especially chain-managed units, can utilize RMS by aggregating representative data from similar properties. A 200-bedroom hotel might have over 2,000 different prices for different room categories and products inputted into the RMS with a price range from $60 to $600 for the next year.

## CASE STUDY 7.1

### Revenue management at the RLH Corporation, USA[2]

Since its 1959 establishment in the Pacific Northwest of the United States, the Red Lion Hotels Corporation has expanded across the U.S. and Canada with eight unique brands encompassing over 900+ locations. To reflect its growing portfolio of brands beyond its eponymously named Red Lion Hotels chain, the company quietly rebranded itself as RLH Corporation around July 2017.

The challenge for RLH Corporation was no different to what the rest of the hotel industry faced. Since 2000, the evolution of Internet hotel distribution had changed dramatically, with customer acquisition costs rising twice as fast as the rate of revenue, meaning that profitability was shrinking. As meta-search sites like KAYAK, trivago, Google Travel and Tripadvisor evolved, the costs and complexities of digital distribution had increased.

At its core, revenue management combines three core disciplines: segmenting customers, forecasting demand and then pricing to optimize revenue. RLH Corporation, like many players in the hotel industry, had been using an approach common for more than a decade. Best-available-rate (BAR) pricing provided hotels with a more advanced approach compared to the 'gut feel' method of pricing in the pre-Internet era. With a fixed-tier revenue management strategy, hoteliers set the BAR, typically the lowest publicly available price you'd find on the hotel's website, and all other rates are adjusted accordingly – usually based on a percentage difference from the BAR. For example, if the BAR is set at $100 for any given day, the loyalty rate might be 15 per cent less, online travel agent package rate 35 per cent less, and opaque channels like Hotwire might be discounted down to 45 per cent. If the BAR goes up or down, all other rates move in tandem. Clearly the benefit of this methodology is its simplicity, but, as distribution has become more complex, the loss of potential revenue is a major disadvantage.

When Greg Mount took over as CEO of RLH Corporation in 2014, he realized that pricing practices and the way hotels use revenue management to determine room rates were outdated. To address the issue, he came up with a very clear goal: 'We will be known for having the leading technology and being best at e-commerce.' As a result, the RLH Corporation introduced open pricing, a new more dynamic approach to revenue management that enables hoteliers to manage the yield in all segments, distribution channels, offers and room types independently of each other, and without the need to close off an option. On compressed dates, hoteliers using a fixed-tier BAR pricing often have to close channels rather than accept heavily discounted rates with higher commission costs. Open pricing allows hotel owners to evaluate the demand that every single market segment has and then manage the opportunities to maximize revenue within that specific segment across all channels.

By moving beyond just historical booking information and bringing in new third party data like competitive pricing, online reviews and ratings, and web shopping data, RLH Corporation has been able to review demand more discretely and accurately forecast the future across all segments and channels.

Combining better data and open pricing has allowed RLH Corporation to move closer to the key aim of revenue management – 'getting the right price for the right customer at the right time and in the right channel' – and the results have been impressive. The company has seen consecutive quarters of revenue per available room (RevPAR) increases.

For more information about Red Lin Hotels, visit www.redlion.com.

*Source*: Duetto Research[2]

The emergence of online transparent pricing and price comparison websites, coupled with the development of databases and improved analytics, has changed the pricing strategies of medium and larger accommodation businesses. Companies flex their rates using the principles of yield management, which involves strategic control of the available inventory by selling it to the right customer at the right time for the right price through building rate fences such as advance booking requirements or specific day of arrival. This process results in price discrimination, where a firm charges customers consuming otherwise identical goods or services a different price. Utilization of yield management principles enables companies to offer specific rates to each target market segment and distribution channel to maximize revenues. The room rate fluctuates as the revenue management system (RMS) continuously estimates the demand forecast for each segment and each distribution channel and changes the room rate either in real time or on a periodic basis, for example, every six hours. This raises an interesting issue for customers staying several nights when each night has a different room rate. One approach is to give the customer a blended rate that averages the rates for each night of the stay into one single nightly rate. For a two-night stay, with one night quoted at $200 and the second night quoted at $220, then the average nightly rate using a blended approach would be $210. The alternative approach is to provide non-blended rates: the rate for each night of the guest's stay is given to the customer separately. In the preceding example, the first night is quoted at $200 and the second night quoted at $220. Although the overall price of $420 is the same, customers naturally respond to the different approaches in different ways. Currently, there is no accepted hotel industry practice about blended and non-blended rates, so different companies adopt their own strategies (see Activity 7.3).

Companies using the principles of revenue management and yield management continuously adjust room rates for most segments and distribution channels based on the changes in forecasted demand. However, negotiated contract rates such as corporate contract, aircrew and group negotiated rates are usually fixed at a specific rate or are discounted from the best available rate. Hence, if the best available rate for a room tonight is $200 and the agreed corporate rate is a 10 per cent discount, then the rate would be $180.

---

### ACTIVITY 7.3

Log on to the following hotel websites and check the room/price availability for a three-night stay – Sunday, Monday and Tuesday – at one of the branded hotels. Look for the 'Best Available Rate' and see whether the rates are blended or non-blended:

- Marriott International

- Novotel.

Now check the rates for the same days, at the same Marriott International and Novotel, using Expedia.

Compare the different approaches to presenting room price information to customers.

Since rates fluctuate over time, save a copy of these rates and then check the same hotels over a Sunday, Monday and Tuesday in three weeks' time. Compare the rate fluctuations over time.

---

One of the consequences of utilizing the principles of revenue management is overbooking of the rooms, selling more rooms than the hotel possesses during high demand periods. A 100-bedroom hotel may book 105 rooms because its historical data suggest that 5 per cent of customers will cancel at the last moment or not arrive, also called no-show rate. From a customer satisfaction perspective and from a front desk employee perspective, overbooking creates problems when the hotel is full and angry guests are 'walked' (booked into a nearby hotel), a situation that front-line employees do not enjoy having to manage.

Traditionally, hotels have always used *seasonal pricing strategies* to stimulate demand in low or shoulder demand periods. Hotels also set length-of-stay restrictions on the booking to during higher demand periods – for example, hotels can impose a three-night stay requirement during a mega convention. It is very common for hotels located in college towns to charge the highest possible rate and impose minimum length-of-stay requirements during graduation weekends. These restrictions are an example of rate fences because they act as a barrier and protect revenues during high demand periods. However, customers must perceive that the pricing strategy is fair, and any rate fences reasonable. Hotels can experience problems when customers book at one price and then become aware of different rates being offered to other customers – due to different booking conditions.

Dynamic pricing is a pricing mechanism designed to tackle the problems caused by the special characteristics of service industries. Hoteliers have always recognized that it is better to sell a room at a low price tonight rather than have an empty room, because of the low marginal cost to service that room for the guest. Computerized revenue management systems (RMS) can prevent reservation agents from making critical decisions for themselves, because prices available in the property management system are usually determined by the computerized revenue management system using complex algorithms. Although there is an override facility to allow some discretion by the reservations manager, any excessive use of the override facility must be justified. In some chain-owned hotels, the management of properties that use the override facility more than three times per month will be asked to explain why.

In the restaurant industry, managers sometimes use duration management (how long customers spend on the premises) to optimize table turnover and to manage demand during off peak hours by flexing prices with special discounts. Duration management focuses on the period between arrival at a restaurant, being seated, ordering and consuming the meal, paying and leaving the restaurant. Restaurants can increase their revenues and profitability by reducing service inconsistencies within service operations, making processes more efficient, or by upselling and serving more customers during busy periods. Restaurants can also increase demand during off-peak hours by offering special discounts to specific groups such as senior discounts during the off-peak hours before the busy dinner time.

### Transparent online pricing

When consumers search online for a hotel accommodation, they have an enormous choice of websites to explore including hotel branded sites, independent hotel sites, online travel agents, specialist distributors and hotel/travel comparison-shopping sites. Consumers can spend a considerable amount of time searching and comparing different product/price offers on different sites. One category of distributors, aggregators, use meta-search engines to interrogate hotel room rates and availability across hundreds of websites, and then provide the potential customer with online price comparisons of different hotels, based upon their search criteria, on one webpage. Examples of major aggregators include Expedia, Booking.com, Hotels.com and trivago. These sites enable consumers to read customer reviews of each hotel and compare competing product/price offers more easily. This aspect of pricing is described as transparent online pricing – both customers and hoteliers can clearly see the prices and customer reviews. Normally the customer will choose the hotel with the lowest price with the best possible customer reviews that matches their search criteria. This is where they find the greatest value.

## Price promotions

The impact of price promotions needs to be carefully evaluated in the planning stage to protect non-promotional revenue streams and brand image. City hotels offering low price promotions to leisure travellers rate-fence the promotion to prevent business travellers from taking advantage of it, by insisting on pre-booking conditions such as a three-week advance booking requirement. Price-led promotions must also make a reasonable contribution towards fixed costs and justify the cost that goes into their development and operation.

One tactic is to use loss leaders to attract customers. Bars typically have a special drink offer – perhaps half-price on quiet evenings or 'doubles' at a single price during a happy hour promotion. Joint marketing initiatives between hotel chains and media outlets make use of other promotions – one example is 'free accommodation' at selected hotels, which is offered exclusively to the readers of a newspaper, providing the customer pays a minimum price for meals whilst staying in the hotel. 'Two for the price of one' or BOGOF ('buy one, get one free') promotions are popular and effective in promoting hotel and restaurant products during low demand periods.

These price-led promotions help boost sales in quiet periods, but they do have limitations and drawbacks. In principle, the promotion should attract new customers who, having enjoyed the hospitality experience, will be expected to return at other times and pay the normal prices. In practice, many (even most) of the customers who enjoy a promotional price do not return and book at the normal price once the promotion has ended. There is also the danger of cannibalizing customers. This means that loyal customers may take advantage of the price promotion, changing their booking and purchasing habits, and consequently the hotel or restaurant loses prime-rate business and suffers a reduction in sales and profits.

### Price cuts

There is considerable research into the effects on company and industry profitability of aggressive pricing, undercutting prices/rates and price wars.[3,4] Although individual companies that initially undercut prices significantly may gain market share in the short-term, eventually competitors are forced to respond. If a price war ensues, customers begin to expect a lower price-point, reacting unfavourably when companies attempt to increase prices later. The evidence suggests that all companies in an industry involved in a price war lose profitability.[5] Undercutting rates in hospitality can be a natural reaction to excess capacity, but the consequences can be damaging if maintained for a long period. While both consumers and hospitality operators recognize that prices constantly change – both downwards and upwards due to utilization of revenue management systems, dynamic pricing and online transparent pricing, once customers form a price point reference, it is very hard for companies to change that price point reference upwards.

## International pricing

The difficulties in setting a pricing strategy for companies operating in more than one country are compounded by:

- Different currencies and variable exchange rates
- Operating costs differing between countries
- Different types of competitors – global, regional, national branded chains and local independents
- Different stages of the product life cycle in each country
- Different inflation rates
- Ability to repatriate profits, which again varies significantly from country to country.

For companies aiming to promote and protect their hospitality brands by standardizing the product offer, a uniform price for each product and service offered across countries presents problems. Whilst the pricing strategy can be consistent – for example, to adopt a market leader strategy and charge the highest prices in the competitor set – the actual price charged will vary across different countries. In Western countries, all customers regardless of their nationality can afford the same price, but in some countries, like Egypt and India, charging the same price for a product or service may not work due to significant differences in buying power. Thus, it may be necessary to charge a lower price for domestic customers and a higher price for international customers.

## Conclusion

While companies determine the prices for their products and services, customers ultimately decide whether the company is charging the right price for a product or service through their buying behaviour. Although pricing decisions are the easiest element of the marketing mix to change, they remain a complex phenomenon. In this chapter, we have explained that:

- Companies need to be clear about their pricing objectives.
- Price is the only element of marketing mix that does not generate cost; price generates revenue.
- Price, in the absence of other cues, is an indicator of quality and sets customer expectations.
- Price is the summation of all sacrifices made by a consumer in order to experience the benefits of a product.
- Companies have little control over the *external* factors that influence pricing decisions, but considerable control over the *internal* factors that influence pricing decisions.
- Pricing decisions should reflect product positioning.
- Medium and larger accommodation-based businesses use dynamic pricing strategies and revenue management systems to drive sales and revenue.
- Meta-search aggregators provide online price transparency to help potential customers to book a hotel.
- Price-led promotions are extensively used to build revenue in low-demand periods.
- International pricing decisions are subject to local country environmental factors.

Now check your understanding of this chapter by answering the following questions:

1 Why is pricing significant in the pre-encounter hospitality marketing mix?
2 Discuss the external and internal factors that influence pricing decisions. Provide examples from the hospitality industry to illustrate your answer.
3 Evaluate pricing and product quality strategies in three hotel markets.
4 Explain the role of RM in larger hotel chains.
5 Evaluate the role of price promotions in the hospitality industry.
6 Describe how online price transparency can influence the customer's booking decision; provide an example from your own experience.
7 Discuss the pricing issues for a standardized international hotel brand.

## References

1. Kotler, P., & Armstrong, G. (2016). *Principles of Marketing*, 16th ed. Harlow: Pearson Education.
2. Duetto Research [Internet]. *Success Stories*. [cited September 16, 2021]. Available from: www.duettocloud.com/success-stories
3. Ma, W., Wang, Q., Yang, H., & Zhang, Y. (2019). An analysis of price competition and price wars in Australia's domestic airline market. *Transport Policy, 81*, 163–172.
4. Van Heerde, H. J., Gijsbrechts, E., & Pauwels, K. (2008). Winners and losers in a major price war. *Journal of Marketing Research, 45*(5), 499–518.
5. Krämer, A., Jung, M., & Burgartz, T. (2016). A small step from price competition to price war: Understanding causes, effects and possible countermeasures. *International Business Research, 9*(3), 1–13.

Chapter **8**

# Distributing the offer

**CHAPTER OBJECTIVES**

After working through this chapter, you should be able to:

- Understand the role of distribution and distribution channels in the hospitality industry
- Describe the evolution of hospitality distribution systems and explain the influence of technologies such as computer reservation systems (CRS), global distribution systems (GDS) and the Internet
- Explain the channel and intermediary options available, as well as the functions and role of different hospitality intermediaries
- Understand the benefits and challenges of employing various distribution channels and evaluate channel relationships between principals and intermediaries.

## Introduction

In this chapter, we define distribution, review the evolution of hospitality distribution systems and explain the channel and intermediary options available to hospitality operations. We use examples from various hospitality sectors to illustrate the impact that intermediaries have on all types of hospitality businesses.

The concept of a distribution channel is relatively simple, but the management of distribution in practice can be extremely complicated. In a nutshell, distribution is concerned with making a product or service available for purchase and consumption when and where customers want

DOI: 10.4324/9781003186342-10

and expect. A distribution channel, in turn, is a configuration of organizations or intermediaries that enable product or service providers to make their offerings available for purchase and consumption where and when customers want and expect.

Hospitality organizations, like airlines, car rental firms and leisure attractions, are principals in the distribution channel. They supply the core products that customers buy and consume. Hospitality principals, especially larger companies, need intermediaries to distribute their products either solely or combined with other travel products in a package. Intermediaries sell the principals' products to customers and are normally paid by the principals.

Managing distribution can be challenging because of several factors. First, since hospitality products are perishable, it is crucial to generate advance bookings. Large organizations, for example major hotel companies with thousands of bedrooms to fill in hundreds of locations, need to employ a wide range of distribution channels, which require careful management and coordination.

The second factor that adds complexity is the expanding number and diversity of intermediaries. Due to the heterogeneous and intangible nature of hospitality offerings, the industry's distribution has become heavily dependent not only on middlemen who sell offerings, but also on an additional set of intermediaries that provide vital information services. Since distribution in the service sector moves customers to the product and not the product to the customer (as it is in the consumer goods industries), these information-providing intermediaries are essential. These additional players introduce extra complexity to the distribution function and make the frontiers between a company's marketing communications and distribution strategy unclear.

Despite some intermediaries having a dual function by providing information and taking bookings, for planning purposes it is still useful to make a distinction between promotion and distribution. Remember that the essential role of distribution is to make hospitality services available when and where customers want them, thus providing time and place utilities or benefits to customers, whilst the role of marketing communication is to influence customer demand by informing and persuading target audiences. To help you develop a better understanding of the different roles that distribution and marketing communication play in the marketing mix, we discuss them in different chapters.

We now review the historical development of distribution in hospitality, describe various types of intermediaries, explain horizontal and vertical integration, and discuss the benefits and challenges of various channel choices in the hospitality industry.

## Evolution of distribution

The way hospitality businesses distribute their services is continuously evolving. In general, that evolution of has consisted of two major periods: a period of intermediation and a period of disintermediation, followed by consequent partial reintermediation.

---

**ACTIVITY 8.1**

From the perspective of a principal with hotel rooms or restaurant seats to fill, what advantages and disadvantages does distribution via intermediaries have? Think of all the possible arguments and write them down. Continue adding new arguments to your list while reading the chapter.

### Intermediation

Intermediation started in the mid-1840s and was pioneered by entrepreneurs such as Thomas Cook, who created the first tourism packages for individuals and groups by combining elements of travel, accommodation and other components into a single-priced offer. These principals' products were sold through networks of bricks-and-mortar travel agents in the pre-Internet era.

In the 1950s and 1960s, these travel agents, who had relied on telephone and mail to make reservations for their customers, underwent a significant transformation. This occurred as the airlines replaced their slow and inflexible manual reservation systems with new electronic computer reservation systems (CRS). These CRSs were designed to store and retrieve global airline inventory. The airline companies recognized that the installation of electronic booking terminals in travel agents, with instant access, real-time availability, prices and reservations, would give their customers a better service and generate increased sales. The system was cost-effective and efficient, and gradually more and more bookings for the airlines were sourced through travel agents.

To further improve distribution, in the late 1970s, airlines developed global distribution systems (GDSs) and encouraged travel agents to cross-sell additional complementary travel products such as hotels and car rentals. Originally, there were four competing systems: Amadeus, Galileo, Sabre and Worldspan. Sabre, the first GDS, was founded by American Airlines in 1960. Today, the number of GDSs has increased, but Amadeus, Sabre and Travelport, which now owns Galileo and Worldspan, remain the leading systems.

The GDSs in hospitality and tourism are large-scale computerized reservation systems, which link principals to travel agents anywhere in the world. A GDS is like a global travel supermarket that provides travel agents with rapid search, booking and confirmation facilities for hotel, airline, car rentals and other travel-related products. In hospitality, links to the GDSs are dependent on hotel property management systems (PMS) that provide computerized reservation systems (CRS) with full details of properties, locations, room types, availability, prices and booking conditions. To resolve the problem of connecting several different hotel companies' CRS to the original four GDSs, a 'switch' mechanism was developed in the Western world by two competitors – Thisco and Wizcom – while DerbySoft was founded in 2002 to provide hotel 'switch' services in China. The 'switch' mechanisms enabled each hotel's CRS to connect with the GDS providers using a single interface, enabling all the travel agent intermediaries who are linked into the GDSs to book hotels in seconds. In 2010, Pegasus, who developed the Thisco 'switch', bought Wizcom to become the sole Western 'switch' provider. Thisco was renamed DHISCO (Distribution Hospitality Intelligent Systems Company). DHISCO switch was acquired by RateGain in 2018. Today, DHISCO and DerbySoft serve as the main switches that connect hotels with the GDS providers.

There are several benefits of distributing through GDSs. GDSs facilitate links between thousands of hospitality and tourism providers, increasing reach for individual hotels, airlines, car rental and cruise companies across borders, and giving access to customers through multiple global intermediaries, including travel agents, tour wholesalers, tour brokers, and national, state and local agencies.

GDS services, however, also have notable disadvantages. First, they are only available to a closed network of partners. Even today, despite the fact that CRS and GDS technologies work in conjunction with online networks to deliver search, booking and payment systems for hotel organizations, GDSs continue to be closed networks, where the information is only available to member principals and travel agents. Many non-travel agent distributors and all end-user customers, therefore, do not have access to the GDSs. Also, GDS transaction fees are high and even though GDSs have driven bookings, hospitality principals have not had access to any customer information, something that further increased the power of GDSs and made principals more dependent on them. For smaller chains and independent hotels, such conditions are highly unfavourable. They therefore continuously sought for alternative distribution options to avoid high GDS transaction charges.

### Disintermediation and reintermediation

The first real opportunity to reduce the power and dominance of GDSs emerged in the 1990s, when the Internet was developed. The Internet transformed the existing hospitality and tourism distribution system and brought new and previously unavailable opportunities for principals to connect with consumers directly and instantly. The Internet became a highly cost-effective tool for direct-to-customer distribution. It allowed cheaper and easier access to markets and provided both large global brands and smaller hospitality players with equal opportunities to promote and distribute their services via their own websites worldwide. Principals could now bypass the expensive GDSs and retain full control of their communication and distribution. It also became easier, faster and more convenient for consumers to find information and book directly through the principals' websites at the time and place convenient for them.

Originally, hospitality companies thought that the Internet would eliminate the need for intermediaries, because end-user customers would book directly with principals via their websites. They also thought that the web would eliminate the high commissions paid to intermediaries and other distribution costs. What they did not realize, however, is that the Internet created just as many opportunities for intermediaries. By exploiting the new technology, the existing intermediaries, including GDSs and travel agents, also quickly adopted an online presence. Additionally, new travel e-intermediaries – such as Expedia and, later Tripadvisor, with improved services and increased customer focus – appeared. As a result, intermediaries once again regained their power in hospitality and tourism distribution. Today, intermediaries continue to dominate hospitality distribution channels. However, both principals and distributors are continually looking for ways to manage their cost structures better, so the process of disintermediation and reintermediation is constantly evolving.

## Direct and indirect distribution

As you may know from your own experience and from the previous discussion, hospitality services can be distributed directly to the customer without the involvement of different intermediaries. Both options have their benefits and problems. In this section we discuss the different ways of organizing distribution and explain the advantages and disadvantages of distribution with and without intermediaries (see Figure 8.1).

### Direct distribution

Direct distribution means that principals and customers transact directly with each other. This is called direct sales. In a direct channel, service providers rely on their own distribution systems and sales force. Hospitality principals often use a combination of direct distribution methods to reach potential customers. Besides traditional methods such as telephone and walk-ins, principals can enable direct online reservations via a company website, a mobile app, company-managed blogs and branded pages hosted on other platforms such as social media sites.

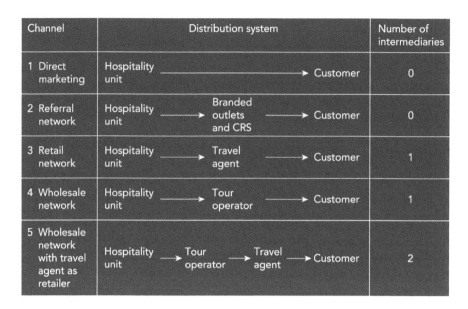

Figure 8.1 Traditional hospitality and tourism distribution channels

Direct distribution is particularly effective when firms want to honour a lowest rate guarantee. Because there are no intermediaries taking a commission and no wholesalers managing the principal's inventory, this channel is the most cost-effective and profitable distribution strategy. Direct distribution leaves the control in the hands of the principal, and thus ensures better brand protection, reduces distribution-related costs and allows direct customer contact which enables principals to capture valuable consumer data and feedback.

Despite all these advantages, few hospitality businesses can afford to rely solely on direct distribution. With the constantly increasing amount of travel options, hospitality providers need to ensure their presence online at all stages of the customer buying process, ensuring they are visible and bring value during inspiration, research, booking, consumption and post-experience stages.

## MARKETING INSIGHT 8.1

### Distribution strategy at Ryanair[1]

For over 10 years, Ryanair, one of the largest low-priced airlines in Europe, has successfully used a direct-only distribution strategy. The model has worked for years and has enabled the low-cost carrier to save costs and capitalize on the growing number of users who make their bookings online. However, while direct distribution has generated large sales volumes, it has only seemed to work with the existing customer base of price-sensitive travellers. In order to tap into a corporate market of business travellers, the company for the first time in many years has had to turn to GDSs and meta-search engines such as Google's Flight Search to reach its potential corporate travellers. As a result, after a long period of direct sales, Ryanair entered an agreement first with Amadeus in 2014 and later in 2015 with Sabre in order to has broaden its distribution base.

In 2021, Ryanair Holdings plc, the parent company of Ryanair, along with Buzz, Lauda and Malta Air, was Europe's largest airline group. Carrying 149 million passengers (pre-COVID -19) on more than 2,500 daily flights from over 80 bases, the group connects over 225 destinations in 37 countries on a fleet of 450 aircraft, with a further 210 Boeing 737s on order, which will enable the Ryanair Group to lower fares and grow traffic to 200 million over the next 5 years. Ryanair had a team of over 16,000 aviation professionals in 2021 delivering Europe's No. 1 on-time performance, and a 35-year safety record. Ryanair claims to be Europe's greenest and cleanest airline group. Customers flying Ryanair can reduce their $CO_2$ emissions by up to 50 per cent compared to the other Big 4 European major airlines.

*Source*: Ryanair Group[1]

## Indirect distribution

A far more common way to distribute hospitality services is through intermediaries. Some major drivers behind the popularity and growth of indirect distribution include:

- Perishability of the hospitality product – hotel managers know that a room unsold tonight cannot be transferred into inventory to sell tomorrow night (a lost revenue opportunity)
- Extremely competitive landscape with well-established international players and emerging new disruptive hospitality business models such as those based on the sharing economy (e.g. Airbnb)
- Complex customer behaviour whereby customers plan, research and book seamlessly using multiple devices (mobile phones, tablets and desktop computers) and channels
- Increased consumer-to-consumer sharing of travel experiences exemplified by the rapid expansion of numerous travel blogs, social media posts and customer review sites, which have over time turned into booking engines in their own right (e.g. Tripadvisor)
- Increased availability of price comparison sites like KAYAK.com or trivago.com.

In conditions where consumers have access to instantaneous choices 24 hours a day, seven days a week and every week of the year, at home, in the office and on the move, the majority of hospitality businesses are left with no other choice than to be present at the different touchpoints, online and offline.

From a hospitality perspective, the benefits of using indirect distribution channels include the following:

- Extensive customer reach through a large number of distribution outlets
- Convenient and instant global/local access points for customers away from the hospitality location
- Provision of relevant information, recommendation and guidance to potential customers by knowledgeable experts and trusted websites

- Bundling of hospitality products into combined but flexible packages
- Advance reservation and payments systems
- Opportunity to work with specialist intermediaries who understand the dynamics of their own markets.

The disadvantages for hospitality organizations using intermediaries include the following:

- Loss of margin paid to intermediaries in the form of commission – distribution can be the highest marketing cost for hotels. Independent and smaller hospitality companies pay higher commissions, GDS and credit card charges. Large hotel companies can negotiate better deals with intermediaries due to the greater volume of booking transactions.
- Loss of margin caused by adopting the merchant model of distribution – charging wholesalers (tour operators) low accommodation rates for volume business – thereby losing control of inventory at low rates
- Losing control of a key element in the marketing mix (distribution), which can lead to an unhealthy dependence on intermediaries. For example, dominant tour operators or major online travel agencies can dictate pricing decisions to independent hotels in some destinations.
- Lack of trust between the managers of hospitality units and distributors, often caused by cultural differences, that leads to non-disclosure of inventory information and inappropriate overbooking practices
- Intermediaries taking 'ownership of the customer' (i.e., privileged and protected access to all customer data) away from the hospitality organization
- Inconsistent pricing – consumers can and do compare prices listed on a hotel website with prices for the same hotel on the websites of intermediaries. The intermediaries' prices can sometimes be lower than those published by the hotel on its own website. This creates confusion for consumers as well as a loss of revenue for the hotel company because most consumers will choose to book a lower, commissionable price via an intermediary.

When there are many distributors of a principal's products, marketers say that distribution is intense. Marketers need to think strategically about the level of intensity that is appropriate for their brands. Generally, inexpensive products are distributed through a larger number of outlets, whereas more exclusive services are only available through selected intermediaries.

Next, we review the different types of intermediaries and discuss their unique functions and roles.

## Typology of intermediaries

Worldwide, the majority of intermediaries are small, independent organizations, yet a small number of major international companies have dominant market positions.

Although it is hard to find an intermediary with no online presence these days (bricks-and-mortar-only intermediaries), a differentiation can still be made between these 'bricks-and-clicks' intermediaries and intermediaries that are 'clicks-only' companies. Bricks-and-clicks intermediaries provide both offline and online distribution services and are still somewhat reliant on face-to-face meetings with potential clients and a physical presence convenient to customers' homes or workplaces. 'Clicks-only' intermediaries have no physical stores and operate purely online. The differences between these types of intermediaries are, of course, diminishing as more

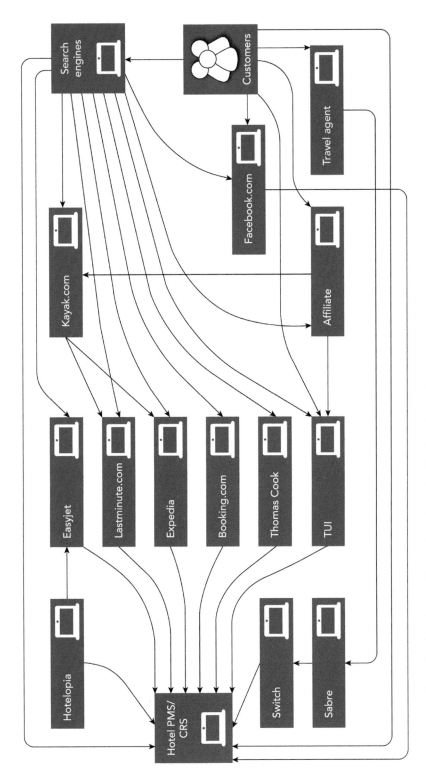

Figure 8.2 Selected online hospitality and tourism distribution channels

and more bricks-and-mortar intermediaries move online and transform into 'bricks-and-clicks' businesses. Overall, the following types of bricks-and-clicks intermediaries play an important role in hospitality distribution:

- Travel agents
- Tour operators
- Conference and meeting planners
- Corporate business travel agents
- Incentive travel houses
- Representative agents
- Tourist boards
- Principals (airlines, hotels, car rental providers).

Additionally, the following purely online intermediaries (see Figure 8.2) are significant in hospitality distribution:

- General search engines, such as Google and Baidu
- Meta-search engines – these are online information retrieval websites that mine the data of other search engines to produce their own results, such as skyscanner and KAYAK.com
- Vertical-specific search engines, a specialized search engine built for a specific type of content, such as Amazon, Pinterest and YouTube
- Online travel agents (OTAs) such as agoda.com, booking.com and orbitz.com
- Price comparison sites such as farecompare.com, KAYAK.com and trivago.com
- Recommendation engines – a system that predicts which hotel/destination a user is most likely to prefer among all hotels/destinations and makes a recommendation based on that prediction
- Peer-to-peer review sites and social media such as Tripadvisor.com, Facebook and Instagram
- Affiliates – also called associate programmes; arrangements in which an online merchant website pays affiliate websites a commission to send them traffic. Most OTAs have a travel affiliate programme.

Although this classification helps you to differentiate between the different types of distributors, the boundaries between the types are not always precise. For example, many firms combine travel agent and tour operations within their range of business activities. Similarly, some airlines that normally act as principals have established intermediary businesses to help their passengers book associated products such as hotels and car hire.

### Traditional and online travel agents

Travel agents are retail businesses that provide information, advice and booking for individual and group travel in both business and leisure markets. They perform the role of a retailer stocking a range of hospitality and travel products online and/or in brochures and act as an intermediary between customers and principals such as airlines, hotels, car rental companies, attractions, entertainment, event and sporting venues. Travel agents are also known as infomediaries, as the travel agent's role is to advise customers, make bookings, collect payments, and provide tickets and accommodation vouchers.

---

**MARKETING INSIGHT 8.2**

### Distribution of an integrated product at TUI Group[2]

Preussag AG, the company we know today as TUI AG, entered the tourism market in 1997 with the acquisition of one of Germany's leading tourism companies, Hapag-Lloyd. Further acquisitions of some of the biggest names in European tourism including Thomson, Fritidsresor and Nouvelles Frontières, and shareholdings in the hotel groups RIU and Magic Life TUI AG created one of the world's leading tourism groups.

In 2007, the tour operating businesses of TUI AG merged with the UK listed First Choice Holidays PLC, a tour operating business started in 1973 which had both mainstream and specialist businesses, to form TUI Travel PLC. As leaders in the travel industry, TUI AG and TUI Travel PLC have cooperated closely. Since the merger in 2007, operations in both businesses have been streamlined to form the TUI Group as the natural progression where two TUIs become one.

Even though the leisure travel market has consistently outperformed world output growth over the last decade and this market is also projected to remain very attractive in the future, the traditional tour operator and package holiday market has become very competitive. Online travel agencies have started to combine hotel and flight offerings by providing customers with dynamic packaging, a method used in package holiday bookings to enable consumers to build their own package of flights, accommodation and car rental instead of purchasing a pre-defined package. In addition, airline operators now provide holiday accommodation as an add-on to de-risk their own flight capacity, increasingly supported by sourcing hotels directly. Meanwhile, it is increasingly likely that there will be new market entrants, for example in the form of global tech companies. Against this background, TUI has strategically moved away from the traditional tour operator model and developed into an integrated provider of Holiday Experiences. TUI has invested in its own product offerings, enabling the company to create unique holidays for its customers, which is a key differentiation factor from its competitors. A TUI customer could be inspired by TUI, and book with TUI, and then experience a TUI flight, TUI transfer in destination, TUI hotel/cruise and TUI activity, as part of TUI's end-to-end integrated product offering. This means TUI customers receive a holistic and seamless experience, while TUI receives more accurate information about what customers truly want, helping TUI to further facilitate individualized offerings. From an end-to-end customer journey perspective, around 70 per cent of TUI's underlying EBITDA (earnings before interest, taxes, depreciation and amortization) comes from revenues generated from its own products and services, and products and services delivered by contracted suppliers.

*Source*: TUI Group[2]

---

Traditionally, travel agents ran local offices where they could meet their customers and help them to plan their travel. However, the number of bricks-and-mortar agencies has been declining rapidly due to consumer preference for online bookings. Many of the surviving bricks-and-mortar agencies have now additionally established an online presence. Examples of such traditional travel agents are TUI and CWT (formerly Carlson Wagonlit Travel), whereas the examples of pure online travel agents are Expedia, Priceline and Booking.com. While many of today's consumers prefer online agencies for routine hotel and/or airline bookings, they may still use bricks-and-mortar agencies for specialized and custom bookings such as honeymoons, once-in-a-lifetime trips, luxury vacations, etc. Thus, bricks-and-mortar agencies that provide customized services have prospered in recent years.

The agency business model is based on the principals paying commission. Agents prefer prompt payment. The lowest commission paid is 8 per cent and the norm is between 10 and 15 per cent. However, up to 25 per cent commission can be paid on specific products, especially during the low season.

Larger hotel chains negotiate with senior representatives of retail travel agent chains on a regular basis. They review sales figures, discuss customers' complaints and guest satisfaction data, and negotiate commission rates. Individual hotels rarely target travel agents since their product offer is too narrow and localized to be of interest.

### Tour operators

Tour operators are tourism industry wholesalers. They package inclusive holidays by combining the travel and accommodation elements with varying elements of food, beverage, activities, entertainment and sightseeing. They are sometimes described as aggregators because they create new travel products by packaging principals' existing products. Some tour operators specialize in particular products (e.g., ski packages at www.directski.com) or destinations (e.g., South Africa tours offered by Wild Planet Safari); others offer a wide range of tours. Tour operators generally work on volume sales, offering attractive, all-inclusive prices to generate high sales, with low margins. This formula implies a high break-even point, which makes tour operators financially vulnerable. Hotels wanting to target tour operators must be prepared to offer low rates and accept that the additional spend in the bar and other areas can be low. To protect themselves, hospitality operators need to transact business with tour operators who are covered by recognized trade indemnity policies and make sure that they are paid on a regular basis.

Often, the tour operator has representatives working in the resort or a tour guide accompanies the tourists on their holiday. These front-line employees play a key role in supporting the relationship between customers and the hotel. Much tour operator business is booked in hotels for a set of nights – in any combination from one to 14 nights – to coincide with working consumers' leisure time and holiday patterns. However, the senior citizens market can book for longer during the low season in large holiday hotels.

The tour operator does not charge principals a commission; instead, the tour operator agrees discounted prices with the principals and makes a profit by charging the customer an inclusive price for the package.

### Conference, event and meeting planners

These specialist agencies provide venue search and expert advice to customers who want to run conferences, events and meetings. Specialist planners do not normally charge the client a venue-finding fee; instead, the venue will pay the planner a commission on the business booked. Planners justify their role by:

- Providing impartial advice as to the suitability of the venue
- Negotiating the contract between the client and the venue
- Ensuring that the venue delivers what the organizer is looking for.

Planners adopt a professional approach to their businesses especially since their customers can be high-spend, frequent users. They will often personally inspect alternative venues, and they develop considerable expertise in this competitive market. The major hotel groups regard conference and meeting planners as a priority target market. Some examples of such planners are Events & Company in France (www.eventsandcompany.com) and Group Seven Events in UK (www.group7events.co.uk).

### Corporate or business travel agents

Business travel agents focus on service quality, in addition to price, in dealings with corporate customers. They arrange air travel and car rental as well as hotel bookings. The globalization of business has increased the demand for corporate travel, and at the same time the cost of travelling and staying in hotels has become a significant cost item. The Global Business Travel Association revealed coming into 2020, business travel had grown for 10 consecutive years, with an average growth rate of 5.1 per cent per year. However, the COVID-19 pandemic had a huge impact on global business travel. As we write, global spending on business travel is expected to show a 52 per cent decrease for 2020 (to US$694 billion), down from US$1.4 trillion in 2019, but business travel spending is forecast to grow 21 per cent in 2021 to US$842 billion, helped by the rollout of COVID-19 vaccines, but will not recover to pre-pandemic levels until the middle of the decade according to the Global Business Travel Association's (GBTA) BTI Outlook.

Although smaller business travel agents still rely on commission payments, the largest have reinvented themselves to provide blue-chip clients with cost-effective travel advice. These business travel agents are less interested in collecting commission from hotels; instead, they charge their clients a management fee for providing a travel management service, just like any other professional organization charges for a service. Business travel agents are keenly interested in negotiating competitive rates with the hotels that their clients want to use, to demonstrate that they are delivering better value to their clients. Examples of corporate travel agents include American Express, CT Business Travel and Travel Solutions International.

### Incentive travel houses

Companies often use travel as a reward to motivate customers, dealers, distributors, salespeople and employees. This idea has developed into a major sub-sector of the tourism industry and is called 'incentive travel'. The demand for incentive travel has increased dramatically during the past 20 years, and specialist incentive houses have developed expertise in this market. To be a successful motivator and 'incentivize' the target audience, the reward should be highly desirable. Many of the most attractive incentive destinations are foreign, unusual and even exotic. This specialized market is not suitable for all hotels; however, exotic hotels in idyllic or unusual locations can seriously target the incentive travel market.

Incentive houses carefully check the facilities and quality of service of hotels in appropriate destinations. Since the promoters of incentive schemes are always looking for unusual themes, venues can help incentive travel houses by packaging distinctive, interesting programmes that are suitable for well-travelled, sophisticated consumers. Some incentive packages involve large numbers of winners all travelling in one party at the same time; others are designed for couples and can be booked on an individual basis as and when it suits the winners.

### Representative agents

Representative agents are another type of intermediary who link hotels, travel agencies and customers. These are independent companies with their own sales teams. One of the largest representative agencies in the world is Pegasus Solutions, which represents their hotel clients to online, GDS and mobile channels. Pegasus helps hotels in other ways too: they offer back-end technical integration to CRSs and GDSs, and website creation to generate reservations and booking. Additionally, they take the responsibility for marketing of the hotels rooms to the end-user using a variety of channels and creative online and mobile solutions.

---

**ACTIVITY 8.2**

The magazine *Corporate & Incentive Travel* provides international coverage of hotel developments, destinations and initiatives targeting the incentive travel market. Visit the magazine's website (www.themeetingmagazines.com/corporate-incentive-travel/) to gain a better understanding of the incentive market.

---

**MARKETING INSIGHT 8.3**

**HonourWay, an independent representation agency**

HonourWay was founded by Honour Schram de Jong as a representative agency for luxury lodges in southern Africa. HonourWay is the public relations, sales and marketing agent for small, exclusive lodges in Malawi, Kenya and Zambia. Principals (clients) include Cottar's 1920s Camp, Kaya Mawa by Green Safaris, Chisa Busanga Camp by Green Safaris and Tongabezi. Each of the lodges is characterized by their remote rural locations in the African bush, proximity to wildlife, high-quality facilities and service, and a passion for responsible tourism. The source markets are primarily the United Kingdom, United States, Germany, France and Australia. HonourWay acts as the European marketing office for their clients. HonourWay has strong working relationships with the travel trade in the UK, Western Europe and around the world. HonourWay supports the principals they serve with trade visits, educational trips, promotions, trade shows, digital marketing, training, all the while raising their clients' profile. HonourWay's focus is on building close personal relationships with clients and the international trade to promote awareness and increase sales. HonourWay carries out sales visits on behalf of clients to existing and potential tour operators in the UK, Western Europe and around the world. The clients are represented at annual events, such as the International Tourism Exchange (known as ITB) in Berlin, Cannes International Luxury Travel Market, World Travel Market in London, the South African INDABA tourism event, and the Asian Luxury Travel Market in Shanghai. Each of the clients pays an annual fee to be represented by HonourWay. HonourWay claims to be an effective agency – one client increased their annual occupancy from 34 per cent to 69 per cent in three years.

*Source*: Honour Schram de Jong and www.honourway.com

## Tourist boards

Local and national tourist boards are destination marketing organizations (DMOs) and have an important role as infomediaries in hospitality distribution channels. Most tourist board websites provide hospitality product information with links and contact information for visitors to make their own booking arrangements. The provision of online booking services has been inhibited due to the complexity of managing a large number of small principals who are unwilling to enter into costly online distribution transactions. Some countries have legislation to prevent their tourist board from providing a booking service (e.g., Australia), although they can still provide very good information about hospitality products: see www.australia.com.

## Principals

As mentioned earlier in the chapter, the boundaries between the different types of intermediaries are becoming more indistinct, particularly online, as more and more of the intermediaries adopt additional features and offer services previously only delivered by specialized middlemen. For example, tour operators no longer only sell packages but also distribute services such as flights and hotels. Equally, online travel agents now sell their own bundled packages that used to be the core offering of tour operators. The main motivation behind this change is the strategy of being a one-stop shop for customers and offering many travel services in one place in order to increase customer engagement and spending. This development is also widespread among the principals.

## Search engines

A search engine is a software programme that searches the Internet for webpages containing keywords specified by the search engine user. Dominant search engines are Google, Bing and Baidu. Search engines use artificial intelligence, spider or web crawler software to search for information that matches users' queries. Search engines use complex proprietary algorithms (Google's algorithm considers over 200 variables) to identify the relevant content and provide a list of results (hits). The results can be listed on many pages, so organizations often advertise to ensure that their offer appears at or close to the top of the list. On Google pages, these paid results may appear at the top, on the right and at the bottom of the screen. The other links listed on the left of the screen occur organically as a result of their conformance to the search engine's algorithm, high-quality content and relevance to the user query.

For companies that do not want to or cannot afford advertising on search engines, search engine optimization (SEO) provides a way of appearing towards the top of the organic listing. The ranking of the links is determined by an algorithm that applies hundreds of variables before serving up relevant pages. Search algorithms consider many factors, including the words of the query, relevance and usability of pages, expertise of sources, and user's location and settings. The weight applied to each factor varies depending on the nature of the query – for example, the freshness of the content plays a bigger role in answering queries about current news topics than it does about dictionary definitions. From an accommodation provider's perspective, effective online marketing is based on an understanding of how search engines work, recognizing the importance of destination links, developing accessible and easy-to-use websites and mobile applications, developing effective booking engines and controlling BAR (see Chapter 7) through the distribution network. Users depend on search engines when looking for information on the Internet. To capture the widest possible online audience, a site needs to ensure that the domain name, property location, text copy, page titles, tags and meta tags are easy for search engines and directories to find. In general, the earlier (or higher on the page) and more frequently a site appears in the search results list, the more visitors it will receive from the search engine. Google is currently the dominant search engine in the West (Baidu is the most popular in China) and hospitality companies need to ensure that their website is ranked highly – preferably on the first page of the search results. For many hospitality operations, the location is a primary search item for potential customers, so links to destination sites, local and national tourist organizations, and local attractions are important.

### Meta-search engines

A meta-search engine is a search engine that searches the content of other search engines. Meta-search engines are often, though not always, developed by owners of the generic search engines. One such initiative from Google is Google Travel. This meta-search service displays rates available from different intermediaries for flights, hotels and vacation rentals; facilitates booking directly from Google maps; offers customer reviews; allows saving information for later retrieval on desktop or mobile; and enables sharing of details with friends.

Other industry-specific meta-search engines, such as KAYAK from Booking.com, trivago from Expedia and kelkoo, are also of growing importance. These sites have no booking facility but provide rich information about the hospitality products and opportunity to compare prices. Often, they are referred to as price comparison sites or infomediaries. The business model of these websites is to charge service providers for displaying their information, something that can be based on a fixed fee or a pay-per-click commission model.

### Recommendation engines

One type of intermediary that has gained considerable popularity in recent years is the recommendation engine. Tripadvisor is an example. Travellers post reviews of the various hospitality service providers they have experienced, and the engine aggregates these reviews so that prospective customers can assess alternatives and make bookings. Studies suggest that most hospitality customers read review comments before making their travel decision.[1]

### Peer-to-peer markets

In recent years a new type of intermediary has emerged. These new intermediaries enable individuals to compete with established service providers. Disruptive innovations like Airbnb have created marketplaces where people can offer accommodation that competes with hotels. Airbnb is a virtual marketplace where travellers can search for and book accommodation provided by local independent people, hence the expression 'peer-to-peer'. Although these intermediaries are similar to specialized meta-search engines, peer-to-peer markets are perceived as more local, authentic and trustworthy. Marketing Insight 8.5 shows how an established hotel brand, Marriott, has responded to the peer-to-peer threat.

---

## MARKETING INSIGHT 8.4

### Tripadvisor[3]

Tripadvisor was founded in the United States in 2000 with the initial idea of offering professional reviews of destinations and other travel services collected from guidebooks, newspapers and magazines, but quickly turned into the largest pool of consumer-generated reviews. Tripadvisor provides travellers and hotel guests with the opportunity to critique their hospitality and tourism experiences and rank the principals' service. Tripadvisor's travel research platform features reviews and opinions from its community of travellers about destinations, accommodation (hotels, bed and breakfasts, specialty lodging and vacation rentals), restaurants and activities throughout the world through its flagship Tripadvisor brand.

Travellers across the globe use the Tripadvisor site and app to discover where to stay, what to do and where to eat based on guidance from those who have been there before. Travellers turn to Tripadvisor to find deals on accommodation, book experiences, reserve tables at restaurants and discover places nearby. Tripadvisor-branded websites include tripadvisor.com in the United States and localized versions of the website in 43 markets and 22 languages, including in China under the brand daodao.com. Beyond travel-related content, Tripadvisor websites also include links to the websites of its travel advertisers allowing travellers to directly book their travel arrangements. In addition to the flagship Tripadvisor brand, Tripadvisor Inc. manages and operates websites under 21 other travel media brands, connected by the common goal of providing comprehensive travel planning resources across the travel sector, including www.cruisecritic.com, www.bokun.io, www.tripadvisor.com/ForRestaurants/ta_singleplatform and www.vacationhomerentals.com. At the time of writing, there are over 887 million reviews and opinions of nearly 8 million businesses, 463 million unique monthly visitors, and Tripadvisor continues to grow.

*Source*: Tripadvisor[3]

## MARKETING INSIGHT 8.5

### Marriott International and the sharing economy[4]

Many hospitality providers see a direct threat in the exponential growth of the sharing economy and are worried by homeowners' willingness to rent rooms or even their entire homes to travellers. In order to compete with companies like Airbnb that offer home sharing and short-term home rentals to travellers, and to capture the growing demand for short-term home rentals,

Marriott International launched Homes & Villas by Marriott International, a global home rental offering, in 2019 with a vision to bring Marriott's 90+ years of hospitality expertise to the home rental market. With a focus only on the premium and luxury tier of rental homes, Marriott works with select professional home management companies to ensure that every home listed can be serviced at a standard expected of Marriott International.

Homes & Villas by Marriott International offers highly curated offerings by working with professional management companies that offer premium and luxury private home inventory. Homes & Villas by Marriott International evaluates each home – either in person or digitally – before it is listed the on their site. Each property listed on Homes & Villas by Marriott International is professionally managed by one of their trusted property management partners, who provide guests a professionally cleaned home with 24/7 local support team for assistance while staying at the booked home or villa, high-speed Wi-Fi, premium linens and amenities, and family-friendly conveniences upon request. Marriott Bonvoy members can earn and redeem points at stays with Homes & Villas by Marriott International.

The launch of Homes & Villas by Marriott International reflects hotel operators' ongoing commitment to innovation as consumer travel needs evolve. Judging by the focus on upscale properties, Homes & Villas by Marriott International is more of a competitor against Airbnb's 'Plus' service, which offers luxury properties to rent in ritzy places like Italy's Amalfi Coast.

*Source*: Marriott International[4]

### Affiliates

Travel affiliates are a considerable influence in hospitality and come in many different forms. Essentially, they either capture web traffic and direct it to principals' websites or sell the principals' product directly on their own website or page hosted on platforms such as Facebook. Some examples of travel affiliates are incentive or loyalty affiliates (e.g., www.aadvantageeshopping.com), cash-back affiliates (e.g. quidco.com), voucher or coupon affiliates (e.g. groupon.com, savoo.co.uk and vouchercodes.co.uk) and content affiliates that run blogs or other communities and offer special interest information (e.g., tripandtravelblog.com).

## Horizontal and vertical integrated marketing channels

A small number of international companies have become dominant players in both hospitality and travel by taking over or merging with competitors in the same part of the distribution channel (horizontal integration), or by taking over or merging with downstream customers or upstream suppliers (vertical integration). The largest global travel organization is TUI. TUI effectively controls all customer touch-points in their proprietary distribution chains by owning the travel agent, tour operator, airline and hotel – this is called a vertically integrated marketing channel (VIMC). The advantages of a VIMC include the following:

- Coordination of all operational and marketing activities across all channel members
- Improved communication between channel members
- Reduction of channel conflict between the channel members, who are all working for the same company
- Cost savings through economies of scale
- Potentially superior customer service
- Opportunity to respond quickly to changes in the PESTE environment.

### ACTIVITY 8.3

Think of the websites you used the last three times you booked travel. What types of principal or intermediary were they? Reflect upon the reasons for your choice of these websites. Why did you select them over the other options? What value do you think they deliver?

The main disadvantage for a dominant travel conglomerate is the threat of regulatory authorities (e.g., the European Commission and the UK Competition and Markets Authority) taking action over monopoly concerns and the lack of consumer choice. For customers, there are potential benefits in terms of a better-coordinated travel experience. Although the travel conglomerates own a range of travel agents, tour operators, charter airlines, hotel operations and customers are not always aware of this common ownership.

## Conclusion

Innovations in technology continue to drive the development of distribution channels in hospitality. The continual evolution of the online world – including the rapid development of social networking sites such as Facebook, Instagram and Twitter, app development, and the widespread adoption of mobile phones – will create new distribution channels in the future. Depending on the size of the business and the market segment targeted, accommodation providers need to use intermediaries to obtain advance bookings to generate occupancy, but the high cost of distribution forces hospitality companies to look for alternatives. The online environment and mobile technologies are important facilitators of hospitality distribution and can help hotels to reduce their distribution costs via direct booking. However, online search engines and intermediaries, travel agents and tour operators have a critical role as intermediaries for most hotels.

In this chapter, we have explained:

- Changes over time in the structure of distribution channels
- Reasons why principals use distribution intermediaries, including the benefits and disadvantages
- Many different types of direct and indirect intermediaries
- Differences between bricks-and-mortar, bricks-and-clicks and clicks-only intermediaries
- Utilities or benefits those intermediaries provide to customers
- Role of computerized reservation systems, global distribution systems and peer-to-peer markets in facilitating online accommodation bookings.

### REVIEW QUESTIONS

Now check your understanding of this chapter by answering the following questions:

1 Discuss the role of online and offline distribution from a hotel company's perspective.

2 Evaluate the relationship between hotel organizations and intermediaries.

3 Who, if anyone, 'owns' the customer – the hotel where the customer stays, the intermediary who makes the booking for the customer, both or neither?

### References

1. Ryanair Group [Internet]. *History of Ryanair*. [cited September 17, 2021]. Available from: https://corporate.ryanair.com/about-us/history-of-ryanair/

2. TUI Group [Internet]. *About TUI Group*. [cited September 17, 2021]. Available from: www.tuigroup.com/en-en/about-us/about-tui-group/

3. Tripadvisor [Internet]. *About Tripadvisor*. [cited September 17, 2021]. Available from: https://tripadvisor.mediaroom.com/us-about-us

4. Marriott International [Internet]. *We Are Marriott International*. [cited September 17, 2021]. Available from: www.marriott.com/marriott/aboutmarriott.mi

Part B

# Communicating the offer

After working through this chapter, you should be able to:

- Understand the role of marketing communication in the pre-encounter hospitality marketing mix
- Explain the marketing communication process
- Evaluate each element of the communication mix
- Understand the role of offline and online promotion
- Plan a marketing communication campaign.

## Introduction

In the marketing mix, communicating the offer is variously known as promotion, the promotional mix, communication, the communication mix, customer communication, marketing communication or marcoms. The public simply thinks of it – wrongly – as advertising and selling. As we made it clear in Chapter 1, there is much more to marketing than advertising and selling; it is also true that marketing communication encompasses more than advertising and selling.

Once the pre-encounter marketing mix has been designed to provide an attractive offer, then communicating that offer should aim to raise awareness, influence expectations and ultimately – through its influence on customer or consumer behaviour – generate sales and

DOI: 10.4324/9781003186342-11

profits. Sometimes companies think that marketing communication campaigns can compensate for deficiencies in other elements of the marketing mix. They are wrong. If the offer does not satisfy customers by meeting their expectations, then investing in marketing communications is a waste of money, which can lead to serious problems with unhappy customers and negative word-of-mouth face-to-face and in online reviews.

We noted in Chapter 8 that companies use the Internet to perform both marketing communication and distribution. Websites have dual purposes – they are both a vehicle for communications and a distribution tool. To help you develop a better understanding of the different roles that marketing communication and distribution play in the marketing mix, we discuss them in separate chapters. Remember that the role of marketing communication is to influence demand by communicating with target audiences and persuading potential customers to buy your company's hospitality offer, whereas distribution focuses on making the offer available for purchase when and where customers want.

In the past, companies aimed to control what was said about their products and brands by dominating communication channels with carefully planned messaging. Companies now realize that message control is impossible to achieve due to consumers' and customers' access to information from alternative non-company sources, particularly online.

Today, customer communication is a multi-lateral process – hospitality companies communicate with customers/consumers, customers/consumers with companies and customers with other customers. While business-to-customer or business-to-consumer communication is known as B2C, customers' communication with companies is known as C2B communication. Customers can communicate with companies face-to-face, by phone, email, text, web form, in online channels and apps and other ways. We have also seen the emergence of powerful consumer-to-consumer (C2C) or peer-to-peer (P2P) communication, which is particularly evident online in blogs, discussion forums, comparison travel shopping websites like Tripadvisor and social network communities such as Facebook and Twitter. Companies no longer control product, brand and corporate messaging, and this creates challenges when promoting a product, or protecting a marketing asset (such as a brand) from negative sentiment.

We now discuss the role of marketing communication and review the different elements of the marketing communication mix.

---

**ACTIVITY 9.1**

Before reading the rest of the chapter, think of how you first heard about a tourism destination or hospitality product which you have already experienced or want to experience.

- Was it a word-of-mouth recommendation from family and friends?
- Was it a recommendation from previous travellers you found on the Internet?
- Was it reading an advert either online or in a newspaper/magazine?
- Was it listening/viewing an advertisement on the radio, television or the Internet?
- Was it hearing/reading/viewing a news item?

# The role of marketing communication

The goal of most marketing communication is to influence customer demand by raising the target audience's awareness of the hospitality brand and building accurate expectations of the hospitality experience. Marketing communication's end goal – influencing demand – can be achieved in different ways, depending on the characteristics of the target audience and their existing knowledge of hospitality companies' brands and products. There are three main classes of marketing communication, depending on whether it aims to inform, persuade or to build relationships with target audiences.

## Inform

Companies need to ensure that potential customers are aware of their hospitality offer. This is partly about building brand awareness and partly about developing product knowledge – both help the prospective customer to form expectations. Awareness of the major hospitality brands is continually researched in company marketing research and omnibus surveys. For companies with low brand awareness, a typical marketing communication objective is to raise brand awareness so that more potential customers will learn and recognize the brand name. Companies also need to ensure that target audiences understand what is being offered. Companies that have successfully communicated their offer to target audiences develop more positive, strategically desirable, reputations. A company with a poor reputation may not have conveyed an appropriate message in its marketing communications. However, trying to change consumers' beliefs about, and attitudes towards, a brand is a very complex task, particularly when these beliefs and attitudes are deeply held.

## Persuade

Consumers who are brand aware and have a favourable perception of the brand still need to be persuaded to buy the company's hospitality product. We have already discussed how consumers have choice and that there are many different competitors vying for consumers' disposable income. Hospitality marketers, therefore, need to persuade target audiences to buy their product instead of competitors' offers. Marketers strive to stimulate buyer behaviour by offering attractive inducements and incentives to book now – often using telephone, email, text, social media and website – rather than later, or never at all.

Companies also monitor and analyze online review comments posted by customers to determine their brand image among their customers. In addition to using user-generated content for research purposes, hospitality companies are also increasingly leveraging user-generated content to promote their offerings to persuade potential customers since it provides a cost effective and authentic way to grow their brand image and revenues. Due to rapid advances in online information sharing opportunities and technology, dissemination of information at a rapid pace to millions of social media users through user-generated content is becoming a common practice.

## Build relationships

Many hospitality companies want to build long-term relationships with targeted customers. Generating repeat and referral sales is crucial in most hospitality markets. Major hospitality companies use a combination of online and offline communication strategies to communicate with recent guests and members of frequent guest programmes. Customer databases hold useful, relevant customer information (club membership details, email and postal addresses, frequency of stay, details of purchases), which enables companies with the right sort of technology to run automated, personalized marketing communications. The right sort of technology is a customer relationship management (CRM) application called *campaign management*. Smaller hospitality companies also compile lists of their customers and reach out to them using email and direct mail (post), text or social media channels. These approaches can be effective in building closer and enduring relationships with customers.

The starting point for any customer communication is to define the target audience. In hospitality, target audiences are typically end-users, intermediaries or other key people in the decision-making unit (see Chapter 3 for more information). Each of these different target audiences has different characteristics and different information needs and is exposed to different media, and therefore different communication channels and messaging strategies need to be used to reach each audience.

For end-users, marketing communications might be used to raise awareness about the recruitment of a new celebrity chef or promote a low season product/price offer; for intermediaries, marketing communications might be used to promote a brand relaunch following refurbishment or to encourage travel agents to book a familiarization visit.

Much end-user communication is intended to create awareness or stimulate demand and, in doing so, it influences customer expectations. This creates a dilemma for campaign managers. Companies' marketing communication activity must attract the target audience's attention, stimulate interest and, most importantly, move them towards purchase, without over-promising what can really be delivered. Unfortunately, because of competitive pressures, some hospitality campaigns make exaggerated promises and raise customers' expectations beyond what can be delivered. Customers who book in good faith, believing the promise, may end up being disappointed when they experience the hospitality service. Many ordinary restaurants make exaggerated claims about the quality of their cooking, which then disappoints discerning customers. Many of those disappointed customers end up posting negative reviews online, which can have disastrous effects on the success and survival of any hospitality business.

## The marketing communication process

Ultimately, the goal of much marketing communication is to move target markets towards purchase of the hospitality product. However, this goal is not as simple as it sounds, because consumers in modern societies are bombarded with thousands of competing messages from hundreds of different sources every day. We call this interference 'noise', and noise disrupts a company's communication with potential customers. Figure 9.1 provides a simple model of the communication process and features the hospitality organization as the sender. The model comprises the sender, a target audience (or receiver), noise in the communication environment, message, medium and feedback process.

- The *sender* is the hospitality organization that wants to communicate with a target audience.
- The *target audience* (*receiver*) consists of the end-users, influencers, decision-makers, gate-keepers or intermediaries. The target audience must be precisely defined to ensure that the message reaches the right people.

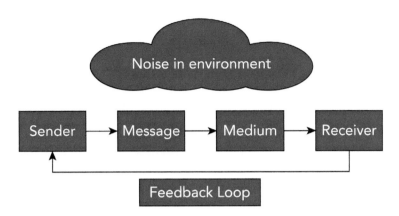

Figure 9.1 The communication process

- *Noise* comprises all the communications from other sources, including both people and organizations, which compete for the target audience's attention and interfere with reception of the sender's message.
- The *message* is the content that the sender communicates to the target audience.
- The *medium* (media: plural) is the communication channel that senders use to communicate with target audiences. Channels include personal communication (such as sales visits) and non-personal communication (websites, social media, brochures, point-of-sale, advertisements in offline and online media and public relations (PR) activity).
- *Feedback* from the audience tells the sender whether the communication objectives have been achieved.

Many marketers have made use of a framework called AIDA to ensure that marketing communication does indeed move audiences towards purchase. AIDA stands for:

- Attention – the message should grab the target audience's attention.
- Interest – the message should arouse the target audience's interest.
- Desire – the message should stimulate desire to take action, such as wanting to experience the product.
- Action – the message should encourage and, preferably, enable the target audience to act in a specific way, for example call a reservation number, jump on a website or make a booking.

Sometimes marketers try to achieve all four AIDA outcomes in a single communication; often they fail. Moving potential customers down the AIDA pathway may involve several different campaigns in different media, over time, employing different messaging strategies for each step. Different communication tools may be needed at each stage of AIDA – for example, advertising might be used to gain attention and sales promotions to generate action.

Before constructing messages and choosing communication tools, marketers need to be clear about their communication objectives. These will be derived from the three core communication strategies we described earlier and may even be informed by the AIDA model. Generally, these can be split into three categories. Communicators want their targeted receivers to learn, feel or do something. Examples include:

- Learn – raise awareness of a new product launch; recall the brand name and recognize the company logo
- Feel – develop a positive attitude to the company; prefer the brand to competitors
- Do – visit the website or telephone the call centre and make a booking.

Messages need to be constructed so that they achieve the specified communication objectives. In devising the message, marketers must decide what to say (message content) and how to say it (message format). This equally applies to the online environment as well as offline.

### Message content

The message content depends first on the objectives of the campaign and then on the characteristics of the target audience and their existing knowledge and understanding of the hospitality product. A campaign for a new brand will most likely stress information that builds awareness of the brand name and business location, or influences expectations by describing the customer experience. For an established brand aiming to fill demand in the low season, the focus will be on price and availability. Audiences who are already aware ('attention' in the AIDA model) are at a more advanced stage of readiness to buy. Message content for them can be more attuned to interest, desire and action outcomes. Different members of the decision-making unit may be at different AIDA stages, and therefore need different messages.

The marketer then needs to decide what type of appeal to use in the message. Appeals can be classified as rational, emotional or moral.

- *Rational messages* appeal to the target audience's practical mindset. This approach is effective in markets where the end-user has a set of tangible requirements. A rational message can provide factual information to reassure the audience: 'Just 50 metres from the beach' to reassure holidaymakers, and 'Close to the airport, but quiet' to reassure corporate markets. 'Great value' price offers aim to appeal to the rational-economic consumer.
- *Emotional messages* are explicitly designed to arouse consumers' passions, interests and desires. This approach is often effective in dining out and leisure markets. Emotional appeals are typically used to target couples for a Valentine's Day meal experience, or to take a relaxing and romantic weekend leisure break.
- *Moral messages* are linked to consumers' belief and value systems. Restaurants that promote non-genetically modified or organic food, and resorts that promise an environmentally sustainable experience, appeal to consumers' core values. Religious organizations sometimes arrange touring vacations for members of their faith, and some faiths have even bought their own properties to cater for their members. Their moral message is essentially a spiritual one.

---

**MARKETING INSIGHT 9.1**

**Creativity in marketing!**

Creativity is an essential ingredient for the professional marketer. Creative thinking uses a combination of situation analysis and thinking outside-the-box to create campaign ideas, which move the target audience towards purchase. The creative element can be copy- or design-led; in a creative treatment of a graphic, still photograph or video clip; a phrase or strapline; the use of humour and an unusual treatment of a mundane topic. Sometimes the wackiest ideas work and other times the creativity can badly misfire. Some communications agencies believe it is best to test the more creative ideas with focus groups representing the target audience to ensure that the message works.

Can you think of any really creative adverts that you liked? What did you like about the advert? Did you tell your friends about the advert?

## ACTIVITY 9.2

Review the advertisements for hotels and restaurants from a newspaper, magazine or the Internet.

- Who is the target audience for these adverts?
- How emotional and how factual are the adverts?
- Using the AIDA framework, which objectives do these adverts aim to achieve?
- Is there a difference between adverts placed by well-known brands and by independent operators?

## Message format

Messages are received using one or more of our five senses – sight, hearing, smell, taste and touch. Message formatting focuses on the design, composition or configuration of the message content, be that an advertisement, brochure, press release, collateral piece, sales promotion, event or sales presentation. Creativity is essential in message formatting and framing in order to create cut-through – that is, to stand out from the noise of all competing messages.

## MARKETING INSIGHT 9.2

### Message framing effects![1]

The 'framing effects' theory suggest that the way an individual reacts to a problem depends on how the problem is framed. Since the introduction of 'framing effects' by Nobel laureate in economics Kahneman in 1981, 'framing effects' has been operationalized in many communications. Many of these framing effects have focussed on travellers' perceptions of risk of terrorism and political instability. The way an advertising message is framed, either as positively or negatively (e.g. enjoy the peace or escape the noise), is reported to result in significantly different reactions from consumers. More specifically, positive messages tend work better in the context of experiential products because a positively framed option generates positive associations and thus seems more attractive than a negatively framed option as in the case of the destination slogan 'Up above, there is paradise; down below, there are Suzhou and Hangzhou' used by Suzhou and Hangzhou in China. Since most hospitality and tourism products are relatively experienced-focused, gain-framed messaging contributes to positive shifts customers attitudes and behaviours.[1]

An increasing number of hospitality marketers utilize Internet, social media, third party sites and search engine marketing in their communications with their target customers due to rapid growth of availability and accessibility of digital data. With online users regularly sharing their personal data online and web cookies tracking every click, marketers have been able to gain unprecedented insight into consumers and present customized messages that are tailored to customers' individual needs.

Website-related considerations include page layout, text, visuals, content such as embedded audio or video files, links to external sites, privacy and personal data use policies, opportunities for interactivity and visitor engagement; and, crucially, ease of navigation and simple-to-use e-commerce functionality so that potential buyers can book when they want. For print advertisements and brochures, important considerations are size, shape, layout, copy and illustrations; for publicity, an important consideration is the storyline that creates interest. Other format considerations include food samples or aromas from the restaurant and the design of the hotel's conference laptop or tablet presentation to meetings and conventions prospects. Attention to detail in designing the appropriate message format is time-consuming and costly, but important.

## Communication channels

There are two main classes of communication channel: personal and non-personal. Personal communication occurs when people directly talk to each other in real time, face-to-face or on the telephone, via online chat and messenger services, or when video-conferencing. It also includes asynchronous (time-lagged) person-to-person interactions by email, text or mail. The main advantage of personal communication is that it provides opportunities for customized interaction. Interaction or dialogue means the customer can ask questions about the hospitality company's brands and products, and the company can find out more about customer needs and wants.

Non-personal communication channels do not allow dialogue and associated learning to occur. They are essentially unilateral and are pre-planned. Non-personal communication channels are used for mediated communications such as advertising, point-of-purchase communications and most public relations/publicity events. Examples of mediated communications include all online, TV, radio and print advertising. The design and production of mediated communications, publicity and point-of-purchase materials require support from specialist suppliers like design companies, advertising agencies, print companies and PR agencies. These agencies offer content development and production expertise in areas such as copywriting, design, artwork, graphics, photography, videography and ad production. Ad agencies and specialist media buying shops enable advertisers to buy access to targeted audiences.

In recent years, a third class of communication channel – technology-abled customized communications – has appeared with the rapid growth of availability and accessibility of digital data. This channel is a hybrid of personal and non-personal communication channels. It is personal in the sense that messaging can be customized for individual target audience members, but non-personal in the sense that dialogue does not always occur. Recent developments in digital data acquisition and data mining technologies have enabled marketers to gain unprecedented insight into consumers' needs and wants and develop customized and interactive messages that are tailored to customers' individual needs. Digital targeting has meaningfully improved the response to advertisements since marketers are able to frame customized and interactive messages that are tailored to customers' individual needs. With the use of artificial intelligence technology, companies can communicate with and answer questions from the customer, once they are online. However, there is evidence that using online tracking to frame customized messages can lead to a consumer backlash. Customers are increasingly aware that companies track their online activities and use information from social media posts to frame customized messages that are tailored to customers' individual needs. Personal experiences with highly specific ads (such as one for wine enthusiast that begins, 'As a wine enthusiast, you might like . . .') or ads that follow users across websites have made it clear that marketers often know exactly who is on the receiving end of their digital messages. Now regulators in some countries are starting to mandate that firms disclose how they gather and use consumers' personal information.

### The hospitality communications mix

Figure 9.2 presents the key communication tools used by hospitality companies, each of which is discussed here in more detail. In small hospitality businesses, the owner/manager will

Figure 9.2 The hospitality communication mix

typically be very involved with the planning and implementation of all marketing communication activity. The owner's control over these activities should ensure that marcom campaigns are coordinated and integrated. This is important to ensure that a consistent message is always communicated to the target audience.

Probably, the most critical communication tool for hospitality marketers is word-of-mouth recommendation (WOM) by family and friends or other customers, or electronic word-of-mouth recommendation (eWOM) through online reviews. Both forms of WOM can be extremely powerful in raising the conversation partner's awareness, interest and desire, and motivating action. Traditionally, word-of-mouth, whether positive or negative, has occurred organically, largely due to the referrer's customer experience. However, there are now specialist word-of-mouth marketing agencies that run product-seeding campaigns in which brand owners give free product samples or experiences to selected members of the agency's panel, with a view to them sharing the product or their experiences with members of their social networks. This type of word-of-mouth is managed, not organic, but can deliver outstanding results.

In recent years, eWOM has started playing a bigger role in the customer decision-making process. As a result, businesses have started playing a more active role in the management of eWOM and their online reputation. Some customers are intrinsically motivated to share their experiences on review sites and social media. They share product information and service experiences voluntarily, generating organic eWOM. However, other customers may require additional reasons or motives to share their experiences of a product or service. Businesses commonly use incentives to motivate and encourage such customers to post comments, which exemplifies the active management of eWOM. However, the use of incentives can result in biased reviews. Furthermore, incentive-driven reviews may be perceived as transactional, trading positive comments for incentives. If eWOM posters are seen as paid agents of businesses, their reviews may not be deemed trustworthy, because their interests converge with those of the businesses. Moreover, offering incentives for reviews may damage the image and reputation of businesses.

Although user-generated content sites take stringent measures against reviews submitted through click farms (an organized group of low-paid workers employed to click on particular parts of web pages), they pay little attention to incentive-driven reviews. Online review sites such as Dianping (the biggest review site in China) and Taobao (the biggest online shopping platform in China) have recently adopted a policy that requires businesses to disclose the type and amount of incentive (if any) that individuals receive for posting reviews, to help customers distinguish organic reviews from incentive-driven ones. This new policy may have a significant impact on how customers perceive these reviews, because the motivation for a post may influence how a message is construed and evaluated by its receivers. This may significantly influence the effectiveness of eWOM because customers have less trust in incentive-driven eWOM than in organic eWOM. However, increasing the quality of eWOM and using third party sites to incentivize the posters can alleviate this low trust issue.[2]

### Integrated marketing communications

The global hospitality giants, such as McDonald's, Burger King, Accor, Hilton, Marriott and IHG, invest billions of dollars, euros, pounds and yen in promoting their products and brands to millions of customers in different target audiences around the world. This creates enormous marketing communication and organizational difficulties. Cultural differences and regulation in different countries are the major barriers to effective marketing communication.

First, there is the issue of language. Some languages need more copy space than other languages – for example, written French and Italian needs up to 25 per cent more space than written English, whereas written German and Scandinavian languages need up to 30 per cent more. This creates different page layout requirements from a visual design perspective. Translating an advertising message can present problems, especially if humour is involved. Humour often involves a play on words that may not convey the same meaning, or even be meaningless, in a foreign language.

Second, there is the issue of cultural symbolism. Not only words, but colours, gender roles, behaviours, objects and symbols vary in meaning between cultures, resulting in audiences potentially creating different interpretations of the same communication. Finally, there is the problem of different governmental and non-governmental approaches to regulating marketing communication. Associations of marketing communications professionals in most developed countries operate voluntary codes of practice setting out what is allowed and disallowed, for example, in advertising and sales promotion. Marketers also face legislative and regulatory controls. Different legislatures impose restrictions on advertising, selling, telemarketing and sales promotion. Even a relatively simple pan-European sales promotion targeting families with children can be difficult to implement because of the different national government restrictions on promotions to young people.

Major hospitality organizations employ their own marketing specialists working in website and online marketing, sales, sales promotion, PR and advertising in their national, regional and international offices. They also have to work with external advertising, PR and design agencies in several countries. With so many marketing communication specialists working on a range of campaigns, but all involved in delivering the global company's branded message, it is easy to see how difficult it is to maintain a consistent message. Most hotel groups have created brand standards manuals that set out the visual requirements for all marketing communications. For example, they specify the precise dimensions and colours of the brand logo, and the font that is to be used in advertising and website content.

The concept of integrated marketing communications (IMC) is a response to this potentially confused approach to organizing marketing communication. Major international advertising agencies like Leo Burnett and WPP provide a global one-stop shop for all the marketing communication services that a national or global client needs and provide an integrated service for international campaigns. Whether a hospitality corporation uses a global one-stop shop or continues to use specialist agencies and their own in-house marketing specialists, the important point is that effective international marketing communication campaigns need to be coordinated across all countries, and all elements of the marketing communication mix, to provide a consistent branded message to the target audiences.

### Projecting the brand image

The quality and design of all communications material must reflect and project the desired brand positioning to target audiences. The use of colour, photographs and graphic design, the style of copywriting and the quality of materials used can all influence consumers' or customers' perceptions of the hospitality brand. Online and offline marketing collateral (collateral is the term used to describe all the print materials designed to support the sales and marketing functions) need to complement each other to project a consistent brand image.

Cloud storage and filesharing technologies have enabled hospitality chains to develop solutions to the problem of delivering brand-consistent marketing communications collateral across all the units in the company. The brand manual and brand standards are provided on the cloud storage in digital format and shared with all appropriate users, with standardized sizes, colours and layouts for logos, brand identities, ads, print material and signage. Some also include a searchable database of marketing or brand assets including photographs, logos, marketing campaigns and press releases to support current marketing activity. Links may be provided or access to files can be granted to external suppliers such as advertising agencies, designers and printers. A unit planning to develop a marcom campaign can access the cloud storage and file sharing site and customize the promotional material, inputting the menus, prices, dates and address/contact details. The final artwork can be shared with the corporate head office for approval. Once approved, the artwork can then be sent to the commercial printers. This use of technology is cost-effective and allows the corporate head office much greater control in delivering consistent brand standards in marketing communications materials.

### Providing information

Both online and offline marketing communications need to provide current, accurate, essential and useful information, which tells the audience what they want to know. Customers will have specific information needs. For example, a conference organizer requires:

- Accurate location maps
- Information about availability of car parking
- Conference/meeting room layout details, including the number of delegates who can be accommodated in boardroom-, horseshoe- and theatre-style layout; the width, length and height of meeting rooms; the location of light fittings and power points
- Information about air-conditioning facilities
- Details of the number of bedrooms and bedroom types suitable for delegates
- Menus
- Details of leisure and spa facilities
- Examples of, or testimonials from, organizations who have recently used the conference facilities
- Information about available technologies and Wi-Fi access
- 24-hour delegate rates.

### CASE STUDY 9.1

#### Integrated marketing communications at IHG[3]

With nearly 5,950 hotels badged under 16 brands operating in 100 countries with over 883,800 rooms, IHG has developed a global approach to marketing communications. The IHG reservation and communication system comprises brand management, channel management, sales and reservations, and – with more than 100 million members – one of the largest hotel loyalty clubs in the world.

The brands are marketed on a global and regional basis using system fund revenues raised by charging each hotel a percentage of rooms revenue. System fund revenues of IHG in 2020 totalled US$765 million, down from US$1.4 billion in 2019, reflecting lower demand as a result of the COVID-19 pandemic. Branding decisions are strategic and set by the IHG head office. For example, the design of the IHG strapline 'Great Hotels Guests Love', which is set in a red heart, was a strategic decision. Each country has its own tactical national marketing and PR, whereas direct guest marketing is driven through the Priority Club Rewards programme. The global sales force comprises 21,000 sales professionals operating from local hotels, local market area sales teams, with key account managers and directors working in regional sales centres. Global account directors build relationships with the largest international corporate clients who often work in the banking, finance and IT sectors.

*Source*: IHG[3]

Although much information is often available in hard copy format (see section later in this chapter on collateral), online technologies enable hospitality companies to provide a vast range of high-quality, customized and sometimes less obvious information, that meets or even exceeds the expectations of target markets. The InterContinental Hotels brand was the first to introduce destination-specific concierge websites and videos for Priority Club Members. In these videos, the head concierge provides customers with interesting, unusual and vibrant commentary about places to visit, where to have a drink or eat out and what makes the destination special. In the videos, the head concierge visits the places they are recommending and introduces local characters who add their own comments to enrich the story. By using the head concierge in this role, InterContinental have exploited a natural and most appropriate voice to provide Club Members with interesting insights into the destination.

## MARKETING INSIGHT 9.3

### Hilton's response to COVID-19 pandemic: 'To New Memories', its first global marketing campaign[4]

The hospitality industry has been one of the hardest hit industries by the COVID-19 pandemic. Hotel chains decreased the size of their workforces as revenues dropped. Seven months into the coronavirus pandemic, Hilton launched its 'To new memories' global marketing campaign that includes TV ads, online videos as well as other digital and social content to inspire customers to make new memories. The 'To new memories' campaign focused on moments of reconnection consumers have been missing since the beginning of the COVID-19 pandemic, positioning Hilton as a place to make new memories. The video content used in the campaign depicted a series of reconnection moments consumers have been missing, highlighting the new memories waiting to be made with Hilton.

The 'To new memories' campaign was initiated based on the results of Hilton's survey of consumers, uncovering that travel memories are some of the happiest memories of consumers' lives (89 per cent of survey respondents), suggesting that most Americans (188 million) would say they are experiencing a travel memory deficit. The results also revealed the optimism and desire consumers have for travelling again soon, a feeling that is reflected in the new campaign and new Hilton packages and promotions.

This insight driven 'To new memories' global marketing campaign reflected consumers' desire to reconnect with the people and places they love. It was first launched in September 2020 in China, the United Kingdom and Germany, and was rolled out in October 2020 in the U.S. and Saudi Arabia. As a catalyst for memories for more than

100 years, Hilton developed the campaign to inspire consumers to move from dreaming to planning their next trip to create new memories. As stated by Chris Nassetta, president and chief executive officer, 'While so much has changed this year, some things remain true – people crave connections, seeking out the reliable, friendly experiences that only our hospitality can provide. Hilton is here to help you make new memories, whenever you are ready.'

In addition to this campaign, Hilton launched new programmes and adopted new protocols to support consumers around the globe and make them feel comfortable with Hilton as their first choice to make new memories. These include:

> Contactless arrival: Through the Hilton Honors app and Digital Key technology, members were given the option for a contactless arrival experience at thousands of participating hotels. Guests had the option of bypassing the front desk by using their mobile phones to choose their room, check in, unlock their door and check-out.
>
> Hilton CleanStay: The Hilton CleanStay programme was created in collaboration with Lysol® and Dettol® maker RB and Mayo Clinic. Hilton CleanStay was implemented across Hilton's 18 brands in July, 2020.

Hilton EventReady with CleanStay: Hilton developed a global meeting and events programme designed to create experiences that are clean, flexible, safe and socially responsible. EventReady with CleanStay provided curated solutions and reimagined environments to meet and gather safely and comfortably.

*Source*: www.hilton.com[4]

### Digital (or online) marketing

The rapid development of information and communication technologies (ICT) and devices including desktop computers, laptops, tablets, smart phones and wearable devices such as smart watches has enabled businesses and consumers to access destination, travel and hospitality information online and make purchases. Although most hospitality businesses have websites, the majority are little more than digital brochures, linked to a booking engine to facilitate reservations, and offering an email address or web form to receive inbound enquiries. These websites are primarily one-way communication tools with limited interactivity, although some small hospitality businesses are also starting to integrate links to their social media pages, where customers can post comments and engage further with the brand.

The larger, more professional hospitality companies and a small number of tech-savvy hospitality entrepreneurs who have access to appropriate resources can experiment with more innovative technological developments, invest in more sophisticated interactive communications and engage in proactive online marketing. Their websites are designed with more imagination, higher specifications, more graphics and better quality, digitally enhanced photographs, greater use of video and greater interactivity. They can adopt the latest channels to engage with consumers and customers and support interaction via social networking sites such as Facebook, Twitter, Pinterest, Instagram and LinkedIn.

The current use of ICT allows hospitality companies to communicate interactively with customers via email, SMS (text), online chat, social media and mobile apps. For example, hotels, especially large chain hotels, can customize guests' hospitality experiences using the historical customer data they have in their databases. During the booking process, almost all hotels offer customization by asking guests to specify their preferences: this helps the hotel to better prepare for the guest's stay. Hotel company directories can link information from satellite navigation systems so that customers can obtain easy-to-follow directions to the hotel they are staying in that night via, for example, Google Maps. This communication activity reinforces the brand's messages and helps to enhance service quality.

---

### MARKETING INSIGHT 9.4

**Marketing to Gen Z and younger millennials: Taco Bell[5]**

Taco Bell is an American-based quick service restaurant (QSR) chain that was founded by Glen Bell in 1962 in Irvine, California. Taco Bell is a subsidiary of Yum! Brands, Inc. The restaurants serve a variety of Mexican-inspired foods, which include tacos, burritos, quesadillas, nachos, novelty and specialty items, along with a variety of 'value menu' items. As of 2020, Taco Bell serves over 40 million customers each week. The chain has over 7,400 restaurants in 31 countries.

Taco Bell is one of the more successful QSR chains when it comes to marketing to Gen Z and younger millennials. With more than 1.3 million Instagram followers, 2 million Twitter fans and 93,000 YouTube followers, Taco Bell has been creating a buzz among Gen Z and younger millennials with some clever campaigns.

Taco Bell's Instagram features new products, mouth-watering pictures, contests, a blog and plenty of event-based marketing such as their #TacoBellFriendsgiving menus. Taco Bell's Cinco de Mayo filter on Snapchat that turned users' faces into giant tacos has been a great success, receiving 224 million views. Taco Bell's content hub features blog posts from fans, employees, dieticians, marketers and fun stories about the restaurants. Taco Bell's YouTube channel tells short fun stories like 'What The Bell Happened'. They successfully operationalized the idea that video content under 1 minute is highly watchable and sharable for their demographic. The brand also puts fans at the centre of their content. The YouTube series 'For Here or To Go' is a great example. They also retweet fan stories knowing that user-generated content is extremely powerful.

The best Taco Bell campaign was the time they opened a pop-up hotel in the summer of 2019. The company took over the V Palm Springs hotel in Palm Springs, California for an extended four-day weekend in August. The plans for an exclusive, Taco Bell-themed resort were released in May. The resort was temporarily named 'The Bell: A Taco Bell Hotel and Resort'. As a marketing campaign, the brand featured exclusive Taco Bell food that no one else had ever tasted before, Taco Bell-inspired nail art and hairstyles and even giant pool floats that look like sauce packets. Taco Bell's ability to successfully market to Gen Z and younger millennials clearly suggests that Taco Bell knows its target audience demographic and creates content for them. The company has segmented the market, targeting youth between the ages of 20 and 30. They specifically target younger men who eat out a minimum of 12 times a month. The market has also been segmented according to income, targeting lower, middle- and upper-class-income groups. Taco Bell's success is a testament to the fact that if you want to be successful in any markets such as the saturated food and beverage market, you must research and understand your target market thoroughly.

*Source*: Dibenedetto[5]

### *Collateral*

In addition to digital versions, hospitality units still use a wide variety of hard-copy print materials, also known as collateral. Print materials include:

- Stationery
- Brochures, tariff and price lists
- Menus and wine lists
- Conference brochures
- Wedding brochures
- Function menus
- Promotional material for the sales team
- In-room information (hotel facilities and in-room service menus)
- Special product brochures
- Special promotional flyers
- Newsletters.

Collateral produced for branded chains includes:

- Corporate directory listing all branded units in the country, region or world
- Corporate leisure breaks brochure
- Corporate conference brochure
- Group business brochure targeting tour operators
- Corporate sales teams' sales support material
- Corporate newsletters
- Loyalty club leaflets, application forms and newsletters
- Special promotions.

Print materials provide different types of information and have different lengths of shelf life. Shelf life is the period of time for which the collateral material performs its communicative function. The design and production costs of a new full-colour brochure will be relatively high and, with reprints, will be expected to have a shelf life of several years. A leaflet promoting a single event for one day or night has a finite shelf life of a few months and is relatively cheap to produce. Only general information should be provided in the long-life pieces of print, whereas price details that change more frequently need to be produced separately.

### *Linking print material to other elements of marketing communications*

Print material is used to support other marketing communication activities. The hotel or corporate sales team need print material when they are discussing potential client needs in sales visits away from the hotel premises. Although these materials are in most cases streamable or downloadable from cloud storage sites and websites, many clients still want to be provided with print collateral to review when the salesperson has left the meeting. There should be a mutually supportive relationship between print material and digital and online materials. Collateral can promote the website address and direct information seekers to the site, whereas the brochure can be downloaded from the website.

**The importance of menu design**

For restaurants, the most important marketing tool is the menu. Indeed, the menu expresses the brand personality of a restaurant and projects the brand promise. However, many menus fail to entice potential customers because of simple mistakes in menu design. The starting point in creating an effective menu design is to research competitor establishments. There is a logic to the menu design of different categories of restaurants. For example, family restaurants need an element of fun to attract children; gourmet restaurants need to present their menu in an elegant, sophisticated style.

Menus must be easy to read. If the menu is in digital format, easy-to-read fonts and high quality attractive pictures should be used, the colour should match the branding of the business and customers should be allowed to customize their orders. If the menu is printed, a minimum font size of 12pt ensures it can be read by most people. The menu structure should follow the typical order of drink and food items (appetizers, main course and desserts) in a natural hierarchy. Effective menu design draws on the principles of newspaper and magazine layouts by using headlines, body text, illustrations and white space to break up the copy and make it easier on the eye. A criticism of many menus is the excess of copy – the descriptions of some menu items are too long and are not always intelligible. Prices need to be clearly labelled. In the competitive world of dining out, restaurants need to project a distinctive experience to encourage customers to return and tell their family and friends. A distinctive menu not only conveys the information that the diner needs but also creates a unique talking point that creates a competitive marketing advantage for that restaurant. Figure 9.3 provides an example of a distinctive menu from Langham's Brasserie.

Advertisements in print media are often restricted in space terms and are mainly used to stimulate prospects to visit a website and/or make a telephone call for further information (the second A for 'Action' in the AIDA model). The brochure, tariff and accompanying sales letter are designed to convert the enquiry into the booking. Another use of print material is in direct mail campaigns, often to members of the frequent guest programme and/or guests who have stayed before. Unfortunately, recipients often throw brochures and leaflets away. Wastage and high costs of producing high-quality hospitality brochures, coupled with inaccurate target marketing, means that companies are always searching for more cost-effective solutions. The online environment represents one such solution, as the Internet and online promotion gradually takes over from print material.

### Sales force (personal selling)

Personal selling uses direct-to-customer communication to present information that moves potential clients towards action and maintains relationships with customers. Although personal selling includes correspondence and telesales, the main focus in hospitality is face-to-face contact with potential clients by the sales force. Employing a salesperson is very expensive, with major costs, including salary, commission and bonuses; travel and accommodation costs; professional presentation equipment to demonstrate the company's products, locations and prices; laptops

Figure 9.3a   Langan's Brasserie menu

or tablets; mobile/telephone charges and administrative support. Indeed, personal selling is the most expensive marcom activity available to hospitality companies, and for this reason most small hospitality companies do not employ salespeople. However, the outward-looking owner/ manager can take on the sales role and actively promote the company to prospective clients.

## WHITE WINES

1. HOUSE WHITE LANGAN'S SELECTION 17·50
2. ½ LITRE HOUSE 12% 14·00/ BY THE GLASS 12% 175ML 7·00
3. MARQUES DE RISCAL RUEDA BLANCO SPAIN '09 21·00
4. PICPOUL DE PINET BEAUVIGNAC '09 23·00
5. PINOT GRIGIO TRENTINO ITALY '09 23·50
6. MUSCADET SEVRE-ET-MAINE SUR LIE
   CHATEAU DU CLERAY '08 24·50
7. MACON-VILLAGES DOMAINE CHENEVIERE '08 24·75
8. BUITENVERWACHTING SAUVIGNON BLANC '09 26·50
   BY THE GLASS 12·5% 175ML 7·50
9. COOPERS CREEK CHARDONNAY '09 26·50
   BY THE GLASS 13·5% 175ML 7·50
10. ST VERAN CUVEE COQ D'OR '08 27·00
11. HUNTER'S MARLBOROUGH SAUVIGNON BLANC '09 N. ZEALAND 27·00
12. TERRA LAZARICA SAUVIGNON BLANC SERBIA '06 27·50
13. GAVI DI GAVI LA MEIRANA '09 ITALY 29·50
14. LANGAN'S CHABLIS LOUIS PETIT '08 32·50
15. SANCERRE LES COFFANTS CHARLES DUPUY '08 35·50
16. MONTAGNY 1ER CRU ALAIN ROY '07 37·50
17. POUILLY FUME DOM GILLES CHOLLET '09 41·00
   CHABLIS 1ER CRU FOURCHAUME '08 44·00
19. MEURSAULT VIEILLES VIGNES VINCENT GIRARDIN '07 65·00

## CHAMPAGNES

46. MUMM CORDON ROUGE 55·00
47. PERRIER JOUET NV 55·00
48. TAITTINGER BRUT 55·00
49. MOET & CHANDON NV 60·00
50. BELLE FON CUVEE DES MOINES BRUT ROSE 60·00
   BY THE GLASS 12·5% 12·00
51. TAITTINGER ROSE 60·00
52. BOLLINGER NV 65·00
53. LAURENT PERRIER ROSE NV 70·00
54. PERRIER JOUET BELLE EPOQUE '02 110·00
55. DOM PERIGNON '00 125·00

## SPARKLING WINES

56. PROSECCO DI 'ALDOBBIADENE 27·00
57. BLANC DE BLANCS RESERVE FERE FRANCE 27·50
58. BALFOUR BRUT ROSE '04 63·00

### A FINE WINE LIST IS AVAILABLE

WINES BY THE GLASS ARE ALSO AVAILABLE IN 125ML MEASURES ON REQUEST

## RED WINES

20. HOUSE RED LANGAN'S SELECTION 17·50
21. ½ LITRE HOUSE 12% 14·00 / BY THE GLASS 12% 175ML 7·00
22. NORTON CABERNET SAUVIGNON ARGENTINA '09 19·75
   BY THE GLASS 13·5% 7·50
23. SANTA RITA MERLOT '09 CHILE 20·50
   BY THE GLASS 14% 175ML 7·50
24. VINA TORCIDA RIOJA '09 22·00
25. COTES-DU-RHONE ST ESPRIT DELAS '08 24·50
26. COOPERS CREEK HAWKES BAY MERLOT NEW ZEALAND '07 24·50
27. TERRA LAZARICA CABERNET SAUVIGNON SERBIA '07 24·50
28. FLEURIE CLOS DES QUATRE VENTS '09 29·75
29. HUNTERS MARLBOROUGH PINOT NOIR '08 NEW ZEALAND 30·50
30. RUPERT & ROTHSCHILD CLASSIQUE '08 SOUTH AFRICA 30·50
   BY THE GLASS 14% 175ML 8·00
31. BOURGOGNE PINOT NOIR GIRARDIN '08 33·50
32. CHATEAUNEUF DU PAPE DOMAINE DU GRAND TINEL '05 34·50
33. RIOJA RESERVA CONDE DE VALDEMAR '04 35·50
34. CHIANTI PEPPOLI CLASSICO '07 38·00
35. CHATEAU DE GIRONVILLE HAUT MEDOC '03 38·00
36. DOMAINE CARNEROS AVANT GARDE PINOT NOIR '08 38·00
37. CHATEAU D'ANGLES A C LA CLAPE '06 39·00
38. CHATEAU LALANDE DE GRAVET GRAND CRU
   ST EMILION '07 40·75
39. CHASSAGNE MONTRACHET LES CHENES COLIN '08 46·00
40. CHATEAU BELLEGRAVE PAUILLAC '06 58·50
41. MOULIN D'ANGLUDET MARGAUX '06 61·00
42. CHATEAU DE SALES POMEROL '02 66·00

## ROSE WINES

43. LES QUATRE TOURS COTEAUX D'AIX-EN-PROVENCE '09 18·50
   BY THE GLASS 12·5% 175ML 7·00
44. COTES DE PROVENCE '09 LES MAITRES VIGNERONS
   DE ST TROPEZ 22·75
45. SANCERRE ROSE GITTON '07 35·50

## DESSERT WINES

MUSCAT DE BEAUMES-DE-VENISE '08 ALC 15%
BY THE GLASS 100ML 8·00    BY THE BOTTLE 37·50
CHATEAU LA FLEUR SAUTERNES '06 ½ BOTTLE 27·50
MISSION HILL RIESLING ICE WINE CANADA '03 ½ BOTTLE 76·00

## PORTS

| | GLS 100ML | BOTTLE |
|---|---|---|
| VINTAGE PORT RAMOS PINTO ALC 20% '91 | 12·00 | 75·00 |
| RUBY PORT RAMOS PINTO ALC 19·5% | 7·00 | 45·00 |

## BRANDIES 50ML

| | |
|---|---|
| HENNESSY *** | 9·50 |
| MARC DE BOURGOGNE JULES BELIN | 7·50 |
| CALVADOS BOULARD | 10·50 |
| HINE VSOP FINE CHAMPAGNE | 11·50 |
| JANNEAU VSOP ARMAGNAC | 11·50 |
| MARTELL VSOP | 11·50 |
| COURVOISIER VSOP | 11·50 |
| MARTELL CORDON BLEU JP MARTELL | 16·00 |
| HENNESSY XO | 16·00 |
| DELAMAIN PALE & DRY GRANDE CHAMPAGNE | 16·00 |
| REMY MARTIN FINE CHAMPAGNE XO SPECIAL | 16·00 |

## MALT WHISKIES 50ML

| | | |
|---|---|---|
| CRAGGANMORE | 40% 12 YEARS | 9·50 |
| GLENFIDDICH | 12 YEARS | 9·00 |
| GLENKINCHIE | 10 YEARS | 9·00 |
| GLENLIVET | 12 YEARS | 9·00 |
| GLENMORANGIE | 10 YEARS | 9·00 |
| MACALLAN | 40% 10 YEARS | 9·50 |
| OBAN | 43% 14 YEARS | 9·50 |
| LAGAVULIN | 43% 16 YEARS | 9·50 |
| TALISKER | 45·8% 10 YEARS | 9·50 |
| DALWHINNIE | 43% 15 YEARS | 9·50 |
| PENDERYN | 46% 12 YEARS | 10·00 |

## LIQUEURS 50ML

| | | |
|---|---|---|
| AMARETTO | 28% | 8·50 |
| BAILEYS | 17% | 8·50 |
| BENEDICTINE | 40% | 8·50 |
| COINTREAU | 40% | 8·50 |
| CREME DE MENTHE | 25% | 8·50 |
| DRAMBUIE | 40% | 8·50 |
| KUMMEL | 39% | 8·50 |
| SAMBUCA | 38% | 8·50 |
| TIA MARIA | 20% | 8·50 |
| GRAPPA | 40% | 8·50 |
| GRAND MARNIER | 40% | 8·50 |

GIN, VODKA, RUM & WHISKEY ARE ALSO AVAILABLE IN 25ML MEASURES
ON REQUEST

" IF YOU REQUIRE AN ALTERNATIVE PLEASE ASK "

Figure 9.3b Langan's Brasserie menu

From a customer's perspective, low-risk and low involvement hospitality products do not really need a detailed personalized explanation in a face-to-face meeting. A quick service restaurant offers relatively simple product purchases and does not therefore need to employ a sales force. However, more complicated or higher value hospitality products – for example, major conference bookings from key corporate accounts and intermediaries who generate volume bookings – require more detailed discussions and negotiations in face-to-face meetings. Prospective clients who can generate large numbers of nights and/or food and beverage revenue expect a salesperson to pitch for their business, and because of the high sales value the competition will almost certainly want to talk to prospective clients as well. In sum, face-to-face selling is appropriate when:

- The product is complex or risky and needs detailed explanation.
- The product specification can be customized to suit the needs of the client.
- The potential value of the sale is relatively high.
- The price is negotiable.
- The sales contact can influence or make the decision to book business.
- The contact expects a sales visit.
- Competitors are likely to pitch for the business.

During the COVID-19 pandemic face-to-face interaction became much less frequent as firms and customers sought to reduce opportunities for infection. Online applications such as Zoom became very widely adopted.

In larger hospitality companies, responsibility for unit sales can rest either with the corporate sales organization or the unit. In the latter case, proactive general managers will join their hotel sales executives when meeting key accounts. Indeed, most medium and large hotels will employ at least one sales executive, unless this function is entirely managed by the corporate office.

### The corporate sales team

All the major hospitality organizations use personal selling as an interactive communications tool in servicing and building or maintaining relationships with clients. Important clients are called *key accounts*, and potential clients are called *prospects*. Selling is a professional art. Effective sales executives follow systematic procedures and use sales force automation (SFA) software to help them plan, conduct and report on sales visits. SFA applications enable the salesperson to monitor progress of opportunities against an approved selling process. Salespeople perform a range of tasks including the following:

- *Prospecting*: This refers to the search for prospective customers. It includes searching for new leads from local or national organizations and companies, and reactivating lapsed customers. Prospects need to be qualified, which means checking that the contact has the authority and budget to buy. Salespeople can also check that the prospect is a good fit with existing customer segments.
- *Sales calls*: Hotel sales executives will occasionally turn up at a prospect's office unannounced, hoping to arrange a meeting by chance. This tactic is called 'cold calling' and can occasionally be effective. However, the most effective sales approach is to pre-book an appointment. This ensures that both the prospect and the sales executive do not waste valuable time. Often, sales executives will have to make several telephone calls before they book a meeting date in the prospect's calendar, and dozens of calls need to be made every day to identify genuine prospects. Sales executives might need to meet a client several times and gradually build up a personal relationship before signing any business. Arranging sales meetings with existing clients is also an important function of the sales executive, in order to continue building and maintaining a close relationship with the customer.

- *Relationship management*: Sales executives not only win new business but are also responsible for maintaining long-term profitable relationships with customers. Sales executives therefore must service accounts, deal with queries and complaints and be proactive in relationship maintenance. Keeping accurate records of contacts, issues or complaints and sales opportunities are important tasks for salespeople and this is made easier through SFA software applications.

Occasionally, a sales force will organize a 'sales blitz'. This is a coordinated sales campaign using a large number of sales executives who work together to saturate a target geographic area, combining cold calling, telesales and pre-booked meetings with prospects and key accounts. Although a sales blitz is an effective tool, it requires a considerable amount of organization.

Prospective customers who want to book significant volumes of business will contact hotels directly and arrange to visit them. The hotel sales executives, the conference and banqueting manager or the duty manager will host the meeting, show the prospect the hotel's facilities and explain the services available. These visits are key opportunities to impress potential customers.

Personal selling is an important part of the marcom mix. The salesperson represents the unit and the brand and can be regarded as the human face of the company.

## Advertising

Advertising is any paid communication in traditional and online media owned by third parties. Although advertising normally reaches a wide audience, the proportion of readers, listeners and viewers who are potential customers can be relatively small. For this reason, advertising can be relatively expensive, and it is notoriously difficult to measure its effectiveness. Although the advertiser does have control over the message content, message format and message source, there are legal, voluntary and social constraints that advertisers need to recognize. Most countries have legal restrictions on advertising, ranging from tight censorship controls in countries like Saudi Arabia to voluntary agreements like the British Code of Advertising Practice. These regulations are designed to ensure that ads do not mislead consumers with inaccurate or dishonest claims. Advertisers need to recognize that inappropriate ads that offend people's religious or cultural values can be extremely damaging to their product and company.

Most hospitality advertising is aimed at consumer and customer (business) markets, but occasionally a major company will communicate with other audiences (such as financial and political stakeholders) by advertising in the business and financial media. When there is a contested takeover battle, both companies will invest in advertising to influence the outcome.

The following media can be used for advertising campaigns: online media (e.g. Google search pages, review websites, social media sites and other digital platforms), newspapers, magazines, tourist board publications, guide books, broadcast media (radio, cinema and television), outdoor media (billboards and posters), transport media (buses, trains and taxis) and non-traditional or ambient media. This term is used to describe a multitude of formats, including adverts on shopping trolleys, washroom walls, pizza boxes, risers on staircases, bus tickets and even cattle grazing alongside highways!

The decision about which media are used depends mainly on the campaign's marketing communication objectives, the audience the medium delivers and the available budget. We will now discuss the advantages and disadvantages of the main advertising media.

## ONLINE ADVERTISING

As consumers have come to rely on online resources for information gathering, socialization and making purchases, so has online advertising become more important. All major hospitality companies use online advertising as part of their integrated communication strategy. Generalist advertising agencies or hotel specialists like TravelClick advise, create and place online adverts for hospitality companies. Campaigns are normally placed across a range of websites, social media platforms and on search engines, as opposed to a single site, to achieve a broader audience reach. Online advertising can take several forms, including text and video, but is more often associated with banner advertising, originally because the advert was placed in a box across the top of the web page. Online adverts can be static, animated or interactive. There are several ways in which the advertiser benefits from banner advertising. First, viewers are exposed either consciously or subconsciously to the brand's message; second, they can click on the advert to obtain more information, which might result in a sale; and third, advertisers can be very targeted in their communication reaching very specific audiences based on their demographics, interests and other behavioural signals. Online adverts can be customized for individual viewers, based, for example, on their research use of keywords for online searches or their browsing history. Each view of the advert is described as an impression. The ratio of viewers seeking more information by clicking on the online advert is called the 'click-through rate' (CTR). The effectiveness of an online campaign is often based on the cost per one thousand impressions (CPM). Alternatively, the costs are based on the number of click-throughs, which is called a cost-per-click (CPC) method. The CPC is regarded as a more cost-effective model because the advertiser only pays for the number of viewers who have behaved by clicking through for more information.

## NEWSPAPERS

Newspaper advertising varies in cost according to:

- Circulation and readership – the number of copies sold and the number of readers per copy. Most major newspapers now have hard copy and online versions reaching different segments of audience
- Geographic coverage – local, regional and national
- Audience profile – socio-economic profile, income and lifestyle
- Size of advert – larger display adverts cost more than classified ads
- Colour – these are more expensive than monochrome adverts
- Location of advert – where an advert is placed in the newspaper (front page, back page and requests for a specific spot are more expensive)
- Timing – Sunday is one of the most popular days to read newspapers, and so it is more expensive
- Number of adverts placed – a series of adverts booked at the same time can qualify for volume discounts.

The key point about newspaper advertising is the short shelf life. This means that yesterday's newspaper has old news; readers quickly throw out old newspapers and the adverts in them.

## MAGAZINES

Magazines have similar cost variables to newspapers, with two important differences. First, whilst newspapers have a broad readership, magazines focus on specialist subject areas and attract discrete, distinct readership profiles. Second, magazines have a longer shelf life; this means they can continue to generate responses months after the publication date. Magazines generally use higher-quality paper and encourage full-page colour adverts particularly for life-style advertising. Hotels and restaurants located in popular city destinations from Abu Dhabi to Zagreb can advertise in magazines like *Time Out*, which targets visiting tourists. Country hotels targeting leisure break consumers can advertise in specialist bird, gardening and walking magazines, whereas adverts aimed at promoting the transformative power of travel as a vital pathway to growth, healing and unity after a pandemic like COVID-19 use appropriate imagery and text that champion travel with a renewed sense of purpose – not just to escape, but to discover ourselves, each other and the world everyone shares (see the Marriott Bonvoy advert in Figure 9.4).

**Figure 9.4** Marriott Bonvoy is championing travel with a renewed sense of purpose of not just to escape, but to discover – ourselves, each other and the world everyone shares

*Source*: Marriott Bonvoy

The international luxury hotel brands create brand image advertising campaigns primarily using colour magazines, such as in-flight airline magazines for business-class customers and the financial media (e.g., the *Financial Times* weekend edition), to project their brand personality. A Four Seasons Hotels campaign targeted both business executive travellers and the family market using appropriate talent (models) in carefully staged leisure settings with the strapline 'What will you remember?' One and Only used a black-and-white shot of a couple having fun with wrap-around hammocks on a private deck in their Maldives Hotel using the phrase 'Live the moment'. Peninsula Hotels use photographs and brief storylines of their employees under the heading 'Portraits of Peninsula', and Mandarin Oriental uses a personality endorsement strategy with the simple strapline – 'He's a fan' or 'She's a fan'.

## TOURIST BOARD PUBLICATIONS

Tourist boards are destination marketing organizations (DMOs) that produce many print and digital publications carrying advertisements for, and listings of, accommodation, attractions, bars and restaurants and events. Potential visitors to the area contact the DMO to request information and they are either sent these brochures or directed to specific websites to view digital communication materials. For smaller accommodation businesses, for example, a farmhouse with bed-and-breakfast, tourist board publications are one of the most effective promotional tools.

---

**ACTIVITY 9.3**

Go to the Mandarin Oriental website (www.mandarinoriental.com). On the home page, click on 'view guest gallery' to discover their destinations through the eyes of their guests. You can also share your experience with #ImAFan and mention @mo_ hotels for a chance to be featured.

Visit the Time Out website (www.timeout.com/). On the website, find and click on 'Advertising' link located under 'Contact us'. Explore the different options hospitality companies have to advertise in *Time Out*.

---

### GUIDEBOOKS

Country and city guidebooks provide tourists with information about travel, where to stay, what to do or see, where to eat and local cultural/historical anecdotes in several different languages. Popular guides include the motoring organizations (AAA and AA), Baedeker, Dorling Kindersley, Fodor, Lonely Planet, Rough Guides and Wallpaper. While printed guides have a very long shelf life, digital versions of those guides provide more up-to-date information. In recent years, digital versions of popular guidebooks have become more popular due to travellers' increasing reliance on online resources and increasing use of smart phones, tablets and other mobile communication devices while travelling. Indeed, real-time mobile technology provides hospitality businesses with the opportunity to advertise their offer 'right now' to visitors. Some guides, like the motoring ones, will only accept advertising from hospitality organizations that have been inspected and are listed in the guide, while others will accept advertising from any source.

### TELEVISION

Television reaches mass audiences and is consequently the most expensive advertising medium. TV advertising costs include both origination costs (for producing the commercial), which can be significant, and media costs for purchasing time. Media costs vary depending on the length of a television commercial, the time it is broadcast and the profile and size of the audience viewing the programme in which it is embedded. The norm for a TVC (television commercial) is 30 seconds, though slots vary from 10 seconds to several minutes. A prime spot during the evening news or in the middle of one of the most popular national programmes costs a significant sum of money, because these programmes attract peak audiences. An advert running during the 'graveyard shift' in the middle of the night on a local television channel is much cheaper, because the audiences are so much smaller. The impact of television advertising can be diminished because viewers channel-hop, use apps that enable them to skip ads, or leave the room during the commercial break. Programming that is recorded and viewed later can be set to omit the adverts. Some networks embed adverts in banners that appear at the top, bottom or side of screen during programming to counter this behaviour. Effective television advertising requires significant budgets to afford the slots and frequency to generate brand name or message recall. Television advertising is appropriate for mass-marketed products and for this reason the most significant hospitality advertisers on major television channels are the QSR brands like McDonald's, Burger King, KFC and Wendy's. Although QSR TV advertising is often used to promote price deals, hotel companies tend to use TV for building brand awareness and enhancing brand image. Travel agents such as Trip.com have developed their own dedicated interactive YouTube channels, which promote package holidays, cruises and destinations that can be booked by viewers as they watch the YouTube programme. You can view the Trip.com YouTube Channel here: www.youtube.com/c/TripOfficial.

---

**MARKETING INSIGHT 9.5**

### Content marketing[6]

More and more hospitality and travel companies realize the importance of offering additional, inspiring and useful travel content to their potential customers. In a quest for the more customer-centric, authentic and creative solutions, many businesses turn to travel bloggers or, in collaboration with creative digital agencies, develop their own innovative promotional content concepts. In 2015, Lawrence of Morocco, an independent family travel business, partnered with the digital agency Moz to reach out to the prospect travellers and to promote their niche travel business. Instead of promoting the company in the traditional way, the agency linked the business to the long-awaited launch of the fifth season of the television series *Game of Thrones*. As a number of scenes in the popular series were shot in Morocco, the agency suggested creating a map showing all the filming locations, including those in Morocco, and promoting it to the right audience at the right time. The campaign resulted in 245 per cent higher referral traffic to the website as compared to the previous year, positive word-of-mouth, increased brand awareness and free coverage on such popular sites as the *Washington Post*, *Business Insider* and *Mashable*.

*Source*: McLoughlin[6]

---

### CINEMA

Cinema advertising has many similarities to TV advertising but is not as expensive. The main hospitality advertisers on cinema are the QSR chains and local restaurants. Production costs can be low because local advertisers simply use stock footage and overdub a relevant local soundtrack. Cinema advertising is a cost-effective promotional tool to reach the young adult (18–30) audience.

### RADIO

In recent years, radio has become a more popular advertising medium because the target audiences have become much more tightly defined. Stations have clearly identified target audiences and formats such as top 40, classics, talk, sport, niche and classic rock music. Because of this, programmes hold the attention of the audience better than television. Radio advertising is not as expensive as television, and the cost of making radio commercials is considerably lower. Most local radio stations offer simple, low-cost advertising production facilities to enable local advertisers to use this popular communication tool.

### Sales promotion

The primary role of sales promotion is to stimulate short-term or immediate sales. Virtually all hospitality organizations use sales promotions at new product launches (to attract trial purchase), during low and shoulder periods (to boost demand) and at customer touch-points (to promote in-house offers). Effective sales promotions are designed well in advance. However, on occasions, for example when there is a sudden collapse in demand, the marketing department needs to respond quickly with a sales promotion campaign. Many sales promotions are bundled products offered at attractive prices, which offer enhanced value for the customer. The design and pricing of a packaged sales promotion must be:

- *Carefully targeted* – in particular, targeted at compatible target markets that will fit in with the existing customer mix.
- *Attractive to customers*, since competitors who have a similar demand pattern and may be planning their own sales promotion.
- *Properly costed* – both the level of the discount and the promotional costs (print material, online and offline advertising and email/surface mail) must be calculated during the planning stage of the campaign; bookings from sales promotions are generally stimulated by an attractive discounted price, but the price must cover the costs of the campaign.
- *Consistent* with the current brand position and brand image.
- *Creative!* The promotion needs to grab the audience's attention and interest and motivate the desired behavioural response. Creativity in designing and publicizing the offer is essential to ensure that the sales promotion stands out from competitors.
- *Of a fixed time period* that is long enough for the target audience to learn about the promotion and have time to book the offer, but not so long that there is little urgency for the customer to book.

Sales promotions that become the principal long-term marketing communication activity eventually become ineffective. Sales promotions lose their vitality, and over a longer period of time repeated price discounting can damage brand positioning.

There are many issues to consider when planning a sales promotion. First, promotional price discounting can be particularly complicated. If two restaurants in the same product class are competing and one restaurant has a sales promotion offering 'two meals for the price of one' (the equivalent of a 50 per cent discount), then the other restaurant cannot compete effectively with a 25 per cent discount voucher. Second, sales promotions do not necessarily generate customer loyalty. Indeed, bargain-hunting customers are unlikely to remain loyal, as they will always be looking to patronize competitors with similar or better deals. Finally, the sales promotion should not generate overfull demand that the business cannot satisfy.

Examples of typical sales promotions include:

- Price discounts on accommodation, food, beverage and leisure activities
- Added value promotions – bundling a range of hospitality products into a single price and package
- Buy one, get one free
- Early bird discounted drinks
- Discount vouchers and coupons.

### Point-of-sale material

Hospitality businesses use a variety of point-of-sale material to promote in-house products. Examples of point-of-sale material include calendars of events (see Figure 9.5), coupons, leaflets, menus and posters at the reception desk, in the lift, bedrooms, bars, restaurants and at leisure outlets. Point-of-sale material is usually a tangible piece of collateral that attempts to cross-sell additional products and services to guests whilst simultaneously projecting the image of the business. Larger properties and chains may have their own in-house TV networks running promotional and informational campaigns. Many hospitality brands produce excellent point-of-sale material, but there are also many units with dated, tired collateral, and this sends out negative signals to customers.

### Public relations

Most PR aims to generate positive publicity for the company in the media. Such publicity is generally regarded as 'free' because space and time are not bought as in advertising media. However, the design, effort, creativity and networking required to generate media coverage are not cheap. Public relations (PR) is a profession with a structured career pathway and specialized education with formal examinations. Many countries have professional associations for their PR professionals, which can provide useful information about career opportunities and professional development for students.

The major hospitality corporations employ PR managers in their national and international head offices. The corporate PR role includes managing publicity aimed at financial stakeholders and political bodies, crisis management (e.g., when a case of food poisoning is reported in the media), as well as promoting the parent company image and specific brands. Although the management of media relations at national and international level is clearly a role for the professional PR executive, individual hospitality owners and general managers can become adept at generating publicity for their own properties. The principles of effective PR are the same regardless of the scale of business. PR activity should:

- *Ensure that the proposition, or the publicity idea, is consistent with the brand's positioning.* Some hoteliers are so keen to be in the news that they forget the purpose of PR activity, which is to generate positive publicity for the business. Inappropriate stunts can generate significant amounts of irrelevant or even negative publicity, which undermines the brand's position in the marketplace.
- *Develop a creative concept that stimulates the media's imagination.* Media journalists and their editors are well informed, very aware and frequently cynical. To capture their imagination, the publicity concept needs to be different, interesting and, therefore, newsworthy.

Belmont House Hotel

# Dates
*for your diary*

## JANUARY

**Jamie's Bar**
Champagne treats,
Live up to your New Year's
resolutions. Carpe Diem!!
House champagnes at
January sale prices! Delicious.

**13th   Cherry Restaurant**
New menus, New prices,
Better value.

**20th   Jamie's Bar**
Jamie's new sandwich menu,
out with the old and in with
the new, except for old
favourites of course.

**25th   Cherry Restaurant**
Burns night supper in the
Cherry Restaurant, with our
own Head Chef, Stewart,
adressing the Haggis!
£24.95pp

**31st   Bowies**
New monthly music rights
start our first evening with
local singer Lindsey Cowlishaw
singing all her favourite classic
pop songs. Book a table for a
candlelight dinner and a
relaxing evening. Dinner
£15.00pp. Engry fee £1.50pp.

## FEBRUARY

**3rd   Bowies**
New menu!

**Jamie's Bar**
Jamies warms up the month
with Claret. A selection of
very special clarets available
from £4 a glass, a real treat.

**14th   Valentine's Night
(or overnight!)**
Choose from a delicious
menu for 2 in Cherry's
Restaurant, or be extravagant
and book dinner and one of
our lovely rooms. Or go
down to Bowies and enjoy a
romantic candlelight dinner
with a hint of blues music
playing. And if you can't
make the 14th come on the
15th! Cherrys £24.50pp
Overnight £130.00 including
dinner, bed and breakfast
for two, half a bottle of
champagne and a rose.
Bowies £19.50 pp

## MARCH

**2nd   The Belmont
Wedding Fair**
A must for all brides, or
even those just contamplating.
A collection of dedicated
suppliers there to help you
with all those tough decisions.
Hopefully you've already made
the most important one and
booked the Belmont.. (Well,
OK, I suppose your partner
could also be the most
important decision.)

**Jamie's Bar**
Jamie's Bar is going Australian,
a few little wines from down
under (is there such a thing as
a little wine from down under!),
and we might have a prawn or
two off the barbie

**21st   Cherry Restaurant**
Tonight is our FUN wine
appreciation night in
cherrys. Come and enjoy
a great meal with an
intriguing selection of
wines, the origins of which
will be described to you
by our experts...but are
they telling the truth?
Dinner including wine is
all inclusive, really good
value at £29.50

**Jamie's Bar**
Great coffee served from
8am weekday mornings.
Coffee & Croissant or
Danish £2.95 Choice of
Teas and cakes £2.95

**28th   Bowies**
Bowie's Jazz night, come
and listen to our singer
and the Sax player in the
candle light.

Don't forget Cherrys serves the
best breakfast around and is a
great way to get through your
first meeting of the day.

**10th–17th   Cherry Restaurant**
Lobster week in Cherrys,
one or two special dishes
of this most delicious of
shellfish to titillate the
palate.

**28th   Bowies**
Bowie's monthly Music
Night! Tonight we have
Karaoke! Dinner £15.00pp

**30th   Cherry Restaurant**
30th is a most important
date, yes it's Mothering
Sunday so book early and
make sure you give her a
great treat. Cherry's
Restaurant will be serving
its usual great food.
£18.50pp 4 courses.
coffee and a gift.

Figure 9.5  Point-of-sale collateral

*Source*: The Belmont House Hotel

- *Make sure that press information is professionally presented and made available at the right time.* Old news is not interesting. The tools that PR executives use include press releases, a press pack with all the relevant company information, photographs and arranging familiarization visits for journalists.

- *Suitable PR stories* include company news (e.g. new hotel/restaurant openings, new product launches), events, new menus and special offers, winning accolades and awards and human-interest stories about customers and employees.

Success is measured by print column inches/centimetres, online exposure, social media likes, number of comments and airtime minutes, though the level of sales generated by PR is more difficult to calculate.

---

**MARKETING INSIGHT 9.6**

**Prêt-À-Portea, Berkeley Hotel, Maybourne Hotels, London[7]**

The Berkeley Hotel, located in a fashionable part of London, created a designer afternoon tea menu called Prêt-à-Portea, which, because of its innovative fun and exquisite cakes, has generated over a million pounds worth of publicity worldwide. Conceived in 2005, the afternoon tea menu is inspired by the themes and colours of the fashion world. A team of leading international designers helps the head chef to select the current season's 'fashionista afternoon tea menu'. The design of the cakes is based on fashion apparel (boots, handbags, hats and shoes) and this has stimulated the interest of the media. The cakes, served on Paul Smith china, are stunning, and each designer gives her or his name to one of the cake designs. One example is the 'Christian Lacroix dark chocolate dress with soft centre and chic golden bow'. Designers include Anya Hindmarch, Paul Smith, Yves Saint Laurent, Christopher Kane, Jean-Paul Gaultier, Jason Wu, Sonia Rykiel and Erdem. The unusual feature of this PR campaign is that, twice a year, a new 'seasonal' tea menu is presented to the media that still generates significant publicity at minimal costs.

*Source*: www.the-berkeley.co.uk

---

#### PR AND CRISIS MANAGEMENT

PR is especially important when a company experiences a newsworthy crisis. Unfortunately, events such as terrorism, natural disasters, food poisoning incidents, hotel fires and high-profile court cases involving customers or employees generate media interest, even though the company does not want this type of publicity. The role of PR during the crisis is to present the hospitality company's version of events as favourably as possible. Journalists are more likely to portray the crisis sympathetically if their questions are taken seriously. When a senior figure in the company acts as the spokesperson and answers the media's questions with open, honest and helpful information, the media are more likely to be supportive. However, investigative journalists and those working for sensationalist media may be more difficult to handle. The major hospitality organizations have developed crisis management protocols that are implemented in the event of a crisis; when an incident occurs, it is easy for unit employees and managers to panic in the glare of the publicity and make inappropriate statements. Companies that respond effectively to a crisis can may even improve their image as a result of positive media publicity.

#### PR AND DESTINATION MARKETING

A relatively new PR activity for DMOs is the promotion of destinations to film and television companies. The popularity of destinations that have been featured in successful film and television programming has increased the number of visitors to these locations. The American entertainment industry has been a key attraction for tourists visiting Hollywood, Los Angeles and Orlando in Florida. Films such as the *Harry Potter* series and the *Lord of the Rings* have helped to promote tourism in Oxford, England and New Zealand. Today, destinations actively promote themselves as ideal locations for film and television productions in the hope that positive exposure will generate an increase in tourism.

---

### ACTIVITY 9.4

Visit the following websites of hospitality companies and look for media, press, press releases or press room (if you have difficulty finding the media/press pages, use the site map):

- www.bk.com/
- www.hilton.com/
- www.icehotel.com/
- www.shangri-la.com/

Review the latest press information – these are real press releases sent out by companies to the media to generate publicity. Evaluate the approach different companies take to create stories, and the content, interest and writing style.

---

### Sponsorship

Sponsorship is often used in conjunction with PR to obtain publicity. It is a major component in the financing of sports/arts/cultural activities and events. Football teams, tennis stars, golf tournaments, music festivals, art exhibitions and literary events depend on other organizations for financial support. Hospitality companies can either provide financial donations or complimentary services such as accommodation as part of a sponsorship arrangement in return for publicity. Sponsored activities promote the name of the sponsor on clothes, equipment, posters and vehicles during the event. The sponsorship can also become the focus of a marketing communications campaign. Indeed, key customers can be invited to the sponsored event and provided with VIP status and exclusive hospitality.

The cost of sponsorship is closely linked to the amount of media coverage generated. Obviously, the higher the sport's or celebrity's profile, the more it costs. Major hospitality companies can afford to sponsor popular national and international events. Many hospitality companies also sponsor local events and organizations that assist unsheltered families, promote racial equity, encourage youth participation in arts and culture, and provide opportunities for community service. For example, Starbucks has developed a long-time partnership with STG, a non-profit arts organization committed to community education programmes, offering opportunities for young people to grow their artistic talents. These sponsorships and partnerships can generate significant media coverage in a wide range of media outlets and enhance the brand's image. Small hospitality businesses can, with a modest amount of money, sponsor local community activities just as effectively; for example, a fast-food franchisee could sponsor a local children's football team and buy their uniforms to generate huge goodwill.

## Direct marketing

Direct marketing (DM) is any form of direct-to-consumer communication, such as direct mail, door drops, SMS (text messaging) and email campaigns. Usually, DM aims to inform and persuade customers to respond to a particular offer. A key benefit of DM is that it generally cuts out the intermediaries and the commissions paid to them, though some DM campaigns do direct recipients to intermediaries for fulfilment of the offer. This type of marketing communication activity remains popular with smaller hospitality businesses. Newsletters and seasonal greeting cards from small hotels, bed-and-breakfast houses and local restaurants are inexpensive and can help maintain customer relationships. The communications can be highly personalized, if somewhat quirky at times. Customer profiles and transaction data underpin successfully targeted DM, ensuring that the right message or offer is made in the right channel to the right customer at the right time.

DM in hotels relies on the company's customer database. Customer details from reservation and booking, and loyalty programme data are linked to customer transactions and accounts, to provide a database of customer activity and the value of each customer for the company. Customer data are usually stored in secure data storage facilities away from the operational units. Most customer data is stored in cloud storage, an off-site storage site that is maintained by a third party. Cloud storage safely and securely saves customer data to a remote database. Cloud storage makes it easy to share content securely with other properties and users. Information stored in a customer database typically includes names, contact details, geo-demographic data, number of visits, purpose of visits, time of visits, average spend, onsite purchase history, requests and personal comments – for example, birthdays, wedding anniversaries or the number and age of children. Data-mining tools can search and analyze the data to identify current customer usage patterns and clusters of customer segments. It can then identify customers who are most likely to be interested in booking specific hospitality products, at specific times. This information can then be used as part of a more accurately targeted DM campaign, assuming that the customers have actually given their permission to be contacted.

In hospitality, DM generates better results in leisure markets where the products have low involvement characteristics and prices are relatively modest – for example, leisure weekends. DM is frequently used in new product launches, such as new restaurant openings. It can also be used when targeting specific business markets, like the conference market. However, if the products have high involvement characteristics, then DM often needs to include a follow-up by the sales force.

Indeed, DM can work effectively with all the other elements of marketing communication mix in an integrated marketing communication campaign. DM is a powerful marketing communication tool for the following reasons:

- The company has complete control of the message, medium and timing of its delivery.
- Recipients of DM can be precisely targeted.
- The message can be more easily personalized.
- The impact of the DM campaign has immediate results, and the costs and return from a DM campaign can be measured.

Finally, over time people's geo-demographic characteristics alter, and their lifestyle patterns change. A major criticism of DM is that customer data can become dated. One estimate suggests that on average people move home at least once every eight years, and many people move much more frequently. This means that databases needed to be 'cleaned' and updated on a regular basis to ensure that people who have died or moved house are removed from them.

### The role of marketing agencies

The marcom agency industry comprises a small number of global players, a large number of regional and national companies and many small local businesses – some with only one employee – and today there is a wide range of specialist marcom companies offering services across advertising, PR, copywriting, media buying, selling, point-of-sale, word-of-mouth, DM, online and social media reputation management, photography and collateral. Online specialist agencies provide web design and development, search engine marketing, search engine optimization, content development, social media marketing, online reputation management and online advertising. There are also agencies that monitor and measure the effectiveness of marketing communication campaigns.

Although specialist agencies focus on one specific service, full-service agencies provide:

- *Research* – this includes research into audience characteristics, campaign effectiveness and new media forms.
- *Creative services* – content-related services include the conceptualization and production of advertising, publicity material, PR events and sponsorship material. Creativity gives the message a good chance of achieving cut-through and being noticed by the target audience. A client-produced creative brief summarizes the task, and the agency's creative team will first brainstorm ideas and then develop those ideas into a storyboard that presents a visual interpretation of the message execution. Storyboards can be used to pre-test the effectiveness of the creative concept, by obtaining feedback from focus groups representing the target audience. Their response indicates whether changes in the basic idea or message execution are needed. Although an agency will be responsible for the creative output, the client needs to be involved and has to give approval at key stages in this process.
- *Media planning* – this means selecting appropriate offline and online media, negotiating and buying the media space and time. Agencies should know which media are more effective to accomplish the task and can obtain better prices for clients because of their bulk buying power. Today, a growing proportion of media buying is automated in what is called programmatic buying. Intelligent software makes decisions that ensure that media spends are cost-effective.

Agencies employ account executives responsible for looking after individual clients and coordinating the agency's services to them. There are three ways in which agencies charge for their work:

1 *Commission*: Media owners pay a commission to agents who place the client's business with them. The commission is usually 15 per cent, but this can be subject to negotiation. The commission system has been criticized because unscrupulous agents can place content with the media that pay the highest commission, which is not always in the client's best interest, or buy more media than is strictly necessary to achieve the campaign's objectives.
2 *Fee*: Here, the client pays the agency a fee for the work. This can be on a project basis, or, in the case of PR agencies, clients may pay a regular monthly/annual retainer to ensure that any publicity opportunities are captured as they happen.
3 *Payment by results*: The quest for greater cost-effectiveness has produced a third alternative, payment by results. However, this is not as simple as it sounds, because measuring the out-

comes of marcom campaigns and attributing sales or other outcomes to specific communication activities is notoriously difficult.

Although all three systems are possible, most agencies use a combination of commission and fee.

## Planning the marketing communication campaign

The steps in developing a marketing communication campaign include setting objectives, agreeing the budget, defining the target audience, approving marketing communication strategies and tactics, implementation and measuring the results of the campaign.

### Marketing communication objectives

As mentioned earlier, communication objectives can be classified into 'learn', 'feel' and 'do' categories. Marketing communication campaigns for most small hospitality companies are short-term and tactical. The marketing communication campaigns for the major hospitality companies, however, are usually part of a long-term, coordinated, planned and professional activity to support the company's marketing objectives. The starting point in planning a marketing communication campaign is setting objectives that support and are consistent with long-term marketing objectives. Most long-term communication objectives focus on the brand, rather than on particular locations, products or customer experiences. Typically, brand owners want to ensure that the customers understand what the brand means and to develop favourable attitudes towards the brand. These are 'learn' and 'feel' objectives, respectively. We discuss objectives in more detail in Chapter 15, but all objectives should be specific, measurable, achievable, realistic and set to a timetable. Examples of marketing communications objectives include

- *Learn* – a new product launch objective for a restaurant opening in September could be 'to generate 15 per cent awareness of the restaurant among the target market of men and women aged 18–30, within a 15-minute drive-time radius of the site, by the end of October'.
- *Feel* – an objective for a conference hotel in an Adriatic tourism destination could be 'to become the destination's preferred conference hotel for Italian small and medium-sized professional associations within two years'.
- *Do* – an objective for a leisure hotel could be 'to generate a 25 per cent increase in domestic leisure break bookings in the next 12-month period'.

Short-term marketing objectives employ tactical activities like sales promotions to drive bookings and sales.

### Setting the marketing communication budget

How do you set a marcom budget? There are four recognized ways: affordability, percentage of sales, competitive parity, and objective and task. The approach taken really depends on the size and ownership of the hospitality business and the sector it operates in. Generally, budgeting methods become more systematic as the business grows in complexity.

#### AFFORDABILITY

Small hospitality operators – like the independent sandwich shop, the farmhouse with bed and breakfast and the wine bar – make promotional decisions based on what is affordable. These entrepreneurial owners may respond opportunistically to media offers and make judgements on a trial-and-error basis. Forward planning is rarely a strength of such businesses, but prudent calculations and 'gut instinct' should keep the marketing communication budget within the bounds of common sense.

## PERCENTAGE OF SALES

Historically, most hospitality businesses set their marketing budgets as a percentage of last year's achieved sales or next year's projected sales. Over time, industries establish norms for marketing costs and expenditure patterns. In hospitality, this process is complicated by a lack of consensus about which budget line items count as marketing communications expenses. For example, the sales force can be budgeted as a payroll item or included in the marketing communication budget. Fees paid to a consortium group and ultimately used for marketing purposes might appear as a general administrative item in the budget. However, the major hotel companies, which use the Uniform System of Accounts for the Lodging Industry (USALI), have adopted an accounting standard for marketing that includes some payroll costs. Hotstats Hospitality Intelligence benchmarking company conducts an annual financial survey of 120 brands located in 600+ markets in the UK, Europe and the Middle East to establish benchmarks for hospitality industry operating ratios. The typical investment in marketing communication budgets, stated as a percentage of total sales, are as follows (www.hotstats.com/):

| | |
|---|---|
| Chain hotels | 2.5–4 per cent (including marketing payroll costs) |
| Independent hotels | 2–6 per cent, depending on the location and business mix |

For example, an independent city hotel with a turnover of $1.8 million, using 5 per cent as the percentage of sales method, would allocate $90,000 to marketing communication activity (see Table 9.1). Franchised hospitality businesses have developed complex formulae, which include fees for national marketing communications activity, and a separate line item for local promotions. However, independent restaurants typically spend 2–3 per cent on their marketing communications activity.

Table 9.1 Typical independent hotel's marketing communication budget. A four-star city-centre hotel with sales of $1.8 million (accommodation sales of $1 million) and a marketing communication budget based on 5 per cent of total sales might allocate the $90,000 like this:

| | |
|---|---|
| Salary for salesperson | 35,000 |
| PR agency fee | 6,000 |
| Local paper and magazine adverts | 8,000 |
| Advertising in directories | 3,000 |
| Christmas advertising | 4,000 |
| Promotional print including brochures, posters, calendar of events | 7,000 |
| Website redesign | 6,000 |
| Social media marketing | 6,000 |
| Search engine optimization | 5,000 |
| Consortium fee | 10,000 |
| Total | 90,000 |

The problem with percentage of sales calculations is that the budget is not linked to the needs of the business. In some years, the budget may be too high, because of economic prosperity, whereas during difficult trading periods the budget will probably be too low. Neither does it consider the company's cost/profit structure, different location issues or potential opportunities that might require an investment in additional marketing communication. However, the percentage of sales method remains the preferred choice of most hospitality organizations.

### COMPETITIVE PARITY

Major hospitality brands competing in mature markets fight for market share. These companies invest heavily in marketing communication and are very aware of each other's campaigns. The competitive parity method recognizes the importance of matching competitors' spending on marketing communication. If one competitor increases its *share of voice* (SOV), then competitors may be forced to match the increase in spending to maintain their SOV. Share of voice is a measure of the amount of money invested in promotion, and particularly in advertising, in comparison to competitors. If total sector spend on advertising is $10 million and your company spends $2 million, your SOV is 20 per cent.

### OBJECTIVE AND TASK

The objective and task approach adopts a systematic method to budgeting. Specific objectives are set, and the marketing communication tasks to achieve those objectives are determined. The costs are then calculated, and the marketing communication budget is agreed. For smaller companies, this can be an overly complicated and time-consuming approach. For larger organizations, the objective and task method is favoured. This approach can be problematic if the costs are higher than predicted and expected sales do not materialize.

### COSTS

Although each budgeting approach has advantages and disadvantages, the important point is that setting a budget is essential when planning any marcom campaign. The costs of a campaign may include but are not limited to:

- Agency fees for advice and content creation
- Production costs – a black-and-white leaflet or a local radio station advert is a relatively low-cost item to produce, compared to printing a high-quality, full-colour glossy brochure or making a 30-second TVC (television commercial) on location with celebrities as part of an international campaign
- Media costs
- Buying or renting mailing lists.

Budgeting often becomes an iterative process, as the costs of different media are evaluated, and campaign decisions are changed to fit the allocated budget.

### ABOVE AND BELOW THE LINE

Marketers often distinguish between above- and below-the-line marketing communications. *Above-the-line* is used to describe advertising activities where the space (the online banner advert, the page in print or the time slot in TV) has to be paid for. *Below-the-line* is used for any other non-personal marketing communication activity. This terminology originates with the agencies and refers to commission-earning activity (above-the-line) and fee-earning activity (below-the-line).

### Defining the target audience

The audience must be carefully defined so that appropriate messaging and media strategies can be designed. Target audiences are normally the same as the hospitality company's target markets, or a subset of them. There are two alternative strategies in prioritizing target audiences for hospitality companies who use intermediaries: push and pull (see Figure 9.6).

A *push strategy* prioritizes intermediaries as the main target audience. Marketing communication activities focus on intermediaries, who are then expected to influence the end-user to choose the company's products ahead of competitors. Hospitality marketing communication campaigns targeting intermediaries use all the elements of the marketing communication mix. A *pull strategy* prioritizes the end-user, aiming to influence the customer's decision directly.

The major hospitality players use both strategies to influence intermediaries and end-users.

### Marketing communication strategies and tactics

Before the marketing communication strategy is devised, appropriate market research and planning need to be undertaken (this is discussed in more detail in Chapters 3 and 15). Normally most, if not all, of the various marketing communication tools we have discussed are used to support the annual marketing plan. Communications strategies can be developed either at the brand level or at the unit level, or more typically a combination of both. A monthly planner setting out the key marketing communication activities is drawn up in an annual marketing schedule (see Table 9.2). For each of these activities, a detailed tactical marketing action plan needs

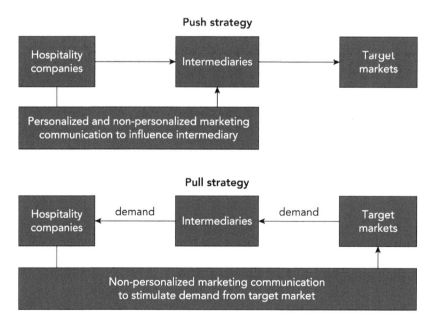

Figure 9.6 Push and pull strategies

Table 9.2 Annual marketing communications activities schedule planner

| Year sales | Jan | Feb | Mar | Apr | May | Jun | Jul | Aug | Sep | Oct | Nov | Dec |
|---|---|---|---|---|---|---|---|---|---|---|---|---|
| Sales visits | | New York | | Paris | | Hong Kong, Shanghai | | | | | World Trade Market, London | |
| Conference sales blitz | | | X | X | X | | | | X | X | | |
| Exhibitions | | | ITB, Berlin | | | Tokyo | | | | | | |
| Print | | | | | | | | | | | | |
| New design and production | X | X | X | | | | | | | | | |
| PR | | X | X | X | X | | X | X | X | X | X | |
| Adverts | | | | | | | | | | | | |
| Leisure breaks | X | X | X | | | X | X | | X | X | X | |
| Conference | X | X | X | X | | | | X | X | X | X | |
| Direct marketing | | | | | | | | | | | | |
| Loyalty club newsletter | | X | | | X | | | X | | | X | |
| Sponsorship | | | | | | | | | | | | |
| Golf events | | | | X | | | X | X | | | | |

to be drawn up, listing the schedule, timing, budget and responsible person. For example, the PR activity to launch a new conference product will require its own brief to the agency and its own budget and implementation plan. However, the PR activity will be coordinated with the sales team, new website copy and images, print and digital collateral, an online and offline DM initiative and in-house launch.

The major hospitality players have continuous marketing communication activity and are adept at managing implementation. Smaller hospitality companies run campaigns during specific periods. During the campaign period, target audience responses must be monitored. Occasionally, a campaign can be adapted to improve the message execution or even 'pulled' if a serious error of judgement has occurred. Regular customers and employees can enjoy the 'buzz' and excitement when an innovative marketing communication campaign generates lots of interest – especially if real employees are actually featured in the campaign.

### Measuring the results

Measurement of results relies on setting measurable marketing communication objectives for what you want the audience to learn, feel or do, and establishing tracking systems to monitor audience responses. There are two main methods of measuring the results of a marketing communication campaign: one is to use marketing research to measure the effectiveness of marketing communication activity, and the other is to measure the return on investment (ROI) by calculating the profit generated from the bookings attributed to the campaign.

#### MARKETING RESEARCH

A company wishing to raise brand awareness ('learn' objective) first needs to establish the current levels of awareness before the campaign starts. This provides a comparison standard for measuring outcomes. Marketing research agencies often conduct this research for hospitality clients. After the campaign concludes, and sometimes during the campaign, the agency measures whether there have been any changes in the levels of brand awareness (see Chapter 4). Similar research tracks the target audience's recall of recent advertising; recall is another 'learning' measure.

#### ROI

ROI is associated with campaigns that focus on 'do' objectives: calls to the 800 number, number of unique (first-time) visitors to a website, number of unique views of an online ad or a video, coupon redemptions, competition entries or bookings. A number of different departments, people and processes can be involved in monitoring and reporting the audience's behavioural response. The reservations department or the central reservation office can record the number of bookings received through the website, or the telephone enquiries generated by each element of the communications mix. Online promotions are easily monitored using tracking technology. This technology allows website owners to record a range of user actions on the website, including sales, bookings and other actions such as sign-ups to newsletters, downloads of menus or video views. Many offline advertisements ask consumers to call a specific 800 number or quote a code when they call for more information, and this allows the responses for each ad to be uniquely monitored. However, some campaigns stimulate lots of interest and enquiries but little in the way of sales. This is why the ratio of enquiries converted into bookings is important. The conversion ratio allows companies to track the actual number and value of bookings generated by each ad in each medium, which in turn allows the marketing team to evaluate the effectiveness of each medium and of different creative executions, to learn what works and to improve future campaigns. The number of customers using vouchers in a bar, club or restaurant also provides a simple tracking system to measure the effectiveness of voucher campaigns.

ROI is estimated by calculating the gross margins earned directly from a campaign as a multiple or fraction of the direct costs of mounting the campaign. The direct costs of the campaign include agency fees, design and production of all content, media space/time, monitoring the campaign results, and associated payroll costs. The formula for calculating ROI is:

$$ROI = \frac{\text{Profit generated by campaign} - \text{Marketing campaign investment}}{\text{Marketing campaign investment}}$$

Table 9.3 provides a hypothetical example to illustrate the ROI for a 1,000-bedroom downtown hotel.

Table 9.3 Return on investment for a leisure break campaign

| | |
|---|---|
| Objective: | To generate a ROI of 140 per cent from this year's $50,000 summer city leisure breaks campaign |
| Strategy: | To target leisure break guests who have stayed at the hotel at least twice during the past three years with a new all-inclusive leisure package |
| Tactics: | To promote the new leisure product to repeat guests via a direct mail campaign, including email and a full-colour leisure break brochure and personalized letter from the hotel's general manager |
| Price: | The price of the leisure break must be set to generate profit – in this example, the targeted profit margin per booking is $80 |
| Costs: | Design, copy, photography, print and postal costs for leisure break brochure; new page for the website; email creative copy; database employee costs |
| Number of mailings | 10,000 |
| Average cost of unit mailing | $5 |
| Total cost of campaign | $50,000 |
| Enquiry response rate | 30% (3,000 enquiries) |
| Conversion rate of enquiries to bookings | 50% (1,500 bookings) |
| Leisure break price, two people staying for two nights | $200 |
| Gross margin per booking | 40% ($80) |
| Total profit | $120,000 |
| Profit after campaign costs | $120,000 – $50,000 = $70,000 |
| ROI | $\dfrac{\text{Profit} - \text{Marketing campaign investment}}{\text{Marketing campaign investment}}$ $= \dfrac{120{,}000 - 50{,}000}{50{,}000} = 140\%$ |

## Conclusion

Marketers are responsible for communicating the offer so that customers know what to expect from the hospitality experience; marketing communications are the most visible part of marketing. When designing a campaign, the hospitality marketer chooses from a wide range of options, and the decision is dependent on the budget available and the campaign's objectives. It is essential to ensure that a consistent message is delivered across the communication elements of a campaign, such as website and collateral. Creativity can increase the cut-through of a campaign. Hospitality marketers work with agencies that provide professional, specialist marketing communication services. All the marketing communication activities should be assessed against whether objectives have been achieved, to ensure that the business learns from experience.

In this chapter, we have explained:

- The strategic role of marketing communication, which is to inform, persuade and build relationships with target audiences
- The communication process, which involves a sender, a target audience, noise in the environment, the message, media and feedback
- Personal communication channels in hospitality, including salespeople and managers interacting directly with prospects and customers
- Non-personal communication channels, including online (website), print, broadcast and ambient
- That the marketing communication mix includes all the online and offline options available for communicating with hospitality customers and other target audiences – including the selling, advertising, sales promotion and point-of-sale material, PR, publicity, sponsorship and direct marketing
- Setting measurable marketing communication objectives is a prerequisite for successful marketing communication planning; marketing communication objectives can be expressed in terms of what the audience will know, feel or do
- Marketing communication campaigns involve several decisions: setting objectives, agreeing the budget, defining the target audience, approving marketing communication strategies and tactics, implementation and measuring the results of the campaign.

---

### ACTIVITY 9.5

At the beginning of the chapter, you thought about how you first heard about a tourism destination or hospitality product that you have already experienced or want to experience.

- Was it a word-of-mouth recommendation from family and friends?
- Was it a recommendation from previous travellers you found on the Internet?
- Was it reading an advert either online or in a newspaper/magazine?
- Was it listening/viewing an advert on the radio, television or the Internet?
- Was it hearing/reading/viewing a news item?

Review what you wrote and think about these questions again. What role did marketing communications play in your answers to these questions?

Now check your understanding by answering the following questions:

1 Discuss the role of marketing communications in the pre-encounter marketing mix.
2 Evaluate the communication process from a hospitality company's perspective.
3 Discuss the hospitality marketing communication mix and explain the role of each tool.
4 Explain the stages in developing, implementing and measuring the effectiveness of a marketing communication campaign for a hospitality product.

## References

1. Zhang, M., Zhang, G. Y., Gursoy, D., & Fu, X. R. (2018). Message framing and regulatory focus effects on destination image formation. *Tourism Management, 69*, 397–407.
2. Ai, J., Gursoy, D., Liu, Y., & Lv, X. (2021). Does offering incentives for reviews effect customer trust? Moderating effects of eWOM quality and the source of incentive. Under Review.
3. IHG Hotels & Resorts [Internet]. *IHG Hotels and Resort Brands.* [cited September 20, 2021]. Available from: www.ihg.com/content/us/en/about/brands
4. Hilton Hotels [Internet]. *Hilton Inspires Travelers to Make New Memories with the U.S. Launch of Insights-Driven Global Marketing Campaign.* [cited September 20, 2021]. Available from: https://newsroom.hilton.com/corporate/news/hilton-launches-new-memories-marketing-campaign
5. Dibenedetto, M.-H. [Internet]. *The Best Marketing Campaigns from the Food & Beverage Sector.* [cited September 20, 2021]. Available from: www.moondustagency.com/knowledge-center/best-food-beverage-social-campaigns
6. McLoughlin, T. [Internet]. *How We Gained More Than 100 Links for a Travel Website Via Content Marketing.* [cited September 20, 2021]. Available from: https://moz.com/blog/case-study-how-we-gained-more-than-100-links-for-a-travel-website-via-content-marketing
7. The Berkeley [Internet]. *Afternoon Tea – Prêt-À-Portea The Couture Cakewalk.* [cited September 20, 2021]. Available from: www.the-berkeley.co.uk/restaurants-bars/afternoon-tea/

# Encounter marketing

DOI: 10.4324/9781003186342-12

Part C

Whilst pre-encounter marketing strategies are designed to attract target customers and inform expectations, the role of encounter marketing is to provide those customers with a service experience that matches or exceeds their expectations and ensures their satisfaction. Encounter marketing focuses on three issues that have a major influence on the experience of the guest: the physical environment, service operations processes and the behaviour of customer-contact employees. Successful encounter marketing creates 'moments of truth' that produce happy customers who are more likely to return and recommend the brand or unit. If customers are unhappy with the ambience, the comfort, the service quality and how employees respond to their needs, then the consequences can range from mild disappointment to anger, and the business can suffer from negative word-of-mouth and poor online reviews.

Chapter 10 provides a discussion on the physical environment, Chapter 11 discusses service operations processes, and Chapter 12 examines the recruitment and management of customer-contact employees.

# 10

# Managing the physical environment

After working through this chapter, you should be able to:

- Understand the role of the physical environment in encounter marketing for a hospitality business
- Have an awareness of design principles used in the development of the hospitality product
- Identify the external and internal elements of the hospitality physical environment
- Recognize the importance of maintenance and refurbishment programmes for hospitality properties in delivering valued customer experience.

## Introduction

The physical environment sends important signals to all of the hospitality organization's stakeholders but, most importantly from a marketing perspective, to customers. Customers intuitively respond to the signals that the external appearance and internal atmosphere project. If the physical environment is appropriate, then target markets are more likely to find the offer attractive and want to buy; at the same time, potential customers who do not 'fit' into the target market profile can be deterred. In this sense, the physical environment helps 'tangibilize the intangible' aspects of the hospitality service. Whilst the physical environment clearly has an impact on customers on the premises – that is why we discuss it in the encounter marketing section of the book – it can also influence customer expectations in the pre-encounter market-

DOI: 10.4324/9781003186342-13

ing stage. Maybe you've walked past a club or bar and felt 'that's not for me'. You are respond-ing to the signals in the physical environment.

In this chapter, we explore how environmental psychology helps hospitality companies to understand consumers' responses to the physical environment. We will then introduce key principles of design and discuss the various elements of the physical environment. Finally, we focus on the crucial issue of maintenance and refurbishment. The physical environment in hospitality is strongly associated with the product element of the marketing mix, and product design decisions thus influence the physical environment.

## Environmental psychology and customers' response to the physical environment

Environmental psychology aims to understand the impact of physical environments on the physiology, behaviours, emotions and cognition (understandings) of people who live, work, move in or otherwise interact in those environments. Buttle[1], Zeithaml and Bitner[2] and Zeithaml, Bitner and Gremler[3] borrowed heavily from environmental psychology to explain the impacts of physical surroundings on service sector customers and employees. Figure 10.1 sum-marizes these influences and helps us to understand the customer's psychological response and social behaviour within the physical environment. There are four elements, which we now discuss – individual behaviour, social interaction, customer responses and the characteristics of the physical environment. Although most of this discussion refers to the 'built environment' that is made up of buildings, furnishings, signage and the like, the principles apply equally to hospitality companies working in a natural environment setting.

### Individual behaviour

Research by environmental psychologists suggests that people respond to the physical envi-ronment with one of two diametrically opposed types of behaviour – approach behaviour or avoidance behaviour. People, to varying degrees, either feel comfortable in a physical environ-ment or they feel uncomfortable. When people feel comfortable, this creates *approach behaviour*. Customers who demonstrate approach behaviour are more likely to enter the hospitality outlet, stay and spend; they may return and/or recommend the experience to others. When people feel uncomfortable with a physical environment, this tends to cause *avoidance behaviour*. These people will probably walk or drive past the hospitality unit without stopping; if they do enter the premises, they may walk out without purchasing anything. Indeed, consumers with an extremely negative response to the physical environment can even become hostile towards that hospitality brand.

Customers aren't the only stakeholders in the physical environment. It is not only impor-tant to create positive responses from the target markets to attract them into and encourage them to stay in the premises but also to create an environment in which it is appealing to work.

### Social interaction

Research also suggests that the physical environment influences how customers and employees interact with each other. The design of the physical environment can encourage or discourage social interactions.

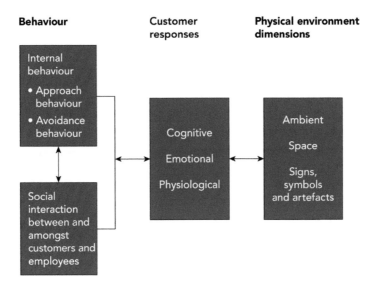

Figure 10.1 Customer behaviour and responses to the physical environment[3]

*Source*: Adapted from Zeithaml et al.,[3] reproduced with permission of the McGraw-Hill Companies

Different types of hospitality products need to generate different types of social interactions. Hospitality products aimed at corporate users – for example, the meetings market – are designed to create more formal social interactions. Customers who do not know each other tend to be polite and adopt more formal behaviour with customer service employees; similar behaviour will be expected from the employees. However, many hospitality leisure products are designed to encourage customers to interact with each other, and with employees, in a much more informal manner. Indeed, social interactions form a significant element of most hospitality leisure product concepts; social interaction is the core product that customers experience in sports bars, clubs and many hospitality businesses that target leisure travellers. If the social aspect of the hospitality experience in these environments fails to meet expectations, this will adversely influence customer satisfaction. Therefore, the character of social interactions needs to be considered when developing the product concept or writing a design brief. Designers need to consider:

- Use of space
- Seating arrangements – the distance between the seating can encourage or discourage conversation between customers
- Décor – the choice of colours, fabrics and furniture
- Lighting and background music.

Ultimately, the physical environment sends signals about how to conduct social interaction, by indicating what is acceptable and appropriate behaviour and what is not.

### Consumer responses to the physical environment

There are three forms of human response to physical environments: cognitive, emotional and physiological.

*Cognitive* refers to mental processes such as thought, understanding and perception. The physical environment influences people's beliefs about places, which in turn impacts on beliefs about the product or brand and the likely behaviour of people in that environment. Therefore, the physical appearance and layout of hospitality premises, signage, the decor and employees' uniforms reinforce or challenge people's prior beliefs about that hospitality offer. Consumers recognize these different combinations of elements of the physical environment that *differentiate* product categories from each other. In this sense, the physical environment acts as a tangible clue for consumers and helps them to evaluate the firm's offer.

Research suggests that the physical environment can, subconsciously or overtly, generate two types of *emotional* response: pleasure and arousal. Arousal refers to a tendency towards feeling alert, excited and energized. Pleasure refers to emotions associated with enjoyment, happiness or euphoria. Figure 10.2 illustrates four emotional responses based on the pleasure/arousal continuum. Different consumers may respond to the same physical environment in different ways – some people will feel pleasure at the sounds and visual stimuli in a fashionable club, whilst others will be distressed. Research suggests that there is a U-shaped relationship between arousal and pleasure. Too little arousal is unpleasant; too much is also unpleasant. The optimal level of arousal lies between these two extremes and will vary between different consumers.

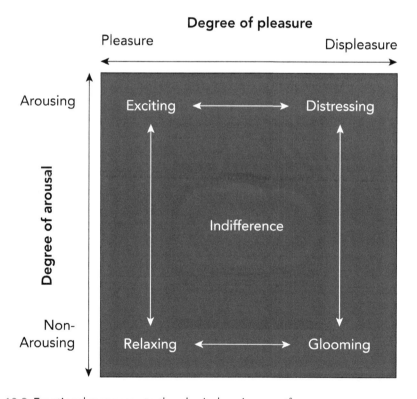

Figure 10.2 Emotional responses to the physical environment[3]

*Source*: Zeithaml et al.,[3] reproduced with permission of the McGraw-Hill Companies

Consumers' emotional responses to the physical environment influence their behaviour, and therefore understanding people's emotional responses is important when designing the physical environment.

---

**ACTIVITY 10.1**

Compare the physical environment of two restaurants you know – one can be a quick service restaurant and the other a fine dining restaurant. What signals does the physical environment send to potential consumers?

---

| Physical evidence | Fast-food branded restaurant | Fine dining restaurant |
|---|---|---|
| Surrounding environment | | |
| External building appearance | | |
| Signage | | |
| Decor | | |
| Table setting | | |
| Staff appearance/uniforms | | |

People also have different *physiological* or bodily responses to stimuli in physical environments. Environmental stimuli take a number of forms:

- Visual stimuli (brightness/darkness; colours and shapes)
- Aural stimuli associated with hearing (the volume, cadence or rhythm of sounds)
- Olfactory stimuli associated with smell (fresh or foul scents and smells)
- Taste or flavour stimuli. Western consumers tend to identify the taste of food and beverages as bitter, sweet, salty, savoury or sour. Asian consumers' palates sense tastes as hot, sweet, sour, spicy, salty, bitter, astringent and 'umami'. Additionally, consumers may identify temperature variations as part of their taste experience.
- Tactile stimuli associated with touch (the texture of food products, the softness in furnishings and the level of comfort with the temperature).

When marketers manage the sensory environment, they are engaged in 'sensory marketing'. Sensory marketing aims to engage consumers' senses and affect their emotions, memories, perceptions, preferences, choices and consumption of products.[4] Sensory marketing is not a new phenomenon and all hospitality brands, whether they consciously plan to do so or not, engage the customer's senses. Some sectors apply considerable thought to sensory marketing: the more luxurious hotel, spa and restaurant brands recognize that combining sensory elements to create a signature environment can add value to the customer experience.

Extreme sensory stimulation, however, can cause consumers varying degrees of physical discomfort, ranging from mildly aggravating to the health threatening. Clearly, these types of physiological responses to elements of the physical environment impact on consumers' initial attraction, enjoyment and propensity to return or reject the hospitality offer.

As consumers have become more sophisticated and markets more fragmented, hospitality operators have recognized the importance of physiological response in designing the physical environment to satisfy the needs and wants of the target markets (see Marketing Insight 10.1).

## MARKETING INSIGHT 10.1

### Hyatt's signature scent[5,6,7]

At the opening of the Park Hyatt Vendôme, Paris, Blaise Mautin, a celebrated French perfumier, created a range of scents for the bedlinen, bath gels, interior sprays and massage oils which 'smell like a wet cement poured over a raw plank of oak, coupled with fresh, ever-so-slightly cinnamoned pastry dough'.[5] This signature scent concept was further developed by the novel idea of blending the scent with taste. Mautin collaborated with Jean-François Foucher, the pastry chef, to create pastries imbued with the Hyatt signature scent, which eventually became the hotel's signature dessert. Upon check-in, a tiny, delicate macaroon was delivered to the guest's room to complement the other scents in the room.

Today, the Park Hyatt Vendôme has further developed its sensory marketing strategy to incorporate music alongside the sense of smell and taste. Jerôme Maitre and Alexandre Sauty de Chalon, founders of the Time 4 Play music design agency, which specializes in creating personalized musical environments for retail brands, have produced a compilation of titles and different genres to reflect the musical ambience of the Park Hyatt Vendôme. The music combines rare titles with different genres of music, including bossa nova, deep house, jazz, pop, soul and trip-hop. A brochure called 'The Universe of the Senses' showcases the signature Blaise Mautin bathroom products, *spray d'ambiance* and perfumed candle; the hotel's Araguani chocolate slabs and 'le parfumeur' macaroons; and the CD *Timeless*, which guests can purchase when staying at the hotel.

Competitor luxury Parisian hotels like the Four Seasons George V, Plaza Athénée and the Royal Monceau have also adopted sensory marketing strategies. The George V appointed Jeff Leatham as the hotel's Artistic Director to design contemporary visual floral displays in the lobby and public areas; each week, over 12,000 flowers are delivered from Amsterdam to ensure the displays are always fresh and vibrant.

*Sources:* Cook,[5] Park Hyatt Paris-Vendôme,[6] Time4Play[7]

### VARIATIONS IN CONSUMER RESPONSES TO THE PHYSICAL ENVIRONMENT

Earlier, we mentioned the differences in consumer response to the same physical environment. Consumer behaviour research into personality traits helps explain why people may respond differently in any given physical environment. Extravert personalities may favour vibrant and sensory-loaded environments; introvert personalities less so. Also, each of us can respond to the same physical environment differently according to changes in our own disposition (good mood/bad mood) and consumption context. A sombre and restrained physical environment may appeal for a wake; a buzzing, noisy environment may suit for a 21st birthday party. Variations in people's responses can also be linked to different lifestyles and different cultural backgrounds.

## Dimensions in the physical environment

Hospitality companies can control the built environment and create a pleasant atmosphere through design. Three environmental dimensions influence consumers' cognitive, emotional and physiological responses: 1. ambience; 2. spatial layout and functionality; and 3. signs, symbols and artefacts.

The *ambient dimension* refers to the sensory elements we have just discussed – features such as colour, scent and lighting (which affect pleasure and arousal) and temperature (which impacts physical comfort) can be linked to consumers' zones of tolerance (see Chapter 3). Relatively minor irritations can be a source of amusement for some consumers, whereas more extreme ambient conditions can create highly distressed customers and even be a health and safety issue, for example, when a customer feels ill when exposed to strobe lighting.

A number of hospitality operations use various scents to improve customer experience. One World Observatory, the top floor of One World Trade Center in New York, for example, offers world-class views of New York City and a specific smell is scented through the air that is reminiscent of the aroma of trees. That scent was commissioned by the venue itself and is named 'One World'. On the other hand, Starbucks hides the odour of the food prepared and served in-house to enhance the in-store experience of customers who enjoy the smell of brewing coffee more.[8]

*Spatial layout* refers to the way in which space is used and how furniture and equipment are arranged in rooms. The scale and size of a hospitality property influence the spatial layout. Consider, for example, the layout of the public lobby area and front desk. Is the lobby a large, formal, spacious are for a grand hotel with high ceilings, chandeliers, many items of furniture and an extensive desk to cater for many customers checking in/out; or is it a smaller, more intimate area for a boutique hotel with low ceilings, darker lighting and a more informal check-in/check-out area. Functionality refers to the effectiveness of the spatial layout to facilitate efficient service and deliver the desired customer experience. Spatial layout achieve an optimal balance between operational requirements and customer expectations. Employees such as kitchen crew and customer service staff need to be able to perform their jobs effectively and efficiently, but the needs of the customer must also be considered.

*Signs, symbols and artefacts* refer to the range of tools that companies can use to communicate with consumers via the physical environment. For example, contemporary hotels can use modern art to convey a contemporary image to customers, and historic hotels can use antique furniture to convey the unique heritage of the property.

These three dimensions need to be coordinated to ensure that a consistent and appealing physical environment is achieved.

## Design and the physical environment

During the development stage of a new hospitality product, factors such as ownership, the site's characteristics and planning permissions/conditions will influence the type of development built. Multi-brand operators will evaluate the market potential for their different branded concepts before selecting the most appropriate brand for a specific site. Hospitality brands vary from formulaic, standardized concepts, where the design component is replicated in each unit, to eclectic collections of units that have no common design theme at all. Ownership attributes can also influence design features. Occasionally, wealthy individuals can afford to be extravagant when investing in an ancillary interest like a hospitality development, but usually the independent sector is characterized by restricted funds. However, the major operators have access to more significant financial resources and have more opportunities to invest in innovative design.

When the product concept and funding have been agreed, the architects, interior designers and management team need to draw up detailed plans for the site. Architects are not hoteliers or restaurateurs, and many new-build hospitality units have problems because marketing objectives are not included in the design brief. Effective encounter marketing relies on the design concept satisfying the needs of target markets, and operational requirements to ensure service processes are effective and efficient. Marketers and operations personnel should be involved in developing the design brief and providing input into the planning stage.

The physical environment has also been described as a 'servicescape'[3] that is equivalent to the 'landscape' of the natural environment. We will now discuss three elements that need to be considered when designing the physical environment:

1  servicescape usage – how each area in the site plan will be used
2  service space complexity – the level of complexity in the operation
3  aesthetics – the creation of the design style.

### Servicescape usage

Different hospitality product concepts have different servicescape characteristics, according to the level of service that is offered and the amount of interaction between customers and employees in the operation. Three broad categories of servicescape are self-service, interpersonal service and remote service (see Table 10.1).

A *self-service operation* relies on customers serving themselves. There are few (if any) employees, and the design of the physical environment focuses on ensuring that customers can conveniently and cost-effectively look after themselves.

An *interpersonal service operation* involves both customers and employees using the same physical environment at the same time. The design of the servicescape needs to ensure that customers are comfortable within the physical environment, and employees can perform their jobs effectively and efficiently. Sometimes poor design of the servicescape creates conflict between customers and employees. Small lobby and front desk areas, which are close to multipurpose customer/service lifts, can inadvertently create conflict if large numbers of customers are arriving/departing at the same time as housekeepers are taking laundry up to service the accommodation.

Table 10.1  Typology of the physical environment for hospitality and leisure

| Servicescape usage | Complexity of the servicescape | |
| --- | --- | --- |
| | Elaborate | Lean |
| Self-service (customer focus) | Self-service restaurant | Vending machine dispensing food |
| Interpersonal services (customer and employees) | Cruise ship | Coffee shop |
| Remote service (employee focus) | Contract catering for airlines | Pizza home delivery |

*Source*: Adapted from Zeithaml et al.,[3] reproduced with permission of the McGraw-Hill Companies

*Remote service*, in this context, means a physical environment where there are no customers. The most common example of remote service in hospitality operations is in contract catering, where food production takes place in large remote kitchens servicing multiple units. The key design issues focus on employee needs and efficient production. Since customers never visit the servicescape, there is limited if any customer/employee interaction.

### Service space complexity

There is a wide variety of different hospitality operations, ranging from small-scale, simple, single-product units to large-scale, complex, multi-product units. The scale and complexity of the operation will influence the servicescape needs. Simple servicescapes are described as lean, and complex servicescapes as elaborate.

> *Lean servicescapes* have a limited number of variables – products, equipment and employees – and only require a limited amount of space. The key focus in design is the effective use of this limited space.

> *Elaborate servicescapes* have many variables and are much more complex. There can be different floor levels, different types of room usage and more equipment, which can be technologically very advanced. Elaborate servicescapes need more space, and the design issues can be complicated and intricate.

---

### MARKETING INSIGHT 10.2

**Hualuxe hotels and resorts – IHG Hotels & Resorts' Chinese luxury brand**[9]

In 2012, IHG launched an upscale hotel and resort brand, Hualuxe, which was designed specifically for the Chinese market. The IHG English website states that the brand name comprises two Chinese words – *hua*, which means 'majestic China', and *luxe* representing 'luxury'. The brand concept is to provide affluent Chinese business travellers with a contemporary luxury Chinese hotel founded upon Chinese values and supported by InterContinental's international scale, management systems and marketing expertise. IHG's local researchers identified four priorities that underpin the design of the hotels:

- *Tradition* – China has a powerful hospitality tradition focused on etiquette that is represented by the tea ceremony. Hualuxe hotels have embraced the tea culture and offer the tea ceremony on arrival and, instead of the typical Western bar, a classic traditional Chinese teahouse acts as a business and leisure meeting facility.

- *Rejuvenation* – natural surroundings are important symbols of rejuvenation in Chinese culture; the design of the green arrival area, with lobby garden and fountains; and resort-style bathrooms with natural woods and stone create a harmonious, relaxed atmosphere for customers.

- *Status* – recognition and respect are core cultural beliefs that the brand's service standards emphasize; employees are trained to provide appropriate recognition and respect to customers.

- *Familiar spaces* – the spatial layout of the hotels is designed to provide familiar traditional spaces, which enable 'distinguished guests' to do business the Chinese way.

At the time of writing, Hualuxe has opened 12 hotels in China with another four hotels in the pipeline. The design concept of Hualuxe is based upon a deep understanding of its target market – affluent Chinese business customers and the unique Chinese culture.

*Source*: IHG Hotels & Resorts

### Aesthetics

Aesthetics is the study of form and beauty. In hospitality design, aesthetics is mostly concerned with the form and beauty – the tastefulness – of the decor. An interior designer may be recruited and given a design brief and budget for a hospitality product concept and invited to create the decor scheme. A decor scheme typically includes floor and wall coverings, lighting, fabrics, furniture and artefacts. It is the interior design that provides the tangible elements of the atmospherics in the hospitality product.

### MARKETING INSIGHT 10.3

**citizenM: A hotel concept that emphasizes common spaces over guest rooms**[10,11]

Headquartered in Amsterdam, citizenM is the brainchild of Rattan Chadha (who founded the fashion label Mexx) and his son Robin, who sought to create a hotel that embraced the idea of affordable luxury for business travellers. The citizenM offers reasonably priced rooms that are small but well thought out, with amenities such as enormous ultra-comfortable beds, unlimited free Wi-Fi and entertainment, Hansgrohe power rain showers, touchscreen Moodpads, and digital screens from Sedition that allow guests to choose which art to display on them.

The citizenM hotel offers only one type of room, but the hotel provides communal areas that are designed to be just as important to the guests' experience as the rooms. Large communal space in the hotel lobby is split up into different zones, including a reading and recreation corner to facilitate a more engaging experience in the lobby. In these communal spaces, guests can gather to work, eat, drink or even just watch TV. The design of the citizenM hotels focuses on guests' behaviours and what is important to them – what luxuries they do not want to compromise on and what they can live without.

*Source*: Sharpe,[10] citizenM

Table 10.2 Innovative design concepts

| Hotels | Examples | Website |
| --- | --- | --- |
| Contemporary designer hotels | Hotel Marques de Riscal, Elciego, Spain<br>Kempinsky Yanki Lake, Beijing, China<br>Tree Hotel, Harads, Sweden | www.marriott.com/hotels/travel/biolc-hotel-marques-de-riscal-a-luxury-collection-hotel-elciego/<br>www.kempinski.com/en/beijing/sunrise-kempinski-hotel-beijing/<br>www.treehotel.se/en |

*(Continued)*

Table 10.2 Continued

| Hotels | Examples | Website |
|---|---|---|
| Art hotels | The ART, Denver, USA | www.thearthotel.com |
| | Miura, Celadna, Czech Republic | www.miura.cz/en |
| City hotels | G-Rough, Rome, Italy | www.g-rough.com |
| | Inntel, Zaandam, Amsterdam, Netherlands | www.inntelhotelsamsterdamzaandam.nl/en/Home.html |
| | The Serras, Barcelona, Spain | https://serrashotel.com/ |
| Grand hotels | The Beaumont, London, UK | www.thebeaumont.com |
| | Hotel de Crillon, Paris, France | www.crillon.com/en |
| Resort and spa hotels | Amanfayun, West Lake, Hangzhou, China | www.aman.com/resorts/amanfayun |
| | Six Senses Zil Pasyon, Felicite, Seychelles | www.sixsenses.com/en/resorts/zil-pasyon |
| | | www.keemala.com |
| | Keemala, Phuket, Thailand | |
| Budget hotels | MAMA Shelter, Bordeaux, France | https://mamashelter.com/bordeaux/ |
| | | www.hoteldebrett.com |
| | Debrett, Auckland, New Zealand | |
| Budget hostels | The Dreamer Hostel, Palomino, Santa Marta, Bogota, Colombia | www.thedreamer.com/ |
| | | www.wombats-hostels.com/london |
| | Wombat's City HOSTEL in London, UK | |

Designers are in the fashion business. At one time, many hotels were considered boring, functional places with unimaginative decor. However, contemporary hotels and restaurants are now more engaged with the fashion industry. Designers have been allowed to use their flair to create visually striking exteriors and interiors for hospitality product concepts in a wide range of different types of hospitality buildings. Visionary hospitality entrepreneurs have championed this design revolution, and global hospitality chains have been influenced by the independents. The 'W' brand, Marriott International's boutique hotel chain and Wyndham's TRYP Hotels are chain-hotel responses to competition from independent boutique hotels. Table 10.2 provides examples of hotels with innovative design concepts.

## Elements of the physical environment

The physical environment for hospitality products and services comprises external features, the internal design, employees and other customers as presented in Table 10.3. Most hospitality businesses use professionally-staged photographs of the unit's physical external and/or internal physical environment on their websites to present the hospitality offer attractively.

### External

The external environment is the equivalent of a shop window in retailing. The visual display in a shop window sends powerful messages about the products available, service quality and price. The shop window reinforces the positioning and brand image. The surrounding environment, the external appearance of the building, landscaping, access routes, car parking facilities, signage and logos and lighting are the shop window for the hospitality business.

Table 10.3 The key components of physical environment for hospitality products and services

| External | Internal | Employees | Customers |
|---|---|---|---|
| Surrounding environment | Internal spatial layout | Appearance | Appearance |
| External appearance of the building | Decor, furnishings and furniture | Dress (uniform) | Dress |
| Access | Equipment | Attitude | Attitude |
| Landscaping | Signage and point-of-sale material | Behaviour | Behaviour |
| Parking | Temperature and air quality | | |
| Signage and logos | Music | | |
| Lighting | Lighting | | |
| Smell | Smell | | |

We considered the local geography (surrounding environment) in Chapter 6, within the context of site selection criteria, and emphasized that the surrounding area must be compatible with the product concept. When the surrounding environment does match the hospitality product concept, potential customers will more likely be attracted to the physical environment. However, through no fault of the hospitality operator, the surrounding area can change over time. Neighbouring properties can be sold, and new owners might change the use of buildings in a way that changes the character of the area. When the surrounding environment becomes incompatible with the existing hospitality product and sales and profits suffer consequently, the operator will have to make a strategic decision whether to sell the property or reinvent the product concept.

The external appearance of the hospitality premises – the building, its size, age, architecture and condition – sends cues to customers. Attractive, well-maintained properties inspire confidence, but buildings that appear neglected can deter potential customers. Effective landscaping can transform the visual appearance of a property. Well-maintained grounds, attractive lawns and gardens, beautiful flower boxes and elegant outdoor swimming pools contribute towards a positive image of a hospitality property. The availability of secure car parking, close to the property, is important for all hospitality businesses that depend on customers travelling by road. Well-maintained attractive signage, including brand logos and effective external lighting, send out positive signals to customers, whereas tired and damaged signage and poor lighting send out negative signals. Investment in the external physical environment can help to attract customers into the premises and give them a sense that their needs will be met.

### *Internal*

Although the external environment creates the first impression for potential customers, it is the internal environment that is most significant in determining whether customers are going to enjoy the hospitality experience. Internal factors include the layout, decor, furniture and furnishings, lighting, equipment, internal signage, temperature and air quality, music and smells, which, combined together, convey the all-important atmosphere of the premises.

The internal layout of a hotel includes floor plans of the lobby area, front desk, lifts, bedrooms and bathrooms, restaurant, bar, conference, function and leisure areas. Although an architect is responsible for drawing the room layouts and making sure all the services (electrics, heating, ventilation and air conditioning, communication systems, water supplies and drainage) comply with local building and safety regulations, it is up to the hospitality management team to ensure that the layout functions effectively to meet the requirements of employees and customers.

Decor is really a matter of personal taste, but in hospitality it is a crucial ingredient in creating the 'feel' in a property. Creating a decor scheme is a job for a professional interior designer. Every element of the hospitality product that is visible to the customer should be designed professionally. The interior designer ensures that the floor and wall coverings, the curtains and lighting, the seating, beds, desks and tables, and the pictures, bric-à-brac and ornaments deliver a consistent positioning message. For the product concept, decor is another tangible cue.

Equipment, in this context, refers to equipment that customers use – for example, the air-conditioning system in the bedroom or the shower in the bathroom. It also includes equipment that employees use in front of customers. Customers expect equipment to work. Faulty or dirty equipment, especially in the bedrooms and bathroom, or slow computer systems at check-in/check-out are serious problems for customers and a major source of complaints.

Today's tech-savvy travellers expect hotels to offer reliable and fast wireless Internet access and be up-to-date with technology. Almost all customers, including the older generations, are well-versed in the use of technology, social media and mobile devices. Customers expect hotels to offer instant communication through online chat and video conferencing software. Customers may also expect to see all the latest tech gadgets, such as service robots, artificial intelligence powered room controls, and keyless entry in the hotel and in their room.

Customers also expect the internal signage to provide clear directions throughout the property. Being lost in a large hotel complex is embarrassing and frustrating for customers. The quality of the internal signage and/or the availability of navigational digital apps are some of the indicators of image and service quality.

We discussed the role of point-of-sale material in Chapter 9. From a physical environment perspective, point-of-sale material should be current, professionally presented and relevant. Unfortunately, hospitality businesses can suffer from dated and tired point-of-sale material, which is counterproductive in generating a positive image. To overcome this issue, many hospitality businesses have started using digital point-of-sale materials that can be managed and updated from a central location.

Air quality and temperature in hotels, clubs and restaurants are governed by local responses to climate and cultural conventions. In guest bedrooms, customers need to be able to control air-conditioning and heating systems for themselves. Customers who experience extremes of heat in bedrooms and restaurants, compared to their normal environment, can be very uncomfortable. If the management does not respond quickly to solve the problem, customers may even leave to find a competitor with a more comfortable temperature.

Background music, live music or no music is another matter of personal taste. However, when designing the hospitality product, music plays a key role in complementing the decor and creating atmosphere in public areas. In particular, bars and restaurants use music to attract target markets and to generate atmosphere. Indeed, sound is such an important atmospheric tool that many hospitality concepts stream music to outlets to ensure that employees cannot interfere with the ambience. W Hotels stream the music in synchronized time to all their properties – so the same music is played at the same time, regardless of time zones, in every W property whether it is located in Hong Kong, Paris, New York or Sydney.

Smell in hospitality is mainly associated with food and beverage outlets. Attractive cooking smells can stimulate the taste buds and attract customers. Foul bar and cooking smells – the combination of stale beer, cigarettes and fried food sometimes found in bars – are a powerful disincentive to many customers.

The combination of all these internal factors creates an overall atmosphere that should, if properly designed, appeal to the target market. However, if some of the key internal environmental factors fail, or do not fit, the customers' expectations, then customers can be dissatisfied.

### Employees

The appearance, attitude and behaviour of employees should complement the positioning, product concept and physical environment. Employees' cleanliness, deportment and dress should reinforce the design theme and send a consistent message to customers. In formal, business-orientated hospitality operations, staff uniforms reflect the business environment – professional attire in conservative colours and fabrics is the norm. In leisure and themed hospitality concepts, casual uniforms designed as part of the theme or no uniforms are appropriate. Contemporary boutique establishments often have contemporary designer-styled employee uniforms. Customers may rarely notice employees' dress and behaviour, when it matches the brand image and other elements of physical environment. However, if the employee's appearance, attitude and behaviour are inconsistent with the design concept, then customers are more apt to notice the inconsistency because it sends out a conflicting message and confuses them.

### Customers

One of the distinguishing attributes of services is *inseparability*, meaning that the service is produced at the same time it is consumed. In most hospitality services, customers must be present whilst the product is produced and served. Since customers are an essential component of the service encounter as they interact with the service staff and each other, contributing to the experience of other customers and creating 'atmosphere', they become co-creators of hospitality experiences. Customers therefore co-create their own experiences and the experience of other customers. Thus, hospitality experiences can be highly variable, another distinguishing attribute of services, in content and quality due to the presence or absence, and behaviours, of other customers. Other customers in the physical environment contribute to atmosphere. Potential customers see and hear other customers. If the customers' dress seems inappropriate and their behaviour in terms of language, loudness, politeness and sobriety is inconsistent with the expectations and standards of the potential customers, this may deter entry. We have already discussed the problems caused by mixing incompatible target markets. In many parts of the world, today's dress codes and expectations of behaviours are more relaxed than for previous generations. This makes it more difficult for hospitality management to control the dress and behaviour of customers. Exclusive clubs, restaurants and hotels still insist on a dress and behaviour code for customers. The Ritz, in London, makes the following statement on their website:

> The Ritz London has a dress code in different areas of the hotel as follows: Gentlemen are required to wear a jacket and tie (jeans and sportswear are not permitted for either ladies or gentlemen) for afternoon tea in The Palm Court and for lunch and dinner in The Ritz Restaurant and Terrace. In all other areas of the hotel (The Ritz Restaurant breakfast service, The Rivoli Bar, The Long Gallery, and The Ritz Garden), smart casual attire is required. Please note that shorts, trainers, and sportswear are not permitted in any of the hotel's restaurants or bars.
>
> *Source*: The Ritz London[12]

---

## MARKETING INSIGHT 10.4

### Hotel and restaurant uniforms[13]

You probably do not think twice about how your bellhop or your front-desk clerk in a hotel or the server in a restaurant looks, as long as they handle your bags, check you in quickly, serve your meal and provide satisfactory service. However, uniforms in fashionable hotels and restaurants are carefully designed to project the desired image. In fact, a lot of effort goes into making hotel employees look good. Just ask Alan Steinger.

His company, Top Hat Imagewear, outfits hundreds of hotel workers around the world, and as the owner and head designer, Steinger is the brains of the operation. Some hotels start the design of the uniforms as they start the design of the hotel. Steinger says that 'with a new build, sometimes we work with the architect or with the interior designer. Sometimes it's the owner, and most often the management team.' However, the inspiration for uniforms can come from the movies, the runway . . . or the owner's closet.

Nicholas Oakwell, Managing Director of No Uniform – a specialist British uniform design company – suggests that 'the uniform tells the customer what the hotel is all about, especially since customers tend to be more fashion and design conscious today'. Uniforms need to be distinctive, easily recognizable and smart. Ideally, if there is a hotel or restaurant new build or major refurbishment project, the uniform designers will be involved five or six months before opening – to allow sufficient time to create a design, which reflects the interior designer's mood boards and the aspirations of the owners/managers.

Uniforms need to be practical as well as stylish. Table service staff need cool uniforms, because they normally work up a sweat whilst running between the kitchen and the restaurant table; managers often need several pockets, because they carry mobiles, keys, pens and memo pads. Uniforms also need a reasonable life span – Oakwell suggests 18 months – and to be available in a range of sizes to accommodate the different heights and shapes of employees.

*Source*: TopHat Image Wear[13]

> ### ACTIVITY 10.2
>
> If you can, visit the two hospitality units that you identified in Activity 10.1. Evaluate the external appearance of the units before entering, and then go into the units and evaluate the internal decor, employees and customers.
>
> - Does the external environment match the internal environment?
> - Do you think the physical environment is appropriate for the target markets?
> - Does it match your expectations of a fast-food restaurant and a fine dining restaurant?

## Maintenance and refurbishment

Earlier, we have referred to the problems caused by damaged furniture, faulty equipment and tired decor. The role of maintenance and refurbishment is to maintain the hospitality product at an acceptable level to guarantee the promised customer experience and ensure effective and efficient operation. Unfortunately, the nature of the hospitality business means that both customers and employees accidentally, and occasionally deliberately, cause damage to the property. In particular, bathrooms and toilets suffer from abuse and accidental water damage. The costs of not maintaining a property include:

- Loss of revenue from current customers who take their business elsewhere
- Negative word-of-mouth and online reviews
- Loss of revenue from potential customers who choose a competitor after reading negative reviews posted online by dissatisfied customers
- Loss of revenue caused by the inability to sell rooms that are out of operation because of maintenance problems
- Lost productivity due to faulty equipment
- Liability for health, safety and other legal infringements.

Although the responsibility for maintenance and refurbishment is an operational issue, marketers can be significantly challenged by tired brands and properties.

### The maintenance and refurbishment life cycle

Effective maintenance should be planned into a new property as part of the design brief. The financial plans of a hospitality business will include a depreciation charge to cover the costs of wear and tear. This depreciation charge is calculated by estimating the reasonable life expectancy of the decor, fittings, furniture and equipment. The life expectancy will be dependent on the quality standards of the original decor scheme and the desired competitive position. Although the depreciation charge is a bookkeeping transaction, companies will also provide a maintenance budget of between 3 per cent to 5 per cent of sales to cover repairs and redecoration. Older inns and hotels that have been converted from other uses can have difficult and costly maintenance issues. New-build properties should have fewer maintenance problems during the first years of operation.

Maintenance and refurbishment plans can be categorized under four headings:

1 *Preventative maintenance* comprises the regular servicing of equipment, such as elevators, kitchen equipment and air-conditioning plant, to ensure they do not break down. These are normally serviced under a contract bought at the same time the equipment is purchased. Indeed, some suppliers sell the service contract and throw the hardware in 'for free'.

2 *Breakdown maintenance* includes all the minor damage caused during the normal daily operations of the business.

3 *Corrective maintenance* includes regular redecoration according to a planned schedule; when elements of the physical environment become tired, a major refurbishment programme is needed.

4 *Designing out faults* is necessary when design faults emerge during the operation of the facility, and can improve guest comfort, operational efficiency, or both.

The refurbishment of public rooms, bars and restaurants varies according to usage and product concept. A popular venue with a short product life cycle might be refurbished every three years, and an established product might need new carpets and furniture as part of a major refurbishment scheme between five and 10 years. Hotel bedrooms should have a planned life cycle for maintenance as follows:

| | |
|---|---|
| Decor and fabrics | 2–4 years |
| Carpets and electrics | 5–8 years |
| Furniture | 7–10 years |
| Bathrooms | Renovated or replaced every 10–15 years |

The implementation of a refurbishment programme can create problems for the hospitality business. Rooms and food and beverage outlets need to be closed whilst the work is undertaken, resulting in a loss of sales. Customers can suffer from the noise and disruption and possibly a reduced service level. Seasonal hospitality businesses can carry out routine maintenance and major refurbishment when the property is closed or during the low season. However, managers of properties in prime locations that enjoy high sales throughout the year must plan refurbishment carefully to minimize the disruption to the business. Unfortunately, financial constraints during economic downturns often mean that the maintenance and refurbishment budgets are cut first, when in fact this is an ideal time for investment, because there is less likelihood of losing revenue and upsetting customers.

## Conclusion

In this chapter, we have discussed the importance of the physical environment in attracting customers into hospitality premises and in contributing to the customer experience during the service encounter. Hospitality businesses that continually invest in refurbishment are more likely to enjoy high-repeat and recommended business and nurture customer loyalty. Hospitality businesses that fail to maintain the physical environment of their premises will eventually become tired and dated, and may have to compete on the basis of lower prices to attract customers. This may result in lower profitability.

In this chapter, we have explained:

- The discipline of environmental psychology is useful for explaining customers' and employees' responses to the physical environment
- The physical environment for hospitality products – external features, the internal design, employees and other customers
- The role of sensory marketing in developing the brand offer
- The importance of design in the hospitality servicescape
- The impact of servicescape usage, servicescape complexity and aesthetics on design of the physical environment
- Characteristics of the external and internal environments in hospitality units
- The importance of maintenance and refurbishment, including preventive maintenance, breakdown maintenance, corrective maintenance and designing out faults.

Now check your understanding of this chapter by answering the following questions:

1 How can environmental psychology explain hospitality customers' responses to the physical environment?

2 Evaluate servicescape usage and servicescape complexity when designing a new hospitality premises for:

- a self-service concept
- an interpersonal concept
- a remote service concept.

3 Explore the concept of sensory marketing in hospitality design.

4 Discuss the role of maintenance and refurbishment in the life cycle of a bar or restaurant.

## References

1. Buttle, F. (1984). How merchandising works? *International Journal of Advertising, 3*(2), 139–148.
2. Zeithaml, V. A. & Bitner, M. J. (2003). *Services Marketing*, 3rd ed. Boston, MA: McGraw-Hill.
3. Zeithaml, V. A., Bitner, M. J., & Gremler, D. D. (2013). *Services Marketing*, 6th ed. New York: McGraw-Hill.
4. Krishna, A. (2010). *Sensory Marketing: Research on the Sensuality of Products.* Hove: Routledge.
5. Cook, R. (2017). Romance in the most romantic city at Park Hyatt Paris. *Focus Daily News Brands.* [cited September 20, 2021]. Available from: www.focusdailynews.com/romance-in-the-most-romantic-city-at-park-hyatt-paris/
6. Park Hyatt [Internet]. *Park Hyatt Paris-Vendôme.* [cited September 20, 2021]. Available from: www.hyatt.com/en-US/hotel/france/park-hyatt-paris-vendome/parph
7. Time4Play [Internet]. *Time4Play – House of Creation.* [cited September 20, 2021]. Available from: www.time4play.fr/
8. Rahmanan, A. B. Y. (2019). *Behind the Science of Scent Marketing: How Smell Changes the Way We Experience Everything from Shopping Malls to Hotels.* [cited September 20, 2021]. Available from: https://fortune.com/2019/11/30/science-behind-scent-marketing-brand-smells/

9. IHG Hotels & Resorts [Internet]. *Hualuxe Hotels and Resorts.* [cited September 20, 2021]. Available from: www.ihgplc.com/en/our-brands/hualuxe

10. Sharpe, S. (2021). *Hotel Concept Emphasizes Common Spaces Over Guest Rooms.* [cited September 20, 2021]. Available from: www.metropolismag.com/interiors/hotel-concept-emphasizes-common-spaces-guest-rooms/

11. citizenM [Internet]. *Company Overview.* [cited September 20, 2021]. Available from: www.citizenm.com/company/overview

12. The Ritz London [Internet]. *The Ritz Experience.* [cited September 20, 2021]. Available from: www.theritzlondon.com/the-ritz-experience/

13. TopHat Image Wear [Internet]. *About Us.* [cited September 20, 2021]. Available from: https://tophatimagewear.com/about-us

Chapter **11**

# Managing service processes

DOI: 10.4324/9781003186342-14

---

**CHAPTER OBJECTIVES**

After working through this chapter, you should be able to:

- Evaluate the importance of effective management of service processes to hospitality marketing
- Analyze service quality in a hospitality context using defined service quality dimensions
- Evaluate the principal reasons for service failure using a gaps model
- Use customer journey mapping to depict hospitality service experiences
- Identify the importance of appropriate service recovery strategies when customers complain.

## Introduction

The management of service production and service delivery processes is generally the responsibility of operations management. However, marketing managers do need to understand the principles of service operations management. Customer satisfaction is dependent on the hospitality operation delivering the pre-encounter marketing promise. Marketing's major contribution to business performance is its influence on customer demand; that is made significantly easier when service operation processes consistently deliver the experience and quality that customers expect. However, when service processes fail to match the promise, marketing becomes much more difficult.

In this chapter, the second in our section on encounter marketing, we discuss the importance of managing service production and delivery processes effectively. We also explore the different dimensions of service quality. We identify operational fail points that can lead to service failures and bad customer experiences. We then introduce the concept of customer experience journey mapping, a customer-focused representation of service delivery processes that depicts step-by-step how a user interacts with a service. The process is mapped from the user's perspective, describing what happens at each stage of the interaction, the touchpoints the customer encounters, and obstacles and barriers they may experience. Clearly describing each stage of the interaction can help hospitality organizations effectively manage each interaction that takes place during service delivery. We also review the crucial role of service recovery when service failures do occur, and when a customer complains about the service received.

---

### ACTIVITY 11.1

Reflect on your own experiences as a customer dining in a restaurant or staying in a hotel.

- Can you remember an occasion when the service quality you experienced was disappointing? Can you explain what went wrong?
- Did you, or somebody with you, complain to the service provider?
- If yes, how did the employee/manager respond to the complaint?
- Were you happy with their response? Did they offer you any compensation?
- If you were happy with the response, did you talk to your family and friends about it? If so, how many people did you tell?
- If you were not happy, did you talk to your family and friends about it? If so, how many people did you tell?
- Did you mention your experience (positive or disappointing) online? If you did, what site(s) did you use to mention your experience?

---

## The importance of managing service processes

In Chapter 1, we discussed the special characteristics of services that present challenges in marketing hospitality businesses. To recap briefly, some of the key characteristics and the challenges include the following:

- *Intangibility* – because the hospitality product is intangible-dominant, customers cannot be certain about the quality of the service they will receive until it has been experienced. For example, a restaurant customer cannot taste the quality of the food or experience the service offered by staff until they order and consume their meal.
- *Inseparability* – this means that the service is produced at the same time it is consumed. In most hospitality services, customers must be present whilst the product is produced and served. Also, as you read in the previous chapter, customers are co-creators of service experiences as they interact with the service staff and each other, contributing to the creation of 'atmosphere'. Customers therefore help to shape their own experience and the experience of other customers.
- *Seasonality* – most hospitality services have busy and quiet periods. During high demand periods, service production and delivery processes can be stressed and fail, resulting in cus-

Part C

tomer dissatisfaction. In contrast, when the operation has too few customers, a vital ingredient of the hospitality product – atmosphere – can be missing, resulting in customer disappointment. In periods of low demand, serving staff may also be overattentive as they try to keep busy, or else inattentive and ignore customers as they attempt to get on with other duties. Understanding and responding to patterns of demand is therefore important for delivering appropriate levels of customer service.

- *Variability or heterogeneity* – the intangibility, inseparability and seasonality of hospitality products contribute to variability in the customers' experience. Variability is widespread in hospitality services. It can confuse and disappoint customers and create uncertainty about what to expect. Customer experiences in the same establishment can vary significantly over different occasions. This variability can have a large impact on customer satisfaction.

A crucial issue for hospitality businesses, therefore, is to try and deliver consistent service quality despite the constraints posed by intangibility, inseparability, seasonality and variability. Academic research in the hospitality industry suggests that delivering consistent service quality that is better than competitors' is a significant antecedent of customer satisfaction and a source of competitive advantage.[1] If a hospitality business does not deliver service quality consistently, customers are likely to be confused about what to expect, leading to an uncomfortable level of perceived risk. If customers think that the service quality is not up to their expectations, they will be less likely to return, or recommend the brand to family and friends. They may even post negative online reviews about their experience of inconsistent service quality. Customer satisfaction is dependent on service quality, and customer loyalty, in turn, is dependent on customer satisfaction. We will discuss customer satisfaction in detail in Chapter 13, and loyalty in Chapter 14, but remember that effective hospitality marketing depends on delivering appropriate levels of service quality consistently by managing service production and delivery processes effectively.

## Understanding processes

Processes can be classified in three ways:

### Vertical and horizontal processes

*Vertical processes* are those that are located entirely within one function or operating department. For example, the food production process resides totally within the food and beverage department in a hotel, and the process of servicing rooms within the housekeeping department.

*Horizontal processes*, in contrast, are cross-functional and involve more than one department. A major three-day conference event will involve sales and marketing, reservations, operations, front desk, housekeeping and general management within a hotel.

### Front-office and back-office processes

*Front-office processes* or front-of-house processes are those that customers encounter or experience directly. The check-in/check-out and complaints management processes are examples of front-office processes. In contrast, *back-office processes* (sometimes referred to as 'heart of house') are hidden from customers who do not experience them directly. For example, procurement or purchasing is a key back-office process that is important to customers, but they do not witness or get involved with it. Some processes straddle both front and back offices – the billing process, for example. The front desk provides the corporate customer with their bill to review and approve, whereas the back-office accounts receivable department will invoice the company and make sure the bill is paid on time.

### Primary and secondary processes

*Primary processes* have major cost or revenue implications for hospitality companies. For example, human resources management processes contribute significantly to the cost base of the business. Given the tendency for high staff turnover in hospitality firms, human resources management processes such as supervision practices have a key impact on talent retention, and thus recruitment costs. One example of a primary process that has a revenue implications is the onboarding process. The term 'onboarding' is used to describe the process of enrolling customers on to a loyalty programme. Many hotel companies consider their loyalty programmes as one of their brands. Research identifies a positive correlation between loyalty programme enrolment and revenue generated through ADR and additional room-night bookings, even when third party programmes, such as Stash Rewards, are used. *Secondary processes*, on the other hand, have minor cost or revenue implications. Customers may have a different perspective from management on what is primary and secondary. Customers typically do not care about back-office processes; they care more about the processes they are visible to them, such as the check-in and check-out processes.

It is useful to understand service processes from a customer perspective and design these processes so that they create positive customer experiences that contribute to customer satisfaction. It is not just front-office processes that have an impact on the customer experience, as back-office processes generally support those of the front office. If the back-office fails, the front-office cannot deliver excellent customer experience. For example, if recruiters in human resources management are not fully aware of the service requirements and the quality expectations of customers, they may fail to recruit staff with the capability to deliver brand standards, or to train staff sufficiently to create acceptable service encounters. Clearly, a major concern for hospitality marketers is that front-office and back-office processes should work together to create service experiences that meet or exceed customers' expectations, especially in terms of quality.

Marketing Insight 11.1 illustrates how upmarket restaurants can make the entire service process (both front-office and back-office) transparent to customers.

## MARKETING INSIGHT 11.1

### The Chef's Table

Some time ago, Eric Marsh, an English hotelier, introduced a table for two customers in the kitchen of the Cavendish Hotel in Derbyshire. By doing so, he encouraged customers to see the back-of-the-house operation and the service processes employed. Since that time, the Chef's Table has become very popular with customers. There are numerous restaurants that offer a Chef's Table in London, including Dinner by Heston (Blumenthal), where guests also enjoy a tour of the kitchen. Some restaurants have altered the experience somewhat by removing the table from the kitchen while ensuring customers have a full view of the kitchen and the back-office service processes. At Benares, customers at the Chef's Table are in a glass-enclosed room that overlooks the kitchen. Marcus Wareing has moved his Chef's Table to provide an elevated view

Part C

over the entire restaurant. At Les Trois Garçons, the Chef's Table is located in the wine cellar, which provides a one-way view into the kitchen. At the Angela Hartnett's Merchants Tavern, guests can dine at a counter with full views into the kitchen. Customers enjoy the experience of dining at the Chef's Table and are willing to pay a premium price for the experience. The restaurant also sends a powerful signal to customers about the high quality of the back-office (food production) service processes.

## Service quality

There are four main perspectives on what counts as 'quality'.

1 Quality means *exceptional*: Service quality, from this perspective, implies high or even outstanding standards. In the hospitality industry, a Michelin-starred restaurant would be considered high or exceptional quality, as would a five-star luxury resort.

2 Quality means *consistency*: Service quality, from this perspective, is considered to have zero defects. In other words, the production and delivery of a service is delivered every time according to the prescribed standard operating procedures or menu specifications. Consistent quality helps customers establish clear expectations.

3 Quality means *fitness for purpose*: Service quality, from this perspective, is when the service meets customer requirements. Customers purchase hospitality products for a wide range of usage occasions. For example, a budget hotel with self-check-in and check-out might be of acceptable quality for an overnight break during a long road trip, but not for an extended vacation.

4 Quality means *value for money*: From this perspective, service quality is a balance of the value experienced by the customer weighed against the price and other sacrifices made by the customer. Consumers make judgements about the different benefits or values derived from the service in relation to the total costs associated with purchasing and using that service. Service quality is therefore based on the customer's perception of value, often relative to competitor offers.

Service quality is thus a complex concept. Nonetheless, understanding how consumers judge service quality is important as these judgements influence levels of satisfaction and repurchase intentions. As a result, a good deal of research has been conducted to identify dimensions of service quality and how to measure it.

## Dimensions of service quality

Because quality can be viewed from the different perspectives identified earlier, it is regarded as a multi-dimensional construct. Measuring service quality is therefore complicated, and researchers have developed several different models over the years as a result. One of the most enduring service quality models developed through extensive multi-sector research is SERVQUAL.[2] In their SERVQUAL model, Parasuraman, Zeithaml and Berry[2] originally identified 10 service quality attributes that they subsequently reduced to five core dimensions – reliability, assurance, tangibles, empathy and responsiveness – also known as RATER. Although the SERVQUAL model has been criticized, it has been used extensively since its development in different sectors, including hospitality, and has served as the basis for the development of other context-specific service quality models. Current arguments suggest that there is a need for industry-specific modelling of service quality that takes account of different country or cultural contexts. Many of the hospitality studies have drawn heavily on these same five dimensions as SERVQUAL, although some have expanded the number of dimensions.

## Service quality dimensions in a hospitality context

### Reliability

During pre-encounter marketing, a promise is made to the customer that informs their expectations of the hospitality product/service offer. Customers therefore expect the hospitality business to deliver on that promise. Reliability is important for repeat customers who judge the consistency of service quality over time. When companies deliver on the promise consistently over time, they are considered reliable; when they do not, consumers consider them unreliable.

### Assurance

This service quality dimension refers to whether employees are knowledgeable and competent, and courteous or polite in their interactions with customers. These characteristics influence whether customers perceive service staff as trustworthy. When employees demonstrate competence, courtesy and politeness, customers have more confidence that the company can deliver its marketing promise. Assured employees inspire customers to trust the advice they receive and to believe the company's promises. Of course, when employees are rude, customers are offended and when employees have insufficient knowledge or skill to deliver the promised hospitality service, customers understandably lose confidence in the company.

### Tangibles

In Chapter 10, we discussed the physical environment and its impact on customers. As a service quality dimension, tangibles are represented by the physical environment. Customers make judgements about service quality based on the appearance and comfort of physical facilities, equipment, employee uniforms, tableware or bedlinen and promotional materials used by the hospitality firm.

### Empathy

Empathy means demonstrating an understanding of customers as individuals, treating them as individuals and providing them with a more personalized hospitality experience. Customer contact staff who make customers feel they are being treated as individuals make them feel important, particularly when they are empowered to respond to customers with some flexibility. Many hospitality firms pride themselves on this service quality dimension, creating heroes out of employees who go out of their way to delight customers. Hotels have promoted stories where staff members have followed guests to the airport to deliver forgotten belongings. Staff members at a Four Seasons hotel went out of their way to photograph a child's stuffed giraffe, named Joshie, that was left behind enjoying his extended stay at the Ritz. These photographs were returned with the stuffed giraffe to the child, so the child would know that the giraffe was looked after in her absence.[3]

### Responsiveness

Responsiveness refers to how quickly and effectively service staff respond to customers and their requests. During the hospitality encounter, customers might ask questions about items on the menu, the location and opening hours of hotel facilities, and many other topics. They may make special requests to substitute menu items in a restaurant or for a late check-out in a hotel; they may raise minor problems or complain. A customer-contact employee's helpfulness in these encounters and ability to respond to customer queries and requests influences the customer's perceptions of service quality.

### Service quality gaps

The SERVQUAL model explains why companies sometimes fail to deliver the service customers expect. Five gaps or weaknesses in management practices are identified in the original SERVQUAL model, as explained next.

#### GAP 1: THE KNOWLEDGE GAP

Hospitality managers often think that they know what customers expect and develop product or service offers on that basis instead of undertaking marketing research to truly understand customers' expectations. As a result, there can be a knowledge gap between what customers truly expect and what managers *think* they expect. Effective marketing research should be able to identify the true expectations of the target market, in terms of the five RATER dimensions. When managers know what customers expect, they can then start to formulate appropriate offers and associated quality standards to match customer expectations thereby avoiding or closing this knowledge gap.

#### GAP 2: THE STANDARDS GAP

When managers understand customer needs and expectations, they must use this to design the operational processes that produce and deliver the service that customers expect. However, sometimes managers find it difficult to translate what the customer expects into operational standards. As a result, a standards gap is created. Hospitality companies can sometimes fail to take the customers' perspective into account when creating service operations standards because the service system is so internally focused that the customer's voice is not heard. Management needs to think creatively to overcome these service design problems and ensure that service standards match customer expectations.

#### GAP 3: THE DELIVERY GAP

This gap occurs when a service standard has been defined but the service production and delivery processes fail to operate to standard. The delivery gap is sometimes caused by poor human resources management, for example, ineffective recruitment, training and reward practices. The gap may also be the result of technological problems, for example, reservation system failure, faulty TV or door keys, or ineffective demand management, for example, too many or too few customers, or an incompatible customer mix. The role of customer-contact employees in delivering a quality service is discussed further in Chapter 12.

### MARKETING INSIGHT 11.2

**Effects of service failure recovery strategies on customers' emotions and satisfaction**[4]

Having service failures is part of doing business for service companies. Even the best service providers cannot completely avoid service failures. Identifying the most critical service failures and then developing strategies to reduce the magnitude and severity of the consequences of those service failures through reliable, timely and satisfactory service failure recovery process can significantly enhance customer attitudes and behaviours. One study that examined airline service failures suggests that service failures caused by internal factors such as aircraft maintenance and overbooking have a larger negative influence on customer perceptions than service failures caused by external factors such as weather. Thus, companies should do everything to minimize service failures caused by internal factors and, in the event of a service failure caused by internal factors, service recovery actions should go above and beyond customer expectations. This research also emphasizes the importance of keeping customers informed about the cause and magnitude of the service failure and what the business is doing to resolve it in a timely manner. Providing adequate information in a timely manner can help ease customers' concerns and create the perception that the company is being honest and doing everything in their power to resolve the issue. This can enhance customers' positive emotions and reduce their negative emotions.

Given the limitations on resources, companies need to set priorities regarding their implementation of various types of service recovery actions. Studies suggest that prompt recovery actions to reduce the magnitude and negative consequences of service failures have more positive impacts on customer emotions. Furthermore, providing compensation for the service failure on the current trip, both monetary and nonmonetary, such as upgrades, vouchers for food and beverages, and waiving certain fees, can reduce customer anger and frustration. Genuine empathy and apologies from employees as well as positive service attitudes and behaviours are especially helpful for alleviating negative customer emotions and enhancing positive emotions. Positive employee attitudes and behaviours have a critical effect on companies' reputations, and many customers mention 'employees saved the company' in their online reviews when they post comments about their service failure recovery experiences.

Thus, it is critical for businesses to develop operational strategies to reduce the frequency of service failures. In the event of a service failure, they should be ready to provide service recovery actions that can minimize the magnitude and negative consequences of the service failure. Timely, reliable and satisfactory service recovery actions, including quick response, constant communication and satisfactory compensation, can have significant impact on customers' perceptions of service quality and their future consumption behaviours.

*Source*: Xun, Liu, & Gursoy[4]

### GAP 4: THE COMMUNICATIONS GAP

This gap is caused when there is a difference between the pre-encounter promise communicated by marketers and the operational expertise of the hospitality firm. It is not unusual for marketers or salespeople to over-promise by making promises that operations cannot deliver. This will surely mean the customer will be disappointed. It is widely accepted that it is better to under-promise and over-deliver than over-promise and under-deliver. In Chapter 9, we discussed the importance of pitching promotional messages appropriately.

### GAP 5: THE PERCEPTION GAP

This gap is the difference between what the customer expects in terms of service quality, and what they experience. If the customer is to be satisfied, there should be no gap between their expectations and their experience of the delivered service. The key to closing gap 5 is to close gaps 1–4: make sure you truly understand customer expectations, make sure service standards match those expectations, design service production and delivery processes to meet those standards, and do not over-promise!

### CLOSING THE GAPS

When customers assess that the service quality they receive is above what they expected, then they become what marketers like to call 'delighted' customers. In contrast, when the service quality received is below what was expected, customers are dissatisfied. As you read in Chapter 3, customers have a 'zone of tolerance' when it comes to satisfaction. As hospitality products are bundles of tangible and intangible elements, consumers may still be satisfied if some elements of their experience fall below their expectations as long as the totality of the experience falls within their zone of tolerance. For example, a restaurant customer may be satisfied overall (the perception gap) even if they waited too long for their food (the delivery gap) and other aspects of the service (intangible) and food and beverage (tangible) was perceived to be of high quality. The gaps model can help hospitality managers to ensure customers are satisfied with the service quality received and importantly, that the totality of their experience falls within their zone of tolerance.

## Service experience journey mapping

The previous section has identified how important it is that service production and delivery processes should satisfy customer expectations. A service experience journey is the process by which a customer interacts with service providers and technology-enabled processes during a hospitality experience. Customer journey mapping is the practice of visualizing customer interactions by mapping out the actions they take to achieve their goals. Customer journey mapping outlines key events, customer motivations, and areas of friction within their experience. Then, this information is combined into a comprehensive visual diagram that describes the stages customers go through, from information search to making online booking to experiencing the service and to sharing their experiences on social media.

Journey maps help service providers visualize and pinpoint critical interaction points that can improve or harm customers' service experiences. Utilizing flowcharting techniques, a customer experience journey map provides a specification of how a service is (or should be) delivered by mapping the customer journey throughout the service experience.

Service experience journey mapping can be used in the design of new hospitality products or to assess current processes and identify actual and potential service fail-points. Service experience journey maps usually chart the customer's actions during pre-encounter information search and reservation processes, their experience of the service encounter, and their exposure to post-encounter processes. They may also chart all the actions that service providers carry out during these same processes as depicted in Figure 11.1. The components of a customer service experience map are presented in Table 11.1.

### Creating a customer journey map

The customer journey begins with customer awareness about a hospitality product or service. Once they become aware that your hospitality product or service may satisfy their specific

## Customer Service Experience Journey Map

| Stages | Awareness | Consideration | Decision | Service Experience | Post Experience Evaluation |
|---|---|---|---|---|---|
| **Actions** | See social media campaign, view online ads, hear radio ads | Conduct information search, compare locations, amenities and prices | Make a booking | Experience hospitality services | Share experiences, make another booking |
| **Touchpoints** | Social media, traditional media, online media | Online review sites, third party comparison websites, social media, OTA websites | OTA, company website, mobile app, phone | Service delivery, service failure, online review sites, mobile app, chatbot | Social media, review sites, word of mouth, mobile app |
| **Emotions and Motivations** | Interested, Hesitant | Curious, Excited | Excited | Happy | Satisfied, Excited |
| **Key Performance Indicators (KPIs)** | Number of people reached | Number of unique visitors to company website, number of online inquiries | Look-to-book conversion rate, online bookings via company website. | Online reviews, social media posts, satisfaction rate, number of complaints. | Retention rate, satisfaction score, positive review comments. |
| **Goals** | Increase awareness, generate interest | Increase number of unique visitors to company website and online inquiries | Increase look-to-book conversion rate and online bookings via company website. | Increase positive online reviews, social media posts and satisfaction rate. Decrease the number of complaints. | Increase customer retention rate, satisfaction score, and the number of positive review comments posted to review and social media sites |
| **Responsible Teams** | Marketing communications, digital marketing and sales, public relations | Marketing communications, digital marketing and sales | digital marketing and sales, marketing, reservation | Frontline service delivery employees, back of the house employees, customer service, digital marketing and sales. | Customer service, social media team, digital marketing and sales, marketing. |

Figure 11.1 Mapping customer service experience journey

Table 11.1 Components of a customer service experience map

| | |
|---|---|
| Customer stages | One of the first steps of creating a customer service experience journey map is to identify stages in the customer service experience journey. There are at least five stages in a customer service experience journey: awareness, consideration, decision, experiencing the service and post-experience evaluation. These stages may have different names such as inquiry, comparison, purchase, consumption and loyalty or advocacy. |
| Customer personas | A customer persona is a semi-fictional profile of your ideal customer in a segment that represents the key traits of that segment. This composite representation of a market segment is usually developed based on research, such as surveying your existing and potential customers and web analytics. A customer persona is an important tool for creating service experience journey maps because you need to understand your customers' expectations from your business, their goals and what they want to achieve from the various processes they experience before developing your map. After building out a few buyer personas, you can start mapping their service experience journey. |
| Customer actions | Determine the route customers would typically take when engaging with your business for the first time. This will help you identify the actions they will take at each stage. |
| Customer touchpoints | These are customers' interactions with a service process, whether delivered interpersonally or by technology. When creating your customer service experience journey map, you need to identify and list common interactions customers have with your organization, including both technologies (e.g., reservation system) and persons (e.g., concierge). You can find this data by polling existing customers, using analytics tools, or by analyzing online review comments. |
| Emotions and motivations | Every action your customers take is motivated by emotion. Customers' emotions will change depending on which part of their service experience journey they are at. One of the main goals of creating a customer service experience journey map is to predict the customers' emotions and feelings in order to determine their motivations. This way, a service provider can pinpoint potential service failure and success points in a customer service experience journey. |
| Potential roadblocks | Identify the touchpoints where customers might be getting lost, confused, misled, or have disappointing interactions, as well as any missing potential touchpoints where you can interact with your customer. By looking at these roadblocks, you can begin to address the issues by simplifying processes or by minimizing or removing these roadblocks and outlining the new ways for customers to navigate the process. |
| Goals and Key Performance Indicators (KPIs) | The customer service experience journey map should also include goals and quantifiable measures for the key performance indicators at each stage of the journey so that the company's performance at each stage against the goals can be assessed. |
| Responsible party | Customer experience journey maps should also identify the key employees and teams that are in charge of interactions at each stage of customer service experience, and the resources they need to perform their responsibilities. |

needs or wants, they become a prospect. The consideration stage is where customers conduct information search using readily available information about different hospitality service providers in any given market to compare image, reputation, features, pricing, customer service ratings and so on. The decision stage is when the prospect becomes a customer, which then triggers the consumption of a service experience. The post-experience evaluation stage is the final stage in the consumer service experience journey when the customer assesses whether they are satisfied or dissatisfied with the service experience. How the customer feels about a service experience journey will significantly influence that customer's willingness to experience the service journey again or consider service experiences offered by competitors. A customer's feelings about their service experiences will also determine whether they will recommend the service experience to others through sharing their experiences face to face or online. We will now discuss the steps and requirements for mapping customer journeys effectively.

## 1 SET CLEAR OBJECTIVES FOR THE MAP

Before you start working on generating your customer service experience map, you need to determine why you are trying to create one in the first place. What is the purpose of the customer service experience map? What are you trying to accomplish? Whose service experience are you going to map? Once you come up with clear objectives for the map, you will need to generate a customer persona, a detailed description of someone who represents a specific customer segment. This semi-fictitious customer profile should embody the demographic and psychographic characteristics of your best potential customer in that specific customer segment. You will be expected to create a customer persona for each of your critical customer segments.

## 2 PROFILE YOUR PERSONAS AND DEFINE THEIR GOALS

Next, you will need to develop detailed profiles of each customer persona. It is important to remember that the purpose of a customer service experience journey map is to identify the specific paths one customer will take during the service experience journey with your company. Thus, the persona you develop for each segment will need to be very specific so that your service experience map can accurately reflect each customer segment's experiences with your hospitality business.

Since a customer persona is a composite representation of a market segment, it should be developed through market research. For example, you can gather information through interviewing and/or surveying your current customers and potential customers or by analyzing online reviews and comments. Your research should specifically focus on people who are interested in experiencing your hospitality products and services, current customers of your hospitality products and services, and those who have already interacted with your company or plan to do so.

Some examples of good questions to ask are:

- How did you hear about us?
- What first attracted you to our hotel/restaurant?
- What sources of information/websites did you use to gather information about us?
- What is the purpose of your visit?
- Did you visit our website/social media sites?
- Have you ever stayed/dined with us? If so, what was your deciding factor?
- Have you ever interacted with our website with the intent of making a booking but decided not to? If so, what led you to this decision?

- Have you ever interacted with our customer service agents? If so, how helpful was the customer service agent?
- Is there any way that we can simplify the booking process?
- How happy were you with your service experience with us? Are there any areas of the service delivery process we can improve to provide a better service experience to you?

### 3 DETERMINE CUSTOMER INTERACTIONS WITH YOUR BUSINESS AT EACH STEP OF THE SERVICE EXPERIENCE JOURNEY

Once you develop customer personas for each target segment, you also need to identify how your customers interact with your business at each stage of their service experience journey. List all interactions and actions each customer persona is likely to experience on their journey. This might be reading online reviews, conducting a search using specific key words or posting comments to a social media channel about their experiences. This process may result in a long list of actions and interactions. From this long list, you will need to identify the most critical interactions each customer persona is likely to have with your business at each stage of their journey.

Creating the first service experience map is usually the hardest. In creating your first customer service experience map, it is always a good idea to focus on your most typical customer segment. Once you have a specific customer persona for your most typical customer segment, identify the route they would typically take when engaging with your business for the first time. Remember to identify the most critical interactions. At this stage, do not worry about the possible interactions you leave out. You can always go back and revise the service experience map.

### 4 LIST OUT ALL THE TOUCHPOINTS

Once you identify how your customers from each segment are likely to interact with your business at each stage of their journey, then you can identify the touchpoints, places, participants and channels your customers use to interact with your business. Touchpoints refer to each interaction your customer may have with your business or brand. Place refers to the location of the interaction such as onsite, online, social media, etc. Participants include customer service agents in contact centres, reception staff, table waitstaff and other frontline employees. Channels refer to any communication technologies used during interactions between the business and its customers. Communication technologies may include traditional media, social media, telephone, text, user-generated content (UGC), email, mobile apps and chatbots, amongst others. You can identify relevant touchpoints, places and channels using research methods such as observation, personal interviews or surveys.

This important step enables you to identify the actions your customers are taking and channels they are using to interact with your company. Identification of the touchpoints can help you understand the most critical sources and types of information your customers use and the channels and places they use to share their service experiences with the company and others. These might include third party review sites, social media, face-to-face and electronic word-of-mouth.

### EMOTIONS AND MOTIVATIONS

Service experiences shape customer attitudes, thinking and behaviours. These service experiences determine how a customer feels about their interactions with a business, which can have a positive, neutral or negative impact on the customer's motivation to move to the next stage of the journey. Understanding a customer's emotions at each stage of the service journey can also help us identify interactions that potentially delight or frustrate that customer.

Identification of potential roadblocks and delight points is critical for ensuring a successful and satisfactory service experience journey. Every action a customer takes throughout the service experience journey is motivated by emotions. Since positive emotions are likely to motivate a customer to move to the next stage in the service experience journey, knowing the triggers of positive and negative emotions at each stage will help you provide the right interaction at the right time so that you smooth the customer's emotional journey.

### Obstacles, problems and delight points

While it is important to identify the roadblocks and problems that may stop your customer from moving from one stage of the service experience journey to the next stage, it is also important to identify the interactions that can result in customer delight, which can provide strong motivation to move to the next stage of the service experience journey. While cost is one of the most common roadblocks, customer service and service delivery failures and how those failures are handled can result in negative customer emotions, which may lower the customer's motivation to move to the next stage of the journey. On the other hand, positive experiences with a company such as satisfactory solutions to service failures or unexpected but welcome initiatives from service employees can result in positive emotions and strong motivation to move to the next stage.

### 5 Determine the key performance indicators, goals, responsible parties and the resources needed

It is important to set measurable goals and key performance indicators (KPIs) for each customer interaction on the journey map. It is critical to identify who or what (technology) is responsible for creating a satisfactory customer interaction at each touchpoint in each stage of the journey and the skills and resources needed. It is helpful to take an inventory of the resources you have and the ones you will need to improve the customer's service experience. For example, you may identify a problem in one of the stages of your customer's journey caused by poor skills or inadequate technological support. Using the map, you could advise management to invest in customer service training or communication tools that are needed to deliver better outcomes for customers.

### 6 Monitor, evaluate and revise the customer service experience journey maps

The final step in the development of customer journey maps is to monitor and evaluate the accuracy and success of the map. It is important for marketers to monitor and constantly evaluate the customer service experience currently delivered by their business at each stage of the customer journey in order to identify weaknesses and opportunities for improvement.

This monitoring and evaluation process must, as a minimum, cover the primary front-office and back-office processes that impact on customer experience. This might include radio, newspaper and online advertising; email communications; in-house and online interactions; third party touchpoints such as online review sites and OTAs; inbound and outbound call centre processes; and much more.

A customer service experience map is a constant work-in-progress. Reviewing it on a regular or continuous basis can help you identify opportunities for improvements in customer experience. Data analytics and customer feedback help you to monitor and evaluate customer experience throughout the journey. This evaluation can help you identify where customer needs and expectations are not being met. Then, you can make the appropriate changes to the journey map to ensure that you are providing the desired experience and make clear that customers can find solutions to their problems with your company's help.

---

### MARKETING INSIGHT 11.3

**Effects of metaverse applications on the hospitality and tourism industry and customers**

The world's hospitality and tourism industry has been undergoing some significant changes not only due to the COVID-19 pandemic but also because of disruptive innovations in the digital sphere such as the evolution of the metaverse from augmented reality (AR), virtual reality (VR) and mixed reality (MR) applications. While the concept of metaverse has been talked about for more than two decades, our collective experience through the COVID-19 pandemic and the intense feelings of disconnection and isolation that they produced has only accelerated our collective imagination around the creation of an alternate reality where one can indeed interact in real-time, at any time with others (potentially thousands or millions of others) and have shared experiences using our digital avatars and experience the virtual world in multiple forms such as AR, VR and MR. A world where one can travel without restriction whenever and wherever they wish to. A world where any experience becomes possible and accessible. Thus, the idea of the metaverse and virtual experiences has radically altered the perspective of people on the future of technology and the opportunities it has in store for consumers and businesses. As a result, customers and companies have been increasingly adopting metaverse applications to deliver and receive experiences. The metaverse market was valued at USD 63.83 billion in 2021. The market is estimated to grow to USD 1,527.55 billion by 2029 at 47.6% compound annual growth rate from USD 100.27 billion in 2022.[5]

There is also a rising trend of consumers adopting metaverse hospitality and tourism experiences, products and services. For example, Japan-based First Airlines has started offering virtual flights from Tokyo and the company reported 100% occupancy for their virtual flights to multiple locations such as Hawaii, Rome, Paris, New York, etc. the National Geographic VR subscription allows you to use your Oculus VR gear to virtually kayak through icebergs in Antarctica, or explore the hidden treasures of Machu Picchu. Similarly, 'Wander' can be used to walk any place in the world if that place is mapped in Google Street View, and the Wikipedia integration also provides location-based information while you walk through your favourite place. Additionally, it also allows you to time travel back in history to witness changes that took place since 2005, that is, when the Google Street view was launched. One can also take part in the expedition of the Arctic Circle and take a guided tour by none other than Dallas Seavey, a veteran, four-time winner of the Iditarod dog sled championship. The metaverse applications are certainly changing the hospitality and tourism industry, virtual hotel and destination tours are changing the way people choose hotels and destinations, make bookings, and attend concerts.

While metaverse applications can be used offer experiences that require low interactivity with others such as customers carrying out activities that do not require active participation or seeking information passively without intrusion, metaverse applications can also be used offer highly interactive experiences that require customers to actively participate in the activities in a live virtual environment such as kayaking, escaping into the wilderness of the Amazon Forest or going scuba diving in the Pacific Ocean virtually.

With the metaverse, people will be able to experience flights, hotel rooms, cooking and food preparation at restaurants, tours, and attend conferences, meetings and conventions all virtually. In fact, several air travel companies like Boeing are working with immersive 3D engineering designs to build production of alien services under a single digital ecosystem through the metaverse. Prospective travellers will be able to play with a try before you buy feature, allowing them to have a trial experience of the accommodation, hotel and restaurant interiors, tourist attractions, flights and other services that they are interested in, all from the comfort of their home. Since customers are able to virtually experience the services, they are interested in during the decision-making phase of their customer journey, metaverse experiences can then be the difference between customers completing a booking or backing out. Thus, metaverse offers significant opportunities to both service providers and customers.

Individuals will be able to go shopping, visit a museum, catch a concert or stroll through an art gallery in the digital world. Pretty cool, right? But will it replace real world hospitality and tourism experiences? Probably not. Though the metaverse cannot replace real travel, with the improvement in technology and sophistication in the quality of VR headsets, the metaverse hospitality and tourism apps are increasingly becoming immersive, pushing digital natives and tech-savvy consumers to sign up for virtual globetrotting. As customers and the technology evolve over time, metaverse applications are likely to play a larger role in the industry, enhancing marketing, customer relationships, communication, customer decision making processes and the guest experience. Therefore, the metaverse would certainly become an integral part of the industry and augment the overall hospitality and tourism experience in multiple ways. The hospitality and tourism metaverse experiences can even become the next disruptor of the industry.

### Complexity and divergence in hospitality services

Service processes vary in their complexity and diversity. The level of service complexity refers to the number of steps and sequences that need to be carried out to perform the service – the fewer the steps, the lower the service complexity; the greater the number of steps, the greater the complexity. Divergence refers to the degree of standardization required during the service process. Some service processes are highly standardized and consequently have a very low degree of divergence. Other processes allow employees more autonomy in delivering the service, and therefore there is greater divergence. Complexity and divergence influence the degree of variability in the service encounter. From a marketing perspective, the promises made to customers must reflect the complexity and divergence of operations, so that the customer's service quality expectations are properly managed. Figure 11.2 provides an example of the complexity/divergence matrix using a pulled pork stall, a sandwich shop, an upmarket restaurant and a customized catered event.

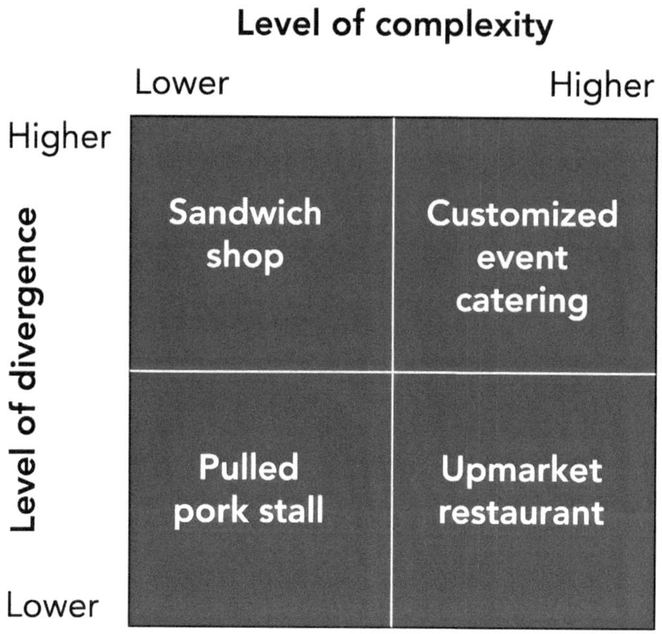

## Level of complexity

Figure 11.2 Complexity and divergence in hospitality services

*Source*: Adapted from Zeithaml, Bitner and Gremler,[6] reproduced with permission of the McGraw-Hill Companies

A person working on a pulled pork stall has a very small number of actions to perform to serve pulled pork in a bun, so the level of complexity is relatively low. There is also a lower degree of divergence because the production process can be very standardized, with a limited number of ingredients. Conversely, a sandwich shop with an extensive menu of different breads and dozens of different fillings offers customers considerable choice. It therefore has a relatively high degree of divergence. However, the operation of making sandwiches is simple, and so the level of complexity is comparably low. The kitchen skills and production processes required to deliver the highest-quality menus in an upmarket restaurant are highly complex, but they must deliver high consistency, regardless of which chef is cooking. The use of standardized recipes is common, and the level of divergence is therefore low. Some services are unique and have high levels of both complexity and divergence. For example, bespoke catering for special occasions, where the customer demands an unusual cuisine using hard-to-find ingredients and exotic recipes, prepared by highly skilled chefs for a customized menu delivered in a unique location, is both highly complex and highly divergent.

### Modifying service operations processes

By mapping service operations processes, a company can quickly establish the levels of complexity and divergence in its service operations. Service processes can often be changed either to increase or decrease the levels of complexity and divergence. There are four alternative strategies:

1  *Complexity reduction strategy.* To reduce the complexity of a service process, the number of steps and sequences used to produce the service are reduced. For example, the complexity of restaurant operations could be reduced by eliminating some menu items. Although this strategy is likely to improve consistency and cost control, it also narrows the marketing offer and risks alienating customers who might transfer their patronage to a competitor.

2  *Increased complexity strategy.* Increasing the complexity of the service process means adding more steps or sequences to the existing service. Adding more menu items might enhance the marketing offer, generate additional revenue and/or enhance customer satisfaction. However, the increased complexity might create service quality problems and increase costs, and some customers may not be interested in paying more for the new offer.

3  *Divergence reduction strategy.* Reducing the level of divergence in the service process implies a greater standardization of the service. For example, a table service restaurant might amend its service processes to have counter service only to achieve a higher degree of standardization and, with that, increased productivity and reduced costs. This type of service process strategy is usually associated with mass marketing or institutional food service. It helps to ensure greater consistency for customers and greater reliability of service quality. However, some customers may resent the changes and react negatively to the standardized service offer.

4  *Increased divergence strategy.* Increasing divergence allows for greater customization of the offer. This strategy can be enabled by empowering employees to respond to individual customers' needs and wants, thereby showing their empathy and responsiveness. It is often associated with a niche positioning strategy as higher prices are usually charged due to the higher costs incurred. However, in recent years, technology has made customization easier for hospitality operations. Many hotels and restaurants offer products and services that can be customized during the booking or ordering stage or even during the delivery stage. While increasing divergence might reduce control over consistency, allowing greater fluctuation in the service quality delivered, it offers greater customization opportunities for customers.

## Service failure

We have already identified several causes of service failure in our earlier discussion of the gaps model. Some service failures are relatively minor for the customer and the overall experience could remain within the customer's zone of tolerance. However, some extremely dissatisfied customers with serious complaints can litigate against hospitality companies. The characteristics of the product, the type of occasion, the price charged, the nature and seriousness of complaints, and the personality of the customer influence whether and how customers complain. Complaining customers generally fall into four categories, as follows.

### The passive customer

Passive customers are generally introverted and prefer to avoid confrontation. As a result, they do not tend to make complaints at the time of a service failure. However, this does not mean they do not complain at all. Rather, they prefer to tell friends and family about their complaints and post negative review comments to review sites, but not to the business itself. As a result, the hospitality business cannot easily identify the nature and cause of service failure and take action to correct it during the service encounter. The passive customer can therefore cause damage to a hospitality firm's reputation. It is important, therefore, that hospitality service staff reach out to these customers by actively seeking their feedback during the service encounter and trying to rectify any issues.

### The constructive complainer

Constructive complainers are not afraid to voice their opinion to serving staff during the service experience. Although critical, they tend to complain in a calm and rational way because they believe that complaining is a positive action benefiting both themselves and the company. They think that complaining helps the company to improve its service, and they give the company the opportunity to recover from the service failure. If the employees or management respond appropriately, these complainers can develop a positive attitude to the company. In other words, the customer's initial disappointment can be turned into a positive incident, and customer loyalty can even be enhanced. In addition, the hospitality business can learn from these complaints, identify the causes of service failure and ensure that they do not occur again in the future.

### The rip-off complainer

These complainers tend to complain in an attempt to 'get something for nothing'. They may or may not have a genuine issue to complain about. If they do have a genuine complaint, however, they generally are not interested in trying to resolve the issue. Rather, they are more interested in receiving something from the service provider by way of compensation. As a result, they often enter into a bargaining position with the service provider, suggesting that whatever is offered in compensation for the service failure is 'not good enough'. They may threaten to expose the company publicly, but in practice these complainers are less likely to use social media to voice their complaints, especially if they are a regular rip-off complainer. They may believe it is better to keep a low profile than be exposed publicly. Many hospitality companies offering a money-back service quality guarantee keep records of complaints so that they can easily spot the rip-off complainer. For example, every time a service guarantee is invoked, firms like Premier Inn and Carlson record the event on a database so that they can identify rip-off complainers. Some highly defensive operations take the view that all complainers are attempting a rip-off, and therefore fail to respond to genuine complaints. It is highly likely that only a small percentage of complainers fit this type.

### The aggressive complainer

Aggressive complainers, sometimes called 'customer terrorists', can be difficult to please. They tend to be extroverted and may even enjoy confrontation with service employees at the time of the service failure. Unlike constructive complainers, they are often more focused on emotional displays than documenting or fully explaining the problem to service staff. As a result, it may be more difficult for serving staff to identify the cause of the problem and to offer suitable compensation to the customer. Aggressive complainers may be dismissive of any excuse offered for the service failure and have also been known to be unreasonable in their demands for compensation. However, they are also more likely to complain to others, telling many people about their poor treatment and posting negative review comments to online review sites. Social media makes it easy for these complainers to publicly document their complaint and unfair treatment. They also encourage other unhappy customers to complain, and some have even set up anti-company websites. Large companies like McDonald's and Starbucks have suffered from the publicity generated by these complainers.

---

### ACTIVITY 11.2

**Online search for poor hospitality service quality**

Log on to the Tripadvisor website.

- Review some of the entries for hotels that contain negative and positive customer feedback.
- Make a list of the main reasons why customers complain.
- What dimensions of service quality (RATER) are the most frequently complained about?
- Identify, if possible, which service quality gaps might be responsible for these complaints.

---

### Customer complaints

From the preceding discussion, it should be clear that dealing promptly and effectively with complaints when the service failure occurs has advantages. Hospitality businesses have the chance to put things right before the customer leaves and, in doing so, often turn a potentially dissatisfied customer into a loyal one. They also have the opportunity to fully understand how the service failure occurred and begin to think through proposals to prevent it happening again.

Not all customers complain during the service encounter. Some customers may wait and contact the hospitality company subsequently via telephone, text, email, in customer satisfaction surveys or social media. With the passage of time some customers feel more strongly about the service failure. The details of the critical incidents can be magnified. However, because the customer has contacted the company and provided details of the complaint, there is still the opportunity for the company to retrieve the situation and win back the customer. Winning back the customer is important because the operation gets to retain future revenue and margin from that customer.

Alternatively, customers can contact other organizations, typically consumer affairs bodies or legal entities. Local or national governments, consumer protection bodies, tourist boards, motoring organizations, hotel and restaurant guidebooks all respond to customers' complaints by discussing the problems with the management of the hospitality business concerned. Normally, a hospitality company will agree a course of action with the third party and respond to the complaint satisfactorily.

---

### MARKETING INSIGHT 11.4

**Chef responds to online complaint at the Pigalle Restaurant[7]**

The Pigalle Restaurant was an upmarket restaurant located in the theatre district of Boston, Massachusetts. The chef prided himself on the quality of food served and ensuring customers had a high-quality experience. After one busy Thanksgiving dinner service in 2012, a diner posted a negative review on Facebook. The diner described the pumpkin pie as really horrible and tasting like vomit, said the $200 meal was awful and thanked the restaurant for ruining Thanksgiving. This complainant soon received a response via Facebook. However, it was not the sort of response she expected. The first response from the chef was an expletive clearly telling the customer where to go. The second response was more detailed. The chef described the unhappy customer as uneducated and unintelligent, complained about her ignorant method of complaining via Facebook and suggested that the other 98 diners left happy.

Many people were quick to take sides in this argument on Facebook, even some in defence of the chef. But others were quick to note that the customer had spent $200 on the meal and had every right to her criticisms, without fear of being verbally abused as a response. This restaurant has now closed.

*Source*: The Boston Eater[7]

Customers can also complain online about their negative service experiences. Many hospitality businesses and online travel agents (OTAs) contact customers following a booking and encourage customers to give positive or negative feedback electronically. Unhappy customers may be able to substantiate their complaint by uploading photographs or a video. Effective managers will monitor these sites to identify and attempt to resolve problems. When they do not, they can aggravate the situation. Customers can post the evidence on social media such as YouTube, where the complaints can go viral and be viewed by hundreds or thousands of people. This negative publicity is extremely damaging to the reputation of a business and could even lead to a collapse in customer confidence, with disastrous consequences for the company (see Marketing Insight 11.4). Because the consequences of online reviews can be so damaging, some hospitality firms have tried to prevent customers from posting negative reviews in the first place (see Marketing Insight 11.5).

## Service recovery strategies

Customer complaints not effectively resolved can be very damaging to a hospitality firm; it is therefore important companies have well-designed service recovery strategies in place. The more professional companies are acutely aware of the importance of handling customer complaints effectively and have procedures that are included in the employees' training programme. Major companies have customer retention teams in their contact centres skilled at complaint handling and resolution. Customer complaints are inevitable in the hospitality industry and the following service recovery strategies can be used.

> **MARKETING INSIGHT 11.5**
>
> ### Union Street Guest House tries to prevent negative reviews[8,9,10]
>
> The Union Street Guest House was a historic inn in Hudson, New York. Built in 1830, the hotel advertised itself as a great option for weddings and other social gatherings. In 2014, however, management of the Guest House implemented a policy of fining guests for posting negative reviews. The policy clearly stated:
>
> > If you have given us a deposit of any kind for guests to stay at USGH there will be a $500 fine that will be deducted from your deposit for every negative review of USGH placed on any internet site by anyone in your party and/or attending your

wedding or event. If you stay here to attend a wedding anywhere in the area and leave us a negative review on any Internet site you agree to a $500 fine for each negative review.

The policy proved to be somewhat disastrous, as news of this policy quickly spread through the press and was written up in the *New York Post*, *Business Insider* and *Time* and picked up by CBC and CNN television networks. The press were quick to publish the policy as follows:

Please know that despite the fact that wedding couples love Hudson and our Inn, your friends and families may not. This is due to the fact that your guests may not understand what we offer – therefore we expect you to explain that to them. USGH & Hudson are historic. The buildings here are old (but restored). Our bathrooms and kitchens are designed to look old in an artistic 'vintage' way. Our furniture is mostly hip, period furniture that you would see in many design magazines. If your guests are looking for a Marriott type hotel they may not like it here.

The press reports interpreted this policy to imply that guests who complained were philistines who did not understand 'hip' and 'vintage'. In addition, the policy itself led to hundreds of negative online reviews, including some from customers who had previously stayed at the hotel and had not complained about their service experience. The publicity surrounding the policy, however, prompted them to write complaints such as the one that follows.

Absolutely the most terrible, unwelcoming environment I have ever experienced. The staff was not very friendly, almost as though they are doing you a favour by helping you. Why would you want to stay at a place that censors your freedom of speech?? Rather than take customer feedback and look to improve the service, the genius in management has taken the practice of fining people for bad reviews. We were here for a wedding and there were so many little issues with the party, food, service, etc. that I couldn't help but share this unfortunate experience. These were only compounded by the policy of not being allowed to write about it. We love the area but would never go near this place again.

Since this publicity, the policy was removed from the website, but not before the damage was done. The hundreds of posts on review sites have brought the rating for the Guest House down. The Guest House was later closed down.

*Source*: CBC News,[8] CNN,[9] Time[10]

## Zero defects (or 'doing it right the first time')

The concept of zero defects is borrowed from manufacturing and is linked to *total quality management* (TQM). The key principle is to design out every potential problem before it can occur. This strategy really reflects the definition of quality as consistency identified earlier in the chapter. However, the special characteristics of hospitality services make the adoption of a zero defects strategy difficult to implement, though the idea of TQM is to create a culture within the company of 'doing it right the first time'. By working to reduce operational service failures, perhaps by customer journey mapping or using the gaps model, companies can reduce the incidence of service failures and therefore customer complaints.

### Encourage customer complaints

This strategy might sound strange, but encouraging customers to complain can improve sales and service quality if a company has systems in place to learn from complaints and make the appropriate changes. Think back to the section in this chapter outlining the types of complainers. Constructive complainers can be very helpful in identifying the causes of the service failure. Passive customers also need to be encouraged to complain before they leave the hospitality premises. A simple way to encourage feedback is to check with customers directly during the service encounter whether everything is satisfactory. Unfortunately, some staff members do not really listen to the answers given or are unwilling or unable to rectify the situation. Other times, customers may feel uncomfortable complaining to the service provider, particularly when in the company of guests. Many companies use customer comment cards or surveys to encourage feedback, distributed either before the customer leaves the premises or via email immediately after their departure. Regrettably, many companies fail to respond to complaints received in this way. Responsive companies, however, will communicate with, and thank, customers for their observations and respond appropriately to the comments. Such a response can potentially turn a critical customer into a loyal customer. Sometimes, negative comment cards and questionnaires can be deliberately 'lost' by employees who do not want to be disciplined if they are responsible for the customer complaint. This is more likely to happen if employee rewards such as bonuses are linked directly to customer satisfaction scores. A key constraint on encouraging customers to complain is the unit manager, who does not want to be seen as having a long complaints record, even though their positive attitude to complaints could mean that their unit is truly providing a better service than units with a lower level of complaints.

### Treat customers fairly

Customers have a sense of 'fairness'. Following their complaint, customers look for three types of fairness from the company:

1 *Outcome fairness* refers to the tangible result the customer expects to receive after a complaint. Hospitality companies use a range of compensation options depending on the type of complaint including apologies, replacing a menu item, providing a complimentary drink, providing a room upgrade, reducing charges or offering complimentary accommodation/ meals. Most customers expect fair compensation relative to the magnitude of the complaint. If the outcome is 'fair', the customer at least feels that the company took the complaint seriously. However, when companies refuse to offer compensation, or the compensation offered is thought 'unfair', then the unhappy customer will be disappointed or even angry, making an already bad situation worse.

2 *Procedural fairness* refers to the company's policy and procedures for handling complaints. Procedural fairness links to the company's policy and processes for responding quickly and efficiently to the complaint. Customers want the complaint policy to be transparent or clear to them. Customer-contact employees and front-of-house management need to find out what the customer's problem is, apologize and take prompt, courteous and efficient action to provide a solution that satisfied the complainant.

3 *Interactional fairness* refers to the ways customers want to be treated by management and staff during the complaint episode. Customers expect to be treated politely and honestly. Customers want companies genuinely to care about their problem. This might seem to be common sense, but some hospitality companies do not provide training in customer care

and do not allow front-line employees to take decisions. Some employees may lie to customers and to management and fail to take customer complaints seriously. When customers feel that they are unfairly treated by customer-contact employees they are more likely to defect to competitors.

Because of this potential for customer churn (defection to competitors) and the associated loss of future revenue and margin, many of the larger hospitality companies do train employees to deal with customer complaints. They may employ acronyms to help employees follow clear steps and respond appropriately. For example, the LEARN acronym encourages employees to:

- *Listen*: to the customer complaint fully, without interruption
- *Empathize*: with the customer's situation to demonstrate you understand how they feel
- *Apologize*: to the customer without making excuses for the service failure
- *Respond*: to the customer's complaint in an appropriate manner; determine what is necessary to resolve the customer's problem
- *Now*: act immediately, instead of promising to find a solution later.

Other firms use the acronym HEAT (hear, empathize, apologize and take action) or LEAP (listen, empathize, apologize and problem-solve). These models essentially take customer service staff through the same step-by-step process.

### Learning from customer complaints

Analysis of customer complaints provides important evidence about the causes of service failure. If customers consistently complain about a certain problem, then management can develop solutions to the problem, reduce customer complaints and improve customer satisfaction. This is called root-cause analysis. Customer complaint data can be used to improve service production and delivery processes leading to enhanced customer experience and satisfaction. Learning from customer complaints is a key element of quality improvement.

### The service recovery paradox

It has been shown that customers who experience and complain about service failure, but are satisfied by the response from the company, can become even more loyal than customers who have enjoyed good service and not had cause for complaint. The service recovery paradox demonstrates that an effective service recovery strategy can redeem a potentially disastrous situation and turn customers with complaints into loyal customers. Excellent service recovery demonstrates two dimensions of service quality – empathy and responsiveness – that are less visible when service is delivered right the first time.

## Conclusion

Designing service production and delivery processes to deliver what customers expect is a crucial component of encounter marketing. Companies need to develop a deep understanding of customer expectations to ensure that the service process delivers satisfaction. However, in the hospitality business, there will always be some customers who complain, so companies must have a service recovery strategy to respond to complaints. Indeed, managing complaints effectively can turn dissatisfied customers into loyal customers.

In this chapter, we have explained the following:

- Service processes can be categorized as vertical or horizontal, front-office or back-office and primary or secondary.
- Managing service processes well is critical to deliver customer satisfaction.
- Service quality can be seen as different things: excellence, consistency, fitness for purpose or value-for-money.
- Five dimensions of service quality – reliability, assurance, tangibles, empathy and responsiveness (RATER).
- The gaps model of service quality and how it can be used to improve service quality.
- Customer service experience journey mapping.
- Complexity and divergence in service operational processes.
- Types of complainers: passive, constructive, rip-off and aggressive.
- The importance of service recovery strategies.

---

### ACTIVITY 11.3

Reflect on the activity you carried out at the beginning of the chapter about your own experiences as a customer eating out. Try now to answer the additional questions, in italics, using the concepts covered in this chapter.

- Can you remember an occasion when the service quality you experienced was disappointing? Can you explain what went wrong? *What dimension of service quality was disappointing to you? Can you relate this to a particular gap in the gap model?*

- Did you, or somebody with you, complain to the service provider? *What type of customer complainer category did you fit into?*

- If yes, how did the employees/manager respond to the complaint? Were you happy with their response? Did they offer you any compensation? *Did they follow a defined service recovery procedure such as LEARN or LEAP?*

- If you were not happy, did you talk to your family and friends about it? If so, how many people did you tell? Did you mention your experience (positive or disappointing) online? If you did, what site did you use to mention your experience? *Was there any response from the company on the social media site? If so, how quickly did they respond? Was the action taken satisfactory to you?*

Do you now understand how your complaint was managed by the employees/management?

---

### REVIEW QUESTIONS

Now check your understanding by answering the following questions:

1 Discuss the role of service operations management in hospitality from a marketing perspective.

2 Apply the gaps model of service quality, using an example from the hospitality industry where you experienced a service failure.

3 Map a hospitality service process that you know either as an employee or as a customer. Evaluate the service from the view of a customer and make recommendations to improve service quality.

4 Discuss the reasons for service failure in the hospitality industry and suggest what companies should do when a customer complains.

## References

1. Chen, S., Han, X., Bilgihan, A., & Okumus, F. (2021). Customer engagement research in hospitality and tourism: A systematic review. *Journal of Hospitality Marketing & Management*, 1–34.
2. Parasuraman, A., Zeithaml, V. A., & Berry, L. L. (1985). A conceptual model of service quality and its implications for future research. *Journal of Marketing*, *49*(4), 41–50.
3. Hurn, C. (2017). Stuffed giraffe shows what customer service is all about. *Huffpost*. [cited September 20, 2021]. Available from: www.huffpost.com/entry/stuffed-giraffe-shows-wha_b_1524038
4. Xu, X., Liu, W., & Gursoy, D. (2019). The impacts of service failure and recovery efforts on airline customers' emotions and satisfaction. *Journal of Travel Research*, *58*(6), 1034–1051.
5. Fortune Business Insight [Internet]. *Metaverse Market 2022–2029*. [cited April 12, 2022]. Available from: https://www.fortunebusinessinsights.com/infographics/metaverse-market-106574
6. Zeithaml, V. A., Bitner, M. J., & Gremler, D. D. (2013). *Services Marketing*, 6th ed. New York: McGraw-Hill.
7. Boston Eater [Internet]. *Pigalle to Customer: 'You Must Enjoy Vomit'*. [cited September 22, 2021]. Available from: https://boston.eater.com/2012/11/28/6516211/pigalle-to-customer-you-must-enjoy-vomit
8. CBC News [Internet]. *$500 Charge for Negative Reviews Doled Out By New York Hotel*. [cited September 22, 2021]. Available from: www.cbc.ca/newsblogs/yourcommunity/2014/08/500-charge-for-negative-reviews-doled-out-by-new-york-hotel.html
9. CNN [Internet]. *A $500 Fine for Bad Reviews? Inn's Policy Pummeled*. [cited September 22, 2021]. Available from: http://edition.cnn.com/2014/08/04/travel/bad-hotel-review-fine-backlash
10. Time [Internet]. *'Historic' Inn Charges $500 Per Negative Online Review*. [cited September 22, 2021]. Available from: http://time.com/3079343/union-street-guest-house-negative-review

# 12

# Managing customer-contact employees

After working through this chapter, you should be able to:

- Understand the importance of customer-contact employees in creating satisfying or memorable customer experiences
- Evaluate service-orientated culture in hospitality companies
- Understand the concepts of internal marketing and empowerment in a hospitality context
- Develop an awareness of the importance of critical incidents and the potential conflicts which employees working in a hospitality customer-contact role need to manage.

## Introduction

A defining characteristic of the hospitality industry is the crucial role played by employees during the service encounter with customers. The behaviours of customer-contact employees can have a significant impact of their customers' impressions of service quality. Furthermore, employees are the personification of the hospitality brand. Although recruiting, training and rewarding employees is a human resource management function, marketers need to understand and influence employment strategies to ensure that employees can represent brand values and deliver the service experience promised to customers. At the same time, human resource managers have increasingly adopted a marketing-like approach to employee recruitment and retention. This type of human resource management strategy is called internal marketing.

DOI: 10.4324/9781003186342-15

In this chapter, we discuss the role of employees in delivering appropriately high service quality during the hospitality encounter. We will then examine service culture, internal marketing and service encounters in hospitality organizations.

---

**ACTIVITY 12.1**

If you are working or have worked in a hospitality unit, reflect on your own experiences as an employee.

- Was the interview/selection process formal, using a range of different methods (online application form/letter, several interviews and applicant tests), or was the process very informal?

- Did the company offer formal induction and training?

- How did you learn about the service culture – from management or other employees?

- Were the managers and employees genuinely passionate about giving customers excellent service?

- What happened if a customer complained?

- We will revisit these questions at the end of the chapter and see what you have learned.

---

## The importance of customer-contact employees

In Chapters 10 and 11, we have repeatedly referred to the key role of employees in delivering appropriate levels of service quality. Considerable research has been undertaken in this area and has established that customer-contact employees have significant influence on customers' perception of service quality and their satisfaction. At the simplest level, as J. Willard Marriott, the founder of Marriott International, has said many times, in the service business you can't make happy guests with unhappy employees.[1] At a more complex level, it is the customer-contact employees who deliver on most aspects of the five RATER dimensions of service quality: reliability, assurance, tangibles (partly), empathy and responsiveness.

The service-profit chain is a model that demonstrates the links between employee satisfaction, service quality, customer satisfaction and business performance. When employees are satisfied with their working conditions and relationships, they are more likely to work productively for the company, giving the service experience the customer expects. Customer satisfaction is enhanced and leads to repeat sales and positive word-of-mouth. Customers like to see familiar faces when they return, and when the same employees greet regular customers by name this helps in the development of loyalty. Loyal customers are more profitable, so business performance improves.

If employees are not satisfied at work, the business can suffer from a cycle of poor employee retention, staff shortages and employees with limited company experience and limited product/service knowledge who consequently deliver service quality below customers' expectations. Customers are less likely to return and if they do return they are unlikely to be recognized. With fluctuating service standards and little continuity of customer-contact employees, the opportunity to develop closer customer relationships is compromised. The business does not generate sufficient repeat and recommended sales, and profits can decline.

The service-profit chain (Figure 12.1) demonstrates the association between employee satisfaction and customer satisfaction. However, this relationship is complex, and there is no simple causal link. For example, some long service employees may fall into a pattern of poor customer service, especially in a hospitality unit that has changed ownership or management several times. Employees can become cynical and bored with their work environment, leading to indifferent service attitudes and lower standards of service.

Figure 12.1  The service profit chain

*Source*: Adapted from Heskett et al.[2]

## Developing a service-orientated culture

A company's culture has a powerful influence on how employees look after customers. There is a limit to management's ability to monitor and control service encounters, so customer-contact employees have enormous scope to interpret the company's rules. What guides customer-contact employees in choosing their behaviour towards a customer is the organization's service culture.

Each hospitality organization has its own culture. Culture, in this context, means the shared core values, beliefs and assumptions that underpin how the organization operates, including the way that it treats its employees. These cultural components are often deeply rooted in the organization's history. Entrepreneurs such as Bill Marriott, whose strong Mormon faith provided the ethical foundation for treating employees in a positive, caring manner, still influences the Marriott Corporation's approach to human resource management. Companies that have been created through a series of mergers/acquisitions, and regard shareholders as the most important stakeholders, can have a culture that values financial performance above all else. This can be unattractive to employees other than the senior managers who own stock (shares) or options.

Case Study 12.1 provides an illustration of service culture and service quality at Red Carnation Hotels.

Employees learn the organizational culture by observing the behaviour and messaging of head and regional offices and the unit's general manager – who represents and personifies the corporate culture. Corporate culture refers to the set of values, beliefs, behaviours, customs and attitudes that govern how people behave within corporations. The culture of a corporation provides boundaries and guidelines that help the employees of the organization to know the correct way of performing their jobs. Organizational climate refers to the atmosphere of an organization that is created based on the employees' perception and feeling of the corporate culture of a particular organization. Although the climate and culture in a company is not normally written down, they nonetheless influence service culture and how customer-contact employees interact with customers and each other. Sometimes a company's senior management will draft a statement reflecting its vision, mission and values. This can encapsulate the culture of the organization.

## CASE STUDY 12.1

### Service culture and service quality at Red Carnation Hotels (RCH)[3,4]

The Red Carnation Hotels Collection comprises 20 luxury hotels and spas around the world, each unique, whilst sharing the founding values that define the family-owned and run business. These four- and five-star privately owned boutique hotels operate in intensely competitive environments. The RCH mission is to provide exceptional, memorable hospitality by meeting or exceeding guest expectations. One of the RCH core values is to give personalized, warm and consistently excellent customer service.

The challenge is how to ensure that over 2,000 employees from 71 different countries working in five different countries and located in three different continents consistently deliver the RCH mission and core values.

The key idea is to invest above average resources in the company's people. RCH have developed a robust human resource strategy and monitoring systems to manage the recruitment, training and motivation of employees. Although RCH does have standard operating procedures, the hotels are managed individually, and the company service culture is customized at the property level.

Recruiting employees with open minds, character, energy and personality as opposed to technical skills is the critical starting point. Although skills can be taught, it is very difficult to change the behaviour of employees who have inappropriate service attitudes. RCH employs its own highly skilled trainers, who conduct training in the hotel properties. Employees are empowered to deliver the RCH mission, but this empowerment is set within precise boundaries, so that employees, supervisors and managers all know what is expected of them. For example, if any guest checking out has a problem with their bill, the front desk employees are empowered to immediately resolve the issue without having to contact their manager. When employees make mistakes, this is accepted provided the employee learns from their error.

Employee/customer ratios are an indicator of service levels in luxury hotels. In the RCH four-star properties, the ratio is above the industry average at 1.5 employees to 1 customer, and in the five-star hotels, the ratio of 2 employees to 1 customer is similar to other leading luxury hotels. To deliver memorable service, RCH carefully observes every customer *touch point* and strives to develop responsive policies that recognize the different types of customer (single, group, business and special occasion), the customer's culture (for example, tourists from the USA have different needs and wants to Mediterranean customers) and what employees should, or should not, be doing. Two ideas help to focus the management thinking: first, to review the customer experience from a BDA perspective (Before, During and After the service encounter); and second, to look to see how the hotels can deliver Tiny Noticeable Touches (TNT). For example, front desk employees are empowered to spend up to £50 on any guest to improve their stay.

One of the challenges is how to deliver consistent service quality in the European, American and South African hotels when each region has such different cultural attitudes to service. To ensure hotels such as the Twelve Apostles Hotel & Spa in Cape Town, South Africa, deliver RCH service standards, many of the South African employees are sponsored to work in front office, bar, restaurant and housekeeping in the RCH hotels in Europe. This not only helps to develop the technical service skills of employees but also exposes the employees to the RCH service philosophy. Many of these employees are then promoted to supervisory and management levels when they return to South Africa. Clearly, this strategy is successful, because the Twelve Apostles Hotel has achieved significant recognition in several reader awards, being ranked number 3 in the 'Best City Hotels in Africa' in Travel + Leisure, number 13 in the 'Top 30 Hotels in Africa' in Conde Nast Traveler.

RCH employees have similar pay and employment conditions to competitor hotels. A key strategy is to ensure that employees are recognized, and this happens in a variety of ways. If an employee is interested in career development, then appropriate opportunities are provided to enable employees to progress. There are initiatives to involve employees in regular social events and many incentives and prizes. For example, upselling at the front office is a major skill. Employees are encouraged to identify customers who might be interested in a room upgrade and then to sell the benefits of the upgrade. The front desk employee receives 10 per cent of the upgrade as a bonus. Therefore, if a guest is upsold from a £200 room rate to £250 and stays five nights, the front desk employee will have a £25 bonus (5 nights × 10 per cent of the £50 upgrade = £25).

RCH monitors its human resource strategy in a variety of ways. Employees have catch-up meetings with their line managers every three months and an annual appraisal. Each year there is a detailed employee survey to track management performance. When employees choose to leave, there is a rigorous exit survey and interview. The monthly department and hotel employee turnover statistics for each property are reported, and the general manager's bonus is partly based on achieving employee retention targets. The departmental/hotel comparative retention statistics are used as a tool to help unit managers to explore retention issues and identify any managerial/supervisory training requirements. RCH employee retention statistics of between 20 per cent and 39 per cent per year are significantly better than for most hotel companies.

*Source*: Pollitt,[3] Red Carnation Hotel Collection[4]

In small- and medium-sized owner-managed hospitality businesses, the 'family' culture will be more visible to employees. The service culture in a family business is often highly personalized and provides guests with a genuinely local hospitality experience (see Marketing Insight 12.1).

### MARKETING INSIGHT 12.1

**The Blunsdon House Hotel, Swindon, England**[5]

Since 1957, the Clifford family has turned a farmhouse bed-and-breakfast business into a major four-star conference and leisure hotel, the Blunsdon House Hotel. Founders Zan and Peter Clifford have always been customer-orientated, and their son John and his wife Carrie continue the tradition, stating: 'We are obsessive in our ambition to provide excellent service.' The founders live on the premises and still take a passionate interest in customers' welfare – demonstrating their commitment and leading by example. They also recognized the need for developing and looking after their employees as the business grew. Key employees, and members of their families, have worked with the Clifford family for generations. Most heads of department have long service awards, and the general manager was also appointed a director. Today the third generation of the family – Ben, Christopher and Grace – are involved in the hotel and the family commitment to customers and employees continues.

Nearly all major hospitality organizations claim to be good employers and suggest 'Our employees are our most important assets'. Employees might not believe these messages when the company's actual human resource practices are poor. Where employees hear company messages that promote a certain kind of behaviour but witness contradictory behaviours from management, then the organization suffers from a kind of cultural schizophrenia. Like a personality disorder, such inconsistency may undermine the organization's aim to deliver high service quality. Clearly, culture and climate reflect the philosophy of the senior management team. The most successful hospitality companies do recognize the strategic value of investing in their employees to ensure that units deliver the high-quality service given the brand's market position.

### The general manager as a role model

Different units within the same hospitality brand can have different cultures and climates. Although the characteristics of a successful hospitality general manager (GM) will vary, the personality, behaviour and actions of the GM send powerful signals to the employees and help to shape the culture and climate of the unit. Employee morale and motivation reflect the general manager; employees respond to the leadership provided and follow the example and direction set by the general manager.

## ACTIVITY 12.2

The Marriott Corporation has developed a Business Conduct Guide and related company policies to provide guidance to all members of the Marriott community on not only what is legal but also what is right. The Business Conduct Guide clearly shows how the company's fundamental commitment to hard work, fair business practices and respect for others has shaped Marriott's everyday decision-making and has guided their relationships with all their stakeholders – associates, owners, business partners, franchisees, customers and the communities in which they work.

Download Marriott International's Business Conduct Guide here and read it: www.marriott.com/Multimedia/PDF/Corporate/Core_Values_Heritage/MBCG_External_Landscape_040919(1).pdf

This Business Conduct Guide clearly reflects the core values outlined in the 'The Marriott Management Philosophy – a living tradition of values and beliefs' publication that is primarily based upon the writings of the founder of Marriott International, J. Willard

Marriott (1927–1985). The quotes it contains illustrate the founder's attention to the minor details critical to delivering high-quality service; his genuine concern for the employees; and his passion for the hotel business. Many of the quotes are still relevant today and they illustrate how a positive service culture can help a company become an industry leader.

Download the document and read the quotes and comments from one of the hospitality industry's great entrepreneurial leaders:

www.docshok.com/uploads/THE-MARRIOTT-MANAGEMENT-PHILOSOPHY1466243113.pdf

### Service myths, heroes and villains

Those hospitality companies aspiring to provide excellent service often use examples of extraordinary customer-contact employee actions in their customer communications such as website, advertising, publicity and newsletters. These stories inform both customers and employees about the service experience the company values. Over time, if repeated, these acts can become part of the dominant service culture. In extraordinary service companies, heroes become the personification of what is best about those companies. However, some maverick companies employ characters, notably celebrity chefs, who become 'villains' through negative publicity, and enjoy their controversial reputation.

### Support systems

Customer-contact employees are dependent on support systems, both human and technological, to help to deliver appropriate levels of service quality. In hospitality, there has traditionally been tension and conflict between front-of-house employees and back-of-house employees, especially between the restaurant and kitchen. Organizations that foster a service culture throughout the company develop and implement strategies to make back-of-house employees think of front-of-house employees as partners or internal customers and not as enemies.

We have already discussed how the company's policies can either nurture or inhibit customer-contact employees' actions towards customers. Companies usually set boundaries to the authority that employees have when dealing with customers. Some companies tightly restrict the authority of customer-contact employees, who must follow rules and regulations and report to the more senior managers who make decisions. Others give customer-contact employees the responsibility, authority and tools to solve customers' problems. Technological support systems include the computer systems, equipment and infrastructure within a property or chain. Clearly it is difficult for customer-contact employees to provide appropriate levels of service quality if computer systems are slow, or food and beverage equipment does not function properly. No matter how pleasant customer-contact employees are, if the support systems do not work, the organization's claim to have a service culture will appear fraudulent to both customers and the employees. Finally, in a genuine service culture, all employees – regardless of their role and status – should be customer-focused. Indeed, some experts contend that all employees in service companies should think of themselves as part-time marketers, even if they don't occupy a formal marketing role.[6]

**MARKETING INSIGHT 12.2**

**Use of artificially intelligent (AI) devices and robots in service delivery[7]**

In recent years, the introduction and integration of artificial intelligence (AI) technology and artificially intelligent robotic devices into service delivery operations has been creating new tensions and conflicts among hospitality employees. Several hospitality companies have already developed robots, empowered by artificial intelligence (AI) technology, to perform certain tasks in order to lower labour costs. For example, Connie, the robotic concierge adopted by Hilton Worldwide Hotel, can provide customers with personalized care and support, such as giving real-time recommendations and answering customer queries. Henn-na Hotel in Japan is currently operated by artificially intelligent robots without any human employees. All service delivery tasks such as greeting customers, checking customers in and out, carrying luggage, cleaning rooms, providing travel information, etc. are provided by robots powered by AI. However, studies suggest that hospitality customers overwhelmingly prefer services delivered by human employees over AI robots, especially in contexts where they seek hedonic value from social interactions with real people. Since AI robots cannot yet provide the level of interaction customers expect in service contexts where hedonic benefits are sought AI robots are not likely to replace human employees any time soon. However, an increasing number of hospitality businesses use AI service devices to supplement and empower human employees by using those robotic devices to perform routine and repetitive tasks.

*Source*: Chi, Gursoy and Chi[7]

**ACTIVITY 12.3**

Building on Activity 12.1, if you have worked in a hospitality organization, think about the service culture you observed whilst working.

- Evaluate the culture and climate of the company, the role adopted by the general manager, the service myths and company heroes and the adequacy of the support systems.
- What do you think the company did well? What could be improved?

## Internal marketing

There is a critical relationship between pre-encounter marketing and marketing during the encounter. The promises made to customers in pre-encounter communications have to be delivered during the service encounter to deliver customer satisfaction. We have already discussed the role of employees, and specifically customer-contact employees, in the service encounter. Increasingly, human resource managers have adopted marketing-like approaches to recruit, communicate, motivate and retain employees. This is called internal marketing.

The main driver of internal marketing is the industry's recognition that it must compete for the best available talent. Because the success of the hospitality offer is significantly dependent on the quality of service, which is in turn highly dependent on employees, hospitality companies need to attract, train, motivate and retain the most appropriate employees for their product concept. Internal marketing involves marketing the organization to current and prospective employees in much the same way as the organization markets its offer to external customers.

## Recruitment

Societal perceptions of working in hospitality vary according to the importance of tourism to an economy. In societies where tourism is a key industry, such as the Caribbean, or where tourism is rapidly developing, such as in Vietnam, careers in hospitality are regarded favourably. Potential employees recognize that hospitality jobs are relatively well paid and enjoy high status. In these societies, employers can select potential employees from a large pool of available talent. In societies where hospitality is generally regarded as lower status with lower pay and prospects, the recruitment challenge is more difficult.

The labour pool for hospitality comprises a mix of professional, trained managers, skilled workers, local unskilled employees, transient and part-time workers, and migrant workers. Operational roles in hospitality are normally low skilled, physically demanding jobs, with work shifts during anti-social hours and often with low pay. However, because of their different backgrounds and personalities, individual employees have very different perceptions about the importance of their role in the hospitality business. Department managers and the human resources team need to recruit employees who have a positive perception of working in hospitality.

The image and reputation of the company as an employer is crucial in attracting appropriate employees. Indeed, the strategic aim is often to be the 'preferred employer in the area'. Marriott International has always nurtured a strong employee focus in their operations and endorses the 'preferred employer in the area' strategy. In recent years, Marriott International has won many international 'Best Places to Work' awards in America and Europe, as well as Asian countries such as China, Dubai, Hong Kong, India, Indonesia, Japan, Korea, Singapore and Thailand.

---

### MARKETING INSIGHT 12.3

**Effective people management at Le Manoir Aux Quat'Saisons, Oxford, England**[8]

Raymond Blanc is the charismatic chef/patron of the Belmond Le Manoir and a celebrity television chef. This luxury 32-bedroom country house hotel is a member of Relais & Châteaux and has held two Michelin stars since 1985. Raymond states that 'the good does not interest us, the sublime does!' To deliver sublime service, Le Manoir recruits, trains and motivates employees using both conventional and unusual tactics. One of the first criteria for customer-contact employees is to 'welcome guests with a smile and make them feel at ease throughout their stay'. Employees must demonstrate a passion for food and service, possess high standards of personal appearance and have excellent attention to detail to ensure that service standards are delivered.

The range of benefits includes employee discounts at Relais & Châteaux and Belmond properties, a 'family and friends' discount at Le Manoir, quarterly staff parties and social events, employee loyalty and recognition awards, special occasion gifts, a day off on the employee's birthday, a guest experience after one year of service and every year afterwards.

Le Manoir is the employer of choice for many aspiring hospitality students and young professionals because of its high reputation as an iconic hotel and its excellent approach to human resource management.

*Source*: Le Manoir Aux Quat'Saisons[8]

## Service-mindedness

An essential quality that employers seek in front-line employees is the 'right service attitude'. Some people seem to have a natural aptitude for service: they spontaneously respond to customers and co-workers and have a cheerful and helpful disposition. They are service-minded. These characteristics are linked to an individual's personality, interpersonal communication skills and initiative, and are developed in life experiences over time. As such, attitude cannot really be taught as if it were a job-related skill such as operating a cash register. Unfortunately, one of the problems for hospitality employers in competitive labour markets is the lack of potential employees with the right service attitude. This means that unsuitable employees, who do not have an aptitude for service, are recruited, and these employees can undermine management's attempts to deliver appropriately high levels of service quality. Another important element in hospitality employment is teamwork – the ability to fit into a team and play a role. Some people enjoy working in a team, they are good team players and are supportive to those around them; however, other people are awkward in teams and are not good team players, which can be demotivating for their co-workers.

## Service competences

Employees need to have skills and knowledge to be able to perform their job effectively. Skills and knowledge in hospitality are called service competences. Historically, most hospitality managers had limited education and learned service competences whilst working in the industry. Today, there is a well-established system of hospitality and tourism education in many parts of the world. Colleges offer craft training and diplomas; universities offer bachelor's, master's and doctoral programmes; and there is a range of study-mode options. The best institutions have very close links to the hospitality industry – for example, in Thailand, the Dusit Hotel chain set up the Dusit Thani College to provide training and higher education for hotel, kitchen and restaurant and tourism management students. These educational institutions prepare students for the industry and provide them with core hospitality competences.

## Training

Each hospitality company has its own service culture, operating systems and service standards. New customer-contact employees need induction training to become familiar with the product (product knowledge training) and service philosophy and to meet co-employees working in the same team. Induction training in larger organizations is more formal, whereas in the smaller hospitality firms it is likely to be less formal. Continuous training and career development is a hallmark of successful hospitality companies. Companies with seasonal operations such as Ski Olympic have particular challenges when inducting their employees (see Case Study 12.2).

## CASE STUDY 12.2

### The training challenge for Ski Olympic[9]

Ski Olympic recruits more than 150 employees each year to work in its Alpine chalets and hotels for a five-month season. Approximately one third of the previous year's employees return for the new season. Other employees are mostly recruited by word-of-mouth from the friends of recent employees and the families of customers. The challenge each year is to train up to 100 new employees how to deliver the Ski Olympic experience, in less than two weeks. The training is conducted at the Ski Olympic chalet-hotel Les Avals. As soon as the employees arrive, they are greeted and treated like guests, following the same schedule, with breakfast, afternoon tea and dinner. The new employees adopt different roles, taking it in turns to be customers and then employees, and teams of chefs prepare the same meals that customers will eat on their holidays (one difficult challenge is cooking at Alpine elevations – it takes much longer to boil an egg!). Each employee learns his or her role during this intensive period, and departments have written job lists to help to ensure that Ski Olympic's operating standards, even in an informal, fun environment, are maintained. Treating the employees as customers is the most effective way to demonstrate the desired customer experience. The success of Ski Olympic is built on customer satisfaction – 72 per cent of sales are repeat business.

*Source*: Gary Yates, Ski Olympic

### Empowerment

Customer-contact employees work within the boundaries of authority allowed by their companies. Some hospitality companies set clear rules about what any given customer-contact employee is allowed to do or not to do. An alternative approach is to empower employees to take responsibility for ensuring customers are satisfied with the service encounter. This responsibility needs to be matched with delegated authority and supported by appropriate resources such as technology, training and budgets.

The concept that any customer-contact employee should take ownership of and resolve customer problems, and respond empathically to customers' individual needs and wants, is attractive. Customers want speedy solutions, especially when complaining, and resent having to repeat their complaint to several different employees. However, customer-contact employees may not necessarily want to take the responsibility for customer satisfaction for several reasons:

- Employees may not be given genuine authority by the company to solve the problem.
- Hospitality companies are traditionally bureaucratic and hierarchical organizations, where the middle managers may resent customer-contact employees undermining their authority.
- Employees may not receive the appropriate training and resources to make correct decisions.
- Employees may feel that they are not paid enough to take this responsibility.
- Some employees may not like the idea of taking responsibility at all and prefer to follow the orders of managers.

Though many companies talk about empowering employees, few have genuinely developed the organizational strategies and culture to support empowered employees. Marriott International's training is recognized as a leader in the hotel industry with customer service as the core theme and empowerment as the strategy to encourage employees to show empathy towards customers' needs and wants. The training takes 40–60 hours and models the guest experience by having employees participate in role plays. Employees learn that guests need to be acknowledged whilst waiting; want to be treated as individuals; want to see employees who they know and who like their job; and, most importantly, do not want 'hassle' when they are staying in a hotel or dining in a restaurant. Marriott International continues to search for new ways to deliver the basic brand values through their associates – all Marriott International employees are called associates.

## Reward systems

Reward systems for employees include both tangible and intangible benefits. Tangible benefits are pay, bonuses, tips, meals provided free of charge and discounted accommodation for live-in employees. The perceived 'fairness' of the distribution of the tips (and/or service charge) in hospitality businesses can be a controversial topic. Many of the intangible benefits of working in a hospitality environment compensate for the unsocial hours and lower pay. Intangible benefits can include the excitement, fun and teamwork that many hospitality employees enjoy (and which many hospitality textbooks forget!). There can be a sense of pride when customers make favourable comments about their experiences and when family and friends respect the company where employees work.

## Communication

One important lesson that human resource management has learned from marketing is the value of regularly updating employees about the company's current situation and future plans. As well as formal communications about company policy, most hospitality companies' employee magazines, newsletters or internal websites (Intranets) include career development opportunities, articles about social activities, fun events, competitions and long service awards, and interesting anecdotes about individual employees. Important achievements are highlighted to motivate employees to get more involved with the company. From a marketing perspective, it is essential for customer-contact employees to be aware of new openings, new-product development and new marketing programmes, so they can inform customers during service encounters.

## Criticisms of internal marketing

Critics of internal marketing challenge the theory and practice on several grounds. They claim that the champions of internal marketing and in particular empowerment have relied on rhetoric to promote an idealized workplace. The reality is that many hospitality premises are unpleasant, and sometimes hostile, places of work. There are often staff shortages, sometimes due to bad planning, which increase the workload for the remaining employees and create stress. Unfortunately, hospitality employees can suffer from physical and sexual abuse from customers and co-workers. Many owner-managers operate under conditions of high stress and can be abrupt, indifferent or aggressive towards staff. Because senior managers are primarily interested in cost control and profits, they stand accused of poor communication with employees and of not genuinely caring for them. Indeed, many employees feel cynical about management and are suspicious of internal marketing innovations, such as delayering, which appear to be more a cost-cutting exercise than genuine empowerment. Also, the Western concept of empowerment is not easily transferred to countries where the cultural heritage is less egalitarian. Employees working in countries with 'high power distance' are accustomed to a hierarchical management system that discourages workers from taking responsibility. Although there are poor employers in the hospitality industry, internal marketing theory incorporates the best practice and demonstrates the advantages of adopting a positive approach in managing employees.

### Emotional labour

Customer-contact employees work long hours, at all times of the day and night, dealing constantly with customers. Working with people can be emotionally tiring, especially if there are staff shortages or if customers complain. Although working in hospitality can be great fun, it can also be very stressful. However, companies expect customer-contact employees to suppress their own feelings and their own identity to ensure that customers are satisfied. Some hospitality organizations even provide cues and scripts – especially in contact centres – to help customer-contact employees say the right words to customers. In particular, empowerment means that customer-contact employees are expected to take on more responsibility, which can lead to more stress. The term *emotional labour* has been used to describe the emotional demands that service-oriented work imposes on employees. Both hospitality managers and customer-contact employees can suffer from the long-term effects of emotional labour, resulting in minor illness, anxiety, depression and fatigue, which can lead to alcoholism, drug dependence, eating disorders and, ultimately perhaps, cancer, heart disease and nervous breakdowns.

---

**ACTIVITY 12.4**

Building on Activities 12.1 and 12.3, if you have worked in a hospitality organization think about the service culture you experienced whilst working.

- Evaluate the company's recruitment and training policies, the service inclination and competences of the other employees. Did the company 'empower' employees?

- How valid are the criticisms of internal marketing in a hospitality company, compared with your own experience?

---

## Service encounters

There is a wide variety of hospitality service contexts, ranging from low customer-contact services to high customer-contact services (see Figure 12.2 for an example of food service concepts). The importance of customer-contact employees rises as the level of contact between customers and employees increases. During every interaction between customers and employees, the customer's perception of service quality is challenged or reinforced. These interactions between customers and employees are sometimes called 'moments of truth'. While the term 'moments of truth' used to refer to the employee/customer interactions when it was first introduced in 1987,[10] the term now refers to the moment when a customer/user interacts with a brand, product or service to form or change an impression about that particular brand, product or service. In every hospitality business, even in the small ones, service delivery processes include hundreds of 'moments of truth' (interaction) opportunities. These moments of truth may last for only a few seconds. Some hospitality experiences, such as staying in a hotel for two weeks during a vacation, can contain thousands of these moments of truth. The majority of service encounters between customers and employees can be described as routinized and, providing service standards conform to customer expectations, customers should be satisfied. However, in all hospitality operations, there will inevitably be occasions when customers experience disappointing service encounters. Many are minor disappointments that do not adversely impact on customer satisfaction, but major disappointments can become critical incidents for hospitality organizations. How effectively the customer-contact employees respond to critical incidents will influence the customer's intention to repurchase.

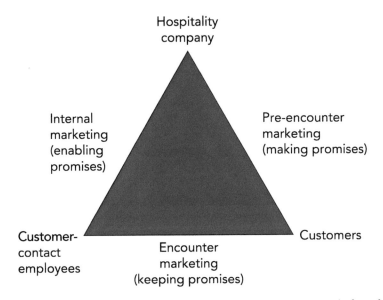

Figure 12.2 Higher and lower customer-contact service contexts – an example from food service

### Critical incidents

When a critical incident occurs, the responses of customer-contact employees can either save the situation or turn the incident into a significant source of customer dissatisfaction. Research suggests[11] that there are three broad categories of critical incidents in service contexts, based on:

1   the employees' responsiveness to service delivery system failures
2   the employees' responses to customer needs and requests
3   unprompted and unsolicited employee actions.

Table 12.1 summarizes employees' responses to customer issues, which can result in either customer satisfaction or dissatisfaction.

Customers want service failures to be resolved quickly, fairly and politely. If the customer-contact employees apologize and provide a satisfactory solution to the problem at the time of the incident, then customers are more likely to forgive the company, and may even develop a more favourable attitude to the business. If the customer-contact employee fails to apologize and empathize or is unable (or even unwilling) to help, then the incident can become a source of a serious complaint.

Inevitably, some customers will have special needs and make special requests that beyond the scope of the hospitality unit's operational norms. Customers who have special dietary requirements

Part C

Table 12.1  Positive and negative responses to critical incidents

| Critical incident | Customer satisfaction | Customer dissatisfaction |
|---|---|---|
| Employee response to service delivery failure | Could be turned into incidents that employees use to advantage and generate customer satisfaction: an employee reacts quickly to service failure by responding sensitively to customers – by compensating the customer or upgrading the customer to a higher status service | Where an employee fails to provide an apology or an explanation or argues with the customer, then the employee's response is likely to be a further source of dissatisfaction |
| Employee response to customer needs and requests | Employee responsiveness, flexibility and confidence that he or she can match whatever is required by the customer are important sources of positive customer responses | Employee intransigence, inflexibility and perceived incompetence are all likely sources of customer dissatisfaction |
| Unprompted and unsolicited employee action | When an employee makes a customer feel special, or where an act of unexpected generosity takes the customer by surprise | Customer dissatisfaction could be the result of a failure to give the level of attention expected, or might involve inappropriate employee behaviour, such as the use of bad language |

or who want to arrange a special event will ask for help and advice. By definition, these requests are unusual; they may even be contrary to the company's standard operating procedures. How customer-contact employees respond to these situations sends signals to customers. If employees can be flexible and have the confidence and expertise to adapt the service to the needs of the customer, then customers are likely to be highly satisfied. If, however, employees appear inflexible and are unhelpful, this can be a source of customer dissatisfaction.

Customer-contact employees can sometimes give customers delightful surprises by their unexpected behaviour, which exceeds customers' expectations. These unprompted and unsolicited employee actions are major sources of customer satisfaction. However, employees who demonstrate a lack of courtesy or use bad language in front of customers can be responsible for major customer dissatisfaction. Of course, unreasonable customers, who can be aggressive, insulting and even threatening, sometimes confront customer-contact employees, especially when customers are under the influence of alcohol or drugs. Good employers do not tolerate bad customer behaviour such as sexual harassment, and airlines such as British Airways have a 'zero tolerance policy' to protect cabin crew from abusive customers.

## Sources of conflict

Customer-contact employees are confronted by both interpersonal and intra-organizational conflicts whilst working for hospitality organizations. Conflict at work can be a source and a symptom of employee dissatisfaction. Continuous or excessive conflict creates powerful emotional responses, including unacceptable levels of stress for employees. Understanding the sources of conflict can help managers to reduce stress in the work environment and promote positive working conditions.

### Personal/role conflict

Employees perform roles at work that may sometimes conflict with their own values and belief systems. Young people may resent a strict dress and grooming code, vegetarians might have an ethical issue preparing meat dishes, people with a strong religious faith may have moral issues with the service and consumption of alcohol, and the behaviour of customers (e.g. female near-nudity at resort hotels in some Muslim countries) can be offensive to social conventions. In these situations, the employee's values are challenged by the workplace. This is a personal conflict that employees need to resolve, or they may have to choose to leave the company or industry.

### Organizational/customer conflict

Organizations have policies, processes and standard operating procedures that regulate the boundaries of employee conduct. Many of these regulations are designed to deliver the brand promise and to help customer-contact employees. Occasionally, customers will make what appears to be a reasonable request of customer-contact employees but which unfortunately breaks the house rules. For example, midmarket hotels with food and beverage facilities normally have opening and closing hours for their restaurant and bar, so when customers want to eat or drink and the facilities are closed, customer-contact employees face a dilemma. Do they maintain the house rules and not serve the customer, causing customer dissatisfaction, or do they break the house rules, serve the customer and deliver customer satisfaction? This type of organizational conflict with customers puts the customer-contact employee in a difficult situation. However, if a customer makes an unreasonable request – for example, asking the employee to help in an illegal activity – then the employee should maintain the company's regulations and not help the customer.

### Inter-customer conflict

Some of the most difficult situations for customer-contact employees arise from disputes between customers. In most hospitality services, customers interact with each other in a myriad of different ways, which can cause problems at times. Customer-to-customer interaction is often a critical component of the hospitality encounter and can have both positive and negative effects on customer experience, satisfaction and future intentions. Customers park their own vehicles in hotel and restaurant car parks, queue for service, consume alcoholic beverages with each other in bars and dance with each other in clubs. Conflict between customers can range from minor irritations, such as queue jumping, to serious abuse and assault. Customer-contact employees need to remain professional and should try and calm difficult situations – but this is easier said than done.

## Conclusion

Hospitality companies need to develop effective strategies to recruit and retain service-minded customer-contact employees. Although many hospitality companies claim to be good employers, the industry suffers from high employee turnover rates, and examples of poor treatment of employees are publicized in the media and spread by negative word-of-mouth. The most successful hospitality companies recognize the importance of recruiting and retaining effective customer-contact employees and nurturing a positive service culture to ensure that the brand's service standards are delivered.

In this chapter, we have explained:

- There is a link between employee satisfaction, service quality, customer satisfaction and business performance (the service-profit chain).
- During the hospitality encounter, moments of truth reinforce or challenge the customer's perception of service quality.
- Each hospitality company has its own culture and climate which guide customer-contact employees in their behaviour towards customers.
- Human resource departments that use marketing-like approaches to recruit and retain employees are adopting an internal marketing strategy.
- Empowerment gives customer-contact employees the authority, responsibility and resources to solve customer problems.
- Critics of human resource management in service industries, and especially of empowerment, suggest that empathic employees can experience high levels of emotional labour, resulting in stress and illness.
- When there is a critical service incident, such as service failure or unusual customer request, the responses and unprompted actions of customer-contact employees influence customer satisfaction/dissatisfaction.
- Customer-contact employees who experience role conflict, organizational/customer conflict and inter-customer conflict can suffer from work-related stress.

---

### ACTIVITY 12.5

At the beginning of the chapter, we asked you to reflect on your work experiences in a hospitality unit. What do you now think about the management's approach in managing employees?

- Was the interview/selection process formal, using a range of different methods (online application form/letter, several interviews and applicant tests), or was the process very informal?
- Did the company offer formal induction and training?
- How did you learn about the service culture – from the management or the other employees?
- Were the managers and employees genuinely passionate about giving customers excellent service?
- What happened if a customer complained?

---

Now check your understanding of this chapter by answering the following questions:

1 Discuss the role of customer-contact employees in delivering the hospitality offer.

2 Discuss the sources of conflict for customer-contact employees whilst working in hospitality organizations. Provide examples to illustrate your answer.

3 Evaluate the role of culture and climate in hospitality companies.

4 Analyze the theory and practice of internal marketing in the hospitality industry.

5 What are the advantages of using 'empowerment' as a human resource strategy in a hospitality business, from each of the following perspectives:

- customer?

- employee?

- hospitality business?

## References

1. Hostage, G. M. (1975). Quality-control in a service business. *Harvard Business Review, 53*(4), 98–106.
2. Heskett, J. L., Jones, T. O., Loveman, G. W., Sasser, W. E., & Schlesinger, L. A. (1994). Putting the service-profit chain to work. *Harvard Business Review, 72*(2), 164–174.
3. Pollitt, D. (2007). Red carnation blooms through management training. *Training & Management Development Methods, 21*(3), 559.
4. Red Carnation Hotel Collection [Internet]. *Our Story.* [cited September 22, 2021]. Available from: https://redcarnationhotels.com/our-story
5. The Blunsdon House Hotel [Internet]. *The Blunsdon House Hotel, Swindon, England.* [cited September 22, 2021]. Available from: www.blunsdonhouse.co.uk/
6. Park, I. J., Yun, D., Kim, P. B., & Hai, S. (2021). How to fuel hotel employees' daily innovative work? The interplay of daily affect and career future time perspective. *Journal of Hospitality Marketing & Management,* 1–25.
7. Chi, O. H., Gursoy, D., & Chi, C. G. (2021). Tourists' attitudes toward the use of artificially intelligent (AI) devices in tourism service delivery: Moderating role of service value seeking. *Journal of Travel Research,* 0047287520971054.
8. Le Manoir Aux Quat'Saisons [Internet]. *Le Manoir Aux Quat'Saisons, Oxford, England.* [cited September 23, 2021]. Available from: www.belmond.com/hotels/europe/uk/oxfordshire/belmond-le-manoir-aux-quat-saisons/
9. Yates, G. (2016). *Personal Interview.*
10. Carlzon, J. (1987). *Moments of Truth.* New York: Harper and Row.
11. Hwang, Y., & Mattila, A. S. (2020). The impact of customer compassion on face-to-face and online complaints. *Journal of Hospitality Marketing & Management, 29*(7), 848–868.

# Post-encounter marketing

DOI: 10.4324/9781003186342-16

Post-encounter marketing strategies aim to retain existing customers, generate repeat and refer-ral business and build long-term relationships with key customer groups. The success of post-encounter marketing depends on customer satisfaction being delivered during the encounter. If the hospitality provider is not delivering satisfaction, then post-encounter marketing strategies will clearly be ineffective. However, satisfied customers play an increasingly important role in providing positive ratings for hospitality firms in third party online review sites like Tripadvisor, hotel booking and travel websites, and in using social media to post stories about their experi-ences to family, friends and followers. Existing customers also represent a significant potential source of future business. Relationship marketing provides the tools for companies to commu-nicate with customers and develop long-term relationships that are mutually rewarding. The alternative strategy, transactional marketing, looks no further than the next sale; its focus is very short-term. Both strategies have a part to play in hospitality marketing.

Chapter 13 provides a discussion on how to measure and manage customer satisfaction and word-of-mouth (WOM), and Chapter 14 explores the concepts of transactional, relationship marketing and customer loyalty.

Chapter **13**

# Measuring and managing customer satisfaction and word-of-mouth (WOM)

**CHAPTER OBJECTIVES**

After working through this chapter, you should be able to:

- Define customer satisfaction
- Understand the importance of satisfying customers
- Explain the features and application of Net Promoter Score
- Recognize the importance of user-generated comments on customers' decision-making process
- Understand the importance of measuring and responding to online reviews
- Evaluate customer satisfaction guarantees in hospitality
- Describe tools for measuring customer satisfaction in the hospitality industry.

## Introduction

The concept of satisfying customers is deeply rooted in the philosophy of marketing and is a key element in most marketing definitions. Academics and practitioners agree that being able to create and maintain customer satisfaction is critical to business performance. In competitive markets where customers have choice, they may choose to take their business elsewhere in search of greater satisfaction. In this chapter, we define customer satisfaction and explain why delivering satisfaction is important, especially given the growing popularity of online customer reviews and user-generated content in social media; we then discuss Net Promoter Score and

DOI: 10.4324/9781003186342-17

the role of customer satisfaction guarantees in hospitality. We explain how companies choose between investing in improvements in customer satisfaction and investing in returns to the other, non-customer stakeholders. Finally, we review measures for capturing customer satisfaction data, and customer complaint processes.

Understanding, measuring and managing customer satisfaction are important elements in the post-encounter marketing mix. Customers generally have pre-encounter expectations of hospitality experiences and after the encounter they evaluate the experience against those expectations, effectively asking: 'Did that experience meet my expectations?' If expectations are not met, dissatisfaction is likely to occur. Dissatisfied customers are at risk of defecting to competitors, generating negative word-of-mouth and posting negative reviews online and via social media. Satisfied customers, whose expectations are met or exceeded, however, will consider revisiting the business in the future and are more likely to generate positive word-of-mouth, both face-to-face and online.

## Defining customer satisfaction

Satisfaction is a complex phenomenon. In Chapter 3, we discussed consumer expectations, which are formed prior to purchase. Expectations are important comparison standards that consumers use to evaluate their hospitality experience during and after a service encounter. At the simplest level, customers are satisfied if the experience matches or exceeds their expectations and dissatisfied if the service performance fails to match their expectations. Customer satisfaction can therefore be defined as *a positive attitude towards a supplier that is achieved when the customer's expectations are met*. Because customers' needs and wants change over time, their expectations of hospitality experiences also change over time. Clearly, customers' perspectives of what constitutes a satisfactory experience will also change.

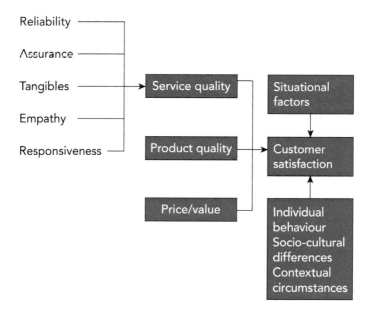

Figure 13.1  Customer satisfaction[1]

*Source*: Adapted from Zeithaml et al. (page: 79),[1] reproduced with permission of the McGraw-Hill Companies

Although we have presented a single definition of customer satisfaction, customers can identify a range of different forms of satisfaction, including the following:

- Contentment, when a routine hospitality service is delivered satisfactorily
- Pleasure, when a hospitality experience makes the consumer feel happy
- Delight, when the experience surprises the consumer and exceeds expectations
- Relief, when a service overcomes a potentially difficult situation and delivers satisfaction.

---

### ACTIVITY 13.1

Identify a number of hospitality experiences that have given you the following feelings:

- Contentment
- Pleasure
- Delight
- Relief.

Can you explain why you felt the way you did?

---

## Why customer satisfaction is important

Customer satisfaction is important to the success of hospitality businesses. Without satisfied customers, most hospitality businesses cannot survive. Remarkably, some hotels and restaurants do manage to survive even though they fail to deliver consistent satisfactory experiences, but this is often due to special circumstances such as being in a prime tourist location where most business comes from transient visitors. Even though the dissatisfied tourists never return, the businesses are able to trade profitably because of their prime location and the number of transient tourists visiting major close-by attractions. However, in today's highly connected digital world, it is becoming harder for businesses to survive unless they deliver consistent satisfactory experiences. An increasing number of customers are sharing their service experiences online, especially if they are not happy with the service they receive, and a large portion of customers read those review comments before making their decisions.

In today's fiercely competitive hospitality marketplace, most customers have a number of alternative providers and since switching costs are relatively low for most hospitality products and services, customers may choose to reduce the amount of business they generate or even not to return at all if they are not satisfied with the service they receive. Furthermore, they may pass on unfavourable word-of-mouth to friends, or post negative reviews online, discouraging potential customers from visiting. Common sense tells us that satisfied customers must be good for business. Satisfactory hospitality experiences are more likely to generate repeat purchase intentions, positive recommendations to friends and relatives, and positive online reviews. Satisfied customers also tend to be less price sensitive. In addition to playing an important role in customers' loyalty formation and choice behaviours, satisfaction can also enhance customers' perception of the brand image of a hospitality business. If customers consistently receive satisfactory services at various locations of a hospitality business such as a chain hotel or a restaurant, they are likely to trust that brand and form a very positive image of that brand.

Considering the significance of customer satisfaction for business survival and prosperity, it is important for marketers to understand, measure and manage the major factors that influence customer satisfaction. The claim that it can cost five to 25 times more to attract a new customer than to retain an existing one is key to understanding the drive toward benchmarking and tracking customer satisfaction.[2] Furthermore, increasing customer retention rates by 5 per cent can increase profits by 25 per cent or more,[3] which further highlights the importance of delivering satisfactory customer experiences.

## Basic principles of customer satisfaction management

The management of customer satisfaction is based on several principles. First, management must decide which customers they are trying to satisfy. Not all customers are equally important: some generate significant revenue and profit; others are important for a range of strategic reasons – maybe they are influential customers or opinion leaders that others follow, or they are the first customers won from a newly targeted market segment. Some customers are much less strategically important. Management generally focuses on satisfying the most important customers first. Critics point out, however, that satisfying all customers can make strategic sense, since tomorrow's most valued customers may be today's casual walk-ins. Furthermore, since many customers, these days, read online review comments before making their purchasing decisions, delivering satisfactory services to all customers can improve a company's online reputation through minimizing the negative comments from dissatisfied customers. Second, management must identify the important drivers of customer satisfaction for the selected customers. For example, do they value restaurant ambience or food quality? Not all customers value the same components of the hospitality experience. Indeed, customers' requirements may change over time, meaning that the drivers of satisfaction also change. Customers generally want faster service at lunch but more leisurely service in the evenings. Third, customers' requirements, once understood, should be satisfied at the first opportunity. 'Do it right the first time' should be the goal. Hospitality firms should try to eliminate the causes of customer dissatisfaction, such as poor hygiene, slow service, ill-informed contact staff and malfunctioning equipment. Fourth, given that there will be inevitable service failures because of broken processes, technology breakdowns and staff problems, management should put in place excellent service recovery processes. Even the best hospitality company will fail to meet customer expectations occasionally, so companies need to have in place recovery processes to mitigate customer dissatisfaction, pre-empt negative word-of-mouth and promote retention. Some companies prefer to use the term 'customer recovery' instead of 'service recovery' to emphasise the end goal is to retain the customer.

## Measuring customer satisfaction

Hospitality companies use a combination of direct and indirect methods to measure and monitor customer satisfaction. Indirect methods include tracking sales and profit figures and monitoring them against forecast or previous period performances. Whilst an increase or decrease in sales can be attributable to several different factors, customers who are not satisfied may not return and negative online and offline feedback can deter potential customers from booking. Properties experiencing a significant decrease in bookings and sales need to investigate the reasons why the business is suffering, and one of those reasons might be customer dissatisfaction. Direct methods include customer research, monitoring online reviews, and analysis of complaints and compliments. Most hotels and many restaurants have customer comment cards or questionnaires that can be completed by customers on the premises. However, the industry does not have a standard approach to measuring customer satisfaction, and companies use a variety of different methods to collect and analyze the data. For example, there is no common scale to collect customer satisfaction data – some companies use a numerical scale (1–5), others use word descriptors (poor, fair, good and excellent), and others rely solely on customers' own comments. Each organization will ask customers different types of questions according to their own needs and may be reluctant to share data on such a commercially sensitive topic. However, companies like BDRC-Continental carry out hospitality omnibus surveys so that each hotel or restaurant brand can benchmark itself against the customer satisfaction standards of its competitor set.

Delivering customer satisfaction consistently is dependent on listening to customers and customer-contact employees to make sure that service standards and performance are aligned with customer expectations. Research can be conducted into current customers from different target market segments, former customers, competitors' customers and potential customers to provide insights into the level and root causes of customer (dis)satisfaction. Techniques include the following:

- *Collecting and analyzing customer reviews and comments* posted online at review sites and in social media.
- *Post-encounter surveys* – customers are emailed questionnaires after the hospitality experience, when they have returned home or to work, with an incentive to complete and return them. The questionnaires obtain post-experience data about customer satisfaction.
- Key account customers, frequent guests and members of loyalty clubs may have a better insight into the level of consistency across a hotel brand than many employees. *Surveying the views of expert customers* can identify underperforming units and highlight important brand inconsistencies.
- *Employee surveys* – employees can also provide feedback on the service operation. Employees are often acutely aware of service problems and understand why performance underperforms customer expectations.
- *Focus groups of customers and employees* allow an expert group moderator to explore customer satisfaction issues in depth.
- *Mystery shopping* is a key tool in auditing the service performance of hotels and restaurants. Mystery shopping involves researchers pretending to be customers and recording their impressions of the service. Mystery shopper surveys report both quantitative variables (e.g., the length of waiting time for service) and qualitative impressions (e.g., employee friendliness and courtesy). At the end of the visit, the mystery shopper scores are reported to the unit manager and to head office. In multi-unit operations, the management uses the scores to identify strong and weak performing units as part of an internal benchmarking programme, and to identify opportunities for improvement. Some companies also use the results as part of the manager's bonus scheme.
- *Internal brand audits* – hospitality chains can employ their own staff or commission external firms to carry out brand conformance audits to ensure that the unit is delivering customer satisfaction (assuming that the brand standards do actually match customer expectations!). The timing of these inspections may be secret. If the general manager and employees know in advance when the audit is scheduled, they may prepare for the inspection. Inspectors have detailed brand performance standards covering all major aspects of the operation and check the unit's performance against the company's benchmarks. In large hotels, several inspectors might stay for three or more days to produce a comprehensive review of the entire

service operation. For franchise operations and hotels in consortiums, the brand audit provides the brand owner with evidence of operator compliance. This is used to make units performing below the minimum brand standards improve performance. Ultimately, if the unit continues to underperform, the brand owner can terminate the agreement and withdraw the brand name and support for the property.

Normally, both quantitative and qualitative research methods are used to collect data from customers. Research should be continuous, providing management with insight into changes in customer satisfaction and an explanation for increases or decreases. Processes for evaluating customer satisfaction include importance/performance analysis (IPA) and using Net Promoter Score.

## Importance/performance analysis

Importance/performance analysis (IPA) starts by identifying the elements of the hospitality experience that contribute significantly to customer satisfaction. Many companies conduct qualitative research, such as focus groups, to identify the important elements of the experience. The elements are then embedded into questionnaires and used to measure satisfaction. There are clearly dangers in using standardized instruments that have not been customized for a particular hospitality organization. The questionnaires are used to assess customer expectations of those elements as well as their perceptions of performance against those elements. The normal format is to ask customers to rate, on a seven-point scale, their expectations of an excellent hospitality company and their perceptions of the researched hospitality company's performance (see Table 13.1).

Table 13.1 Importance/performance questions

| Item | Strongly agree | | | | | | Strongly disagree |
| --- | --- | --- | --- | --- | --- | --- | --- |
| *Expectation*: Excellent budget hotels provide quiet sleeping accommodation | 1 | 2 | 3 | 4 | 5 | 6 | 7 |
| *Perception*: Hotel XYX provides quiet sleeping accommodation | 1 | 2 | 3 | 4 | 5 | 6 | 7 |

Analysis can then focus on identifying where the company falls short of meeting customer expectations. For example, if a customer were to rate an expectation item at 7 and the same perception item at 4, this would mean a three-point negative gap (4 − 7 = −3) between the perception and expectation scores. Customers are invited to identify the relative importance of each element or a group of similar elements, such as those relating to responsiveness of contact staff. It is a mistake to believe that every negative gap is equally important to customers. For most customers, a noisy bedroom is a much more important issue than a non-smiling employee. For this reason, many satisfaction questionnaires invite customers to identify not only expectations and perceptions but also the importance of each element.

This information can be used to guide customer satisfaction improvement strategies. For example, where customers have identified a particular attribute as important and the company is not meeting expectations, there is a potential source of customer dissatisfaction, and the gap should be closed. However, where the company is exceeding customer expectations on some attribute that is unimportant to customers, there may be a case for reducing investment in that attribute.

Results from this sort of analysis can be mapped on to an IPA matrix, as in Figure 13.2. Cell I of the matrix represents competitive strengths – an area where the customer is satisfied with the company's performance on important attributes. Cell II includes threats – the company is failing to satisfy customers on important attributes. Cell III describes the situation where the company is meeting or exceeding customer expectations on attributes that customers think are unimportant. The options here are to educate the customer as to the attribute's importance or to reduce investment in that attribute. Cell IV includes attributes that are not up to customers' expectations, but the attribute is not a priority for customers. It would make sense to monitor the importance of that attribute, because if customers come to regard it as important in the future it will become a threat. Figure 13.3 provides an example of seven IPA attributes, for an upscale full-service hotel brand, mapped on an importance/performance matrix.

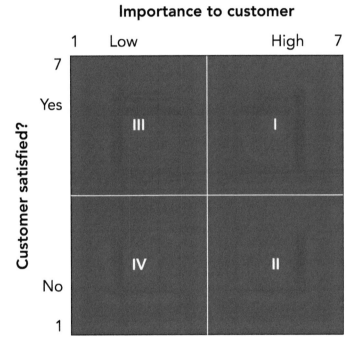

Figure 13.2 Importance/performance matrix

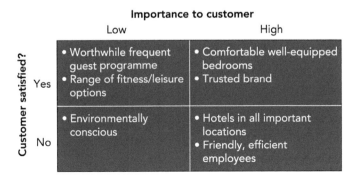

Figure 13.3 Importance/performance matrix, hotel example

## MARKETING INSIGHT 13.1

### Can the use of self-service technologies and service robots improve customer experience and service quality perceptions?[4]

It is commonly believed that the level and quality of interactions between customers and employees during service experiences is one of the most critical determinants of experience and service quality. However, this may not be true for all market segments because a large portion of restaurant customers use dining out as means for socializing with friends, family or colleagues.

There is no question that the level of interactions between employees and customers can improve quality perceptions for some market segments. However, not all customer-employee interactions result in positive evaluations of service experiences. Excessive and unnecessary employee-customer interactions can lower customers' evaluation of service experiences of market segments whose main purpose is to socialize with friends, family or colleagues by interrupting the flow state of social interactions. While small interruptions may have minor impacts on the social interaction flow state, major interruptions may bring the flow state to a halt. These interruptions can have significant impacts on customers' evaluations of their dining out experiences.

Utilization of self-service technologies and service robots may enable restaurants to minimize employee interruptions to the social interaction flow state while maintaining an open communication line with customers, which can further foster a positive climate for social interaction flow among the members of a dining out group. However, utilization of self-service technologies goes against the conventional conception of the service quality and customer satisfaction. Some people might argue that lowering the number of employee-customer interactions will lower service quality perceptions and customer satisfaction. However, research suggests providing a dining out environment in which social interaction flow state reaches its peak can have significant positive impacts on perceived experience quality, perceived service quality and customer satisfaction with the dining out experience. Too many customer-employee interactions interrupt the social interaction flow state, and thus, lower perceived experience quality, perceived service quality and customer satisfaction with the dining out experience.

Utilizing self-service technologies instead of employees can strengthen the social interaction experience flow state between customers. Self-service technologies and service robots might also lower the operating cost for restaurants, which can result in significant increases in profits.

*Source*: Wu, Gursoy and Zhang[4]

### Net Promoter Score (NPS)

Net Promoter Score (NPS)[5] is a metric that tells companies how likely their existing customers are to recommend their products, services or brand. Word-of-mouth is regarded as a predictor of business performance and is highly correlated to customer satisfaction. NPS data are based on responses to a single question: '*On a scale of 0 to 10, how likely is it that you would recommend [brand, company, product, or service] to a friend or colleague?*' This presents respondents with an

11-point scale (0 = Not at all likely, 10 = Extremely likely). This question requires customers to place a value on their experiences with the brand, company, product or service and asks them to stand by it.

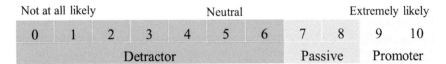

$$\text{Net Promoter Score (NPS)} = \% \text{ Promoters} - \% \text{ Detractors}$$

Figure 13.4  Net Promoter Score

Based on the responses, customers are grouped into 'promoters' who provide ratings of 9 or 10, 'passives' who provide ratings of 7 or 8, and 'detractors' who provide ratings of 6 or lower. Promoters are considered to be loyal enthusiasts who will keep buying and refer others, fuelling growth. The passives group represents customers who are satisfied but not really enthusiastic about the service or product. They tend to be vulnerable to competitive offerings. Detractors are unhappy customers who can damage a brand and impede growth through negative word-of-mouth.

Usually, users of NPS perform a calculation that involves subtracting the proportion of detractors from the proportion of promoters collected by the survey item, and the result of the calculation is typically expressed as an integer rather than a percentage.[6] In other words, subtracting the percentage of detractors from the percentage of promoters yields the Net Promoter Score, which can range from a low of -100 (if every customer is a detractor) to a high of 100 (if every customer is a promoter). The NPS is typically interpreted and used as an indicator of customer loyalty. The NPS is widely used to determine what customers really think about a brand, company, product or service. Its popularity and broad use have been attributed to its simplicity and transparent methodology of use.[7]

---

**ACTIVITY 13.2**

You are the general manager of an upscale restaurant. You want to find out what your customer really thinks about your restaurant. You randomly selected a group of customers and asked then the following question: 'On a scale of 0 to 10, how likely is it that you would recommend this restaurant to a friend or colleague?' Results indicated that 20 per cent of your customers are detractors, 40 per cent are passives and 40 per cent are promoters. What is your NPS score? What does this score suggest?

---

### Word-of-mouth recommendations

Word-of-mouth (WOM), as we all know, is a form of interpersonal communication that can have considerable effect on its recipients. Personal influence carries great weight especially for hospitality and tourism consumers due to the level of uncertainty associated with hospitality and tourism products and services. Traditionally, word-of-mouth refers to information that is passed orally from person to person in an informal manner. Positive word-of-mouth occurs when people tell friends, family and associates of their positive experience with a service, product or organisation; negative WOM is the opposite. Positive *word-of-mouth* can have significant impact on the success of hospitality and tourism services and products. With the advent of social media, the term *word-of-mouse* has been coined, as well as *electronic word-of-mouth (eWOM)*, to describe informal endorsement of products, services or organisations online in social media channels, micro blog sites, digital forums, review sites, and other publicly available online peer-to-peer communication channels. Electronic word-of-mouth recommendations tend to have far-reaching and longer-lasting consequences than face-to-face word-of-mouth recommendations because they are capable of reaching more people over a longer period of time.

A word-of-mouth recommendation from a satisfied customer, whether face-to-face or online, is the most cost-effective form of customer acquisition. When friends or relatives tell us that a restaurant served really good quality food at reasonable prices or that the atmosphere, drinks and music at a club were excellent, then the next time when we decide to go out for a meal or go clubbing, we will consider following that word-of-mouth recommendation. Word-of-mouth has a positive influence on customers because the source of the message (our friends, relatives and associates) is highly trusted. They have no reason to lie to us, and we know them so well that we are likely to believe their advice. Customers who give positive word-of-mouth are also less likely to switch; they are more likely to be loyal customers. Although word-of-mouth is effective at customer recruitment, face-to-face recommendations are unlikely to reach large numbers of people, so other forms of customer acquisition normally need to be used.

User-generated content (UGC) such as reviews, photos and videos posted on a wide range of third-party websites, such as Booking.com, Expedia, Hotels.com, Priceline, Travelocity, Tripadvisor and trivago, and social media platforms such as TikTok, Instagram, Twitter and Facebook have become a critical concern for hospitality marketers. An increasing number of customers share their satisfactory and dissatisfactory experiences by writing reviews and posting them to online review and social media sites, to help others make better buying decisions, to voice their concerns or to reward a company for good performance. As a result, online reviews posted by others have become one of the most important sources of information in customers' decision-making processes. Consumers usually consider only a small portion of the available information sources in their pre-purchase information search, meaning that their increasing reliance on online reviews is having a significant impact on hospitality marketing.

The widespread practice of sharing hospitality and tourism experiences in online reviews, pictures and videos, and the increasing reliance of prospective customers on those posts for decision-making have significantly decreased hospitality marketers' ability to control messaging about their brands, especially to prospective customers who may not be very familiar with the brand. Customers who are not very familiar with a brand or a destination rely relatively more on online reviews in decision-making compared to customers who are more familiar with the brand or destination in order to minimize the perceived risk associated with this unfamiliarity. Thus, customers who share their experiences online have significant power. Although site visitors will rarely know the persons posting the content, the number of posts and overall ratings/rankings of a brand or a destination provide powerful impressions. Potential consumers can form judgements about hotels and restaurants entirely based upon previous customers' comments without ever personally visiting the business or its website. Therefore, customer satisfaction becomes even more critical for the success of the business. Clearly, positive comments and high customer ratings create favourable impressions when potential customers are evaluating different hospitality options since prospective customers tend to see such reviews as more reliable than other marketing sources.[8] Thus, eWOM has more influence on potential customers' decision-making process than do other marketing efforts.[9]

Businesses may assume that providing satisfactory customer experiences will result in positive eWOM behaviour.[10] However, all customers expect to have satisfactory experiences when they visit a hospitality business. Thus, satisfaction with a product or service may not necessarily result in an increase in eWOM posting behaviour. It is rare that someone takes the time to talk or write about an experience that merely met their expectations. Customers are more likely to talk or post comments about experiences that are unexpectedly good or bad. Furthermore, eWOM is not limited to user reviews. Photos and videos showing people using a hospitality brand's services or products that are posted on Instagram, Reddit, Facebook, YouTube or TikTok are also viewed as eWOM.[11] Considering the fact that an average user spends 2 hours and 24 minutes per day on social media in 2020,[12] and over 80 per cent of all travel bookings are made online via a mobile app or website without human interaction,[13] it is not surprising that almost all consumers are exposed to some form of eWOM, whether they are seeking it out or not, at some point in their consumer journey. Almost all of today's customers in advanced economies form their first impressions of brands on digital properties and social media platforms. Thus, it is important to keep track of your brand's online reputation.[14]

## MARKETING INSIGHT 13.2

### Importance of responding to online customer review comments[15]

Online reviews carry a lot of weight when consumers are deciding where to dine. Customers are reading dine out experiences posted by their social media friends, monitoring hashtags, reviews and digital images posted to review sites before determining where to dine. Around 90 per cent of consumers state that they read reviews before selecting a restaurant and more than 55 per cent of consumers report that online reviews play a very influential role in their restaurant selection behaviour.

As the number of customers who mainly rely on online reviews during the restaurant selection process continues to increase, effective digital reputation management is becoming an important tool for survival and success in a very competitive restaurant market. Understanding the influence of online reviews on customers' perception of restaurants, the impacts of negative online reviews and how restaurateurs can use customers' increasing attention to online reviews to their advantage are critical.

Online reviews are more than short descriptions of customers' experiences with a star-based rating. They show customers' commitment to the business and their social network by sharing experiences that are worthy of feedback, both good and bad. Thus, management needs to give careful attention to those reviews. Restaurateurs often fail to respond to online comments. Considering that around 94 per cent of consumers reported that they avoided certain business because of bad reviews and 53 per cent of customers expect businesses to respond to negative reviews within a week, there is clear importance of paying close attention to customer reviews and replying to them in a timely manner for the current and would-be customers. Since 45 per cent of consumers report being more inclined to visit those that respond to negative reviews, timely, well-thought and considerate response could be the difference between acquiring new customers and losing the chance forever.

Hospitality is all about service. Thus, customers expect to receive quick responses to their online comments that assure them that they are valued, and companies will use those inputs to make products and services better. Failing to respond can have devastating effects on brand image, revenues and customer retention considering the fact that a large portion of dissatisfied customers could share their dissatisfactory experiences online through various social media channels and third party online review sites such as Yelp.

There is no question that recovery efforts can turn a dissatisfied customer into a satisfied loyal customer by changing their attitudes toward service providers. Since businesses can easily identify dissatisfied customers on review sites, responding to their complaints promptly with action items and number to call can initiate a conversation that can motivate a dissatisfied customer to reach out to the business for further help with a concern. Expressing gratitude for their willingness to share their experiences and apologies for falling short of their expectations goes far in diffusing hostility, too, as does taking responsibility for the negative situation. Ensuring dissatisfied customers that appropriate actions have been taken to resolve their issues will not only affect those dissatisfied customers' perceptions of the company but also influence the decision-making process of prospective customers who read those review comments and company responses.

*Source*: www.pymnts.com

Analysis of online accommodation reviews reveals that most negative comments are derived from poor housekeeping and maintenance. Descriptions using words like 'dirty', 'bad smells', 'stains' on bedlinen, carpets and fabrics; 'mould' in bathrooms; 'broken equipment' or furniture; 'noise' and 'indifferent service' are frequently cited by unhappy customers to critique their stay in a hotel. On the other hand, customers who provide positive feedback focus on the friendly and helpful employees, the ambience, the high-quality food and service and unexpected, and delightful surprises. Since negative comments can lead to lost revenue opportunities as potential customers take their business elsewhere, it is vital to understand and manage online reputation. In today's highly connected business environment, it is critical to understand how people feel about your brand and what they think of when they come across your company's products and services.[16]

Online reviews represent the voice of the customer and are very influential in shaping brand reputation. Thus, monitoring online reviews about your brand across multiple websites is a must for brand reputation measurement. However, simply monitoring review comments posted by customers may not be enough. Brand reputation management also requires a thorough understanding of what customers are trying to say through their review comments. Sentiment analysis or opinion mining is an extremely useful tool that is used by researchers and marketers in social media monitoring as it allows them to gain an overview of the wider customer opinion about a brand, product or service. Companies use sentiment analysis to capture positive and negative customer emotions from online customer reviews. Sentiment analysis enables marketers and managers to capture and measure customer emotions behind everything from review posts to social media posts to news articles. Sentiment analysis tools such as SentiStrength software can make that process quicker and easier than ever before. There are also a number of companies that can provide sentiment analytics data to businesses with real-time monitoring capabilities.

Sentiment analytics data generated through market research can help brands identify their strengths and weaknesses and enable them to develop unique customer service approaches and experiences. Sentiment analysis of UGC can help hotel managers to identify the most critical problems to fix. Since, in general, the majority of complaints is linked to poor hygiene and maintenance, operational managers need to ensure that bedrooms and bathrooms are serviced properly so that they are clean and that all equipment works. Managers can use the negative feedback to improve customer experience. Ultimately, it is customer experience during the hospitality encounter that delivers customer satisfaction and generates positive word-of-mouth/mouse referrals. Sentiment analytics data can also be used to see what consumers think about competitors services and products. The ability to quickly understand consumer attitudes and react accordingly is something that brands can take advantage of when there is a jump in negative feedback and reviews to the services, products or experiences they offer. Sentiment analysis can easily identify negative trends, allowing hospitality managers and marketers to make timely and accurate adjustments to their operations and guest experience. It also allows them to quickly identify mixed sentiment reviews that require a response.

---

### MARKETING INSIGHT 13.3

**Online Reviews Statistics and Trends: A 2022 Report by ReviewTrackers**[17]

- **Google is (still) the top review site.** 63.6 per cent of consumers say they are likely to check Google reviews (through Google Maps and Search) before visiting a business location – more than any other review site.

- **88 per cent of all reviews come from only four review sites.** After Google (73 per cent), Yelp (6 per cent), Facebook (3 per cent) and Tripadvisor (3 per cent) follow. Marketers should focus on top directories that hold domain authority and impact reputation.

- **Review interaction is up by 50 per cent from pre-COVID-19 pandemic levels.** Review interaction entails actions like searching for or filtering reviews, or clicking to expand and read the entire review. It's one of the many signs demonstrating consumers' heightened sensitivity about where to go or what to purchase in the wake of the pandemic.

- **Reviews are (a lot) shorter.** They're now about the length of an expanded tweet.

- **Companies aren't responding fast enough (or at all) to reviews.** 53 per cent of customers expect businesses to respond to negative reviews within a week. 1 in 3 have a shorter time frame of three days or less.

- **Responsive industry leaders get higher ratings.** Faster review response times are closely linked to having a positive reputation.

- **Customers don't trust companies with lower than 4-star ratings.** The most common filter applied is to see only companies with 4-star ratings and higher.

- **Reviewers demand greater value from businesses.** Reviews about value tend to be more critical than reviews that talk about other aspects of the customer experience (product, service, location).

*Source*: ReviewTrackers

Almost all customers rely on online reviews in their decision-making process. Consumers not only use online reviews to discover great hospitality businesses, products, services and brands to patronize, but they also use those online reviews to identify hospitality businesses to avoid as evidenced by the fact that 94 per cent of consumers say that a bad review has convinced them to avoid a business.[18] However, a large portion of consumers (45 per cent) say that they are more likely to visit a business that responds to negative reviews. This makes it extremely important for hospitality companies to learn how to respond to negative reviews as well as positive customer feedback and make smart business decisions based on review insights.

Although some hospitality operators feel that extremely negative comments might have been posted by competitors or disgruntled employees, there is limited evidence to support this claim. Regardless of what the operator thinks about the source of the negative review, responding to negative reviews before they drive potential customers away is critical for improving consumer perceptions and patronage intentions immediately. It is important to realize that if customers choose to write a review, then the property should respond as a matter of courtesy and to show potential and actual customers that the business recognizes the importance of customers' feelings. Positive reviews provide an opportunity to reinforce and spotlight the things customers already love. Thanking the customer for their review and adding a personalized response helps build a stronger relationship and encourage repeat visit. When comments are negative, an apology followed by the promise to undertake action to resolve the problem demonstrates that the business does genuinely care about customer satisfaction. A thoughtful response to customer feedback shows that the business cares about the experience of every customer and wants to use reviews to improve it for future patrons. Even though responding to reviews offers an opportunity to build a trusting relationship with the customer, only 36 per cent of customers actually get a response from a business. The right response can turn a one-time customer into a loyal patron or even convince a critic to come back for a better experience. Data show that responding to negative reviews specifically makes it 44 per cent more likely for someone to visit the business in question.[18]

The decision as to who is responsible for replying to customer feedback depends upon the size, ownership and type of property. In smaller, independent businesses the owner/manager will respond; in some larger units the job will be delegated to the duty manager, social media marketer or reputation manager; another approach is for the public relations or marketing manager to be responsible; and occasionally the general manager will respond.

## MARKETING INSIGHT 13.4

### How to respond to negative reviews[19]

Managing and responding to negative reviews are important components of online reputation management since posting negative reviews is increasingly becoming the preferred channel for consumer complaints, making customer service inquiries the norm on review sites and social media.

While the content and the context of the negative reviews will dictate how you will respond, it is important to read the review carefully and calmly. Make sure you respond in a professional manner. Do not let your emotions influence your response to a negative review.

When responding to negative reviews:

> Make sure you address the reviewer personally and individually. Try to use the name of the reviewer, if you know the name, if not, use the reviewer's online handle. Try to avoid the generic 'Dear guest' or 'Dear customer'.

> Make sure you show customers that your company appreciates and values candid unsolicited feedback. Always remember to say thank you in responses to reviews (even the bad ones).

After thanking the customer, apologize and sympathize with the customer even if it is not your fault. Being apologetic shows that you care about your customers and that you are not too proud to own up to your mistakes. This offers a great opportunity to establish and strengthen trust between your company or brand and the customer.

After apologizing, take responsibility without making any excuses. Acknowledge the customer's dissatisfactory experience and provide reassurance that your company aims to provide exceptional service. Ensure the customer that you will use the feedback to become a better service provider and you will not let this happen again.

When responding to negative feedback, include details about the customer's experience in your response (when relevant), and communicate any changes or improvements you have made or will make as a result of their feedback. Make sure you take ownership, and promise to make things right in the future:

Provide an opportunity to reviewers to talk to you directly about the problem they had and take the issue offline. For this reason, you should provide direct contact information for customers in your review response.

Negative online reviews offer you an opportunity to show how much you care about your customers and the length you are willing to go to fix the issue, which can help potential customers establish confidence in your ability and willingness to deliver an exceptional experience. Extend a digital hand to reviewers who posted negative comments by inviting them to come back. Provide your direct contact information so that those customers who posted negative comments can let you know when they are back. Make sure you welcome them with open arms. After providing exceptional service to those customers, share those experiences as a response to the negative reviews.

Here is a template that you can use to learn how to respond to negative reviews:

> *Dear [NAME OF REVIEWER], thanks for bringing this to our attention. We are very sorry to hear that your experience didn't match your expectations. Please know that your situation was an exception. We are normally known for our exceptional service and caring deeply about our customers. We cannot fix the past, but you have my personal commitment to improve the way our staff serves every customer. Until then, please accept my sincerest apologies on behalf of everyone on the team.*

> *Please feel free to reach out to [INSERT CONTACT INFORMATION] with any further comments, concerns, or suggestions you wish to share. We would love to make things right if you give us another chance. Please call me or ask for me next time you're at [Company Name].*

*Source*: ReviewTrackers

Brands typically do not have control over user-generated content found in review and social media sites. However, they can be proactive about ensuring the accuracy of their information across top directories and review sites (Google, Yelp, Facebook and Tripadvisor), which can help the customer to experience a well-informed and smoother journey. Companies can easily apply local search engine optimization (SEO), a practice of improving online local presence. They can easily improve their online local presence by publishing updated business information on sites where their business locations are listed since having wrong location and operating hour information (address) is a recurring complaint found in online reviews. A customer shows up in a restaurant only to find that it is closed that day, but the management did not update its hours of operation online.

## Customer-satisfaction guarantees

When consumers buy manufactured products, the manufacturer provides a guarantee and will normally repair or replace the product or refund the customer if the product fails or if the customer is not satisfied. However, satisfaction guarantees in service industries are less evident. Many hospitality managers are intuitively opposed to the idea of customer satisfaction guarantees. They believe that too many guests will be dishonest and make bogus complaints, even when they have enjoyed their stay or meal. However, most hospitality providers do compensate customers when they have a genuine complaint. This implies that most hospitality providers do offer an implicit customer satisfaction guarantee. In the next section, we will explain the different types of service guarantees that companies can adopt.

### Implicit satisfaction guarantee

When customers book a hotel or restaurant, they assume that they will enjoy a satisfactory customer experience, even though the hospitality outlet has not given the customer any documented guarantee. There is an implicit understanding, grounded in experience, education and consumer protection legislation, that the hospitality provider will deliver a particular kind of experience, and compensate a customer with a genuine complaint. The problem with this informal type of customer satisfaction guarantee is that neither the customer nor the company knows what an implicit guarantee covers. There are no rules or guidelines setting out what the company offers and how customers will be compensated if something goes wrong.

### Explicit satisfaction guarantee

An explicit satisfaction guarantee is based on specific, measurable performance. Time-based promises, such as a maximum of a 30-minute wait for a room service delivery, are a good example of an explicit satisfaction guarantee. The length of time to deliver the service can be explicitly incorporated into the guarantee, and it is then simple to establish whether the service has been delivered as guaranteed – on time or not. These guarantees have been used with varying degrees of success.

Clearly, before a company introduces an explicit time-based satisfaction guarantee, the operation must be able to deliver the promise within the time agreed and at an acceptable performance level.

---

**MARKETING INSIGHT 13.5**

### Ibis '15-minute promise to get it right'

Ibis offers a '15-minute promise to get it right' or guests stay free. Ibis's guarantee is also ISO9001 quality-assured, which, with 1,200 hotels in 67 different countries, demonstrates a major commitment to customer satisfaction. Ibis asks: 'Didn't get what you expected? We have 15 minutes to set this right or the service is on us.' The 15 Minute Guarantee applies to any service which is included within the cost of the room. The guarantee is promoted on the website. There is a leaflet in each bedroom promoting the promise, and whenever a new Ibis Hotel opens, the promise is used as a key publicity tool.

*Source*: www.ibis.com

---

### Unconditional (100 per cent) satisfaction guarantee

An unconditional (100 per cent) satisfaction guarantee promises customers complete satisfaction or their money back. An unconditional guarantee makes a powerful statement about the confidence a hospitality service provider has in the integrity of the offer and the ability of the service delivery system – people, processes and technology – to deliver as promised. An unconditional guarantee gives consumers the following:

- Confidence to purchase the service (by reducing risk) with the knowledge that a full refund is available if they are not satisfied
- Reassurance that the company can deliver on the promise, or it would not provide a service guarantee
- Preference over competitors who do not provide a similar guarantee.

Before a hospitality company can introduce an unconditional guarantee, the following conditions must be fulfilled:

- The customer group for whom the guarantee is created must be clearly defined – for example, is it all guests or just corporate clients who are hosting an event?
- The hospitality company must understand the most significant drivers of customer satisfaction for the products and services under guarantee.
- Product or service quality standards must be set to match customer expectations.
- Service operations must enable the guaranteed products or services to be delivered faultlessly.
- Employees must be aware of the guarantee and be capable of fulfilling their role in the promise.

A hospitality company intending to introduce an unconditional guarantee must be prepared to invest significantly in marketing research to evaluate the drivers of customer satisfaction, competitive standards and consumers' perceptions of price and value, as well as investment in product quality and training. It must also ensure that there is an effective quality audit process. Most importantly, if a company cannot deliver consistent customer satisfaction, then it simply cannot afford to offer an unconditional service guarantee. In fact, very few hospitality companies offer unconditional service guarantees.

To successfully introduce an unconditional service guarantee, a company should do the following:

- Develop a true understanding of customer experience
- Review customer experience to identify and eradicate failure points (areas of customer dissatisfaction) perhaps by using customer journey mapping
- Use the service guarantee as a differentiator in marketing communication campaigns
- Monitor revenues lost (refunds) under the terms of the guarantee
- Use customer feedback from the guarantee to identify and correct the root causes of customer dissatisfaction
- Give managers and employees measurable customer satisfaction performance goals
- Ensure employees understand that a failure by any team member can cause the guarantee to be invoked
- Maintain a stable team of staff who understand the guarantee, and the service standards that are required
- Maintain a list of customers who abuse the unconditional satisfaction guarantee and let them know that the unconditional satisfaction guarantee will not apply to future bookings.

From a quality perspective, unconditional guarantees force companies to 'do it right the first time' or the costs of the guarantee would be unacceptably high. However, despite all these advantages, few hospitality companies can seriously entertain the notion of providing a 100 per cent satisfaction guarantee. Many hospitality organizations do not have the product/service consistency to be able to offer an unconditional guarantee, and in these cases the costs of refunding dissatisfied customers would be too high. Such companies should not consider introducing an unconditional guarantee.

Hampton Inns in the USA and Premier Inn in the UK pioneered the introduction of unconditional guarantees in hospitality (Case Study 13.1). Both operate in the budget accommodation market, with a price-led strategy, a relatively standardized product, simple pricing policies and few employees. This brand formula delivers a homogeneous marketing offer, which lends itself to an unconditional guarantee.

## CASE STUDY 13.1

### Customer satisfaction at Premier Inn

The Good Night Guarantee money-back promise was such a successful marketing strategy that, when Travel Inn took over Premier Lodge and later became Premier Inn, the policy was retained as a key proposition and differentiator in the UK budget market. Premier Inn have made (and continue to make) a significant investment in their hotels to ensure that the 100 per cent 'good night's sleep' satisfaction promise is deliverable and profitable. Recent improvements include the introduction of Hypnos beds and the choice of firm or soft pillows in each bedroom. An interesting finding from Premier Inn marketing research is that customers who are aware of the 100 per cent satisfaction guarantee are *more satisfied* with their experience than customers who are not aware.

Each of the 800+ Premier Inn sites is audited twice each year to monitor cleanliness, comfort, decor, equipment, furniture maintenance and friendliness and service levels of its on-site team members. An external company conducts the audit, and units do not know when it is going to be carried out. Each hotel starts with 1,000 points, and points are deducted when performance in a certain area (e.g., bathroom cleanliness) is below satisfactory levels. The inspection checklist is used to identify areas for improvement, and if the overall site score is unsatisfactory then the general manager needs to take action quickly to remedy the problem areas – before a new inspection is carried out.

Premier Inn sends customers satisfaction surveys to evaluate the performance of each site. These achieve a 33 per cent response rate, which is high compared to most other firms. The results are used to drive new marketing, product and investment initiatives.

*Source*: Premier Inn

---

### ACTIVITY 13.3

Log on to the following hotel brand websites and evaluate their approaches to providing customer satisfaction guarantees:

- https://ibis.accor.com/
- www.premierinn.com/

---

Most midmarket hotels target many market segments. They have a complex range of accommodation, food, beverage and leisure products, with a wide variety of prices and price bundles, and a relatively large number of employees, sometimes a multiple of the number of guests. Since these types of hotels deliver a heterogeneous marketing offer, it is difficult for them to provide an unconditional guarantee, even if the management were interested in offering one.

Luxury hotels and restaurants providing high-quality service and well-maintained facilities do not need to introduce an unconditional guarantee. The reputation of Four Seasons Hotels, or the Savoy Hotel in London, carries an implicit guarantee of complete customer satisfaction.

### Constraints on customer satisfaction

Although most companies could almost certainly improve their level of customer satisfaction, there are constraints that restrict such improvements. Customers want competitive prices, and there are limits to how much customers are prepared to pay for higher levels of satisfaction. Hospitality companies have other stakeholders who compete for the funds that could be invested in delivering higher customer satisfaction: shareholders and owners want an increase in dividends, management and employees want higher wages and bonuses, and suppliers want prompt payment. Therefore, investment in improving customer satisfaction is balanced against the needs of other stakeholders. Financial constraints frequently inhibit investment in improvements in customer satisfaction.

### Complaint capture and analysis

In Chapter 11, we explained that encouraging customers to complain and then responding effectively to the complaint helps to improve customer satisfaction. We also provided an example of a chef who responded to complaints inappropriately (see Marketing Insight 11.2). Companies that take complaints seriously need to develop a policy and processes to capture, analyze and interpret customer complaints. These data can then be used to identify and correct the issues that cause dissatisfaction. In hospitality, one source of complaint data is the post-encounter questionnaire. Another source is complaint emails and letters, which often describe a catalogue of critical incidents. Unless there is a formal process for recording complaints, those that are made face-to-face with a service employee may go unrecorded, meaning that the company has incomplete data on customer complaints. Worryingly for hospitality marketers, unhappy customers might also vent their disappointment online. Online complaints that go viral can be very damaging. Often, however, customer-contact staff and unit managers can address the complaint at the time it is expressed, thereby preventing the risk of reputational damage online. Being empathic, courteous, honest and responsive are important behaviours in resolving complaints and retaining the customer.

Companies should therefore monitor review websites and social networks for complaint data. Companies can conduct sentiment analysis on the online review and social media data to capture positive and negative customer emotions. Capturing and measuring customer emotions from customers' verbal, face-to-face complaints and textual reviews is a technique that is successfully used by a growing number of hospitality operations. After identifying customer emotions, companies can conduct a content analysis to identify the causes of those negative emotions. Once the causes are identified, companies can take steps to eliminate those causes.

These sources provide the management with important information about service failure points. However, the problem with customer questionnaires, online reviews and complaint letters is that they are unrepresentative of most customers. Typically, they only represent very unhappy or very happy customers, those who are so (dis)satisfied that they are willing to spend time to send an email, write an online review or respond to a survey. An effective complaint capture system will employ many channels, such as post-encounter questionnaires, email, telephone calls, chat, face-to-face and web form. It will also include a channel to facilitate employee feedback on customer complaints.

## Customer satisfaction's influence on repeat business

In highly competitive industries with commoditized products, low differentiation, many competitive or substitute offers and low switching costs, providing satisfactory service may not be enough to retain customers. Satisfied customers may still defect. Many hospitality sectors suffer from these characteristics, so while delivering customer satisfaction is essential for survival it is no guarantee of spectacular success.

In hospitality, completely satisfied customers may never return to the unit or to the destination for a variety of reasons. For leisure products, many of today's travellers want to explore the world and visit new destinations rather than returning to the same destination. They are variety-seeking customers. Given the industry's over-capacity, price-sensitive consumers can choose from a wide range of competitively priced deals anywhere in the world. Customers attending unique events, such as wedding receptions, sports events and exhibitions, will stay at or near the venue and may never have another reason to visit the area. However, this does not mean that customer satisfaction is unimportant to these customers. If these customers are not happy with their experiences, they may still share their dissatisfactory experiences through posting online reviews to review sites or social media sites. Thus, hospitality businesses have to take customer satisfaction seriously and should not lower their service standards because of the transient characteristics of customers.

## Conclusion

Customer satisfaction is a complex topic, which will continue to be the focus of research because of its important role in generating repeat sales, word-of-mouth recommendation and enhancing profitability. Although most hospitality companies have difficulty in offering 100 per cent unconditional guarantees of customer satisfaction, virtually all of them provide implicit service guarantees. The cost of improving customer satisfaction must be balanced against the willingness of customers to pay more for higher satisfaction, and the needs of other stakeholders. Customer satisfaction is the foundation of a successful hospitality business, but satisfied customers may never return.

In this chapter, we have explained the following:

- A definition of customer satisfaction
- Four different types of satisfaction – contentment, pleasure, delight and relief
- Why customer satisfaction is important – because of the consequences of online reviews, the high costs of acquiring new customers, and the economic and non-economic benefits of repeat customers
- Net Promoter Score
- Characteristics of an implicit satisfaction guarantee, an explicit satisfaction guarantee and an unconditional satisfaction guarantee
- Constraints on improving customer satisfaction due to the needs of other stakeholders
- Tools for visualizing and measuring customer satisfaction, including the importance/performance matrix and complaint capture and analysis
- Some satisfied hospitality customers may never return.

### REVIEW QUESTIONS

Now check your understanding by answering the following questions:

1  Discuss the importance of customer satisfaction to a hospitality business.

2  Evaluate the concept of service guarantees for the following hotel market sectors:

- budget
- midmarket
- luxury.

3  Discuss the role of customer satisfaction measures in improving customer satisfaction for a hospitality brand.

4  Discuss the importance of understanding and responding to online customer reviews.

# References

1. Zeithaml, V. A., Bitner, M. J., & Gremler, D. D. (2013). *Services Marketing*, 6th ed. New York: McGraw-Hill.
2. Gallo, A. (2014). The value of keeping the right customers [online]. *Harvard Business Review*. [cited December 14, 2021]. Available from: https://hbr.org/2014/10/the-value-of-keeping-the-right-customers
3. Bain & Company [Internet]. *Prescription for Cutting Costs*. [cited December 14, 2021]. Available from: https://media.bain.com/Images/BB_Prescription_cutting_costs.pdf
4. Wu, X., Gursoy, D., & Zhang, M. (2021). Effects of social interaction flow on experiential quality, service quality and satisfaction: Moderating effects of self-service technologies to reduce employee interruptions. *Journal of Hospitality Marketing & Management, 30*(5), 571–591.
5. Reichheld, F. F. (2003). One number you need to grow. *Harvard Business Review, 81*(12), 46–54, 124.
6. Bain & Company [Internet]. *Measuring Your Net Promoter Score*. [cited December 14, 2021]. Available from: www.netpromotersystem.com/about/measuring-your-net-promoter-score/
7. Colvin, G. (2020). The simple metric that's taking over big business. *Fortune*. [cited December 14, 2021]. Available from: https://fortune.com/longform/net-promoter-score-fortune-500-customer-satisfaction-metric/
8. Bruyn, A. D., & Lilien, G. L. (2008). A multi-stage model of word-of-mouth influence through viral marketing. *International Journal of Research in Marketing, 25*(3), 151–163.
9. Lee, E. J., & Shin, S. Y. (2014). When do consumers buy online product reviews? Effects of review quality, product type, and reviewer's photo. *Computers in Human Behavior, 31*, 356–366.
10. Aakash, A., Tandon, A., & Gupta Aggarwal, A. (2021). How features embedded in eWOM predict hotel guest satisfaction: An application of artificial neural networks. *Journal of Hospitality Marketing & Management, 30*(4), 486–507.
11. Hu, X., & Yang, Y. (2021). What makes online reviews helpful in tourism and hospitality? A bare-bones meta-analysis. *Journal of Hospitality Marketing & Management, 30*(2), 139–158.
12. US data reported in Deyab, G. (2021). How much time do people spend on social media in 2021? *Techjury*. [cited December 14, 2021]. Available from: https://techjury.net/blog/time-spent-on-social-media/#gref
13. Online Travel Booking Statistics 2020–2021. (2021). *Explore the Online Travel Market, Including Growth, Technology & The Future of Online Travel Bookings*. [cited December 14, 2021]. Available from: www.condorferries.co.uk/online-travel-booking-statistics
14. Luo, J., Huang, S., & Wang, R. (2021). A fine-grained sentiment analysis of online guest reviews of economy hotels in China. *Journal of Hospitality Marketing & Management, 30*(1), 71–95.
15. PYMNTS.com [Internet]. *How Customer Reviews Provide Lifeblood to Restaurant Operations*. [cited October 25, 2021]. Available from: www.pymnts.com/restaurant-innovation/2020/how-customer-reviews-provide-lifeblood-to-restaurant-operations/
16. Pitt, C., Plangger, K., & Eriksson, T. (2021). Accommodation eWOM in the sharing economy: Automated text comparisons from a large sample. *Journal of Hospitality Marketing & Management, 30*(2), 258–275.
17. ReviewTrackers. (2021). *Online Reviews Statistics and Trends: A 2022 Report by ReviewTrackers*. [cited December 14, 2021]. Available from: www.reviewtrackers.com/reports/online-reviews-survey/
18. ReviewTrackers. (2021). *Powerful Examples of How to Respond to Negative Reviews and Positive Reviews*. [cited December 14, 2021]. Available from: www.reviewtrackers.com/guides/examples-responding-reviews/
19. Reichheld, F. F., & Sasser, W. E. (1990). Zero defections: Quality comes to services. *Harvard Business Review, 68*(5), 105–111.

Chapter **14**

# Relationship marketing

After working through this chapter, you should be able to:

- Understand the differences between transactional marketing and relationship marketing
- Identify the components of transactional and relationship marketing strategies
- Evaluate the concept of attitudinal and behavioural loyalty in the context of hospitality
- Analyze the role of frequent guest programmes in branded hospitality chains.

## Introduction

This chapter explores and contrasts the concepts of transactional marketing and relationship marketing. Transactional marketing focuses on a short-term, sales exchange process with customers; the business is not interested in developing a long-term relationship with customers. Relationship marketing takes a different perspective and regards customers as revenue-generating business assets who should be nurtured. Relationship marketing recognizes that some customers have the potential to generate significant value for companies over the long term. Therefore, the goal of relationship marketing is to create and maintain durable and profitable customer relationships.

We start the chapter by further explaining and differentiating between transactional and relationship marketing. We then discuss the economics of customer retention, the defining char-

DOI: 10.4324/9781003186342-18

acteristics of relationship marketing and what multi-unit hospitality companies need to do to implement a relationship marketing strategy. Finally, we consider the role of loyalty and frequent guest programmes in hospitality.

## Transactional and relationship marketing

In Chapter 1, we briefly introduced the concepts of transactional marketing and relationship marketing. Transactional marketing is based upon the traditional exchange/transaction process and is associated with single sales transactions. There is no expectation that a long-term customer relationship will be developed. Transactional marketing aims to make the sale, earn a margin and then make another sale. The focus is on the sale, not the customer who makes the purchase. There is no strategic effort to develop the relationship further; the transaction is complete from the company's perspective. This used to be the dominant approach to marketing practice and is still quite common today. Many small hospitality businesses located in resort destinations where there are transient visitors intuitively adopt this approach to marketing. Budget brands have also adopted a transactional marketing approach by providing product and service standardization, with no added value facilities or personalization, which enables the business to drive costs down and deliver the offer at a relatively low price. Since price-sensitive customers focus only on price they are not likely to come back if they find another offer that is cheaper. A transactional marketing approach is therefore appropriate when the potential customer lifetime value (CLV) is low and when customers are not interested in, and will not benefit from, a long-term relationship with the provider.

Relationship marketing is a critical component of customer relationship management (CRM) that focuses on customer loyalty and long-term customer engagement rather than shorter-term goals like customer acquisition and individual sales. It is both an approach to managing a business that stresses the importance of customer retention and loyalty, and a marketing strategy that aims to establish a long-term mutually beneficial relationships with customers. Businesses apply the principles of relationship marketing in their everyday operations in order to create strong, even emotional connections with customers that can lead to repeat patronage, positive word-of-mouth promotion both online and offline and loyalty.

In many hospitality businesses, frequent or regular customers have always been recognized as important. The owners and managers of small hotels, bars and restaurants are able to develop a close rapport with regular customers, giving them a special welcome, knowing their preferences and making sure they are looked after well. However, for branded hospitality chains, this recognition of key customers at the unit level was not easily transferred across all the other units in a chain until the Information and Communication Technology (ICT) revolution provided the computer systems and data storage facilities to create and share guest histories and manage loyalty programmes. Although independently owned and managed units can build on their traditions of hospitality and implement relationship marketing strategies, most of the discussion in the following sections is concerned with multiple-unit-branded chains.

It is important to remember that relationship marketing is a business strategy that aims to create and maintain profitable relationships with customers by designing and delivering satisfactory experiences. It's common to find that a small portion of customers generate a large portion of revenues. This is known as the 80/20 rule, or the Pareto Principle. This 'rule' implies that 80 per cent of company sales will come from 20 per cent of customers. Whether the 20 per cent who generate the most sales are profitable depends on their cost-to-serve. The 20 per cent might be more demanding in terms of expecting lower prices and higher levels of customization and service, all of which can add cost-to-serve those customers and have negative effect on profitability. Thus, it is important to recognize and identify repeat customers who have a high profitable lifetime value. CLV is the present-day value of all past, present and future profit derived from sales to a particular customer or segment. Building close relationships with retained customers should be mutually rewarding for both the company and the customer.

Table 14.1 contrasts the traditional transactional approach to marketing with relationship marketing.

Table 14.1 Relationship and transactional marketing

| Transactional marketing | Relationship marketing |
| --- | --- |
| Single sale focus | Customer retention focus |
| Focus on product features | Focus on customer value |
| Short-term promotions | Long-term relational marketing communication |
| Customers tend to be price sensitive | Customers tend to be less price sensitive |
| Short timescale | Long timescale |
| Discontinuous customer contact | Continuous customer contact |
| Limited commitment to customer relationships | High commitment to customer relationships |
| Quality is an operations issue | Quality is an issue for all employees |

A relationship marketing strategy should be targeted at selected hospitality customers or segments. Not all customers want a relationship, and not all customers merit a relationship. We mentioned in Chapter 13 that hotels and restaurants have many customers who are unlikely to return, and therefore trying to build a long-term relationship with these customers makes no strategic sense and cannot be cost-effective. There are two other customer segments that are unlikely or unwilling to want to develop relationships with a hospitality company. Some customers are aware of the availability of wide choice of competitor products in hospitality markets, do not want to limit their options by developing a relationship with a single brand or provider, and prefer to switch providers accordingly. Others might be very price sensitive. These price-sensitive customers' sense of value is strongly associated with low prices and they do not value other components of the offer. Thus, they are not interested in any type of relationship with any company and simply make their purchasing decisions based on price. Online search and comparison sites help this type of customers easily find low-price, convenient hospitality choices.

On the other hand, there are several circumstances when a business customer may want a long-term relationship with a hospitality supplier. These include the following:

- *When the hospitality product is strategically important* – for example, it may be a component of a bundled offer in a critical location for a tour operator or as a location for an international conference.
- *To avoid switching costs* – switching costs are incurred when customers change to another hospitality provider. Switching costs are very low for individual business and leisure travellers who book their accommodation online, but the switching costs for a corporate client who arranges major conferences/hospitality events and for intermediaries who handle large volumes of room-nights can be significant due to search, evaluation and negotiation costs. A strong relationship also means that customers are less willing to incur switching costs. Provided the hospitality organization is delivering customer satisfaction at a competitive price,

and the relationship is strong, then it is more convenient and cost-effective for the corporate clients and intermediaries to continue to purchase from their existing supplier.

- *When reciprocity is expected* – a local company may want to build a close relationship with a hotel so that they can offer accommodation to visiting customers. In return for free or heavily discounted accommodation for its customers, the local company offers the hotel its own products and services either free or at low cost. In many Asian markets, this type of reciprocal business relationship is common. For example, a hotel might plan an advertising campaign on the local radio station in return for letting the radio station have an equivalent value of accommodation, food and banqueting. Barter like this is a simple form of relationship marketing.

In a consumer context, relationships may be sought when the consumer values benefits over and above those directly derived from the hospitality experience. For example,

- *Recognition* – a customer may feel more valued when recognized and addressed by name.
- *Personalization* – for example, over time a restaurateur may come to understand a customer's particular preferences or expectations.
- *Risk reduction* – a relationship can reduce, or perhaps even eliminate, perceived risk. For example, a customer may develop a relationship with a branded restaurant chain to reduce the perceived performance and physical risk attached to eating when away from home.
- *Status* – customers may feel that their status is enhanced by a relationship with an organization, such as an elite health club.

## The economics of customer retention

Hospitality companies lose customers each year, for many reasons. Customers grow older and move through the family life cycle, changing their employment, home, lifestyle and consumption habits. Corporate customers and intermediaries go through similar changes, with growth, mergers, takeovers, relocation, downsizing and demise. In addition to this natural loss of customers, competitors lure customers away with new-product initiatives, new openings, price deals and attractive marketing communication campaigns. For these reasons, hospitality companies traditionally have relatively high customer defection rates (also known as customer churn). Although companies need continually to attract new customers to replace lost ones, customer retention is critical.

The fundamental reason for companies wanting to build relationships with customers is the profit those customers generate. Companies generate better results when they manage their customer base to identify, satisfy and retain profitable customers. This is the core goal of relationship marketing strategies. Improving customer retention rates has the effect of increasing the size of the customer base. If competitors lose customers at the rate of 20 per cent each year and your business loses customers at 10 per cent each year, then in a few years, other things being equal, your business will have a significantly larger customer base. However, there is little merit in growing the customer base aimlessly. The goal must be to retain existing customers who have future profit potential or are important for other strategic purposes. Not all customers are of equal importance. Some customers may not be worth recruiting or retaining at all – for example, customers who have a high cost-to-serve or are debtors/late payers or are promiscuous in the sense that they switch frequently between suppliers.

As customer retention rates increase (or defection rates decrease), so does the average tenure of a customer. *Tenure* is the term used to describe the length of time a customer remains as a customer. The impacts of small improvements in customer retention are magnified at the higher levels of retention. For example, improving the annual customer retention rate from 75 to 80 per cent grows average customer tenure from 10 to 12.5 years.[1] Managing tenure by reducing defection rates can be critical for business performance. Research suggests that an increase in customer retention of 5 per cent increases profits from 25 to 95 per cent for some service firms.[2] One of the reasons this happens is the high-fixed and semi-fixed cost structure of the hospitality industry. This means that the marginal costs of servicing a repeat customer are relatively small. Managing customer retention and tenure intelligently generates two key benefits:

1  Marketing costs are reduced. Less needs to be spent on advertising, distribution, selling and sales promotion to replace lost customers. In addition to reducing the costs of customer recruitment, costs-to-serve existing customers also tend to fall over time.
2  As tenure grows, companies accumulate customer data and insight, meaning they better understand customer requirements. Consequently, the hospitality provider is better placed to identify and satisfy customer requirements profitably. Customers also come to understand what a company can do for them. Over time, as relationships deepen, trust and commitment between the parties is likely to grow. Under these circumstances, revenue and profit streams from customers become more secure.

## Characteristics of relationship marketing

Hospitality companies that want to implement a successful relationship marketing strategy need an effective segmentation strategy, a strong service culture including a commitment to internal marketing, an interactive relational database in all properties, trust from their customers and associated customer recognition/reward strategies. We will discuss each of these factors in more detail.

### Segmentation

The segmentation strategy should focus on customers who have a potentially high lifetime value or are strategically significant in other ways. For example, they might be reference customers (customers whom other customers copy) or customers who initially enable a hospitality company to enter a new market segment. The Pareto principle (80/20 rule), which we mentioned earlier, is often used to identify customers who are strategically significant. The top 20 per cent of customers by volume (room-nights or revenue) includes frequent travellers, corporations and intermediaries. The branded chains are aware that frequent business travellers, who have a high CLV, are important customers and highly sought after. National and international corporations and key intermediaries also generate substantial volumes of hotel room-nights. Hospitality chains' sales and marketing executives liaise regularly with these key accounts, nurturing the relationship and trying to protect the business from competitors. However, hospitality companies need to be very careful in applying the 80/20 rule, as these key customers/distributors may not, in fact, be the most profitable – they may require costly pre-, during and post-encounter service as well as deeply discounted rates, thereby reducing their profitability. Firms are advised to estimate the customer management costs associated with these accounts, and not jump to the conclusion that they are the most profitable customers.

High frequency customers who have a relatively low spend-per-transaction and a relatively low management cost may be more profitable than high frequency customers who have a relatively high spend-per-transaction but a relatively high management cost over the lifetime of their patronage. Thus, it is important to analyze the profitability of each segment before determining the market segments to target.

Customer profitability analysis helps businesses estimate the net profit generated by each customer segment. The net profit is calculated by subtracting the cost spent on each customer segment from the revenue each customer segment generates. The cost includes all the expenses involved in serving a customer segment, such as customer acquisition and retention, marketing, sales and distribution in addition to production and delivery of services. Customer profitability analysis can also help you identify unprofitable customer segments. Some customer segments might generate high revenue but cost more than the revenue they generate. On the other hand, some customers might generate low revenue but cost less than the revenue they generate. Managers can identify and eliminate or reduce the cost spent on customer segments that do not generate adequate profit for your business based on the results of customer profitability analysis.

## MARKETING INSIGHT 14.1

### How to analyze customer profitability

Analyzing customer profitability requires a lot of time and effort. Customer profitability analysis can be difficult to implement, but it can still provide useful insights to help your business maximize its profit.

The steps involved in customer profitability analysis are:

1 Segment your customers into groups: Start your customer profitability analysis by dividing your customers into approachable segments. Market segmentation creates subsets of a market based on specific criteria such as demographics, needs, priorities, common interests and other psychographic or behavioural criteria used to better understand the target audience. An easy way to segment and define market segments is to create a customer persona. As discussed in Chapter 11, a customer persona is a semi-fictional profile of your ideal customer in a segment that represents the key traits of that segment. This persona should be developed based on market research and real data about the customer segment.

2 Identify the cost of each customer segment: The next step in the customer profitability analysis is to determine the cost associated with each segment. This includes costs such as sales and marketing costs (e.g., cost per customer acquisition, per customer retention costs), customer service cost, distribution cost, in addition to cost of production and delivery of services. You need to find relevant data for each segment or come up with realistic estimates. You will use this data to estimate the average cost per customer.

3 Determine how much revenue each segment generates: After you identify the cost of each segment, you will need to estimate how much revenue each segment will generate using the relevant revenue data. These data will give you the average revenue per customer in each segment.

4 Calculate customer profitability: Based on all the data you have collected, let's assume that you have developed two customer personas (segments).

    1 Persona A with a lower average revenue per transaction

    2 Persona B with a higher average revenue per transaction

By looking at the summary information provided earlier, Persona B looks like a more attractive customer segment than Persona A due to higher average revenue per transaction. However, when you calculate customer profitability, you see that Persona A is relatively a more profitable segment because it costs less than Persona B.

Let's simplify it:

|  | Persona A | Persona B |
| --- | --- | --- |
| Average revenue per transaction | $80 | $100 |
| Marketing cost | $6 | $10 |
| Distribution cost | $10 | $15 |
| Service production and delivery cost | $45 | $65 |
| Total Cost | $61 | $90 |
| Net Profit | $19 | $10 |

The net profit generated by Persona A is $19, while the net profit generated by Persona B is $10. Persona A is a more profitable segment than Persona B, even though it did not appear to be that way at first.

Figure 14.1 illustrates appropriate marketing strategies based upon a customer's level of frequency and their lifetime value.

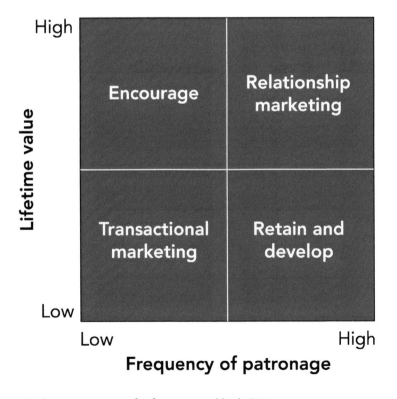

Figure 14.1  Marketing strategies for frequent and high CLV customers

### Service culture

Successful relationship marketing strategy also depends on the company's service culture. The company needs to invest in a genuine customer-orientated service philosophy that delivers the product and service quality customers expect. This means making appropriate investments in the people, technology and processes that deliver the desired levels of service quality. If the company cannot deliver the experience customers expect, it cannot hope to develop long-term relationships with them.

Internal marketing is an essential component of an effective relationship marketing strategy. In Chapter 12, we discussed the crucial role of customer-contact employees in delivering customer satisfaction, and the importance of internal marketing programmes to communicate with, up-skill and empower employees. A service culture that fosters employee involvement and encourages employees to build close relationships with customers provides a strong foundation for a successful relationship marketing strategy.

### Database

ICT is another prerequisite for multiple-unit companies aiming to develop and implement a relationship marketing strategy. Hospitality companies often have customer-related data in different databases: rooms, food and beverage, sales, marketing and customer service, for example. This information needs to be assembled so that the firm has a single view of the customer, providing ICT users with insight into the customer's purchases, payments, enquiries, complaints, demographic and contact details, contact history and communication preferences. Customers often mention their preferences to customer-contact employees during their stay in a hotel, for example, their preferred salutation (formal 'Mr Smith', or informal 'Joe'), a favourite type of pillow or a food allergy. This information must be added to the customer database. It is essential for building a successful customer relationship featuring relevant, timely, customized face-to-face and mediated interactions and communications. Some communications will focus on cross-selling and upselling opportunities, but it is important to understand that customers do not want to be 'sold' at every opportunity. Analysis of the aggregated customer data can create insights that guide communications and management actions: for example, analysis might be able to identify lead indicators of customer churn, for example a disputed invoice or an unresolved complaint. Management can then respond with appropriate actions. The effect of these actions on churn can then be assessed and, if necessary, modified over time. Analysis of the profile and transactional history of key accounts throughout a chain's properties would enable management to identify potential new key accounts having the same profile, reward those customers who maintain current high-value sales and incentivize accounts that are declining in sales volume.

In Chapter 9, we discussed the role of the database in personalizing communications with key customers. The database is crucial in identifying key customers to target with specific promotions and in providing accurate contact information. Indeed, many owner-managed units build simple, cost-effective email lists to provide regular communication with customers.

### Trust and commitment

Trust and commitment are core concepts in relationship marketing. Customers must trust and have complete confidence in the company's competence and integrity. It does help for the customer and the company to have shared values. It is less likely that a customer will develop a relationship with a company whose activities conflict with the customer's own values. Trust is built up over time and depends on the company being competent in delivering on its promises and not exploiting the customer. A long-term relationship provides opportunities for the company to demonstrate its values, competence and integrity to the customer. As trust develops over time, the customer feels secure in the relationship and the company earns the customer's commitment.

A long-term relationship implies that both parties have been prepared to make short-term sacrifices. From a hospitality company's perspective, this means that opportunistic behaviours to make short-term profits should be avoided – for example, a hotel company will maintain a price commitment to key customers during high season periods, even though it could sell the rooms to a guest paying higher rates. Clearly, delivering consistent customer satisfaction is an essential condition for building a long-term relationship. Customers who suffer from inconsistent service standards cannot give their trust to a company that is incompetent.

### Recognition and reward

Customers who have a relationship with a company generally expect recognition. The customer record enables key customers to be identified as, or even before, they check in to the hotel. Rooms on executive floors and individually named suites easily identify key customers for all customer-contact employees, who should be trained to recognize, greet and look after them appropriately.

A mutually beneficial relationship implies that there are rewards for both parties. We have already discussed how the company aims to secure better sales and profits by cultivating long-term relationships with strategically significant customers. Loyal customers should also be rewarded for their patronage. Although recognition plays an important role in rewarding customers, tangible reward systems can help build customer loyalty and increase switching costs for the customer.

## Attitudinal and behavioural loyalty

We will now discuss the concept of attitudinal and behavioural loyalty, the relationship marketing ladder of loyalty, frequent guest programmes in hospitality and customer disloyalty.

### The concept of loyalty

Most hospitality companies are keen to encourage customers to repeat purchase and generate positive word-of-mouth, both online and face-to-face. However, there is a distinction between a frequent customer and a truly loyal customer. For example, frequent business travellers might be compelled to stay at a particular brand because of their employer's policy. Others become frequent customers because there are no effective competitors in the area; these customers could easily defect if serious competition emerged. Indeed, some frequent customers might even be extremely dissatisfied with their hospitality experience, and complain, but still stay because of the lack of alternatives. While they may be frequent customers, they may not be willing to recommend it to others. This type of loyalty is described as behavioural loyalty because it is simply based on frequent behaviour.

A truly loyal customer is emotionally committed and does not seriously consider competitor alternatives. This type of loyalty is described as attitudinal loyalty because of the strong preference the customer has built towards the brand or unit. Ideally, hospitality businesses want customers who have both attitudinal loyalty and are frequent guests. There is evidence to suggest that totally satisfied customers are six times more likely to repurchase and have a greater propensity for loyalty than partially satisfied customers.[3] Loyal customers will often take ownership of the relationship and refer to the brand in first person terms (e.g., loyal pub customers often describe their bar as 'my local'), they tune into the marketing communication messages sent out by the brand and shut out the messages from competitors.[4] If there is a service problem, loyal customers are more likely to report it because they genuinely want to help. Price is less of an issue for loyal customers. Most importantly, loyalty creates a major barrier to switching behaviour. True loyalty can override rational behaviour, as customers who are truly loyal to their hospitality brand have become emotionally involved with the brand and its values. Customer loyalty is therefore a powerful indicator of marketing success.

However, customer loyalty is a complex phenomenon. A key issue is to build loyalty with customers who belong to the target market profile; attracting loyalty from the wrong customers can be dangerous and embarrassing. Building customer loyalty to the brand, and to the unit, is important for the hospitality marketer. In hospitality, customers can be both brand-loyal and loyal to specific units from several brands. While harder, more standardized brands generate customer loyalty to the brand, softer, less standardized brands tend to generate loyalty towards individual units. Brand loyalty refers to the tendency of some consumers to keep using the services offered by the same hospitality brand even when they have choices of competing alternatives. Consumers continue to use services from the same brand not because the brand is the only option but because they trust the brand. Consumers stay loyal to the brand because they feel that the brand is trustworthy and offers better services and high-quality products compared to all other brands in the market. This may be through reputation, various promotional activities and customers' previous experiences with the brand.

Customers can also be loyal to specific units at different locations regardless of their brand due to quality and price of services and products offered by each unit. Customers can use services offered by a certain unit in a specific location because of the benefits they can get from that unit. For example, frequent travellers who visit certain destinations on a regular basis can become hotel-loyal but not brand-loyal. An international frequent traveller might therefore have preferred, first-choice hotels from a range of brands depending on the location, choosing the Hilton in New York, the Crowne Plaza at Birmingham, the Marriott in Athens, the Novotel in Sydney and the Shangri-La at Kowloon, Hong Kong.

It is a common misconception that all companies should adopt a relationship marketing strategy. There is a role for transactional marketing, and in practice most branded hospitality businesses combine both relational and transactional marketing strategies according to the needs of different market segments. Building frequency is a legitimate marketing objective and strategy, just as building loyalty is an appropriate objective and strategy for companies seeking to develop a relational approach to marketing. Table 14.2 presents the different marketing approaches that can be adopted when developing a frequent or a loyal customer base.

Table 14.2 Marketing strategies targeting frequent versus loyal customers

| Marketing activities | Frequent customer base | Loyal customer base |
| --- | --- | --- |
| Objective | Build traffic, sales and profitability | Build brand desirability, sales and profit |
| Strategy | Incentivize repeat transactions | Build personal brand relationships |
| Focus | Segment behaviour | Individual emotional and rational needs |
| Tactics | Sales promotions, focus on free offers/discounts/ rewards; frequent guest programme with incentives | Customized communications, preferred status, emotional rewards, added value upgrades; loyalty guest programme with recognition and rewards |
| Measurement | Transactions, sales growth | Individual customer lifetime value, emotional responses and attitudinal change |

*Source*: Reproduced with permission from Lewis and Chambers[5]

---

### ACTIVITY 14.1

Think about your relationships with hospitality brands.

● Can you identify brands where you have a transactional relationship?

● Are there any brands to which you feel emotional loyalty?

● If you work for a hospitality brand, has your relationship with the brand changed because of your experience as an employee?

---

### The relationship marketing ladder of loyalty

Researchers have categorized customers into six different types according to their usage and loyalty behaviours. Different marketing strategies are required for these different types of customers. The bottom of the ladder of loyalty starts with 'prospects'; they need to be persuaded to make a first purchase and experience the offer. Once on the ladder the task is to encourage them to become regular 'clients', and then to turn clients into 'supporters' and supporters into 'advocates'. Finally, 'advocates' become 'partners' in the ultimate, mutually rewarding relationship (Figure 14.2). The idea of the loyalty ladder is to progress appropriate customers further up the ladder. However, customers can also move down or off the ladder, and some customers will choose not to move at all. The loyalty ladder recognizes the need for segmenting customers in terms of their propensity for loyalty and their lifetime value. Although CLV can be calculated using the customer retention rate, achieved spends and variable costs, it is much more difficult to determine a customer's propensity to be loyal.

## Frequent guest and loyalty programmes

Earlier in this chapter, we explained the difference between frequency and loyalty. This distinction can also apply to any discussion of frequent guest programme (FGP) and loyalty guest programme

(LGP). However, in everyday usage, these expressions are virtually interchangeable, and hospitality companies use the term FGP to apply to any loyalty programme.

Figure 14.2 The relationship marketing ladder of loyalty

*Source*: Peck et al.[6]

Rewarding customers for their patronage in tourism dates from the 1970s, when American Airlines introduced a successful frequent flyer programme that was quickly imitated by competitors. The airlines' system of managing their frequent flyer programmes provided hotel companies with a template that they copied. Today's FGP enables frequent travellers to receive points and/or air miles whenever they stay at a hotel in the scheme. FGPs tend to adopt one of two approaches: they are either part of a consortium scheme offering rewards for a wide range of service purchases, including hotels and travel, retail and financial products, or they are property or chain-specific. In this case they invite regular customers to join a club and receive recognition and reward as a privileged guest in the form of added benefits during the stay at the hotel.

All the international hospitality corporations recognize the importance of offering a FGP to reward regular customers (see Table 14.3), and regular customers are very aware of their importance to the hotels. All these programmes provide different levels of membership, which are determined according to the number of nights a customer stays and/or amount of money the customer spends in the hotels. The higher the number of nights and/or the amount of money spent, the more generous the benefits become as a customer graduates to the top tier of membership. Some programmes allow customers to 'double dip' – this means that a customer who has an airline frequent flier programme membership can earn air miles whilst staying at the hotel, and at the same time earn points from the hotel, which are credited to their FGP. We will review two different programmes here: Hilton's Honors and Shangri-La's Golden Circle.

Table 14.3 The FGPs of international hotel corporations

| Corporation | Programme |
| --- | --- |
| Accor | ALL – Accor Live Limitless |
| Best Western | Best Western Rewards |
| Hilton | Hilton Honors |
| Hyatt | World of Hyatt |
| IHG Hotels & Resorts | IHG Rewards |
| Marriott International | Marriott Bonvoy |
| Shangri-La | Golden Circle |

### Hilton Honors

The Hilton programme is open to customers staying in any of their current lodging brands, ranging from the budget properties to luxury hotels. However, customers who are on discounted rates booked through channels such as wholesalers, tour operators, aircrew and Internet auction sites are excluded from the scheme. There are four levels of membership:

1 *Member* – there is no minimum qualifying number of stays; benefits include digital check-in, choose your own room, free Wi-Fi, guaranteed Hilton Honors discount rate, points toward free nights, travel partners and more, no resort fees on reward stays, Digital Key and access to exclusive Hilton Honors experiences.

2 *Silver* – a customer needs a minimum of two qualifying stays, five qualifying nights or 12,500 base points. In addition to Member benefits, Silver members get the fifth night free, 20 per cent bonus Hilton Honors points, free bottled water and elite rollover nights.

3 *Gold* – a customer needs a minimum of 10 qualifying stays, 20 qualifying nights or 37,500 base points. In addition to Member and Silver benefits, Gold members get 80 per cent bonus Hilton Honors points, daily food and beverage credit in US hotels or free continental breakfast in non-US hotels, space available room upgrades and milestone bonuses.

4 *Diamond* – a customer needs a minimum of 15 qualifying stays, 30 qualifying nights or 60,000 base points. In addition to Member, Silver and Gold benefits, Diamond members get 100 per cent bonus Hilton Honors points, guaranteed reservations availability up to 48 hours before booking, executive lounge access, premium Wi-Fi, elite status gifting, space-available room upgrades and diamond status extension.

Each level of membership must be earned in each calendar year. Because of the differences between Hilton's brands (market segment, product offer and rates), there are several exclusions and different rewards according to the brand and the location. For example, a Diamond member can choose a room upgrade at a Waldorf Astoria Hotel, but only a non-alcoholic beverage or one snack item at a Hampton Inn. Hilton has agreements with more than 60 airlines and encourages double dipping. The rewards for staying in the budget brands are considerably lower in value than those in the mid- and upscale brands. Hilton has negotiated an extensive network of partners to provide customers with the opportunity to either earn Hilton Honors bonus points when using their services or redeem points. Hilton Honors partnered with several credit card companies, airlines, rental cars companies, Lyft and Amazon.

Although Hilton promotes its guest programme as a 'guest loyalty program like no other' the scale of the programme, with many millions of members from a wide range of hospitality target markets staying at over 5,900 hotels around the world and able to redeem their points from a variety of products and services, suggests that this is really a transaction-orientated FGP.

### Shangri-La Golden Circle

Shangri-La's loyalty programme, called Golden Circle, is only for the *most valued* guests who stay at Shangri-La Hotels and Resorts, Traders Hotels, Kerry Hotels and Hotel Jen. The focus is on guest recognition and individual personal preferences. Golden Circle (GC) membership is free and gives access to a range of benefits the second a guest joins the programme. Status upgrades are awarded according to the number of nights spent or the number of points earned at hotels that participate in the programme, opening the door to even more benefits and perks. GC has three membership tiers: Gold, Jade and Diamond.

Gold membership is activated by earning a minimum of 50 GC points at any Shangri-La hotel, Kerry hotel, Traders hotel and Hotel Jen, and entitles guests to the following benefits: pre-registration for easy check-in, priority waitlist for room reservations, cash advance of up to US$250 per stay on major credit cards (no hotel commission or handling fee), complimentary local calls and welcome fruit platter.

Jade membership is awarded after 20 qualifying nights or 10 qualifying stays in a calendar year at any Shangri-La hotel, Kerry hotel, Traders hotel and Hotel Jen, and comes with all the Gold benefits, plus: priority check-in and check-out at an exclusively designated area, daily buffet breakfast served at Café Restaurant or designated restaurant, upgrade to the next best room category, if the reserved room type is not available at check-in, priority waitlist for room reservations, guaranteed room availability for reservations made 72 hours prior to arrival, early check-in/late check-out – 11am/4pm, 25 per cent bonus GC Award Points and choice of three welcome amenities (e.g. chocolates, fresh fruits, etc.).

Diamond membership is awarded upon 50 qualifying nights or 25 qualifying stays in a calendar year at any Shangri-La hotel, Kerry hotel, Traders hotel and Hotel Jen, and comes with all the Gold and Jade benefits, plus: access to Horizon/Traders Club Lounge, where available, priority check-in and check-out at Horizon/Traders Club Lounge or in-room check-in, where available, daily buffet breakfast served at Café Restaurant, Horizon/Traders Club Lounge, where available, partner enjoys access to Horizon/Traders Club Lounge, where available, concierge services for non-staying guests, guaranteed room availability for reservations made 48 hours prior to arrival, guaranteed bed type at time of reservation, early check-in/late check-out – 8am/6pm, pressing for one suit upon arrival, use of selected resort facilities, a bottle of red or white wine as welcome amenity, cash advance of up to US$300 per stay on major credit cards (no hotel commission or handling fee), long distance calls and faxes at cost price, and 50 per cent GC Award Points.

With over 100 owned or managed luxury hotels in 76 destinations, four complementary brands and focused target markets, the Golden Circle is a genuine relational marketing programme aimed at recognizing and rewarding loyalty for their most valued guests.

### Disadvantages of FGPs

The main disadvantages of FGPs include the following:

- Benefits are awarded to individual guests, but most frequent guests are travelling on business – so their companies pay for the hotel accommodation but do not gain the rewards.
- Guests have potential liability for tax on the benefits accrued from a FGP.

- Company has potential liability of unredeemed rewards eventually being claimed (this is limited when companies require benefits to be earned and points redeemed with a calendar year).
- Customers may join the FGPs of many hotel companies, which erodes competitive advantage and encourages switching behaviour.
- Significant costs are usually incurred when setting up and administering the scheme.

---

## ACTIVITY 14.2

Log on to Hilton Hotels (www.hilton.com/) and Shangri-La Hotels (www.shangri-la.com/). Both the Hilton Honors FGP and the Golden Circle FGP FGP are accessible from the home page and in several languages.

- Compare the language used by Hilton and Shangri-La to describe their FGPs.
- Review the rewards offered and the conditions in both schemes.
- What differences can you identify between these hotel companies' approach to marketing their FGPs?

---

## CASE STUDY 14.1

### The rewards programme at BJ's Restaurant and Brewhouse

BJ's Restaurants, Inc, was founded in 1978 in California as a pizza restaurant and currently owns/operates more than 200 casual dining restaurants in 29 states throughout the USA. The original concept has been further developed to include a broader range of menu items. The company serves BJ's award-winning proprietary handcrafted beers, brewed at its brewing operations in five states and by independent third-party craft brewers. Some of the restaurants have their own microbrewery on the premises. Despite operating in a highly competitive market, annual sales in 2019 (before the COVID-19 pandemic) increased by 4 per cent year over year to $1.2 billion. With the strength of their brand and positioning, BJ's comparable restaurant sales growth outperformed the casual dining industry as measured by the Black Box Intelligence survey in 2019, for the fifth consecutive year.

BJ's has a simple, but effective, rewards programme where members earn one point for each $1 spent on eligible transactions such as food and non-alcoholic drinks and the BJ's logoed merchandise, but not alcohol. For every 100 points customers earn in the programme, they are automatically issued a non-transferable reward for $10 off a qualifying purchase at a BJ's restaurant or on their website. BJ's will send an email to customers' registered address when each reward is issued.

Customers can earn additional points by signing on to BJ's social media and they can easily access their online account to see how many points they have earned. BJ's reward programme has 1 million members and won a COLLOQUY Recognizes Award for delivering valuable, relevant rewards and nurturing a better customer experience.

*Source*: www.bjsrestaurants.com, www.colloquy.com

## Criticisms of relationship marketing

Relationship marketing has been criticized for several reasons. First, there is a limit to the number of relationships a customer can sustain with companies. Consumers are bombarded with many competing messages and cannot possibly have a one-to-one relationship with every brand they buy. Hence, some hospitality companies may have unrealistic expectations about their customers' willingness to give them trust, commitment and loyalty. In reality, customers can only give their loyalty to a small number of brands. Some consumers are also concerned about organizations' use of personal information, which has to be disclosed when staying in a hotel. Unsolicited communication in the form of direct mail, email and text messages, which aim to build a relationship with customers, may in fact be counterproductive and turn customers away. Other criticisms include the following:

- Hospitality companies generally want customers to be loyal, but often fail to deliver the services that customers expect.
- Special introductory offers to attract new customers are not offered to existing loyal customers, who then feel that they have been treated unfairly.
- Customers can change their preferences, and do not always want the same magazine or drink every time they check-in.
- Preferential treatment given to customers in the FGP can be upsetting, or even offensive, to other customers.

## Conclusion

Despite the legitimate criticisms of relationship marketing, customer loyalty is an appealing goal. Those hospitality companies that can develop meaningful relationships with customers do gain a competitive advantage. However, a relationship marketing strategy is not appropriate for all branded hospitality organizations. Companies developing a relationship marketing strategy must have a strong service culture that delivers high customer satisfaction, and relevant recognition and reward policies, in order to create customer trust, commitment and loyalty.

In this chapter, we have explained:

- Relationship marketing strategies focus on customer retention and recognize the long-term value of loyal customers.
- Transactional marketing strategies focus on customer acquisition.
- Increases in customer retention can enhance profitability significantly.
- Hotel companies are aware of the importance of repeat guests and have developed FGPs to attract and reward them.
- Frequency is not an indicator of loyalty.
- Loyal customers are less price sensitive and more resistant to competitors' offers.
- Frequent guests may be loyal to individual hotels, as well as to hotel brands.
- There are limits to the number of relationships customers can have with companies.

REVIEW QUESTIONS

Now check your understanding of this chapter by answering the following questions:

1 Highlight the differences between a relationship marketing strategy and a transactional marketing strategy within the context of hospitality.

2 A hotel company is planning to develop a relationship marketing strategy. Explain what is required to implement a relationship marketing strategy successfully.

3 Discuss the concept of customer loyalty in the hospitality industry.

4 Evaluate the role of FGPs in the international hotel industry.

## References

1. Dawkins, P. M., & Reichheld, F. F. (1990). Customer retention as a competitive weapon. Directors & Board, Summer, 42–47.
2. Reichheld, F. F., & Sasser, W. E. (1990). Zero defections: Quality comes to services. *Harvard Business Review*, *68*(5), 105–111.
3. Jones, T. O., & Sasser, W. E. (1995). Why satisfied customers defect. *Harvard Business Review*, *73*(6), 88.
4. Shen, Y., Huang, S., Choi, H. S. C., & Morrison, A. M. (2021). Does brand love matter to casual restaurants? A multi-group path analysis. *Journal of Hospitality Marketing & Management*, *30*(5), 630–654.
5. Lewis, R. C., & Chambers, R. E. (2000). *Marketing Leadership in Hospitality: Foundations and Practice*. Chichester: John Wiley.
6. Peck, H., Payne, A., Christopher, M., & Clark, M. (1998). *Relationship Marketing for Competitive Advantage: Winning and Keeping Customers*, 2nd ed. Oxford: Butterworth-Heinemann.

# The marketing plan

DOI: 10.4324/9781003186342-19

The marketing plan (Chapter 15) is where the marketing manager assembles data and reveals strategies and tactics that focus on the achievement of pre-encounter, encounter and post-encounter marketing objectives. The marketing plan relies on marketing research (Chapter 2) to underpin the analysis of the current situation, including consumer research that supports the targeting decision (Chapter 3), and research into the competitive environment (Chapter 4) and customer satisfaction (Chapter 13). Each element of the hospitality marketing mix (Chapters 5–12) is carefully evaluated and modelled for its influence on customer expectations and experience, and its contribution towards the company's relational or transactional marketing strategy (Chapter 14).

# 15

# Marketing planning

After working through this chapter, you should be able to:

- Understand the contexts and types of marketing planning in hospitality organizations
- Describe a generic process for marketing planning
- Carry out the research needed to develop a strategic or tactical marketing plan
- Explain how analytical tools are used to evaluate a hospitality business's current and potential situation
- Recognize the limitations of marketing planning and the importance of contingency planning.

## Introduction

Planning is widespread in businesses of all sizes. Larger companies have more formalized planning processes, but smaller companies also perform planning essentials. A plan can be thought of as a set of decisions about what a company wants to achieve and how it is going to achieve it. The essence of a plan is, therefore, a goal with accompanying strategy and tactics. The goal defines what the company wants to achieve, whereas the strategy and tactics set out how the goal will be achieved. A marketing plan sets out the marketing objectives that a company wants to achieve and the strategy and tactics that will be used to reach those objectives.

DOI: 10.4324/9781003186342-20

In this chapter, we build on your learning from the pre-encounter, encounter and post-encounter hospitality marketing activities discussed in previous chapters. We will explain how marketing plans consist of objectives, strategies and tactics across the three stages of a customer relationship: pre-encounter, encounter and post-encounter.

## Contexts of marketing planning

Although unit-level marketing plans are the major focus of this chapter, it is important to acknowledge that marketing planning is carried out within a hierarchy of levels in the more complex hospitality organizations such as Marriott International including the corporate head office, the division and the unit.

### Corporate marketing planning

Corporate-level strategic marketing plans are concerned with major decisions such as which brands to acquire, develop, sell or close down; which geographic markets to enter and which hospitality formats to offer in those markets; and strategies for market entry including joint venture, acquisition or organic development. Decisions are also made on the allocation of resources to support the marketing activities of divisions.

### Divisional marketing planning

A divisional marketing plan focuses on the goals of a major division of a hospitality company; these goals are usually set by, or negotiated with, corporate head office. A division is a profit centre comprising one or more core businesses, often a brand, run by a dedicated chief executive and management team. Major hospitality groups, like Whitbread, will produce marketing plans for each of its brands – for example, Beefeater, Premier Inn, Brewers Fayre and Table Table. Each brand will set its own goals, often in terms of sales and profit growth, and develop strategies for goal achievement. These strategies will consist of decisions to open (or close) operational units, to focus on particular market segments, to position against named competitors and to compete by employing a particular set of competitive advantages. The divisional marketing plan is evaluated and monitored by corporate executives to ensure that it is consistent with corporate strategy and goals.

### Unit marketing planning

Unit marketing plans can be developed for a particular chain-owned branded hotel or restaurant, or an independently owned and managed business. Typical marketing and operational objectives employed at the unit level include sales revenues, occupancy levels and RevPAR. Sometimes, objectives may be set for pre-encounter marketing (raise awareness, develop expectations, develop preference), encounter marketing (achieve revenue and average spend targets) or post-encounter marketing (satisfaction, Net Promoter Scores, intention to buy again, share of customer spend). Strategies focus on segmentation, targeting and positioning, and developing strong pre-encounter, encounter and post-encounter marketing mixes.

Within a hotel, different departments (such as the rooms division or food and beverage) may produce their own marketing plans. The focus at departmental level is generally much more tactical. The core strategic marketing decisions of segmentation, targeting and positioning (STP) will have been made at divisional or unit level. Departments operate within the parameters of those strategic decisions. For example, the rooms division manager may need to find a solution for an unexpected loss of business. If a tour group suddenly cancels, the manager needs to develop a rapid tactical response to win additional business from targeted customer groups, such as airlines, transients or meetings and conventions.

## Strategic and tactical marketing plans

A distinction can be made between strategic and tactical marketing plans. As the focus of marketing plans shifts downwards from corporate through division to unit and department, plans become much more tactical. Strategic plans set the broad goals for the company, whereas tactical marketing plans focus on the detailed actions required to achieve those goals. Strategic planning in major hospitality businesses is normally the responsibility of the corporate or divisional office. Units just receive budgets for tactical marketing. In single unit enterprises, both strategic and tactical plans are the responsibility of the owner/manager.

### *Strategic marketing plans*

Strategic marketing plans (SMPs) are generally established for a minimum three- to five-year term. They focus on long-term goals, such as growing market share, building yield and lifting revenues. Core marketing decisions are made about market segmentation, target markets and brand positioning, and these decisions establish the foundations on which tactical plans can be built. When an international hospitality corporation decides to grow one of its brands by entering a new country market, this is a major strategic decision with significant financial and operating consequences. SMP decisions, once made, are not easy to reverse. A company that changes its strategic position in the marketplace too frequently runs the risk of confusing customers and alienating investors.

There have been two significant efforts to identify generic strategies that are associated with business success. Both have a strong marketing focus. The first was produced by Michael Porter; the second by Michael Treacy and Fred Wiersema. Companies can choose to adopt one of these strategies as the basis of their presence in a market. Each strategy has different implications for marketers.

### *Porter*

Porter[1] claims that there are three core generic strategies for success – overall cost leadership, differentiation and focus.

#### OVERALL COST LEADERSHIP

Firms adopting a low-cost position relative to competitors need to pursue a strategy of cost control in every aspect of the business. In hospitality firms, this means that food and beverage costs, payroll, location, utilities, maintenance, administration, marketing and distribution overheads, decor, fabrics and furniture costs are all minimized and kept under strict control in order to achieve the lowest cost position in the market. Cost control allows the business to attract and retain customers who are price sensitive.

Companies adopting a cost–leadership strategy need to generate economies of scale in marketing and purchasing; this implies that the company should be seeking to obtain a high market share. A cost–leadership strategy is most suitable for companies and properties that target price-sensitive markets like the budget accommodation market. This strategy is best delivered by designing new-build hospitality premises; Accor's very low-priced French budget brand hotelF1 locates low-cost areas; has low construction costs with minimal fixtures, fittings and furniture; and is designed to maximize operational efficiencies.

## DIFFERENTIATION

Porter found that some successful firms adopt a product–service differentiation strategy that results in the company's offer being perceived by customers as significantly different from competitors. In hospitality, differentiation is closely linked to branding and offer formulation. Firms adopting a differentiation strategy strive to deliver a clearly defined experience that differs from that of competitors. We have already discussed the role of differentiation in Chapter 4 and have provided examples from the hospitality industry.

## FOCUS

The focus strategy, Porter's third generic strategy, describes firms that concentrate on one narrow market segment such as a particular customer group or geographic area. The benefits of a focus strategy are derived from serving that segment more effectively than either differentiated or low-cost firms. We discussed a focus (or niche) marketing strategy in Chapter 4.

If firms do not adopt any one of these strategies, Porter suggests that they will be 'stuck in the middle', losing price-sensitive business to low-cost leaders and higher-margin business to firms adopting a differentiated strategy. Porter claims that firms 'stuck in the middle' are not as profitable as firms that have adopted one of the generic strategies.

### *Treacy and Wiersema*

Treacy and Wiersema[2] also identified three major strategies that companies can adopt. Each is defined by the way the business orients itself to its customers. Called 'market disciplines', the three strategies are: operational excellence, innovation and customer intimacy.

## OPERATIONAL EXCELLENCE

This strategy calls for doing a limited number of things extremely well. It implies the development of a well-defined customer offer based on clearly understood customer expectations, and the repeated production and delivery of the product-service that complies with exact specifications of a Standard Operating Procedure Manual. Companies such as McDonald's, Taco Bell and Pizza Hut fit this model.

## INNOVATION

The innovation strategy is founded on the belief that relevant, customer-focused innovation will win buyer preference. Companies that stress product–service innovation nurture ideas, translate them into product concepts and market them successfully. These companies experiment and think 'out-of-the-box'. The Yo! Company, which developed Yo! Sushi, YOTEL, Yo! Japan (a clothing brand) and Yo! Home, is constantly looking for innovative ideas in hospitality and retail to take to market.

## CUSTOMER INTIMACY

The third strategy, customer intimacy, is based on the provision of solutions that are customized for individual customers. In these companies, empowerment is pushed to the front line and the company is flexible, doing whatever it takes to produce satisfied customers. Marriott International's Ritz-Carlton brand prides itself on being such an organization.

## CASE STUDY 15.1

### Airbnb's response to the COVID-19 pandemic[3,4]

Since its creation, Airbnb has reshaped the world of travel and challenged some of the age-old principles of the lodging business. However, the COVID-19 crisis hit Airbnb just as badly as the rest of the hospitality industry: a quarter of its workforce had to be let go and the company reported a 30 per cent decrease in revenues in 2020 compared to 2019.

Airbnb responded to the COVID-19 pandemic crisis by adapting and innovating. As many countries introduced lockdown measures and travel restrictions Airbnb started to highlight the risks of travelling during a pandemic on their website. When the situation became dire on a global level, it was obvious that short-term rentals would be compromised for the foreseeable future. Airbnb completely revamped their website in a matter of a few days. Under normal circumstances, such change would take months to implement, but the situation called for a much swifter response.

To keep its business afloat in a world without nearly as much travelling, Airbnb decided to take part of its services online. Through the new Online Experience feature, Airbnb's users were able enjoy a wide array of activities, which would in normal times be suggested as part of a trip, from the comfort of their home.

The company also decided to move away from short-term rentals towards longer-term stays. This decision was a direct response to an emerging demand trend: people were looking to get away from crowded cities to remote locations. By rethinking its services to match customer expectations in the post-COVID world, Airbnb was able to turn a desperate situation into an opportunity to generate new revenues by pivoting its business and diversifying its offers.

While many governments and companies alike had struggled to find the right way to pass along information, Airbnb was able to convey a message of solidarity and empathy. Airbnb doubled down on communication through multiple channels and involved top managers, such as CEO Brian Chesky, to speak up and show a more humane approach to the pandemic. Airbnb also set up newsrooms for hosts and travellers, providing key information regarding their policies during the pandemic. Throughout the crisis, they strove to make sure that all stakeholders, hosts and guests alike, were adequately kept up to date with the situation and supported in navigating through the crisis.

In doing so, Airbnb stood out from many OTAs, whose clumsy handling of the pandemic (especially regarding last-minute cancellations) bred distrust among their customer bases. Due in part to its effective communication, Airbnb may emerge stronger out of the crisis and stands to gain even more market share online in the long run.

As the pandemic changed the way people travel, and much of that new behaviour may be permanent, Airbnb has also been evolving. Airbnb's travel trends report suggested that one quarter of Americans would consider travelling during off-peak times of the year or the week, and in 2021, more than one third of the people searching on Airbnb have been flexible in terms of date and location. To address this change in travel search pattern, Airbnb introduced Flexible Search, which allows users to forgo putting in exact dates when they look to book lodging on the platform. Instead, users can search for a weekend getaway, week-long vacation, month-long vacation or months-long vacation without setting specific dates. Airbnb had also introduced a global resource hub dedicated to helping hosts secure bookings in this new environment. The global resource hub provides key information about current and future booking trends from its research to help hosts to understand where the market is headed.

During the pandemic, the hospitality industry underwent a major transformation; customer expectations shifted significantly. Airbnb's navigation of rough waters during the pandemic confirm that it is vital for hospitality operations to adapt their offerings to match these new expectations and needs. Hospitality companies should keep this in mind when establishing their long-term and short-term marketing strategy and plan.

*Sources*: hospitalitynet, https://news.airbnb.com/

### Tactical marketing plans

Tactical marketing plans (TMPs) differ from strategic plans in both their time frame and content. The typical TMP operates within a short time frame, normally no longer than one year. The TMP is subordinate to the SMP and, therefore, operates within the segmentation, targeting and positioning parameters established by the SMP. TMPs consist primarily of campaigns that are unit or department specific. A campaign is a promotion that runs for a short period of time. Campaigns are carefully targeted and timed customer or prospect communications. A campaign might be a sales promotion designed to fill rooms during the shoulder period or a sales blitz designed to generate prospects for a salesperson to follow-up. Typically, a campaign is designed to produce specific behaviours in the targeted audience – for example, to visit the website and make a booking.

## A generic marketing plan structure

In this section, we present a generic framework (see Table 15.1) for marketing planning. This offers a structured approach for carrying out all the activities associated with researching and devising a marketing plan. Not all the components of the framework appear in every marketing plan. For example, unit plans are unlikely to include corporate objectives. The framework consists of four major elements and 12 embedded activities. This framework provides direction for what the company wants to achieve by some predetermined future point. It focuses on the development of marketing mix strategies and tactics and addresses the questions of cost, implementation and control. Each element and all the activities are now discussed.

### Goal setting

There are two elements to goal setting. The first is an articulation of the business's mission, vision and values; these provide the organization with clear statements about why it exists, what it wishes to become and the values the business will exhibit in its operations. The second is the setting of corporate objectives that are continually revised on at least an annual basis.

#### VISION, MISSION, VALUES

Many leading hospitality companies have developed vision statements, mission statements or sets of values. These are enduring statements about what the organization is *en route* to

Table 15.1  A generic framework for marketing planning

**Goal setting**
  vision, mission, values
  corporate objectives
**Situational review**
  marketing audit
  strengths, weaknesses, opportunities and threats
  assumptions
**Strategy formulation**
  objectives
  strategies including objectives, segmentation, targeting and positioning
  expected results
**Resource allocation**
  implementation
  budget
  control
  evaluation

becoming sometime in the future (the vision statement); why the organization exists (the mission statement); and how the organization shall act in relationships with its stakeholders, such as shareholders, customers, employees and local communities (the values statement). Many organizations do have policies like these but merge them into a single generic statement that contains elements of all three. Increasingly, mission statements contain references to a company's corporate social responsibility (CSR) and sustainability efforts to satisfy a range of different stakeholders. These statements serve as both a guide and constraint on marketing planning. The pursuit of diversity in employment might favour the recruitment of indigenous populations to work at all levels of a unit, whereas corporate values such as respect for the environment might rule out the development of a hotel resort close to an endangered reef.

Mission statements are succinct 'philosophical' statements, sometimes a paragraph or at most a page in length, and often presented in short bullet points. Mission statements are typically published on corporate websites, featured in annual reports and displayed in prominent places for customers to view, for example, in front desk and lobby areas. Mission statements are also given to new employees as part of their induction process. Smaller independent hospitality organizations are less likely to have a formal mission statement, although owners and managers may have a very clear vision of what they want their business to achieve.

A mission statement can include the following elements:

- Definition of the broad scope of the business, the markets served, the products and services offered, and the distinctive benefits provided by the organization to its customers
- Summary of the distinctive competences the business has developed, for example, a service ethos (Marriott), quality (Four Seasons) or product consistency (McDonald's)

- Description of the desired market position vis-à-vis competitors
- Statements about the company's values.

Pret A Manger developed the following mission statement: 'Pret creates handmade, natural food, avoiding the obscure chemicals and preservatives common to so much of the "prepared" and "fast" food on the market today.' Pret A Manger's mission statement, which emphasizes the company's environmental ethics and passion for fresh, healthy and natural food compared to their fast-food competitors, was established in 1986 and has provided a strategic direction for planning for more than 35 years and remains relevant in today's marketplace.

Many hospitality companies have developed a unique set of values, which are often derived from their origins and built up over a long period of time. However, some hospitality companies produce bland mission statements lacking originality (or even copied from another organization) to conform to societal expectations. The development of a mission statement that does not reflect the company's historic values or its distinctive competences and that the employees clearly do not endorse can be legitimately criticized. Indeed, meaningless 'motherhood' statements, providing solemn assurances of service and quality, are faulty exercises in public relations and do not convince employees or customers.

## ACTIVITY 15.1

Log on to the following hotel websites and evaluate their vision, mission and value statements using the criteria outlined earlier:

- At the bottom of the Marriott home page, click on 'Our Company' and then select 'About Marriott' and review the 'Core Values & Heritage' pages – www.marriott.com
- At the bottom left of the Shangri-La home page, click on 'About Us' under 'About Shangri-La', and review the Shangri-La Heritage, People, Culture pages – www.shangri-la.com

## MARKETING INSIGHT 15.1

### Corporate objectives[5]

IHG identified a potential growth market in travellers wanting to stay in 'happier and healthier' hotels. The global health and wellness market was estimated to be a US$3.31 billion market in 2020. Health and wellness refers to the state of complete wellbeing of the body, mind and spirit. Some of the important aspects of the health and wellness industry include personal care/beauty, nutrition, weight management, fitness and preventive/personalized medicine.

IHG recognized the growth potential of this market and invested over $150 million in researching this market and developing a brand concept to target wellness conscious travellers. The brand name – EVEN™ Hotels – reflects the balanced lifestyle that wellness conscious hotel guests seek when travelling. EVEN Hotels aims to help travellers embrace wellness and even renew their motivation by giving them choices designed to help them stay on track. Athletic Studio, in-room training zones and group classes offer personalized activities to fit a customer's routine. The gym provides a range of cardio, strength training and mat exercises; the nutritionally designed menus offer healthy options and different sizes, including tapas-style portions; and the rooms are described as having a 'premium sleep system' with natural eucalyptus fibre bedding and hypoallergenic linens. The IHG Executive Board set a corporate objective of developing a wellness hotel brand and approved the investment of $150 million; the EVEN™ brand management then delivered on this corporate objective. By early 2021 there were a total of 16 EVEN Hotels locations with 2,415 rooms in the United States. A total of 32 hotels were in the pipeline, suggesting a rapid growth of the EVEN hotel locations after the COVID-19 pandemic.

*Source*: www.ihg.com/evenhotels/hotels/us/en/reservation

## CORPORATE OBJECTIVES

Corporate objectives are what the enterprise is aiming to achieve over the planning period. For example, the executive board of major international and national hospitality corporations may focus on group-level financial targets such revenue and profitability, or more operational goals such as growing the number of hotels in each brand and in each country of operation (often described as the 'pipeline'), withdrawal from certain geographic markets, and investment in the development of new brands (see Marketing Insight 15.1). Each division or brand is then responsible for contributing to the corporate objectives; each unit in turn contributes to divisional objectives; and each department contributes to unit objectives.

## Situational review

The situational review for any marketing plan comprises three activities: carrying out a marketing audit; compiling a strengths, weaknesses, opportunities and threats (SWOT) analysis; and providing an assumptions statement.

### MARKETING AUDIT

An early step in creating a marketing plan is to answer the question 'Where are we now?' Hospitality managers must try to be objective and rational about their company when evaluating the business's strengths and weaknesses. Too often, an emotional attachment to the business can influence owners and managers who see the weaknesses identified by customers as being minor, irrelevant or even attractive, rather than the negative attributes they really are. Although managers normally prepare their own marketing plans, the use of outside consultants can bring impartiality to the marketing planning process. Ideally, the situation audit for a property should be written up as brief factual statements covering all the key aspects of the hospitality business. The marketing audit comprises an internal audit and an external audit, and the key issues are summarized in a SWOT (Strengths, Weaknesses, Opportunities and Threats) analysis.

### INTERNAL AUDIT (STRENGTHS AND WEAKNESSES)

The internal audit assesses all aspects of the hospitality unit's operations, with the aim of establishing what the business is doing well – the strengths – and the parts of the business performing poorly – the weaknesses. Managers can usually identify their business's strengths and, more often than not, know their weaknesses, but the difficulty is recognizing the difference between the symptoms of a problem (e.g., low food sales) and the cause of the problem (in this case, perhaps, unpopular menu items, high prices, poor service, unappealing decor or a combination of all of these factors). By identifying the causes of the problem, managers can plan remedial actions to correct the poor performance and improve customer experience. Strengths and weaknesses can be identified in a rigorous way, first by vertical analysis (e.g., within business functions – finance, operations, marketing, human resources) and then horizontally, by looking at cross-functional processes and issues such as leadership and culture.

Most medium and larger hospitality companies are composed of a number of strategic business units (SBUs), some of which will be in the early stages of their life cycles and some of which will be mature. Some will be heavy users of cash striving to build market share, others will be powerful generators of cash surpluses. A healthy, well-managed company will have a balanced portfolio of SBUs and the internal audit should assess the health of the product–service portfolio. One tool that has been developed to help in this assessment is the Boston Consulting Group (BCG) matrix.

The BCG matrix is an analytical approach to assessing a SBU's cash flow, based on its relative market share and the industry sector's market growth rate. The rate of market growth indicates the attractiveness of a market; higher-growth markets are usually more attractive than low-growth markets. Relative market share indicates the degree of dominance a SBU holds in its marketplace and the share of the company in comparison to the market leader. The combination of these factors provides companies with a tool to evaluate possible strategic directions and, most importantly from a marketing planning perspective, to calculate the cash generation and cash usage of each SBU. This model's four quadrants have been labelled as follows and as shown in Figure 15.1.

1 *Star* (high market growth/high relative market share). A star is a successful SBU that has a relatively high share of a high-growth market. The company will need to reinvest the cash generated from this SBU to continue to maintain the brand's position by acquiring/building additional outlets. A star is self-financing, but all the cash generated by this SBU is used within it.

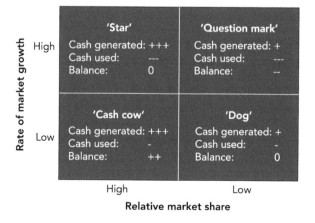

Figure 15.1 BCG portfolio analysis – cash generated and cash used

*Source*: Boston Consulting Group[6]

2  *Cash cow* (low market growth/high relative market share). Cash cows operate in mature, stable markets with low growth rates and high relative market share. They generate cash and high profits, because of their economies of scale and low marketing costs. The profits generated are reinvested by the parent company to fund the development of the next category – question marks.

3  *Question mark* (high market growth/low relative market share). Question marks operate in high growth markets but suffer from a low relative market share and do not occupy a dominant market position. Most new products start out as question marks. Companies may develop many new product concepts, and those that are retained require significant marketing support and, therefore, use more cash than they generate. If they succeed, they can eventually turn into stars and ultimately into cash cows to support additional innovation.

4  *Dog* (low market growth/low relative market share). Dogs operate in mature markets and have low relative market share. These businesses must be tightly managed to ensure that they do not become a liability. Dogs can be cash-neutral; but if they continue to make losses they need to be disposed of quickly. Dogs are rarely able to generate the profits and growth expected by major companies. Although it does not generate sufficient return for its current owners, in the hands of new owners (who might have different performance measures) a dog may make a satisfactory return.

Strategic planners strive to achieve a balanced portfolio of SBUs with sufficient cash cows to generate profits to satisfy shareholders and fund investment in question marks, which might eventually become stars and later become cash cows. The disposal of dogs is essential to prevent them from becoming a financial drain on the resources of the company.

The BCG model has been criticized because of its narrow focus in only using two factors, relative market share and market growth rate, to evaluate a company's SBU portfolio. The fragmented nature of the hospitality industry also creates market definition problems, and trying to establish the rates of market growth and accurate market share figures is not always easy. Although the BCG has limited practical use, the language of question marks, stars, cash cows and dogs is widely used in business, and the principles of cash generation and cash usage are helpful to understand the importance of having a balanced portfolio of SBUs.

Marketers who create a group or divisional plan also compile information on strengths and weaknesses, based to some degree on data collected from the group's operational units. A key issue for head office marketers is delivering a consistent quality standard across hotels carrying the same brand. A particular difficulty is when hotels under a single brand are a mix of owned, contracted and franchised units.

### External audit (opportunities and threats)

The external environment includes all the factors over which the company has no control. The purpose of an external audit is to identify potential opportunities that might be exploited by the firm and any threats that might damage the business. The external factors are applicable to all companies operating in the same competitor set. The external influences impacting on a company can be classified under two headings: the macro-environment and the micro-environment, as originally described in Chapter 1.

#### The macro-environment

The macro-environment includes major regional, national and global trends influencing business and society in broad general terms. In Chapter 1, we referred to these as PESTE factors. The macro-environment analysis evaluates current and future PESTE conditions that might require or encourage the hospitality business to adapt its operations.

THE MICRO-ENVIRONMENT

A hospitality company's micro-environment includes external stakeholders and, most importantly, customers, competitors and suppliers. Local or regional influences in the micro-environment can have an impact upon a firm's trading situation.

## SWOT ANALYSIS

Although the situation audit described earlier requires considerable in-depth research and the accumulation of extensive data about the company, only a summary of the audit needs to be presented in the marketing plan. This is described as a SWOT analysis. The 'Strengths' and 'Weaknesses' are internal factors; and the 'Opportunities' and 'Threats' are external factors. The situation audit, with commentary, focuses on the key factors influencing the current and future performance of the company. Appendices containing more detailed analysis, for example, the customer analysis or profiles of new competitors, can be added. A thorough understanding of 'Where are we now?' forms the basis of effective marketing planning, and this is the purpose of the situation audit. Table 15.2 illustrates some of the key SWOT data that can emerge from a situation analysis.

Table 15.2 Extract from hotel SWOT analysis

|  | Strengths (internal) | Weaknesses (internal) |
| --- | --- | --- |
| Positioning | Brand reputation increased by 2% over key competitor according to independent research | Brand image suffers due to lack of consistency, caused by wide variety of standards in group's units |
| Location | Most convenient access to motorway network | Problems of noise from passing traffic |
| Product | Recently refurbished bedroom decor is superior to competitors | Standard bedrooms are smaller than those of two newly built competitors |
| Price | Customer ratings and comments on Tripadvisor suggest leisure breaks are high 'value for money' compared to our competitors | Family rates 10% higher than our competitors |
| Distribution | Contract with high-profile international third-party intermediary distributor has increased leisure bookings from three key source countries | Conference agents' high commission levels eroding profitability on conference bookings |
| Marketing communication | Recent online advertising and offline public relations campaign has raised brand awareness by 2% compared to our competitor set | Website design and photography dated compared to competitor's new website |
| People | Key heads of department have worked at the unit for 15+ years | High turnover of housekeeping staff is preventing effective staff training |
| Processes | Improved check-in/check-out at front desk, according to mystery shopper analysis | Banqueting suite does not have adequate hot food storage facilities |

|  | Strengths (internal) | Weaknesses (internal) |
|---|---|---|
| Physical evidence | Excellent landscaping and lighting and prominent signage on major road | Kitchen waste storage and bin area always untidy, creating sanitation problem |
| Customer satisfaction | High (and increased) level of repeat business travellers staying compared to two years ago | Post-experience customer questionnaires and Booking.com comments identify problems of inconsistent standards of housekeeping |
| Key relationships | Sales manager has successfully built close relationships with three key intermediaries in the conference market | Lost one key account due to inconsistent housekeeping standards |

|  | Opportunities (external) | Threats (external) |
|---|---|---|
| Political | Changes in the Chinese government's approach to tourist visas allowing Chinese consumers more opportunity to travel to foreign countries | Changes in health and safety legislation mean that kitchen equipment specifications will have to be adapted |
| Economic | Increased consumer disposable income from Asian markets is generating more demand for long haul holidays in the Americas, Australasia and Europe | High exchange rate makes cost of foreign holidays relatively cheap and negatively influences demand for domestic holidays |
| Socio-cultural | Demand for vegetarian meals is growing due to increased public concern about animal rights | Sophisticated consumers are bored with hotel restaurants |
|  | Increasing COVID-19 vaccination rates is resulting in higher demand from leisure travel segments | Omicron and other variants of the COVID-19 virus may result in lockdowns and property closures |
| Technological | Growth of smart mobile technology and new apps create opportunities to reach hospitality consumers whilst travelling | Business travel agents directing web links to corporate client's booking site is eroding customer loyalty to hotel brand |
| Environmental | Concern for environmental issues means consumers will value sustainable tourism initiatives | Concern about air pollution might discourage tourists from staying in downtown locations |

The situation audit also helps to identify *critical success factors* (also called key factors for success), which are company-specific (see Chapter 4).

## ASSUMPTIONS

Marketing planning is a future-orientated activity that is based in part upon assumptions about consumers, competitors, markets and the PESTE environment; these assumptions are projections of what might happen over the time frame of the plan and are derived from the preceding analysis. There is no guarantee that the assumptions upon which objectives, strategies and tactics are made will actually happen. Therefore, a small number of key assumptions should be assembled. Examples of key assumptions are:

- As COVID-19 vaccination rates increase, the number of leisure travellers will continue to increase.
- Easing of international travel restrictions that were imposed due to COVID-19 pandemic will increase demand from international travellers.
- Many business travellers who have learned to use ZOOM and other conferencing applications during the COVID-19 pandemic will be slow to return to business travel.
- Outbound Chinese tourism will continue to increase.
- Competitors in the economy accommodation market will grow their capacity by 10 per cent annually over the next five years.
- Inflation will increase significantly over the planning time frame.

### Strategy formulation

Having conducted the 'Where are we now?' audit, the next step in the marketing planning process is to formulate strategy. This element of the marketing plan comprises objective setting, strategy development and an evaluation of the expected results to ensure that corporate goals are delivered.

#### OBJECTIVE SETTING

Objectives are statements that translate the hospitality company's mission and corporate objectives into targets regarding profits, sales and occupancy. Objectives provide answers to the question 'Where do we want to go?' Companies that do not have objectives fail to provide managers and employees with a clear direction. Objectives should be Specific, Measurable, Achievable, Realistic and achieved within a set Timetable (SMART). SMART objectives provide managers with clear targets to achieve, and act as a control mechanism in determining whether they have been effective. Examples of strategic and tactical hospitality marketing objectives are provided in Table 15.3.

Table 15.3 SMART marketing objectives

| SMART strategic objectives (3–5 years) | SMART tactical objectives (within 1 year) |
| --- | --- |
| To increase sales from $165 million in the current year to $280 million in year 3 | To increase room occupancy from 69% to 72% within 12 months |
| To acquire 20 upscale, 100-room properties in target South American city centre locations within 4 years | To acquire four upscale properties, with rooms ranging from 80 to 130, in Barcelona, Manchester, Prague and Stuttgart within 12 months |
| To develop a new food and beverage lifestyle concept suitable for residents and non-residents within 2 years | To test-market a new food and beverage lifestyle concept in Sydney between March and September next year |
| To increase brand awareness amongst European conference and event agents from a current level of 55% to 65%, in the BVA BDRC Continental European Business Travel survey, within 3 years | To launch a new dedicated conference and event agent website for European distributors, in January, with new online booking options and video clips of key conference facilities |

SMART objectives are formed using quantified metrics like money, percentages, ratios and other numbers. The timetable can either refer to the time period during which the target should be achieved ('to achieve $1 million sales within the next 12-month trading period') or to the date by which a target should be achieved ('to achieve one Michelin star for the restaurant by June 2024').

Marketing objectives will vary across the customer relationship from pre-encounter, through encounter to post-encounter. Managers need to think carefully about what is relevant for each stage.

- Pre-encounter objectives focus on achievements such as raising awareness, generating understanding and knowledge, creating expectations, building interest and stimulating first purchase.
- Encounter objectives focus on generating customer satisfaction, influencing the level of spending, cross-selling and upselling.
- Post-encounter objectives focus on building customer retention rates, growing share of spend and promoting positive word-of-mouth.

Marketing objectives will also vary according to whether the business is a lifestyle business or a business with ambitious owners or investors who want to grow the business. Lifestyle entrepreneurs are content to see their restaurants busy with regular customers, their staff happy and secure, and enough money coming in to repay any borrowings and to sustain their lifestyle. For many small hospitality businesses, the lifestyle of the owner/managers is integrated with the needs of the operation. Growth-oriented businesspeople are more likely to set ambitious 'stretch' targets that, if achieved, will see the market value or capitalization of their business improve.

## SALES GAP ANALYSIS

Company records tell the marketer the level of sales achieved in the past and currently. An examination of the SWOT conditions should give a good idea of what will happen to sales in the future if the identified threats and opportunities actually impact on the business, and if the company continues to pursue the same strategies. Very often, companies find there is a 'gap'

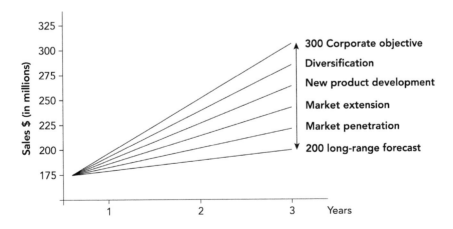

Figure 15.2 Gap analysis

*Source*: McDonald and Wilson[7]

between where they want to be in terms of sales and where a forecast based on the SWOT analysis tells them they will be. Gap analysis computes the size of the gap. For example, a parent company of a budget lodging company could set a divisional objective of increasing room revenues from $175 million to $300 million within three years. However, the division's forecast shows that in three years' time, sales will be $200 million if the present marketing strategy is pursued. There is, therefore, a gap of $100 million ($300 million objective − $200 million forecast) that must be filled through additional revenue generation activity (Figure 15.2).

## FILLING THE GAP: THE ANSOFF MATRIX

There are four key strategic options that a company can use to fill a sales gap, and in the process grow the business; these options require changes to markets, products or both. H. Igor Ansoff[8] developed a matrix that encapsulates these options. It is often described as the Ansoff matrix, but is also called a market/product analysis. Ansoff's four strategic options to close the gap are market penetration, market extension, product development and diversification. Businesses need to identify which of these options is most likely to succeed given what they have identified during their SWOT analysis. If this analysis suggests the business is unlikely to close the sales gas but still not reach the objective the company would have to re-evaluate the objectives and perhaps set a revised, lower objective. A similar approach to sales gap analysis can be used to identify and bridge 'profit' gaps. The profit gap can be closed using strategies to reduce costs, improve the sales mix with higher margin products and services, increase prices and improve productivity. Ansoff's four growth options are discussed here.

## MARKET PENETRATION STRATEGY

A market penetration strategy aims to grow the business by increasing sales of the current offer(s) to current target markets. There are three ways to increase sales to existing markets. The first is to focus on selling more to current customers. This can be achieved in several ways: 1. increase the frequency with which current customers patronize the establishment (i.e., increasing repeat visits); 2. increase current customers' spend (i.e., increasing achieved room and meal rates) or, 3. ideally, both. The second method is to attract your competitors' customers. The third route is to grow the market by convincing non-users to buy the product (Figure 15.3). Examples of strategies and tactics used for market penetration include:

- Yield management
- Frequent guest programmes
- Staff training to upsell
- Sales promotions
- Departmental cross-selling (rooms division selling food and beverage, for example)
- Campaigns and events targeting current competitors, non-user and ex-customers.

A market penetration strategy is the safest and least risky strategy to adopt. Relying on a market penetration strategy is problematic when market conditions and customer expectations are changing.

## MARKET EXTENSION OR DEVELOPMENT

A market extension strategy features the roll-out of existing offers to new markets. In hospitality, there are different approaches to market extension, depending upon whether the strategy

| | Products | |
|---|---|---|
| | **Existing** | **New** |
| **Existing** (Markets) | Market penetration or concentration (same markets/same products) Increase market share by: (a) Increase frequency and spend from existing customers (implement revenue management system; improve internal marketing; enhance brand loyalty programs; develop frequent-stay promotions; promote in-house product/price bundles) (b) Attract competitors' customers (promote special offers, raise brand image/brand awareness) (c) Convince non-users to buy products (educate market by informing non-user of the product benefits) | Product development (same markets/new products) Introduce product improvement programs by: (a) Replacement and refurbishment of rooms, food and beverage, and leisure facilities – targeting existing customers (b) Introduction of new technology to improve service quality Introduce product extensions by: (a) Development of new menu items aimed at existing customers |
| **New** | Market extension or development (new market/same product) (a) Target new customers: Identify new target markets and develop marketing communication programme to promote existing product, e.g. early-bird diners (b) Target similar customers in different geographic areas: Identify geographic areas with similar demographic profile and roll out existing product (c) Use new distribution channels to reach new markets: e.g. work with intermediaries on joint-marketing initiatives | Diversification and innovation (new market/new product) (a) Intensive (inside the existing firm) Innovative, new bar and food concepts aimed at new target markets, e.g. new leisure center at hotel targeting new local customers (b) Extensive diversification (outside existing firm) Vertical integration (i) Forward (ii) Backward Diversification (i) Horizontal (ii) Concentrated (related) (iii) Conglomerate (non-related) |

Figure 15.3 Ansoff matrix

is focused on growth within existing units or on expanding the number of properties in the group. In existing units, market extension refers to promoting the existing property to new target markets. Most hospitality businesses will target the same primary markets each year, but secondary target markets can change in line with changing market trends. These secondary target markets represent new opportunities for the existing product. Creative product/benefit bundles targeting new market segments can highlight the benefits of the company's offerings.

A typical restaurant example is a competitively priced, all-inclusive meal promotion aimed at attracting 'early-bird' diners.

Another approach to market development that is particularly relevant to hospitality chains is geographic expansion of existing product concepts. When the product concept is proven, the key issue in expanding geographically is to ensure that the characteristics of the new target market are similar to those of existing successful markets. Hospitality companies also expand geographically by acquisition, which can be riskier, because the newly acquired properties may not conform to the requirements of the branded hospitality chain. You can read more about this in Chapter 4.

Another strategy for reaching new markets is to develop new distribution channels. Joint marketing initiatives with intermediaries who have access to new markets can be effective. For example, an independent hotel can join a consortium like Best Western Hotels to participate in their established domestic leisure break programme and attract new customers by distribution through their international travel intermediaries.

## PRODUCT DEVELOPMENT

The product development strategy features enhancement of the existing offer, or the introduction of new products aimed at existing customers. Managers in hospitality operations are constantly looking for ways to increase customer satisfaction and improve customer experience by improving their offering. Product development strategies and tactics for existing customer markets include:

- Refurbishment of existing operations
- New menus or menu items
- New technology to improve service operations (e.g., self-check-in)
- New product concepts.

## DIVERSIFICATION

The diversification strategy focuses on creating new product – service offers for new target customers. This is the riskiest growth strategy, because the company has no existing customer or product knowledge to exploit. Diversification within hospitality units is described as intensive diversification, meaning that new products are offered inside the existing unit. For example, intensive diversification might involve the building of a new facility on the premises, designed to attract new segments of customers. Examples of intensive diversification in an existing hotel might include:

- A new restaurant concept aimed at new target markets (e.g., non-resident customers)
- A new leisure complex aimed at people living in the local neighbourhood
- New banqueting/conference and exhibition facilities aimed at new corporate markets.

Diversification outside the scope of the existing firm is termed 'extensive' and can take many different forms:

- *Vertical backward integration* occurs when a hospitality business acquires a supplier – for example, a contract catering firm taking over food distributors.
- *Vertical forward integration* involves acquiring firms that are closer to the end-user – for example, when a third-party intermediary (TPI) such as an online tour operator acquires hotels.

- *Horizontal diversification* is the acquisition of a competitor operating in the same market – for example, a midmarket hotel chain taking over another midmarket hotel chain.
- *Concentric diversification* is the acquisition or start-up of companies that exploit the hospitality company's core competences – for example, a restaurant starting up a delicatessen using its kitchen brigade's skills.
- *Conglomerate diversification* is diversification into an unrelated area – for example, a hotel company buying an engineering company.

The Ansoff matrix enables marketers to evaluate systematically the gap-closing growth options facing the company. When management has decided which market/product options to pursue, then detailed marketing mix strategies must be developed to achieve the objectives. For example, in competitive hospitality sectors, companies strive to obtain competitive advantage by constantly investing in product development and continually improving the offer to customers. Once this strategy has been decided, the detail of the new product development strategies needs to be considered.

### SEGMENTATION, TARGETING AND POSITIONING (STP)

Having set objectives, which may involve closing a sales or profit gap, the next step of this generic marketing planning process is to make the core strategic decisions about how to segment the market, which customer segments to target and how to position effectively against competitors. These issues have been addressed in earlier chapters (see Chapters 3 and 4 particularly), but it is worth stressing a few points here.

- Market segmentation involves dividing up the market into homogeneous subsets, so that marketing strategies and tactics can be developed for one or more segments.
- Companies that are innovative in the way they segment a market can enjoy first-mover advantage, as they exploit opportunities that have not been recognized by competitors.
- Companies can choose to focus on one or more market segments, depending upon the attractiveness of the opportunities and the competences of the company.
- Positioning is concerned with identifying a competitive set and establishing a competitive platform.

Until the STP decisions are made, companies cannot begin to develop marketing mix strategies and tactics for pre-encounter, encounter and post-encounter stages of the customer journey. STP strategies are based on the findings from the situation audit, and the positioning strategy provides the core theme that integrates all the elements of the marketing mix.

### EXPECTED RESULTS

Before tactical plans are developed and resources are allocated, marketing planners need to assess whether the strategic plan will deliver the company's objectives, and that the costs are within its resource capabilities. If not, the strategy or the objectives need to be modified.

### Resource allocation

When the objectives and strategies have been agreed, resources need to be allocated so that the plan can be executed at both strategic and tactical levels.

## IMPLEMENTATION

There are three main aspects to the implementation of any marketing plan:

1  assigning the roles and responsibilities for resourcing and executing the plan to individuals, departments or external agencies

2  engaging and obtaining the commitment of those individuals, departments or external agencies to ensure that the plan is successfully implemented

3  designing a process to track the performance of the plan against revenue targets and cost assumptions.

Marketing plans do not simply involve marketing people. Operational units (such as food and beverage) and service departments (such as front office) influence customer experience and need to understand their roles in meeting the marketing objectives, delivering customer satisfaction and creating customer retention. Marketing plans also need the support of those who control the allocation of resources. A unit marketing plan might need to be endorsed by the division, whereas a divisional marketing plan might need to go to the corporate level for funding.

All the hard work in researching and compiling a marketing plan can be wasted if a company fails to communicate with its employees. Customer-contact employees are often unaware of the marketing plan's goals, strategies and tactics, and of their role in it. Chapter 12 emphasized the importance of effective employee/management communications. Involving employees in the preparation of the marketing plan provides a good opportunity to facilitate that communication process. Hospitality employees can – indeed they should – be involved in the situation audit. The employees can provide useful insights into how customers view the facilities and service, and often know the strengths and weaknesses of an operation better than management. Also, employees are very aware of competitors. They may have worked for the competition or have friends working in competitor organizations or even patronize competitors' food and beverage outlets. Finally, customer-contact employees need to be aware of what is happening during the implementation of events and campaigns in case customers ask them any questions.

External persons and organizations may also need to be educated about their role in the plan's execution – for example, intermediaries, consortium partners, franchisees, management contractors, independent sales representatives and advertising and public relations agencies. Management also needs to communicate their plans effectively to other stakeholders, especially banks and any institutional shareholders.

## MARKETING MIX DECISIONS

Marketing mix decisions should be compatible with the overall STP strategy and designed to achieve the agreed marketing objectives. Strategic and tactical marketing mixes will vary according to the stage of the customer relationship – pre-encounter, encounter or post-encounter. Table 15.4 provides a useful framework that can be used to construct appropriate marketing mixes. The eight elements of the hospitality marketing mix are listed vertically, and the three journey stages are listed horizontally. The check marks within the cells indicate the marketing mix elements that are more widely deployed at each stage of the relationship.

Throughout this text, we have explained the responsibilities of the marketing team and stressed how marketers need to work with other departments to ensure the marketing offer is consistent and delivers the desired customer experience. The marketing office plays a major role in the pre-encounter marketing that aims to stimulate demand for the hospitality offer, and the

Table 15.4 The hospitality marketing mix matrix

| Marketing mix elements | Pre-encounter marketing mix | Encounter marketing mix | Post-encounter marketing mix |
|---|---|---|---|
| Product/service offer | ✓ | ✓ | |
| Location | ✓ | ✓ | |
| Price | ✓ | ✓ | |
| Distribution | ✓ | | |
| Marketing communications | ✓ | ✓ | ✓ |
| Physical environment | ✓ | ✓ | |
| Process | ✓ | ✓ | ✓ |
| People | | ✓ | |

The symbol '✓' indicates which element is important in a particular marketing mix

post-encounter marketing that builds customer relationships and generates word-of-mouth and repeat sales. During the encounter, the primary responsibilities for service delivery lie with operations and the human resource functions although marketers will want to influence decisions about the physical environment, service processes and internal marketing.

Broadly, there are three different approaches to planning the marketing mix.

1 In the first approach, the focus is on each stage of the customer journey: pre-encounter, encounter and post-encounter. Marketers will consider the SMART objectives and how the eight-element marketing mix will be structured for each stage.
2 In the second approach, the focus is on the marketing mix components. The strategy for each element of the marketing mix in the unit is discussed in turn – for example, the product strategy, the price strategy, the distribution strategy, the marketing communications strategy.
3 In the third approach, the marketing mix for each functional area of the unit is considered – for example, the marketing mix for the accommodation, the marketing mix for the restaurant operations, the marketing mix for the conference facilities.

Many marketers merge all three approaches into their planning processes, enabling them to answer such questions as 'what is the role of pricing strategy in attracting new customers to our accommodation facilities?' or 'how can we use marketing communications to build longer-term repeat relationships with customers who have attended functions hosted by our food and beverage department?'

Strategies and tactics need to be developed for each element of the marketing mix, but marketers must ensure that each strategic element complements the other marketing mix strategies – inconsistencies between marketing mix elements will send the target markets mixed messages and will inevitably be self-defeating.

Just as there is a choice of different marketing objectives, there can also be a choice of different marketing strategies that can achieve the same objective. For example, if an annual accommodation sales objective of $10 million has been set for a 200-bedroom hotel, there are different revenue management strategies that can achieve the sales objective (Table 15.5).

Table 15.5 Accommodation strategies

| Strategy 1: lower occupancy/higher achieved room rate | Strategy 2: higher occupancy/lower achieved room rate |
| --- | --- |
| 200 rooms at 50% annual room occupancy and an achieved room rate of $273.90 = $10 million | 200 rooms at 80% annual room occupancy and an achieved room rate of $172.23 = $10 million |

Unit and departmental marketing plans will normally include the detailed tactics that support the broad strategy. These will include events and campaigns that are scheduled for the year ahead. Sales and marketing personnel implement these tactical plans and typically want answers to the following questions:

- What action is going to be undertaken? (tactical campaigns)
- What are the campaigns designed to achieve? (SMART objectives)
- Where will the actions take place? (location, units, departments)
- When will the action take place? (timetable)
- How much will it cost? (budget)
- Who will run the events and campaigns? (responsibility and authority)

Table 15.6 illustrates a template for a tactical marketing plan.

Table 15.6 Template for a tactical marketing plan

| Objectives (SMART) | | | |
| --- | --- | --- | --- |
| • Target market(s) | | | |
| • Positioning | | | |
| • Financial | | | |
| • Marketing | | | |
| Actions | Timetable | Budget | Who is responsible? |
| | | | |

## BUDGETING

Companies need to create a budget for the implementation of their strategic and tactical marketing plans. Budgets include two classes of forecast data: revenues and costs. Revenues are generated by departmental sales (rooms division, food and beverage, entertainment, shops, etc.), and these appear on the top line of a budget. The budget will also identify and quantify the cost elements that will be incurred in reaching the revenue targets. Not all cost elements are regarded as marketing costs – for example, food and beverage input costs are reported as operational department costs. The costs that are usually attributable to the marketing function are

- Marketing research expenses
- Distribution (commissions to intermediaries)
- Marketing communication costs (advertising, newsletter, website, public relations)
- Sales team (salaries, travel costs, support materials and training)
- Customer database management costs (customer lists, data entry, data cleansing, storage, and compliance with privacy regulations).

In Chapter 9, we provided a detailed discussion of marketing communication budgets. Budgets for a unit's marketing plan are usually within limits set by division. Marketers typically work within industry norms of 4–8 per cent of revenue.

## CONTROL

The penultimate stage of this generic marketing planning process is to design a system to monitor and control the plan's implementation. The key concerns here are to ensure that there is no unacceptable variance between the plan's revenue targets and anticipated costs, and those that are actually achieved. When there is unacceptable variance, a tactical response may be initiated. Unfortunately, there is no such thing as a perfect marketing plan. External events beyond the marketer's control can have a major impact on both revenues and costs – for example, governments may alter their tax regime, resulting in lower consumer disposable income and reduced expenditure on leisure products; or suppliers may increase prices, resulting in higher costs. COVID-19 was a massive surprise and burden on the entire hospitality and tourism sectors. Equally, hospitality companies can be the beneficiaries of unanticipated changes in the marketing environment, for example, when a foreign airline is granted rights to use a nearby international airport. Internal conditions can also influence performance against plan: key employees might leave the company, or there might be publicity about a company's failure of a kitchen hygiene inspection. Controls are necessary to detect, correct and prevent unacceptable variances from the plan's objectives and cost profile. The key to control is setting SMART objectives. Without SMART objectives, managers have nothing against which to compare performance. There are five stages in the control process:

1  Set SMART objectives.
2  Establish a reporting regime that reports to management on progress against budget.
3  Monitor performance.
4  Identify significant variations from target.
5  Take corrective action.

SMART objectives and associated control measures can include a wide variety of financial, customer, process and people metrics, including: sales, achieved room rate, occupancy and RevPAR, customer mix ratios, market share, brand awareness and brand reputation, number of unique visitors to the website, number of bookings, conversion ratio from enquiries to bookings, number of complaints, speed of complaint resolution, staff turnover, employee satisfaction, customer satisfaction, and positive and negative posts on social media.

Providing the objective is SMART, then variance from the plan can easily be detected when it occurs. Marketing managers need to establish whether variance is minor or major, and whether it affects one market segment or all customer groups. If the variance is a minor underperformance for a short period in one market segment – for example, weekend leisure breaks in the North, during the Winter season, due to poor weather – then it might be tolerated. If it is significant and affects all markets, then urgent action needs to be taken. Appropriate actions might include adapting the tactics, revisiting the strategy or, in extreme circumstances, changing the SMART objectives if they are no longer realistic. Overperformance against plan can also be problematic. This happens when there is too much demand on a property. Figure 15.4 summarizes the stages and monitoring and control mechanism in the marketing plan.

### EVALUATION

This is the final step of the generic marketing planning process. Shortly after the conclusion of a planning period, event or campaign, the marketing team needs to evaluate results. The comparison of actual performance with the SMART objectives across relevant areas of the business, with a commentary explaining the reasons for variance, provides useful information for the preparation of the next marketing plan. Companies often repeat successful tactics of previous years and aim to learn from less effective activities. Indeed, marketing is a continuous learning activity. The cycle of forward planning the next campaign while implementing the current marketing action plan and evaluating recent activity is carried out simultaneously.

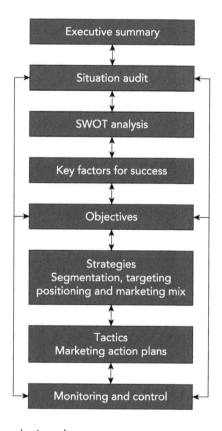

Figure 15.4 Summary of marketing plan

### Contingency planning

Although the generic marketing planning process described here is founded upon rigorous analysis, many companies also develop contingency plans. Contingency planning recognizes that the key assumptions upon which the marketing plan is formulated may be incorrect and contingency plans are formulated on various 'what if?' scenarios – for example, what would happen if a serious environmental issue or a public safety incident such as a terrorist attack affected our business? Only major risks are considered in contingency planning.

Contingency planning forms part of crisis management and has become more important because of recent dramatic events that have had a serious impact on hospitality companies. Environmental disasters such as hurricanes and tsunamis, health scares caused by global epidemics and pandemics, and terrorist incidents like suicide bomb attacks, temporarily destroy demand for hospitality and tourism. In these circumstances, public health and safety are the most important issues and price does not influence demand. Hospitality companies generally respond to these crises by reducing costs as far as possible – especially payroll costs. As consumer confidence gradually returns, companies reignite their marketing activity to encourage customers to return, often using price-led promotions. The strategic marketing plan should always include a budget item for contingencies. This provides funds to enable the company to take advantage of an unforeseen opportunity or to respond to a downturn in demand by increasing marketing activity.

## CASE STUDY 15.2

### Contingency planning at IHG[9,10]

On Thursday 15 April 2010, airspace across most of central and northern Europe was closed for five days due to volcanic ash clouds from Eyjafjallajökull in Iceland. Ninety-five thousand flights were cancelled and 5 million passengers were stranded, not only in Europe but also around the world. The disruption to air travel was greater than that caused by the attacks on the United States on 11 September 2001.

Although some hoteliers simply thought of this incident as an immediate opportunity to fill their hotels at higher than normal prices, IHG recognized that this crisis was both an opportunity and a threat. On the Friday immediately following the closure of European airspace, IHG's crisis management planning team evaluated the potential threats from both a business and a consumer perspective. They soon realized that the long-term consequence of the disruption to their brands and customers was significant. An IHG corporate level virtual meeting of senior vice-presidents and executives on Sunday 18 April, agreed a strategic and tactical response that was rolled out across all brands and hotels affected by the crisis.

The tactical response included the decision not to take advantage of stranded travellers by overcharging them on room prices and to even provide customers with discounted food offers of between 20 per cent and 25 per cent. To implement this response quickly, the IHG team had to ensure that all their franchisees were properly informed about the crisis and adopted IHG's policies. The fact that franchisees endorsed these pricing policies was in part due to the IHG's corporate values.

Although the widespread travel disruption due to the volcanic ash was limited to approximately one week, the effect of room cancellations – especially on conference business – created potential long-term negative financial consequences for some IHG hotel owners. IHG was sympathetic to hotel owners who experienced financial difficulty and supported them in a variety of ways. The IHG crisis management team had already identified the threat of business disruption to franchisees and initiated a special sales initiative to support the vulnerable hotels to help them rebuild occupancy during the aftermath of the volcanic ash cloud incident.

IHG was able to respond quickly to the travel disruption and initiate an effective response because they had an experienced contingency planning team in place that identified the immediate and long-term issues confronting all their brands. The IHG corporate culture also enabled the team to implement the response strategy with the support of their franchisees.

*Sources*: BBC Online[9], IHG, Times Online[10]

## Criticisms of marketing planning

Critics of marketing planning claim that the uncertainty of the future makes long-term planning unreliable and costly, and that marketing strategies should emerge as a management reaction to changes in the environment. Clearly, a strategic marketing plan can be completely undermined when disease, terrorism or war suddenly break out. However, the planning methods and tools we cite here can be helpful because they provide a framework for organizing marketing activity on a regular basis. Other critics of formalized marketing planning portray examples of successful entrepreneurs who use their flair, intuition and vision in building dynamic businesses and suggest that marketing is all about spontaneous ideas. However, companies cannot rely upon spontaneous thinking to solve all their problems, and the marketing planning process can allow opportunities for creativity and flexibility, via contingency planning, within a systematic framework. Although many companies pay lip service to the concept of a customer-orientation, the reality is that budgeting, with its emphasis on sales generation, cost control and profit engineering, is dominant in the hospitality industry, and the influence of marketing often seems to be subordinate to financial imperatives.

## Conclusion

Marketing planning provides hospitality companies with a structured approach to creating a desired future. Although the future is uncertain, environmental trends can be identified and their impact on the hospitality company can be consequently evaluated. Although marketing planning has its critics, primarily because it can be a costly, time-consuming process, there is little doubt that such planning in any organization improves the chances of survival and success. However, marketing planning alone cannot be a guarantee of success.

In this chapter, we have explained:

- Contexts within which marketing plans are constructed – corporate, division, unit and department
- Two different types of marketing plan – strategic and tactical; strategic marketing planning typically takes a three- to five-year time frame; whereas tactical planning covers a 12-month period or less

- A generic marketing planning process comprising four major elements and 12 activities
- Key tools in strategic marketing planning, including the BCG matrix, SWOT analysis, PESTE analysis, gap analysis and the Ansoff matrix
- That objectives should be Specific, Measurable, Achievable, Realistic, and carried out within a set Timetable (SMART)
- That contingency planning provides an alternative in the event of a major deviation from plan
- That marketing planning has been criticized as pointless, given the unpredictability of the future
- That marketing planning provides a structured approach to organizing marketing activity.

## REVIEW QUESTIONS

Now check your understanding by answering the following questions:

1 Discuss the role of marketing planning in hospitality organizations.

2 Explain the SMP process, illustrating your answer with examples from the hospitality industry.

3 Explain why control is important in marketing planning.

## References

1. Porter, M. E. (1980). *Competitive Strategy: Techniques for Analyzing Industries and Competitors*. New York: Free Press.
2. Treacy, M., & Wiersema, F. (1995). *The Discipline of Market Leaders*. New York: HarperCollins.
3. Mauguin, M. (2020). What hotels can learn from Airbnb's response to the COVID-19 crisis. *Hospitalitynet*. [cited December 6, 2021]. Available from: www.hospitalitynet.org/opinion/4100678.htm
4. Airbnb [Internet]. *Building on Our Commitment to Trust*. [cited December 6, 2021]. Available from: https://news.airbnb.com/building-on-our-commitment-to-trust-2/
5. EVEN HOTELS [Internet]. *Meet EVEN®Hotels: Where Wellness Is Built in*. [cited December 6, 2021]. Available from: www.ihg.com/evenhotels/hotels/us/en/reservation
6. Boston Consulting Group [Internet]. *Growth Share Matrix*. [cited December 6, 2021]. Available from: www.bcg.com/about/overview/our-history/growth-share-matrix
7. McDonald, M., & Wilson, H. (2016). *Marketing Plans: How to Prepare Them, How to Use Them*. Chichester: John Wiley & Sons.
8. Ansoff, H. I. (1965). *Corporate Strategy*. New York: McGraw Hill.
9. BBC Online. (2010). *Ash Cloud Chaos: Airlines Face Huge Task as Ban Ends*. [cited December 6, 2021]. Available from: http://news.bbc.co.uk/1/hi/uk/8633892.stm
10. Times Online. (2010). *Volcanic Ash Grounds Britain for Days to Come*. [cited December 6, 2021]. Available from: www.thetimes.co.uk/tto/travel/news/article2480786.ece

# Index

Page numbers in *italic* indicate a figure and page numbers in **bold** indicate a table on the corresponding page

*For Product Safety Concerns and Information please contact
our EU representative GPSR@taylorandfrancis.com Taylor & Francis
Verlag GmbH, Kaufingerstraße 24, 80331 München, Germany*

T - #0181 - 230425 - C424 - 246/174/20 - PB - 9781032030265 - Gloss Lamination